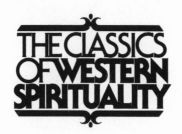

WilliamLaw

A SERIOUS CALL TO A DEVOUT
AND HOLY LIFE · THE SPIRIT OF LOVE

EDITED FROM THE FIRST EDITIONS
BY
PAUL G. STANWOOD

INTRODUCTION
BY
AUSTIN WARREN
AND PAUL G. STANWOOD

PREFACE
BY
JOHN BOOTY

PAULIST PRESS
NEW YORK ◆ RAMSEY ◆ TORONTO

Cover Art:
The artist EDWARD F. BARBINI studied painting and advertising art and design at Pratt Institute and The School of Visual Arts before embarking on a career as a designer and Art Director for various New York ad agencies. In 1966 he became a principal of the Barbini, Pesce and Noble Advertising Agency, where he is currently Executive Art Director. Mr. Barbini is a member of the New York Art Directors Club and winner of various advertising awards including the prestigious "Andy" award. Mr. Barbini has exhibited his paintings at various art shows in the New York Metropolitan area. Of his cover painting he says, "The multi-colored quill symbolizes the essence of Law's inspirational writings. The flowers symbolize his role as a simple country parson. In the painting I have attempted to convey the strength of his thoughts that are manifested in his mystical treatises."

Design: Barbini Pesce & Noble, Inc.

Library of Congress
Catalog Card Number: 78-61418

ISBN: 08091-2144-1 (Paper)
ISBN: 08091-0265-X (Cloth)

Published by Paulist Press
Editorial Office: 1865 Broadway, New York, N.Y. 10023
Business Office: 545 Island Road, Ramsey, N.J. 07446

Printed and bound in the
United States of America

CONTENTS

The Editor of this Volume:

PAUL G. STANWOOD is Professor of English at the University of British Columbia, Vancouver, Canada. Born in Des Moines, Iowa, after completing his Ph.D. at the Univeristy of Michigan he did advanced studies at Oxford University and Cambridge University. He has been a recipient of two Canada Council Leave Fellowships, is a Member of the High Table at Peterhouse, Cambridge University, where he is a permanent member of the College. He is a Senior Fellow, Folger Shakespeare Library and a Reader, Humanities Research Council of Canada. He has contributed numerous articles to scholarly journals. His books include *John Cosin, A Collection of Private Devotions* (1967), *Henry More, Democritus Platonissans* (1968). Dr. Stanwood is married and the father of two children. He is Clergy Warden of St. James' Anglican Church, Vancouver.

The Author of the Introduction:

AUSTIN WARREN was born in Waltham, Massachusetts, in 1899, and completed his A.B. at Wesleyan University in Connecticut in 1920, his A.M. at Harvard in 1922, and his Ph.D. at Princeton in 1926. His long and varied academic career spans fifty years and includes Professorships of English at Boston University, and the Universities of Iowa and Michigan. He received a Literary Award from the American Academy of Arts and Letters in 1973 and an honorary Litt.D. from Brown University in 1974. In 1975, he was elected to membership in the National Institute of Arts and Letters. He has published numerous books and essays including studies of Alexander Pope, Nathaniel Hawthorne, Henry James, and Richard Crashaw. In 1970, he moved to Providence, Rhode Island, and resumed work on his autobiography, *Becoming What One Is, 1899-1939*.

The Author of the Preface:

JOHN E. BOOTY is Professor of Church History, Episcopal Divinity School, Cambridge, Massachusetts. Since 1974, he has been Acting Director of the Institute of Theological Research. A native of Detroit, Michigan, he became an Episcopal priest in 1953. He completed his Ph.D. at Princeton University after a Fulbright Fellowship at the University of London. Dr. Booty is the author of *Yearning To Be Free* (1974) and *John Jewel as Apologist of the Church of England* (1963). He has contributed numerous articles to such publications as *Encyclopedia Britannica, World Book Encyclopedia, Westminster Dictionary of Church History, Church History, Theological Studies,* and many others. He has edited many books and is presently on the Editorial Board of the Folger Library edition of *The Works of Richard Hooker*. Married and the father of four children, he lives in Concord, Massachusetts.

Preface

William Law's importance as a master of the spiritual life was acknowledged in the eighteenth and nineteenth centuries by persons as diverse as John Wesley, the founder of Methodism, Samuel Johnson, the renowned lexicographer, and John Henry Newman, the leader of the Oxford Movement, subsequently Cardinal, although such admirers did not follow Law's teachings blindly and without criticism. An Anglican who remained loyal to the dethroned Stuarts, and thus a non-Juror, Law represented the heart of Anglican spirituality as it developed during the sixteenth and seventeenth centuries. *The Book of Common Prayer*, the major instrument for the development of Anglican piety, and the teachings of the Caroline Divines, especially their exposition of moral theology, influenced Law. He was also influenced by the Protestant mystic Jacob Boehme, French mystics such as the famous Madame Guyon, and English men of science such as John Newton. Thus influenced Law viewed the condition of English society and of the Church and religion in his time with alarm and made his fervent plea for reform. *A Serious Call to a Devout and Holy Life* is at one and the same time such a plea for reform and also a work of spiritual guidance describing the way to reform. The book was very much relevant to the situation Law confronted in eighteenth century England and it possesses relevance for us, living in the twentieth century, because in it Law demanded reform—a constant, fundamental theme in the history of religions—and prescribed the way to achieve it in concrete, profoundly spiritual terms.

Reform in a spiritual sense involves recovery of humanity's lost integrity and innocence, that which was ours before Adam's fall. Now, by virtue of God sending his Son—the second Adam—to us it is possible to be reformed after the image of God in Christ, to return to the Garden, regaining the integrity and innocence which

1

God intended. The Greek Fathers, who also influenced Law, understood this. Gregory of Nyssa wrote of reform in such words as these: "It is indeed possible for us to return to the original beatitude, if we now will run backward on the same road which we had followed when we were rejected from Paradise together with our forefather [Adam]" *(De Virginitate,* 12,13). Such a return is made possible through Christ, but it is not easy. Reform involves renunciation, leaving behind the things of the flesh, the world, and the devil. It involves devotion and discipline of the most rigorous sort.

At times of decline and decay in the Church and in society, such as Law recognized in eighteenth century England, when Christian committment is nominal and the pursuit of holiness ignored and ridiculed, there arise prophets such as Law to expose hypocrisy and apostasy and to lead the way toward reform. Law was especially concerned for the "leisured classes"—the idle rich who also concerned St. Jerome in fourth century Rome—who attend Church and make their modest contributions to assist the poor and believe that such outward display is sufficient. Law knew better. The true Christian is devout, striving to live a life wholly devoted to God, through humility and renunciation returning to Paradise.

In being critical of mere attendance at Church services, Law does not mean to deprecate public worship. Rather, he seems to emphasize the New Testament teaching that for the Christian *the* place of worship is that place where God confronts us in Christ and we respond to that confrontation. Worship in spirit and in truth involves all of life. St. Paul understood this: "I appeal to you therefore, brethren, by the mercies of God, to present your bodies as a living sacrifice, holy and acceptable to God, which is your spiritual worship. Do not be conformed to this world but be transformed [reformed] by the renewal of your mind, that you may prove what is the will of God, what is good and acceptable and perfect" (Romans 12:1-2, NEB).

The radical nature of Law's understanding of such Biblical wisdom is vividly displayed in the contrast of two sisters, Flavia and Miranda. The former is conceited, worldly, and selfish, considering herself to be admirable in works of charity, which she believes she can ill afford. Miranda is wholly devout, devoting all of

2

her life to the doing of God's will, giving with the same magnanimity with which God has given all that she has and all that she is. God gives without regard to the worthiness of the recipients. "And shall I," says Miranda, "withhold a little money or food from my fellow creature, for fear he shall not be good enough to receive it of me? Do I beg of God to deal with me, not according to my merit, but according to his own great goodness, and shall I be so absurd as to withhold my charity from a poor brother because he may perhaps not deserve it?" (p. 85)

Miranda's devotion is grounded in large part in private prayer, in study of the Bible, especially the New Testament, and in imitating the lives of the saints. Prayer is central to her spirituality. For Law "Prayer is the nearest approach to God and the highest enjoyment of Him that we are capable of in this life. It is the noblest exercise of the soul, the most excellent use of our best faculties, and the highest imitation of the blessed inhabitants of heaven" (p. 171). Prayer is the way to devotion in all of life and should imbue all of life. It need not be confined to special times and forms of prayer. "Sometimes the light of God's countenance shines so bright upon us, we see so far into the invisible world, we are so affected with the wonders of love and goodness of God that our hearts worship and adore in a language higher than that of words, and we feel transports of devotion which only can be felt" (p. 180).

Law's special wisdom and continuing worth consists in part in his recognition of the depths and heights of true devotion and in part in his acknowledging that on account of our imperfection in this life we need forms and a routine of daily prayer. Like Richard Hooker who preceded him in the development of Anglican spirituality, Law was aware of human frailty, but unlike Hooker seemed not to go so far as to prefer public worship as the best aid available. He had witnessed too many people in his time attending the Church's services without being influenced by them to cultivate true devotion. Like Lancelot Andrewes in his *Preces Privatae*, Law affirmed a routine of private devotions sanctifying the day and the night from early morning praise and thanksgiving to evening confession and penitence and to the remembrance of death's certainty upon retiring at day's end. The latter part of *A Serious Call* concerns six specified times of private devotions, relating the uniqueness of

3

each to the specifics of the devout life. Prayer in this context is routine but more than routine. It is, in the words of George Herbert, "Gods breath in man returning to his birth,/The soul in paraphrase, heart in pilgrimage" ("Prayer I").

In *The Spirit of Love*, which is perhaps Law's best writing, a deeper level of understanding is achieved, reflective of the developing mystical experience in Law's life. Greatly influenced by Boehme, Law here writes of our union, which is our reunion, our returning, our renewal and reform. It is union with God who is love and not a wrathful Father who must be appeased. The wrath which separates us from God is not in God but in us. Redemption consists in the removal of this wrath and thus in reconciliation with God. The process of redemption involves Christ living triumphantly through every sort of temptation, suffering and evil which is experienced by humanity, living through it all in humility and with patient love. And this is what happened culminating in Christ's death and resurrection, the culmination of redemption. In the Second Dialogue, Law set forth a view of redemption which is reminiscent of Richard Hooker, whose theology of participation involved a view of Christ as the second Adam, through whom we are saved and in whom we are restored to participation in the Divine nature.

Law refutes the legalistic view of atonement, calling it "the grossest of all fictions," clearly contrary to the Word of God: "the infinite love, mercy and compassion of God toward fallen man is not purchased or procured for us by the death of Christ, but the Incarnation and sufferings of Christ came from and are given to us by the infinite antecedent love of God for us and are the gracious effects of His own love and goodness towards us" (p. 93). This view of God as love, so much in tune with the teachings of the Greek Fathers and so agreeable to many modern Biblical theologians, goes far toward explaining Law's understanding of devotion, the heart of his spirituality. Surrender to God's will is not simply (and harshly) a necessary duty. It is the irresistible human response to God's love. Theogenes put it well: "the God of patience, meekness and love is the one God of my heart. It is now the whole bent and desire of my soul to seek for all my salvation in and through the merits and mediation of the meek, humble, patient, resigned, suffering Lamb of God who alone hath power to bring forth the blessed birth of these heavenly virtues in my soul" (p. 169).

Law's teachings are not beyond criticism. He has been accused of undue rigorism, of stressing good works to the detriment of justification, of neglecting the humanist elements in the Christian faith, and of stressing faith to the neglect of reason. There were those who objected to his view of the atonement and there were those who resented his preoccupation with the "leisured classes." But for anyone sensitive to the ways in which life in the modern world seduces would be Christians into believing that the comfortable way of self satisfaction is the way of the Cross, the way of light and life, Law's clear, challenging definition of devotion as entire dedication to God—spelled out in concrete ways applicable in many instances to life in the twentieth century as well as the eighteenth—is powerful, disturbing, and inspired.

Law is most helpful in the ways he details the cultivation of devotion, appealing to reason and common sense as well as to duty. His plan of devotional exercises in *A Serious Call* may seem impossible given the conditions of our modern lives. But then, true devotion may seem impossible. *The Spirit of Love* concerns the motivation which makes the impossible more nearly possible. God as compassionate and persistent, giving his Son that we might be set free from the tragedy which is ours through the first Adam, inspires the response of genuine devotion. It is in union with Christ, He in us and we in Him, that we rise to the life eternal, to "the life of God in the soul" (p. 174). This is Christian spirituality according to William Law.

John Booty
Episcopal Divinity School
Cambridge, Massachusetts

Foreword

William Law (1686-1761) was born in King's Cliffe, North-amptonshire, near the cathedral city of Peterborough. He was educated at Emmanuel College, Cambridge, of which he became a Fellow in 1711 (B.A. 1708, M.A. 1712), the year also of his ordination; but he declined to take the Oath of Allegiance to George I on the king's accession in 1714, and thus as a Nonjuror he had to resign his college position. He later retired to Putney, next to London, and lived in the household of Edward Gibbon from 1727 to 1737, where he was tutor to the father of the historian. Here he published *A Serious Call to a Devout and Holy Life* in 1728, a devotional work stimulated by his reading of such writers as Johann Tauler, Jan van Ruysbroeck, and Thomas à Kempis. Law's book, full of practical wisdom on the Christian life, and pleasing for its plain style, its memorable aphorisms, and its literary portraits of the character types around him, proved enormously popular in his own lifetime and has won for him a wide and lasting audience. Of English devotional classics since the Reformation, *A Serious Call* is one of the most significant, for it may be compared with John Bunyan's *Pilgrim's Progress* (1678) because of its great influence on the lives of generations of readers, and its ability to demonstrate how to live the noblest ethical and ascetic ideals in terms of ordinary Christian experience. Law returned to his home in King's Cliffe in about 1740, where he lived quietly and benignly for the rest of his years. He continued to write, but with a new spiritual direction determined by his reading of Jakob Boehme and his enthusiasm for the works of this German Protestant mystic of the 17th century. *The Spirit of Love* (in two parts, 1752-54) is among the last of Law's books, and it illustrates with particular subtlety and power his understanding of Boehme and the concerns of his later years, emphasizing especially the indwelling of Christ in the soul and His universal

FOREWORD

Atonement, now in a style more abstract than that of *A Serious Call*, but no less urgent, somber, and persuasive.

This present edition, based upon the earliest and best texts, brings together for the first time in this century, in an unabridged and definitive form, Law's two greatest works. Written under different spiritual influences in widely separated and contrasting times of his life, one explores the daily life of practical devotion, the other sets forth the mystery of life in God. Together they reveal to us a devotional way made up of much "head-work" and "heart-work" (to adapt Richard Baxter's description of Herbert's poetry)—the two opposing but complementary actions of the Christian pilgrim who at the same time looks for and celebrates the joy and glory of God.

Paul G. Stanwood
University of British Columbia

Introduction

William Law:
Ascetic and Mystic

by Austin Warren

In many ways, the 18th century was like our own. Joseph Butler wrote, in the 'Advertisement' to the first edition of his famous *Analogy* (1736), "It is come, I know not how, to be taken for granted by many persons that Christianity is not so much as a subject for inquiry, but that it is now at length discovered to be fictitious. And accordingly they treat it as if, in the present age, this were an agreed point among all people of discernment and nothing remained but to set it up as a principal subject of mirth and ridicule, as it were by way of reprisals for its having so long interrupted the pleasures of the world."

In England, the 18th century was the age of the 'Enlightenment,' of 'reason,' of common sense and easy compromise. And the Church was the profession for a gentleman, the younger son of a landed family, who needed no other qualifications for his office than an education at Oxford or Cambridge and the absence of an openly scandalous life; it involved no claims or aspirations to devoutness, still less to sanctity. The Anglican priest was an official of the state, just as the Anglican layman was an Anglican precisely and only because he was a loyal Englishman. 'Enthusiasm,' the being 'filled with God,' was viewed by clergy and people alike as being un-English—fanatical or at least whimsical and 'peculiar,' like the Papists, the Methodists, the Quakers, and those "lesser breeds," the Seekers, the Anabaptists, and the Ranters.

In such times, the danger to the Church is not persecution by pagans or atheists but the flattery and compliance of the world. No longer beheaded or otherwise martyred, 'Christians' are publicly honored for their compromise with Caesar and Mammon, with the powers that be. The enemies of the Church are within. Those Christians who are loyal to their principles are spiritual heroes and saints, admired by almost all, though followed by very few. Such men in the 18th century were Bishop Butler, Samuel Johnson, John Wesley, and William Law, Anglican saints who kept the faith in difficult times. It is not strange that these men, especially Butler and Johnson, were somber, even melancholy, of temperament; that Law was an austere and religious moralist till he became a mystic; that all were sober and cautious thinkers. And, living when they did, these men had to be 'inner-directed,' quietly independent thinkers who had, like Pascal, Kierkegaard, and Simone Weil, to examine the very foundations of their faith.

William Law (1686-1761), born in King's Cliffe, a village of Northamptonshire, was a graduate of Emmanuel College, Cambridge, which, in the reign of Elizabeth, had been a nursery of Puritanism, English and American, and which, in the early 17th century, had been the center of the Cambridge Platonists— Whichcote, Cudworth, Henry More, and John Smith. It is strange that Law never mentions these men of an earlier generation at his own college. The reason is probably their churchmanship, which was Puritan while his was High Church; for, being moralists, and, two of them, mystical philosophers, they should have had a strong appeal for him.

A serious young man, Law, before he set out for Cambridge in 1705, drew up a set of "Rules for My Future Conduct" which reminds one of the "Resolutions" young Jonathan Edwards drew up for himself. Among Law's "Rules" are these:

> To avoid all concerns with the world, or the ways of it, except when religion requires. To remember frequently, and to impress it upon my mind deeply, that no condition of this life is for enjoyment, but for trial; and that every power, ability, or advantage we have are all so many talents to be accounted for to the Judge of the whole world. To avoid all excess in eating and drinking. To be always fearful of letting my time slip away without some fruit. To avoid all idleness.

Time must not be wasted. If he says nothing about money, it is probably because he then had none; but in *A Serious Call*, waste of money becomes almost as important as that of time: 'voluntary poverty' becomes a definite part of his mature scheme for Christian living. The "Rules" continue:

> *To think humbly of myself, and with great charity of all others. To think often of the life of Christ, and propose it as a pattern to myself. To spend some time in giving an account of the day, previous to evening prayer: how have I spent this day? what sin have I committed? what temptations have I withstood? have I performed all my duty?*

Characteristic words are 'sin' and 'idleness,' 'duty' and 'Judge.' These are ascetic notes, all essentially negative. "The fear of the Lord is the beginning of wisdom." But where are the peace and joy of the spiritual life? They lie far ahead, but eventually they are to be attained.†

Law took his B.A. in 1708. In 1711 he was elected to a fellowship of his college, but in 1716 he resigned it, finding himself conscientiously unable to take the oath of allegiance to the Hanoverian George I. He was ordained a priest by Nonjuring Bishop Gandy in 1711. Law belonged to the second generation of the Nonjurors, that group of High Church men who, believing that the Stuarts were by Divine Right the legitimate monarchs of England, refused to take the oath of allegiance to William and Mary and to the Hanoverian Georges. This Nonjuring schismatic Church, far more Catholic minded in doctrine and liturgy than the Establishment, continued in England and especially in Scotland, where Jacobite sympathies were strong, well into the latter part of the 18th century; and it was the bishops of the Nonjuring Episcopal Church of Scotland who, in 1784, ordained Samuel Seabury as the first prelate of the American Episcopal Church.

This stance, at once political and religious, of the Nonjuror, made it impossible for Law to hold any university or church ap-

---

† Law's "Rules" survive in the autograph, and they are contained in the Walton Manuscripts (186.4) in Dr. Williams's Library, London. Christopher Walton, who assembled many of Law's papers and unpublished writings, described his collection and quoted copiously from it in his *Notes and Materials for an Adequate Biography of the Celebrated Divine and Theosopher William Law* (London: privately printed, 1854). The extracts from the "Rules" are from Law's own copy, but Walton was first to give them in full (pp. 345-46).

pointment. Like other Nonjuring priests, he had to earn his living as a tutor, private chaplain, or writer. Between 1716 and 1740 he was all three. For ten years, he was the tutor, at Putney in Surrey, of Edward Gibbon, the father of the great historian. "In our family," writes the sceptical historian, "he left the reputation of a worthy and pious man who believed all he professed and practiced all that he enjoined."

About 1740, Miss Hester Gibbon, the historian's aunt, and Mrs. Hutcheson, a rich and pious widow, took a house in Law's native village, King's Cliffe, and the celibate Law joined them as their spiritual director and chaplain. This small household, a kind of 'Protestant nunnery,' resembled the family community of Nicholas Ferrar at Little Gidding and continued that 17th-century experiment in 'holy living' into the 18th century, forming a link between it and the revival of the monastic life after the Oxford Movement of the 19th century. The members of the household at King's Cliffe pursued a 'regular' and methodical regime, assembling three times a day, morning, noon, and evening, for corporate prayers. With money given him by an anonymous benefactor, a grateful reader of his writing, Law had earlier founded a school for poor girls, who were taught to read, knit, and sew, and to study the catechism and attend church service regularly. Mrs. Hutcheson added another school and almshouses. Of their large joint income they lived on a tenth and gave the rest away. The three gave clothes and soups and money to the poor. They were, indeed, so generous in their charity, and so uncritical of the merits of applicants for it, that King's Cliffe gained, it is said, a reputation for attracting the idle and the worthless. The time of the little community was divided between pious exercises and 'works of mercy.'

Law rose at five, and spent much of the day in a small study occupied at his reading and writing. He was already absorbed in writing meditations on the works of Boehme, which he had begun to read some seven years before. But he possessed, besides these works, a large and choice library of other mystical books. He wrote, "I thank God I have always been a diligent reader of those mystical divines through all the ages of the Church, from the apostolic Dionysius the Areopagite down to the great Fénelon, Archbishop of Cambray . . . ." Deeply attracted to the Desert Fathers, he owned *Les Vies des Saints Pères des Déserts* and the *Spiritual Homilies* of Saint Macarius of Egypt; he owned also the medieval mystics, Ruysbroeck (his copy of the *Opera Omnia* is underlined and evidently much read), and Tauler (both in Latin and German), and the *Theologica Germanica*, which he valued highly and recommended to the more advanced among his disciples. He knew well the *Imitation of Christ* and Saint Francis of Sales' *Introduction à la Vie Dévote*, the Catholic counterpart of the *Serious Call*. His spiritual life was nourished by the books of his spiritual ancestors, and by what nourished them as well as him, a life centered in prayer and meditation.

Though Quakers, actual or virtual, can find warrant for their views in Law's writings, Law lived and died an Anglican. Ready to find testimony to the truth in Papist and Protestant writings, and at the end an ecumenical spirit, he was unwilling to separate himself from the specific regional church into which he was born. And though as a matter of private conscience a Nonjuror, he took no part in the characteristic Nonjuring activities, which were markedly liturgical enrichments or attempted reunion with Eastern Orthodoxy. Instead, with the two ladies under his direction, he attended all the services at the parish church of King's Cliffe, this despite the fact that he and the resident rector were not on personally friendly terms.

Law's *Serious Call* (1728), his second book, which was written at Putney, has received all manner of encomia. When Samuel Johnson went to Oxford, he picked it up "expecting to find it a dull book (such books generally are) and perhaps to laugh at it. But I found Law quite an overmatch for me." Boswell, who reports this saying, adds, "From this time forward, religion was the dominant object of his thoughts." Dr. Johnson later pronounced the *Call* "the finest piece of hortatory theology in any language." In 1789 John Wesley speaks of it as a "treatise which will hardly be equalled in the English tongue, either for beauty of expression or for justice and depth of thought"; and in his *Christian Library* of fifty volumes, published in 1749, he included abridged versions of both *Christian Perfection* and *A Serious Call*—as well as, later, in 1768, two volumes of extracts from Law's later writings, including the final *Address to the Clergy*, *The Spirit of Prayer*, and *The Spirit of Love*. But the highest tribute is probably that from Leslie Stephen, who in his *English Thought of the Eighteenth Century* says *A Serious Call* "may be read with pleasure even by the purely literary critic"; but its "power can only be adequately felt by readers who can study it on their knees."

This book is substantially as readable and as pertinent today as it was when it was written. The most entertaining parts are the 'characters' which portray permanent human types: The shrewd businessman, the man of fashion, the easygoing clergyman, the literary scholar, the cultivated dilettante, the worldly and un-worldly women are all still with us. In these portraits, and in the literary skill with which Law draws them, Law was in a great tradition going back to the Greek writer Theophrastus and down through the French La Bruyère, to whom he has been likened, and the English 'character' writers, Overbury, Earle, and Thomas Fuller—especially in his *Holy and Profane State*; Law's 'characters,' like those of La Bruyère, carry Latin or Greek names as signs of their being traditional types—Miranda (wonderful), Flavia (ex-travagant), Calidus (cold and wasteful), Penitens (penitent), Mundanus (worldly), Flatus (sanguine), Succus (dispirited), Eusebius or Eusebia (reverent), Paternus (fatherly). Among these, there are few persons downright evil, and but a very few who are wise and saintly; most of them are at neither pole but in between, com-promisers between the Spirit and the World, the Laodiceans of Revelation; and it is these compromisers, ordinary, normal, well-adjusted members of society, who are Law's chief and most effec-tive butts. The keen knowledge of the human types which Law displays was based upon his years at the Gibbon estate at Putney—the family and their middle-class guests, businessmen and their wives; on his visits to nearby London (where he later lived for a few years); on his memories of the university, with its assem-bly of Fellows at once scholars and clergymen; and lastly on his knowledge of his own heart.

"Enter in at the strait gate" is Law's virtual maxim and motto. He admits no comfortable distinction between the Counsels of Per-fection enjoined by the Sermon on the Mount, by which monks are to live, and the accommodations permitted by Roman Catholics to lay people living in the world, who are to keep the Ten Commandments of the Mosaic law and the commandments of the Church but nothing more rigid. Law knows of no 'two ways' of life. He takes the Counsels of Perfection as applying to all who "profess and call themselves Christians," and makes no real distinction between priests and their parishioners except what might be termed an occupational one: All are alike called to holiness. "Be ye perfect, even as your Father in Heaven is perfect." Law seems ever mindful of him whom he calls "the young gentleman in the gospel"—the rich young ruler who came to Jesus in search of eternal life, the ruler who, having kept the Commandments from his youth up, was still lacking peace, but, because he could not bring himself to sell all his goods, went away sorrowful. Law does not interpret this as dividing those called to the 'religious' life (with its poverty, chastity, and obedience) from those who follow only the Commandments but as dividing true Christians from nominal adherents.

No more than Jesus will Law allow compromise between God and the world. "Ye cannot serve God and Mammon." "No man can serve two masters." There can be no peace of mind for the half-hearted, for those whose eye is not single. Law takes his stand upon such texts from the New Testament; and though he quotes the Epistles of Saint Paul, chiefly from the mystical passages, for example, "Not I live, but Christ liveth in me," he chiefly quotes the sayings of Jesus—the sayings, not the narrative of his life, or his miracles, or the facts of his birth or Resurrection; and he seeks to exposit and apply the spirit of Jesus' unequivocal teaching.

A Serious Call is written in a style plain, manly, and "nervous" (in the 18th-century sense of sinewy), to be paralleled, among Restoration writers, perhaps by Isaac Barrow; among his contemporaries, by Swift; among his successors, by Johnson in his *Rambler* essays. Law writes like the clear and forcible thinker he is. He is often witty, never for show but for point. Thus he speaks of "Mundanus" as always busy improving the "clearness and strength of his understanding," yet still praying the same "little form of words" which, when he was six years old, he was used to say, night and morning, at his mother's knee; and, of "Classicus," that, though he is so versed in "the best authors of antiquity" that he can "very ingeniously imitate the manner of any of them," yet "the two Testaments would not have so much as a place among his books but that they are both to be had in Greek."

A "devout and holy life," Law makes clear in his very first chapter, is not primarily one of churchgoing or pious exercises. "Prayers whether private or public are particular parts or instances of devotion. Devotion signifies a life given, or devoted to God." "It is very observable that there is not one command in all the gospel for public worship; and perhaps it is a duty that is less insisted upon in scripture than of any other. The frequent attendance at it is never so much as mentioned in all the New Testament. . . . Our blessed Savior and His Apostles are wholly taken up in doctrines that relate to common life".

There are three classes of people whom Law addresses—the clergy, aristocrats and gentlefolk, and "tradesmen"—the bourgeois; and Law never wearies in pointing out that the same general principles apply to the life of them all, though he addresses advice to each class. "Let a clergyman be . . . pious, and he will . . . no more talk of noble preferment than of noble eating or a glorious chariot." The "gentleman of birth and fortune . . . does not ask what is allowable and pardonable but what is commendable and praiseworthy." "Let a tradesman have this intention, and it will make him a saint in his shop." But all must, if they would be true Christians, live by method and rule, wasting neither time nor money. "You see one person throwing away his time in sleep and idleness, in visiting and vain diversions. . . . You see another careful of each day, dividing his hours by rules of reason and religion. . . ." Certainly "scrupulous anxiety" is wrong, but we should have "a just fear of living in sloth and idleness"; he "that has begun to live by rule has gone a great way toward the perfection of his own life." And for a summary epigram, "It is better to be holy than to have holy prayers."

It is the world which, more than the flesh or the Devil, is the chief enemy of true Christians. It "was the spirit of the world that nailed our Lord to the cross." "The world, to be sure, now professes Christianity, but will anyone say this Christian world is of the spirit of Christ?" Indeed, the world "has, by its favors, destroyed more Christians than ever it did by the most violent persecutions."

Law applies this practically by remarking how afraid a man is of not advancing his wealth and his ownership of great houses and fine clothes "lest the world should take him for a fool" and how "many a man would drop resentment and forgive an affront but that he is afraid, if he should, the world would not forgive him."

As a spiritual teacher, Law is a master of Christian seriousness, in this respect at least the equal of Kierkegaard, whose *Training in Christianity* has been called the closest parallel to *A Serious Call*. Law is, like Kierkegaard, the exposer of the futility—and danger—of compromise in all its manifold forms. But while Kierkegaard affords extrareligious pleasure, by his brilliant analyses of such neurotic states as anxiety and by his little parabolic narratives, and flatters the pride of the reader who can follow his subtleties, Law affords no such flattery; he lays bare and flays one's innermost motives, the motives by which one lives. He recalls a man to his adolescence, when right and wrong, sin and holiness, seemed sharply differentiated and there was no either-or; he exposes equivocations and half-truths, saying "but one thing is needful."

And yet: with all his genuine ecumenism, his revolt against sectarianism, his catholic elevation beyond and above even the distinction between "Papist and Protestant," between which Western Christendom is divided, he is still too narrow to be truly catholic. One cannot but contrast him with Bishop Jeremy Taylor, who, in his *Holy Living* and *Holy Dying*, quotes almost as much from the Greek Stoics as from the Jewish Scriptures, Old and New; and with the Cambridge Platonists of the English 17th century; and with their greater ancestors, the Christian Platonists of Alexandria; and with the Russian Orthodox thinkers who, writing in the 19th and 20th centuries, are debtors both to speculative philosophy and to a long tradition of liturgical and mystical piety; and with Fénelon, Maritain, and Baron von Hügel—all great Christian Humanists. What is Christian—or spiritual—Humanism but the reconciliation of three deeply essential movements of man's spirit, at every time likely to split asunder: learning, or erudition; poetry, or culture; and high religion? It can't honestly be claimed that the Jesus of the Synoptic Gospels reconciled these three; yet the author of the Fourth Gospel and Saint Paul began to do so, and a rich and long-continued tradition holds that the wisdom of 'pagan' aspiration

19

is completed and fulfilled, but not cancelled, by Christian 'revelation.'

It is in the light of this Christian Humanist tradition that Law seems an obscurantist. He abrogates human reason, human learning, and human culture (literature and the arts) in the name of true religion. Not a Fundamentalist in the sense of an adherent to an infallible Bible literally read, he is one in his attitude toward humanistic culture, the servant and complement of religion.

According to the traditional wisdom of Christian Humanism, in things religious and moral, some things are commanded, some recommended, some permitted, and some forbidden. Between the commanded and the forbidden, there is, for Catholic casuists, a middle ground governed by the old classical principles of decorum and moderation. Pascal accused the Jesuits of laxity in what they permitted; Jonathan Edwards and Law are rigorists for whom there is really no middle ground between virtue and vice. The latter find, too, no middle ground between industry and sloth, no 'innocent' amusements or 'play'; and, in so ruling, they virtually rule out the fine arts — not only the theater but painting, all music except hymn tunes, and literature — poetry and the novel: in a word, culture. And they rule out cards and all other games, and dancing, and sports and other athletic exercises, performances, and entertainments. The bow must always be taut, never relaxed.

The impression must not be given, however, that Law is either a dour fanatic or an advocate of ascetic extremes. He is very English in his sobriety. He does not advocate, like the Shakers, universal celibacy. Marriage is to go on, and families are to be reared. Virtuous women have their choice of marriage or a 'virgin state.' His ideal of family life seems that which became familiar in the 19th century among Quakers, Wesleyans, and other Non-Conformists, and some High Anglicans. Nor does he want to attack 'right reason' (the rational) or 'happiness,' but indeed to show, as he undertakes to do in chapter 11 of *A Call*, that great devotion fills our life with "the greatest peace and happiness," while their enemy, the "passions, in rebellion against God and reason, fill human life with imaginary wants." The holy life is also the happy life.

If one asks whether Law's picture of the holy life seems a happy one, an attractive one, the answer must be that such a life cannot be viewed, still less judged, from outside. To a neurotic, a normal life seems commonplace and dull, without excitement; a neurotic, under therapy, fights to retain his anxieties, without which, so he thinks, he will not feel alive, will not feel himself: He is asked to find a new center. To a man of the world, a life either of study or of good works is a boring one. Both the neurotic and the man of the world must be converted, turned around, born again, before they can judge of the happiness proposed by a holy life. To both, the saints in the *Paradiso* are far less individuated and less piquant than the sinners in the *Inferno*. Sanctity has its own leveling, a leveling, however, at the highest elevation.

Law's two practical and devotional treatises, *Christian Perfection* (1726) and *A Serious Call* (1728), were preceded and followed by polemic works, published between 1717 and 1740, good accounts of which are given in the critical histories by Stephen and Elton (see the Bibliography). In 1717, in *Three Letters to the Bishop of Bangor* (Dr. Hoadly), Law defended the apostolic succession of the bishops and the spiritual authority of the Church against an Erastian prelate asserting the ecclesiastical supremacy of the state. In 1723, he attacked Mandeville's *Fable of the Bees*, which proclaimed that "private vices were public benefits." In 1726, he maintained *The Absolute Unlawfulness of the Stage-Entertainment*, the theater of the Restoration. In 1731, he replied to Tindal's Deistic book *Christianity not Mysterious* with his *Case of Reason and Natural Religion Fairly and Fully Stated*. And lastly, Dr. Trapp being the enemy addressed, he assailed that fellow-Anglican's book *Folly, Sin and Danger of being Righteous Over-much*. In short, Law took on all the enemies of the orthodox Anglican Church, whether theoretical or practical; and he is credited with having argued forcibly and with acute, persistent logic.

But meanwhile Law was himself undergoing a deep change. He lost faith in the use of the external historical evidences for Christianity, which at best reached the reason and left the heart unaffected. Even intellectual orthodoxy came to seem an affair not at the center of things, any more than correct ritual. What mattered was a change of heart, a new and regenerate holy life; and having reached this conclusion, he gave up arguing and addressed himself

21

to testifying, persuading, converting. It is a commonplace that polemic works date rapidly, while ascetic and mystical works remain fresh. And, though Law was without literary ambition, this has happened to his own books.

In his years of controversy, between *A Serious Call* and *The Spirit of Prayer* and *The Spirit of Love*, Law accepted the standard 'evidences' of the Christian apologist, the fulfillment of Old Testament prophecy and the miracles wrought by Christ and His Apostles. But these finally came to seem to him external, as not touching the inner reality of the spiritual life. One could know all the arguments, defend them intellectually, and still live like other people. As Jesus says of giving presents to your friends (as we all do at Christmas, the reputed date of His birth), "Do not even the Gentiles do the same?" The mark of the Christian is that he gives to the undeserving and to those hostile to him.

All of Law's mystical writings were composed at King's Cliffe in that semimonastic retirement into which he withdrew at the age of fifty-four. There, living in a country village, he continued to live by rule and method, alternating study and meditation and writing with his practical office as almoner, writing letters to a few spiritually minded friends, seeing a few friends like Dr. Byrom and Mr. Langcake. His later writing, in all of which he expressed his admiration for and indebtedness to Boehme, alienated him from former admirers like John Wesley, who attacked him in a printed *Letter*, and Dr. Johnson, as well as, in our century, from that great French historian of Christian spirituality Fr. Louis Bouyer, who says of these books that, though they "contain passages of high spirituality, Boehme's bizarre genius here turns into a very British kind of mild dottiness." On the other hand, Aldous Huxley, author as well as compiler of that remarkable book *The Perennial Philosophy*, who probably quotes more passages from Law than any other writer—passages of "high spirituality"—holds the later writings in highest esteem and regards their author as "not only a master of English prose" but as "one of the most endearingly saintly figures in the whole history of Anglicanism."

Law certainly damaged his general reputation in his own time by his loyal and dogged adherence to Boehme, whom he variously calls "illumined" and "blessed"; of whom he says, in *The Spirit of Love*, "the mystery of all things [was] opened by God in his chosen instrument Jacob Boehme." What is it to be "illumined"? What status did Law assign to Boehme? Not of equal authority with scripture, we may safely suppose. Why then was he of more authority than any other mystic, such as Fénelon's friend and inspiration Mme Guyon, whom on one occasion Law also called "illumined"? The word had a special technical meaning in the 17th and 18th centuries, shifting though that meaning was. It signified one with claims to esoteric knowledge through "openings," visions, or private revelations. Boehme had three or four such openings, during the earliest of which he said he learned more in a quarter of an hour than he could have learned in all the universities. It was on the basis of these brief openings, and the insights they gave him, that he constructed his philosophy.

To accept these visions and their authority, Law was already prepared by a lifelong sympathy with mysticism. What such sympathy requires is belief in two things—the possibility of union with God, temporary or permanent, in this life, and the belief that religious inspiration or revelation did not stop with the end of the New Testament, but continues, as the Holy Ghost discloses truths which the world was not earlier ready to understand. Both of these beliefs Law appears to hold.

He is said to have begun his reading of Boehme—or Behmen, as he calls him—about 1734. Why did Law so avidly seize upon the writings of this 17th-century German shoemaker when all his life he had been acquainted with the great line of mystics from Dionysius the Areopagite down to Fénelon, the apostle of pure love?

My first answer is that it was exactly the humble status of Boehme and his supposed absence of book learning which attracted Law. I say "supposed," for modern studies show that, thanks to the erudition of his more highly placed friends, Boehme was versed in Paracelsus and the spiritual alchemists and in pietistic theologians like Weigel. But Law must have thought of him as taught directly by God through his own intuitions, a mystic in the most exact sense, and thus the direct opposite of the bishops and scholars like Hoadly and Warburton, who, exegetes and reasoners, spoke by hearsay.

Most deeply, however, Law was attracted to Boehme because the shoemaker combined Evangelical theology with speculative theories about ultimate realities, and Law felt the need of a framework for his own thinking—a framework both intellectual and imaginative which can be called either a myth or a system—a framework indeed conceptual-imaginative. He needed a philosophy of religion, and this Boehme provided him with. Though he did not like his views called a 'philosophy,' such they were.

The system of Boehme can here neither be given adequate exposition nor yet entirely omitted; it can but be sampled. Its speculative theology is divided, by his most thorough modern expositor, into "Good beyond Nature and Creature: Theogony," "Eternal Nature," and "Temporal Nature"; only after these do we reach "Man" and "Redemption." It is in the first two of these that Boehme is most original. God begins as the Godhead, an Abyss, an *Ungrund*; then develops a Will; then comes a Trinity of Persons; then a fourth person is added, Sophia, or Divine Wisdom, a female principle named and characterized in *Proverbs* and the *Wisdom of Solomon*. Between these persons there is a "love-play": Wisdom acts as a mirror in which the ultimate God comes to consciousness.

Nature, first imagined, becomes actual through the operation of the Seven Natural Properties, so often dwelt upon or mentioned by Law—a dark ternary and a light ternary, the intermediate fourth between the two ternaries being fire, the lightning flash. First comes Desire, or contraction, which is harsh and hard; then Movement or expansion; then (born out of the conflict of the first two) Anguish or rotation. The lightning flash, or contact between Nature and Spirit, transfigures the dark ternary into the light which consists of: the fifth property, Wisdom or love-fire; the sixth, intelligible sound; and the seventh, Essential Wisdom. Law is concerned only with the first three, which characterize the unrest of the physical world and the unrest of man's restless, desirous nature.

This is heady stuff but it satisfied the hitherto undeveloped speculative part of Law, though he did not immediately find it easy going. He writes: "When I first began to read him [Boehme], he put

me into a perfect sweat. But as I discerned sound truths and glim-
merings of a deep ground of sense even in passages not then clearly
intelligible to me, I found in myself a strong incentive to dig in
these writings, I followed the impulse . . . till at length I discovered
the wonderful treasure that was hid in this field." The reader of
Law's later writings will remember this passage and take heart.

Most of *The Spirit of Love*, like its predecessor (to which Law
calls it an 'Appendix') *The Spirit of Prayer*, also nominally in dialogue
form, is difficult to read, not taken sentence by sentence, or paragraph by paragraph, but as a whole. In contrast to the *Call*, these
works lack any clearly defined method of organization or logical
progression. Called "dialogues," they come nearest to being
monologues of a rhapsodic kind. Later, Law lived for the most part
a quiet and solitary life. His habitual companions were two women
and a few men, not his equals in character or intellect, his disciples,
to whom he discoursed. This absence of method, associated in his
mind perhaps with his increasing distrust of reasoning and criticism, makes his later works prolix and repetitious; and it is doubt-
less for that reason that they are better known today in the form of
selected passages (such as those anthologized by Scott Palmer and
Hobhouse, and Aldous Huxley) than they are as wholes. Yet at
least one of them, and preferably the shorter, *The Spirit of Love*,
should be read as a whole for the sake of the ecstatic flow of Law's
own spirit, which desires to break all its trammels, to move at will
among the grandest themes—the fall of man, or man's redemption,
the creation of the universe and its apocalyptic reunion and trans-
figuration.

In literary style, the Law of these later works was what literary
historians used to call a 'pre-Romantic.' His prose style still largely
uses abstract words, but he uses them to different effect; and nature
breaks into his consciousness, even though he lacks the specific
natural imagery which is so characteristic of Romantic poets. His
sentences become longer and looser, one clause or phrase added to
another; all rigidity dissolves. The man is less talking than meditating, and addressing himself rather than any audience, willing to be
overheard but adapting his discourse only to those who (unlike the
readers supposed by the *Call*) are already eager to hear, and near
conversion to the 'heavenly doctrines' the master proposes. The

modern reader should endeavor to let Law glide into his soul; put the book down for a time when he finds it boring; take it up again. The total effect will be larger than the sum of such intermittent reading.

We speak of the mystical writings of Law. What was their authority? Law made no claim ever to immediate inspiration, to visions or auditions such as those of Saint Paul, Saint Teresa, or Julian of Norwich. He had no known period of ecstasy like that after which Saint Thomas Aquinas wrote no more on his *Summa Theologica*. I see no clear evidence that he was an actual mystic. Yet it is difficult to relegate him to the rank of literary mystics like Richard Crashaw and Evelyn Underhill, persons widely read in mystical authors, the composers of poetry with mystical overtones: Even in these cases, we cannot be sure that they were not themselves mystics using the language of their predecessors out of modesty rather than coining a new terminology. Law speaks with authority, and in a language and a sentence structure his own. He sounds like no one else.

His deep sense of being an interpreter of Boehme needs interpretation beyond lists of parallel passages between them, such as Hobhouse has collected. The general sense of commentaries on their relationship would have it that Law selects from Boehme, omits the too esoteric, and gives a simplified version of the system; and I think this by and large true. But the doctrine of Boehme, chiefly, when stripped of its alchemy and theosophy, is good Evangelical Protestant mysticism (cf. Boehme's "Of the Supersensual Life: Two Dialogues"). In my own judgment Law professed and felt an indebtedness and a reverence for Boehme which was partly adventitious, and he attributed to Boehme much which he had already read in the earlier mystics but was earlier not ready to accept—his 'pride of intellect,' his logical powers, and his sheer English common sense had first to give way.

The Spirit of Love is divided into four sections—a 'letter' to a friend who is having difficulties with Law's teaching, who finds his "doctrine of pure and universal love" too refined and imaginary (fanciful), and who cannot reconcile that doctrine with the scriptural accounts of God's wrath. These are the problems which continue to engage us through the whole work; but after the letter

26

follow three dialogues in which Law, or Theophilus, is replying at great length to the objections of his companions. These men are Eusebius, easy to be convinced of the doctrine, which, because of his affectionate nature, he embraces with open arms, and Theogenes, who is shocked to find, despite his progress in the doctrine, that "all the passions of his corrupt nature [are] still alive in him." One is too easily made glad; the other, too discouraged by the fight he has before him. Law has to distinguish firmly between accepting the doctrine and putting it into practice, and, using characteristic mystical imagery, he reminds Eusebius that if he really possessed spiritual love he would know "how many deaths you had suffered before the spirit of love came to life in you."

In this whole book, divided into sections only to give semblance of reality to the dialogue-device of conversation, Theophilus is always the master, never doubting that he is in possession of the truth, and the other two are his students or disciples, men seriously in search of religious truth but with their intellectual difficulties as well as their difficulties in putting even what they see into practice. Their responses are of two kinds: Eusebius complains in the Second Dialogue that "your censure upon us seems to be more severe than just," and, in the same dialogue, Theogenes says "I could willingly hear you on this subject till midnight." The topics discussed run through all four parts, though Law says the Third Dialogue is to concern itself with "the practical part of the spirit of love, that so doctrine and practice, hearing and doing, may go hand in hand."

In actuality, Law's mind, even in the First Dialogue, goes back and forth constantly between theory and practice, between cosmic metaphysics derived from Boehme, and concerned with the seven properties of nature, and controversial references to current doctrines of the Calvinists and the Methodists and objections (unacknowledged) to his own earlier teaching in the *Call* about methods of life. And these same subjects are also discussed in *The Spirit of Prayer* (which is the spirit of love) and in the *Way of Divine Knowledge*. All Law's later works constitute a continuous meditation; he delights to repeat, with variations, these same motifs over and over, as does Boehme, so that if one has read one book attentively, and repeatedly, one has the system.

Law neither here nor elsewhere undertakes to prove the existence of God, an existence not denied even by Deists, who rejected revelation but held to 'natural religion,' which they maintained was "as old as creation" and "not mysterious." The existence of God was for Law certainly 'proved' by scripture; yet he did not, I feel sure, rely upon scripture, but upon the negative argument, the presence of evil in the natural world—storms, hail, floods, and earthquakes—and the sin of man, and especially his desire, his restlessness, and dissatisfaction. As Saint Augustine said, "Our hearts are restless till they find their rest in Thee."

There is a striking passage in Newman's *Apologia* which contrasts the certainty of the being of "God, as certain as his own existence," and the dismal sight of the world and the confusion and futility of human history. How account for the contrast? Newman answers: "*If* there is a God, *since* there is a God, the human race is implicated in some terrible aboriginal calamity. It is out of joint with the purpose of its creator." So too felt Boehme and Law.

This "aboriginal catastrophe" for Boehme and Law was the fall in prehistory, first of Lucifer and the other rebellious angels, and then of man, who in Adam was created perfect (and so, like the Godhead, androgynous). This double fall brought into being the physical world as we know it: The fall of the angels brought into being matter; and the creation described in Genesis is really a second creation, that of a material world in contrast to the first creation, which was of ideas and forms in the imagination of God. The fall, first of the angels and then of men, has disordered God's intention. But at the end of time, the universe will be restored to its original order and harmony. As Saint Paul wrote, "We know that the whole creation groaneth and travaileth in pain together until now"; and "the earnest expectation of the creature waiteth for the manifestation of the sons of God." The end of the return movement is the "glassy sea of unity and purity in which Saint John [in *Revelation*] beheld the throne of God in the midst of it" (the phrase "the glassy sea" is dear to Law and is repeated over and over like a kind of mantra). But before that redemption, creation must pass through its seven properties of nature. "Nature can have no rest but must be in the strife of fermentation, vegetation, and corruption, constantly doing and undoing, building and destroying, till the

spirit of love has rectified all outward Nature." These passages
come from the first section of *The Spirit of Love* .

Both Boehme and Law, in his later period, were obsessed with
the problem of evil, a problem cosmically antecedent to and inclu-
sive of sin. How not to end up by attributing evil as well as good to
God, or to postulate, like the Manichaeans, two gods, one good, the
other evil? Boehme in effect solves this partly by removing the
Deity by intervening stages from his creation, partly by supposing
in God the principles both of love and of "wrath." But Law seems
to reject both of Boehme's solutions, and to take his stand on a God
who is "pure love."

As Law does not undertake to prove the existence of God, so
he does not attempt to prove that God, the supreme principle of the
universe, is love on the basis of New Testament texts such as "God
is love" or "God so loved the world"; he proclaims it, explains away
all texts to the contrary, which chiefly come from the Old Testament, and then develops the implications of the doctrine that God
is Love, unmixed and pure and therefore incapable of "vindictive
wrath." And "the Spirit of God and the spirit of goodness are not
two spirits," while wrath and evil are but two words for one and the
same thing.

Though he never discusses figurative exegesis, Law's attitude
toward the interpretation of scripture requires some comment. Jesus' ethical teaching in the Sermon on the Mount he took with the
literalness of the later Tolstoi; but the 'history' in the Bible, and in
general the Old Testament, he treated with an unacknowledged but
generous allowance of figurative 'accommodation.' At the beginning of *The Spirit of Love*, he quotes a correspondent as objecting to
his "doctrine of pure and universal love" on the ground that so
much is "said in scripture of a righteousness and justice, a wrath
and vengeance of God that must be atoned"; that scripture seems to
deny a "Being that is all Love." This objection Law never directly
answers or rebuts; but from what he indirectly says it is clear that,
like Swedenborg, he interpreted the wrath of God, his anger and
jealousy, as not in God but in us, who are angry at God, who see
God as made in man's image. Whatever the Old Testament may
say, the New Testament proclaims a God of love. Says Law, speaking of both man and God, "The spirit of love can only love . . . it

knows no difference of time, place, or persons, but whether it gives or forgives, bears or forbears, it is equally doing its own delightful work, equally blessed from itself".

Like Boehme and the older Protestant mystics, Law strongly opposed all forensic theories of the Atonement, those commercial and legalistic theories that Christ paid upon the cross our debt to God the angry Father, thus freeing us from our debt of guilt; and he opposed, too, all theories of Christ's righteousness being 'imputed' to sinners. In *The Spirit of Love* Law writes: "The whole Truth . . . is plainly this. Christ given for us is neither more nor less than Christ given into us. And He is in no other sense our full, perfect, and sufficient Atonement than as His nature and spirit is born and formed in us, which so purgeth us from our sins that we are thereby in Him, and by Him dwelling in us become new creatures having our conversation in Heaven".

Law does not accept the Calvinist doctrine that fallen man is totally corrupt: There is in man "a seed of life"; there is "a smothered spark of heaven in the soul of man." "The Christ of God" lies "hidden in every son of man," for the very desire for a heavenly life argues "something of Heaven hidden in his soul." That man is not wholly corrupt is 'proved,' for Law, by the fact that Adam had two sons, Cain and Abel—Cain, who murdered his innocent brother; hence, both principles must have come from Adam; and similar pairs appear in Ishmael and Isaac, and in Esau and Jacob: such "strife and contrariety" appeared in the sons of the same father. Nor does he accept, in their Calvinistic form, the doctrines of election and reprobation. He denies that they are eternal decrees relating to "any particular number of people." They relate, he says, "solely to the two natures that are . . . in every individual of mankind"—his bestial nature and "the incorruptible seed of the world, or the Immanuel in every man."

Of Wesley and the Methodists, who owed so much to the earlier Law but broke away from the latter, the mystic, Law seems to be thinking when he says that men should judge their "state of love" by "these angelical tempers, and not by any fervor or heat that you find in yourself."

Law attacks bibliolatry in a fashion that caused Eusebius to say, "It seems to   to derogate from scripture". What Law is concerned to do is to distinguish between the written word and the Word. If Saint Paul could say of the law that "it was a schoolmaster to bring us to Christ," then "one thing can be affirmed of the letter of the New Testament; it is our schoolmaster unto Christ, until Christ, as the dawning of the day . . . arrives in our hearts."

At the end of the third, the 'practical' dialogue, one of Theophilus's disciples requests of him some rules or methods for attaining perfect love, or holiness. The earlier Law might have proposed some recipes, but not the later. Mrs. Stow says of Jonathan Edwards, of whose late treatise *The Nature of True Virtue* Law and his *Spirit of Love* strongly remind me, "he knocked out every rung of the ladder [to heaven] but the highest, and then, pointing to its hopeless splendor, said to the world, 'Go up thither and be saved.' " Both these rigorists felt mankind to be in search of easy ways. But the "one true way of dying to self is most simple and plain; it wants no arts or methods, no cells, monasteries, or pilgrimages . . . ." "Covetousness, envy, pride, and wrath are the four elements of self . . . or Hell." What is the cure—"the way of patience, meekness, humility, and resignation to God. This is the truth and perfection of dying to self".

In *The Spirit of Love*, Law is impatient of advice about not wasting time or money. He is forgetful of how many years he lived methodically in the Purgative Way, and now calls for total surrender of the self without 'aids to devotion.' He does not believe in instant conversion to a second birth, but wants to fix the mind of the spiritually minded only on that one end, the abolition of the carnal self. "Work out," as Saint Paul says, "your own salvation—with fear and trembling."

The teacher of love died on April 9, 1761, with appropriate 'last words,' recorded by his companion, Hester Gibbon: "He said he had such an opening of the divine life within him that the fire of divine love quite consumed him."

There is no shift in Law's uncompromising position, his rigorism, from the first of his eighteen books to the last; the deviation is in method and tone, which depend on the audience addressed and the purpose. Like that other rigorist, Jonathan Edwards, he is the controversialist, the preacher to the many (in Edwards's case through actual sermons; in Law's, through his written homily the *Call*), and finally, in both cases, the mystic and the apostle of disinterested benevolence or pure love. In the *Call*, he addresses all professed Christians, summoning them to take their profession seriously, to "come up higher"; and he gives variety to his book by alternating straight instruction and illustrative portraits, not devoid of entertainment. The later books are addressed to a smaller audience, men presumed already in the Purgative Way, who are eager to be enlightened in the higher reaches of the spiritual life.

Law never makes the relation between the two stages that his books represent as clear as it might be, and the modern reader needs the help of the traditional Catholic wisdom in spirituality to comprehend the relation between asceticism and mysticism. The higher stages presuppose the lower. Reared in the Church, nourished by the sacraments, a lifelong reader of the mystics, Law forgot the ladder by which he had himself climbed to his spiritual altitude.

Law seems never to have been read so much as in the last hundred years—that, I think, because we live now in a post-Christian period, as Bonhoeffer has called it, when, as in the 18th century, the truth of Christianity can no longer be taken for granted, and when the practical inefficacy and the sham of nominal Christianity is everywhere apparent. Law appeals to fundamentals, and the religion he preaches makes men take sides. So his appeal today is to Quakers, members of the Charismatic movement, and Evangelicals, but also to the spiritually minded, both within and without the Church. Like the Christian Humanist Fénelon, although unlike him in temper, he has an ecumenical audience. Law speaks to all as a writer of almost unique force, penetration, and insight.

On the Texts of This Edition

by Paul G. Stanwood

A Serious Call. Law's most popular work has appeared in numerous editions, both during his own lifetime and frequently thereafter. Evidently Law interested himself only in the first edition of 1728, and possibly the second or "revised" one of 1732, a paginary reprint of the first edition whose revisions may simply be the work of the printer. In most cases, the corrections of 1732 are trivial and remove obvious errors (sometimes introducing new ones), but an occasional substantive alteration suggests the hand of the author (see for example, p. 315, n. 56, where "for" replaces "with"). The copy text of the present edition is that of the first edition of 1728, with substantive corrections from the second edition of 1732 as indicated in the notes. The title page of the second edition, in all essentials the same as the first, is illustrated at the beginning of this text. The copies used for the Paulist Press edition are both in the University Library, Cambridge; the collation of these first two editions is the same: 8° A^4 B-Z^8 2A-L^8 2K^4 = 256 leaves; pp. *1-3* ii-vi *1-499 500-504* = 512 pages.

The third edition appeared in 1733; it was set from the first in a new duodecimo format. The fourth edition of 1739 and the fifth of 1750 were set from this third edition. The sixth edition of 1753 returns to the octavo format of the first two editions, and it faithfully reprints the first edition of 1728. After Law's death in 1761, another edition appeared in 1762, with the whole works, styling itself the "Tenth Edition," collating exactly with the first; but I cannot locate the three editions supposedly appearing between 1753 and 1762. The subsequent publishing history of *A Serious Call* down to our own time is of little or no textual interest. Only John Wesley's abridgement in 1744 (published again in 1784 and 1794) and Samuel Johnson's appreciation in 1741 should be mentioned, and these are not editions so much as responses to Law. Dr. Johnson, indeed, discusses Law in the "Doctrine of the Holy Eucharist vindicated and explained in a sermon [on John 6:51] with a prefatory discourse addressed to . . . Law." The various 19th-century editions of *A Serious Call* have as their ancestor the 1762 edition, but in 1892-93, "G. Moreton" reprinted it among the nine volumes that included all of Law's works. It is this edition which apparently lies behind such later editions as that in the Everyman's Library (1906) and other, often very informal and careless editions of this century. Unfortunately, "G. Moreton" produced a very imperfect text, for he frequently gives readings which are not in the first edition, and he obviously purifies Law's language of its "quaintness": Law, for example, prefers the distinctive "you was" for "you were," and such familiar contractions as "don't" and "it's." The present edition gives Law's words as he wished them to appear by trying to recover the text of the first edition, and not by simply reprinting a previous and almost certainly corrupt text.

But this is not, strictly speaking, a "critical edition," although I think it is certainly the best one available. While every effort has been made to preserve all the substantive features of Law's text, I have modernized his spelling, punctuation, and capitalization in accordance with current American usage. Law's own punctuation is extremely heavy by contemporary standards, with commas separating almost every clause; his tendency is to capitalize most nouns and italicize them indiscriminately. On the other hand, Law does not capitalize such words as "Christian" (or only rarely does so), nor the pronouns referring to God or Christ; nor does he use the possessive apostrophe consistently. But he frequently writes in sentence fragments, which I preserve as well as his paragraphs (except for one instance on p.125, 11. 7-10, where a question and an answer appear in two paragraphs in the original, but here are fused); for I believe the fragments and the brief paragraphs reflect Law's "nervous" and aphoristic style in *A Serious Call*.

Law makes two kinds of references, the first to the scriptures, the second to his own or to others' writings. The first I give within parentheses following the quotation, silently correcting any errors; but I do not locate or give scriptural references other than those Law provides. The second I put at the bottom of the page, along with brief explanatory notes where necessary. Law normally follows the King James or "Authorized" Version of the Bible, and I follow its usage, occasionally correcting Law. He also regularly uses "but" where we would give "unless," as on page 2, 11. 9-10, "there is no other reason for this, but that," a feature which I have, of course, left unchanged. He also uses "farther" where we would nearly always prefer "further"; I alter this word to the modern use, for it involves no verbal (or substantive) change, but rather an external (or accidental) difference, and also "an" to "a" before such words as "human," and "towards" to "toward."

The Spirit of Love. The Spirit of Love originally appeared in two parts. The first was published in 1752, and it was bound with some copies of *The Spirit of Prayer* (1749), though separately paginated. This first edition of Part 1 was called on the title page "An Appendix to the Spirit of Prayer"; in the second edition of 1759, the title page is slightly revised, and it is illustrated in this present edition. But the text is an exact (that is, paginary) reprint of the first edition; for this part, or the "Letter to a Friend," I have collated the two editions, the first in Dr. Williams's Library, the second in the University Library, Cambridge, and followed the first edition as my copy text. For Part 2, or *The Second Part of the Spirit of Love*, I follow the first edition of 1754, the original title page given at the beginning of this text. This edition was usually bound with either the 1752 edition of Part 1, or else and most commonly with the 1759 edition (thus we see the combinations 1752, 1754; and 1759, 1754). For my copy of this second part of 1754, I use that in the University Library, Cambridge; the collation of the two parts, in the editions of 1752 and 1754, is as follows: The | Spirit | of | Love, | Being an | Appendix | to the | Spirit of Prayer. | [Rule] | *In a* Letter to a Friend. | [Rule] | By William Law, A. M. | [Rule] | London: | Printed for W. Innys, and J. Richardson, in | *Pater-Noster Row.* | [Rule] | MDCCLII. | 8° π^1 B-E^8 = 33 leaves; pp. [*i-ii*] 1-63 *64* = 66 pages.

The Spirit of Love appeared again with the *Works* of 1762, a third edition of Part 2 in 1772, and of Part 1 in 1781. It was largely ignored in the later years of the 18th century, and in the 19th century, too, along with Law's other mystical writing. It occurs in the reprint by "G. Moreton" in 1892, which occasioned the publication in excerpts (by Hobhouse, in 1938 and 1948) or as a whole (by S. Spencer, in 1967), but never to my knowledge has any edition until this present one attempted to recover Law's original text. The conventions described above for the normalization of *A Serious Call* are followed again with *The Spirit of Love*.

In the later and mystical writing, we see Law developing longer paragraphs, avoiding the sentence fragments and aphoristic comments of his earlier work. *The Spirit of Love* is a gleaming and radiant book, and in spite of its repetitions, or possibly because of them, Law presses his message of God's infinite love and mercy and His generous Atonement. Law's own dedication to the spiritual life is full, exuberant, and joyful; his wish is to see others give themselves to that God who is creating, quickening, and reviving all souls. Not so much for its doctrine but for its atmosphere, *The Spirit of Love* must be distinguished and set apart from *A Serious Call*. Together the two works speak as one, in different directions. In a similar manner, George Herbert joined the moral teaching of the first part of *The Temple* (1633), the aphorisms of "The Church-Porch," with the second part, the spiritual wrestlings of "The Church." On the threshold of the "Superliminare," Herbert looks back but anticipates; here is a fit epigraph for describing the junction of two ways, and especially for illuminating Law the ascetic and mystic:

Thou, whom the former precepts have
Sprinkled and taught, how to behave
Thy self in church; approach, and taste
The churches mysticall repast.

Avoid, Profaneness; come not here:
Nothing but holy, pure, and cleare,
Or that which groneth to be so,
May at his perill further go.

The editor gratefully acknowledges the assistance of various libraries: the Bodleian Library, Oxford; the British Library; Dr.

INTRODUCTION

Williams's Library; and especially the Cambridge University Library for providing microfilm or xerox copies of the works edited for this edition; and the Librarian of Emmanuel College, Cambridge (Law's own college) for permission to consult books there and to the Master and Fellows for the reproduction of the Law window in the College Chapel which was used to inspire the cover artist. I owe a special debt to Austin Warren for his encouragement of my studies over many years, and for his introduction to this edition; to Dorothy Stanwood who collated some of the texts and typed a great part of the manuscript; and, finally, to the Paulist Press whose vision and faithfulness made all this work possible.

* * * *

Bibliographical Note

The best general book on Law is Walker's 1973 monograph, excellent and comprehensive for the facts of Law's life and with useful if pedestrian summaries of his eighteen volumes, but inadequate in interpretation. For that, most valuable are the twenty-four "Studies" appended to Hobhouse's *Selected Mystical Writings* (1938; second edition, revised, 1948), which include "The Fall of the Angels and the Corruption of Nature" and "Mystical Experience and Mystical Philosophy." Talon's book deals adequately with Law's literary craftsmanship.

37

List of William Law's Works

1. *Three Letters to the Bishop of Bangor* (1717-19)
2. *Remarks upon the Fable of the Bees* (1724)
3. *The Absolute Unlawfulness of the Stage-Entertainment fully demonstrated* (1726)
4. *A Practical Treatise upon Christian Perfection* (1726)
5. *A Serious Call to a Devout and Holy Life* (1728)
6. *The Case of Reason, or Natural Religion, Fairly and Fully Stated* (1731)
7. *A Demonstration of the Gross and Fundamental Errors Of a late Book* [by Hoadly], *called A Plain Account* (1737)
8. *The Grounds and Reasons of Christian Regeneration* (1739)
9. *An Earnest and Serious Answer to Dr. Trapp's Discourse of the Folly, Sin and Danger of being Righteous Over-much* (1740)
10. *An Appeal To all that Doubt, or Disbelieve The Truths of the Gospel . . . To which are added, Some Animadversions upon Dr. Trapp's Late Reply* (1740)
11. *The Spirit of Prayer* (1749)
12. *The Way to Divine Knowledge* (1752)
13. *The Spirit of Love* (1752, 1754)
14. *A Short but Sufficient Confutation Of the Reverend Dr. Warburton's Projected Defence (As he calls it) of Christianity* (1757)
15. *Of Justification by Faith and Works: A Dialogue between a Methodist and a Churchman* (1760)
16. *A Collection of Letters* (1760)
17. *An Humble, Earnest, and Affectionate Address to the Clergy* (1761)
18. *Letters to a Lady Inclined to enter into the Communion of the Church of Rome* (1779, written 1731-32)

William Law

A SERIOUS CALL TO A DEVOUT
AND HOLY LIFE · THE SPIRIT OF LOVE

THE CLASSICS
OF WESTERN
SPIRITUALITY

A Serious Call
To a Devout and Holy Life:
Adapted to the State and Condition
of All Orders of Christians

He that hath ears to hear, let him hear **(Luke 8:8).**
And behold, I come quickly, and my reward is with me
(Rev. 22:12).

A Serious

CALL

T O A

D E V O U T and H O L Y

L I F E.

Adapted to the State and Condition of

All Orders of CHRISTIANS.

By *W I L L I A M   L A W,* A.M.

He that hath ears to hear, let him hear.
St. Luke viii. 8.
*And behold, I come quickly, and my reward is
with me.* Rev. xxii. 12.

The Second Edition, *Corrected.*

LONDON:
Printed for William Innys, at the *West*
End of St. *Paul's.* MDCCXXXII.

The title page from the second edition of 1732.

The Contents

CONTENTS

CONTENTS

CONTENTS

Chapter 1

Concerning the nature and extent of Christian devotion.

Devotion is neither private nor public prayer, but prayers whether private or public are particular parts or instances of devotion. Devotion signifies a life given or devoted to God.

He therefore is the devout man who lives no longer to his own will, or the way and spirit of the world, but to the sole will of God, who considers God in everything, who serves God in everything, who makes all the parts of his common life parts of piety by doing everything in the name of God and under such rules as are conformable to His glory.

We readily acknowledge that God alone is to be the rule and measure of our prayers, that in them we are to look wholly unto Him and act wholly for Him, that we are only to pray in such a manner for such things and such ends as are suitable to His glory.

Now let anyone but find out the reason why he is to be thus strictly pious in his prayers and he will find the same as strong a reason to be as strictly pious in all the other parts of his life. For there is not the least shadow of a reason why we should make God the rule and measure of our prayers, why we should then look wholly unto Him and pray according to His will, but what equally proves it necessary for us to look wholly unto God, and make Him the rule and measure of all the other actions of our life. For any ways of life, any employment of our talents, whether of our parts, our time, or money, that is not strictly according to the will of God, that is not for such ends as are suitable to His glory, are as great absurdities and failings as prayers that are not according to the will of God. For there is no other reason why our prayers should be according to the will of God, why they should have nothing in

47

them but what is wise, and holy, and heavenly, there is no other reason for this but that our lives may be of the same nature, full of the same wisdom, holiness, and heavenly tempers that we may live unto God in the same spirit that we pray unto Him. Were it not our strict duty to live by reason, to devote all the actions of our lives to God, were it not absolutely necessary to walk before Him in wisdom and holiness and all heavenly conversation, doing everything in His name and for His glory, there would be no excellency or wisdom in the most heavenly prayers. Nay, such prayers would be absurdities, they would be like prayers for wings when it was no part of our duty to fly.

As sure therefore as there is any wisdom in praying for the Spirit of God, so sure is it that we are to make that Spirit the rule of all our actions; as sure as it is our duty to look wholly unto God in our prayers, so sure is it that it is our duty to live wholly unto God in our lives. But we can no more be said to live unto God unless we live unto Him in all the ordinary actions of our life, unless He be the rule and measure of all our ways, than we can be said to pray unto God unless our prayer look wholly unto Him. So that unreasonable and absurd ways of life, whether in labor or diversion, whether they consume our time or our money, are like unreasonable and absurd prayers and are as truly an offence unto God.

'Tis for want of knowing, or at least considering this, that we see such a mixture of ridicule in the lives of many people. You see them strict as to some times and places of devotion, but when the service of the church is over, they are but like those that seldom or never come there. In their way of life, their manner of spending their time and money, in their cares and fears, in their pleasures and indulgences, in their labor and diversions, they are like the rest of the world. This makes the loose part of the world generally make a jest of those that are devout because they see their devotion goes no further than their prayers, and that when they are over they live no more unto God till the time of prayer returns again, but live by the same humour and fancy and in as full an enjoyment of all the follies of life as other people. This is the reason why they are the jest and scorn of careless and worldly people, not because they are really devoted to God, but because they appear to have no other devotion but that of occasional prayers.

Julius is very fearful of missing prayers; all the parish supposes Julius to be sick if he is not at church. But if you was to ask him why he spends the rest of his time by humor and chance? Why he is a companion of the silliest people in their most silly pleasures? Why he is ready for every impertinent entertainment and diversion? If you was to ask him why there is no amusement too trifling to please him? Why he is busy at all balls and assemblies? Why he gives himself up to an idle gossiping conversation? Why he lives in foolish friendships and fondness for particular persons that neither want nor deserve any particular kindness? Why he allows himself in foolish hatreds and resentments against particular persons without considering that he is to love everybody as himself? If you ask him why he never puts his conversation, his time, and fortune under the rules of religion, Julius has no more to say for himself than the most disorderly person. For the whole tenor of scripture lies as directly against such a life as against debauchery and intemperance. He that lives in such a course of idleness and folly lives no more according to the religion of Jesus Christ than he that lives in gluttony and intemperance.

If a man was to tell Julius that there was no occasion for so much constancy at prayers and that he might without any harm to himself neglect the service of the church as the generality of people do, Julius would think such a one to be no Christian and that he ought to avoid his company. But if a person only tells him that he may live as the generality of the world does, that he may enjoy himself as others do, that he may spend his time and money as people of fashion do, that he may conform to the follies and frailties of the generality and gratify his tempers and passions as most people do, Julius never suspects that man to want a Christian spirit, or that he is doing the Devil's work.

And yet if Julius was to read all the New Testament from the beginning to the end, he would find his course of life condemned in every page of it.

And indeed there cannot anything be imagined more absurd in itself than wise and sublime and heavenly prayers added to a life of vanity and folly, where neither labor nor diversions, neither time nor money, are under the direction of the wisdom and heavenly tempers of our prayers. If we were to see a man pretending to act wholly with regard to God in everything that he did, that would neither spend time or money or take any labor or diversion but so far as he could act according to strict principles of reason and piety, and yet at the same time neglect all prayer, whether public or private, should we not be amazed at such a man and wonder how he could have so much folly along with so much religion?

Yet this is as reasonable as for any person to pretend to strictness in devotion, to be careful of observing times and places of prayer, and yet letting the rest of his life, his time and labor, his talents and money, be disposed of without any regard to strict rules of piety and devotion. For it is as great an absurdity to suppose holy prayers and divine petitions without a holiness of life suitable to them as to suppose a holy and divine life without prayers.

Let anyone therefore think how easily he could confute a man that pretended to great strictness of life without prayer, and the same arguments will as plainly confute another that pretends to strictness of prayer without carrying the same strictness into every other part of life. For to be weak and foolish in spending our time and fortune is no greater a mistake than to be weak and foolish in relation to our prayers. And to allow ourselves in any ways of life that neither are nor can be offered to God is the same irreligion as to neglect our prayers or use them in such a manner as makes them an offering unworthy of God.

The short of the matter is this, either reason and religion prescribe rules and ends to all the ordinary actions of our life, or they do not. If they do, then it is as necessary to govern all our actions by those rules as it is necessary to worship God. For if religion teaches us anything concerning eating and drinking or spending our time and money; if it teaches us how we are to use and contemn[1] the world; if it tells us what tempers we are to have in common life, how we are to be disposed toward all people, how we are to behave toward the sick, the poor, the old, and destitute; if it tells us whom we are to treat with a particular love, whom we are to regard with a particular esteem; if it tells us how we are to treat our enemies, and how we are to mortify and deny ourselves, he must be very weak that can think these parts of religion are not to be observed with as much exactness as any doctrines that relate to prayers.

It is very observable that there is not one command in all the gospel for public worship; and perhaps it is a duty that is least insisted upon in scripture of any other. The frequent attendance at it is never so much as mentioned in all the New Testament. Whereas that religion or devotion which is to govern the ordinary actions of our life is to be found in almost every verse of scripture. Our blessed Savior and His Apostles are wholly taken up in doctrines that relate to common life. They call us to renounce the world and differ in every temper and way of life from the spirit and way of the world. To renounce all its goods, to fear none of its evils, to reject its joys, and have no value for its happiness. To be as newborn babes that are born into a new state of things, to live as pilgrims in spiritual watching, in holy fear, and heavenly aspiring after another life. To take up our daily cross, to deny ourselves, to profess the blessedness of mourning, to seek the blessedness of poverty of spirit. To forsake the pride and vanity of riches, to take no thought for the morrow, to live in the profoundest state of humility, to rejoice in worldly sufferings. To reject the lust of the flesh, the lust of the eyes, and the pride of life; to bear injuries, to forgive and bless our enemies, and to love mankind as God loveth them. To give up our whole hearts and affections to God, and strive to enter through the strait gate into a life of eternal glory.

This is the common devotion which our blessed Savior taught in order to make it the common life of all Christians. Is it not therefore exceeding strange that people should place so much piety in the attendance upon public worship, concerning which there is not one precept of our Lord's to be found, and yet neglect these common duties of our ordinary life which are commanded in every page of the gospel? I call these duties the devotion of our common life, because if they are to be practiced, they must be made parts of our common life; they can have no place anywhere else.

If contempt of the world and heavenly affection is a necessary temper of Christians, it is necessary that this temper appear in the whole course of their lives, in their manner of using the world, because it can have no place anywhere else.

If self-denial be a condition of salvation, all that would be saved must make it a part of their ordinary life. If humility be a Christian duty, then the common life of a Christian is to be a constant course of humility in all its kinds. If poverty of spirit be necessary, it must be the spirit and temper of every day of our lives. If we are to relieve the naked, the sick, and the prisoner, it must be the common charity of our lives, as far as we can render ourselves able to perform it. If we are to love our enemies, we must make our common life a visible exercise and demonstration of that love. If content and thankfulness, if the patient bearing of evil be duties to God, they are the duties of every day and in every circumstance of our life. If we are to be wise and holy as the newborn sons of God, we can no otherwise be so but by renouncing everything that is foolish and vain in every part of our common life. If we are to be in Christ new creatures, we must show that we are so by having new ways of living in the world. If we are to follow Christ, it must be in our common way of spending every day.

Thus it is in all the virtues and holy tempers of Christianity; they are not ours unless they be the virtues and tempers of our ordinary life. So that Christianity is so far from leaving us to live in the common ways of life, conforming to the folly of customs and gratifying the passions and tempers which the spirit of the world delights in, it is so far from indulging us in any of these things that all its virtues which it makes necessary to salvation are only so many ways of living above and contrary to the world in all the common actions of our life. If our common life is not a common course of humility, self-denial, renunciation of the world, poverty of spirit, and heavenly affection, we don't live the lives of Christians.

But yet though[2] it is thus plain that this and this alone is Christianity, a uniform, open, and visible practice of all these virtues, yet it is as plain that there is little or nothing of this to be found, even amongst the better sort of people. You see them often at church, and pleased with fine preachers; but look into their lives and you see them just the same sort of people as others are that make no pretences to devotion. The difference that you find betwixt them is only the difference of their natural tempers. They have the same taste of the world, the same worldly cares and fears and joys, they have the same turn of mind, equally vain in their desires. You see the same fondness for state and equipage,[3] the same pride and vanity of dress, the same self-love and indulgence, the same foolish friendships and groundless hatreds, the same levity of mind and trifling spirit, the same fondness for diversions, the same idle dispositions and vain ways of spending their time in visiting and conversation, as the rest of the world that make no pretences to devotion.

I don't mean this comparison betwixt people seemingly good and professed rakes, but betwixt people of sober lives. Let us take an instance in two modest women: Let it be supposed that one of them is careful of times of devotion and observes them through a sense of duty and that the other has no hearty concern about it but is at church seldom or often, just as it happens. Now it is a very easy thing to see this difference betwixt these persons. But when you have seen this, can you find any further difference betwixt them? Can you find that their common life is of a different kind? Are not the tempers and customs and manners of the one of the same kind as of the other? Do they live as if they belonged to different worlds, had different views in their heads and different rules and measures of all their actions? Have they not the same goods and evils, are they not pleased and displeased in the same manner and for the same things? Do they not live in the same course of life? Does one seem to be of this world, looking at the things that are temporal, and the other to be of another world, looking wholly at the things that are eternal? Does the one live in pleasure, delighting herself in show or dress, and the other live in self-denial and mortification, renouncing everything that looks like vanity either of person, dress, or carriage? Does the one follow public diversions and trifle away her time in idle visits and corrupt conversation, and does the other study all the arts of improving her time, living in prayer and watching and such good works as may make all her time turn to her advantage and be placed to her account at the last day? Is the one careless of expense and glad to be able to adorn herself with every costly ornament of dress, and does the other consider her fortune as a talent given her by God which is to be improved religiously and no more to be spent in vain and needless ornaments than it is to be buried in the earth?

Where must you look to find one person of religion differing in this manner from another that has none? And yet if they do not differ in these things which are here related, can it with any sense be said the one is a good Christian and the other not?

Take another instance amongst the men. Leo has a great deal of good nature, has kept what they call good company, hates everything that is false and base, is very generous and brave to his friends, but has concerned himself so little with religion that he hardly knows the difference betwixt a Jew and a Christian.

Eusebius, on the other hand, has had early impressions of religion and buys books of devotion. He can talk of all the feasts and fasts of the church, and knows the names of most men that have been eminent for piety. You never hear him swear or make a loose jest, and when he talks of religion he talks of it as of a matter of the last concern.

Here you see that one person has religion enough according to the way of the world to be reckoned a pious Christian, and the other is so far from all appearance of religion that he may fairly be reckoned a heathen; and yet if you look into their common life, if you examine their chief and ruling tempers in the greatest articles of life or the greatest doctrines of Christianity, you will find the least difference imaginable.

Consider them with regard to the use of the world because that is what everybody can see.

Now to have right notions and tempers with relation to this world is as essential to religion as to have right notions of God. And it is as possible for a man to worship a crocodile and yet be a pious man as to have his affections set upon this world and yet be a good Christian.

But now if you consider Leo and Eusebius in this respect, you will find them exactly alike, seeking, using, and enjoying all that can be got in this world in the same manner and for the same ends. You will find that riches, prosperity, pleasures, indulgences, state, equipage, and honor are just as much the happiness of Eusebius as they are of Leo. And yet if Christianity has not changed a man's mind and temper with relation to these things, what can we say that it has done for him?

For if the doctrines of Christianity were practiced, they would make a man as different from other people as to all worldly tempers, sensual pleasures, and the pride of life as a wise man is different from a natural;† it would be as easy a thing to know a Christian by his outward course of life as it is now difficult to find anybody that lives it. For it is notorious that Christians are now not only like other men in their frailties and infirmities; this might be in some degree excusable, but the complaint is, they are like heathens in all the main and chief articles of their lives. They enjoy the world and live every day in the same tempers and the same designs and the same indulgences as they did who knew not God nor of any happiness in another life. Everybody that is capable of any reflection must have observed that this is generally the state even of devout people, whether men or women. You may see them different from other people so far as to times and places of prayer but generally like the rest of the world in all the other parts of their lives. That is, adding Christian devotion to a heathen life: I have the authority of our blessed Savior for this remark, where he says, "Take no thought, saying what shall we eat, or what shall we drink, or wherewithal shall we be clothed? For after all these things do the Gentiles seek." But if to be thus affected even with the necessary things of this life shows that we are not yet of a Christian spirit but are like the heathens, surely to enjoy the vanity and folly of the world as they did, to be like them in the main chief tempers of our lives, in self-love and indulgence, in sensual pleasures and diversions, in the vanity of dress, the love of show and greatness, or any other gaudy distinctions of fortune is a much greater sign of a heathen temper. And consequently they who add devotion to such a life must be said to pray as Christians but live as heathens.

NOTES

1. Contemn: view with contempt or scorn.
2. But yet though: although.
3. State and equipage: pomp with all its display, specifically with a fine carriage and servants, features of "impertinence," that is of vanity and irrelevence.

†see footnote 63.

Chapter 2

An inquiry into the reason why the generality of Christians fall so far short of the holiness and devotion of Christianity.

It may now be reasonably inquired how it comes to pass that the lives even of the better sort of people are thus strangely contrary to the principles of Christianity.

But before I give a direct answer to this, I desire it may also be inquired how it comes to pass that swearing is so common a vice amongst Christians. It is indeed not yet so common amongst women as it is amongst men. But amongst men this sin is so common that perhaps there are more than two in three that are guilty of it through the whole course of their lives, swearing more or less, just as it happens, some constantly, others only now and then, as it were by chance. Now I ask how comes it that two in three of the men are guilty of so gross and profane a sin as this is? There is neither ignorance nor human infirmity to plead for it. It is against an express commandment and the most plain doctrine of our blessed Savior.

Do but now find the reason why the generality of men live in this notorious vice and then you will have found the reason why the generality even of the better sort of people live so contrary to Christianity.

Now the reason of common swearing is this: It is because men have not so much as the intention to please God in all their actions. For let a man but have so much piety as to intend to please God in all the actions of his life as the happiest and best thing in the world, and then he will never swear more. It will be as impossible for him to swear whilst he feels this intention within himself as it is impossible for a man that intends to please his prince to go up and abuse him to his face.

It seems but a small and necessary part of piety to have such a sincere intention as this, and that he has no reason to look upon himself as a disciple of Christ who is not thus far advanced in piety. And yet it is purely for want of this degree of piety that you see such a mixture of sin and folly in the lives even of the better sort of people. It is for want of this intention that you see men that profess religion yet live in swearing and sensuality, that you see clergymen given to pride and covetousness and worldly enjoyments. It is for want of this intention that you see women that profess devotion yet living in all the folly and vanity of dress, wasting their time in idleness and pleasures and in all such instances of state and equipage as their estates[4] will reach. For let but a woman feel her heart full of this intention and she will find it as impossible to patch or paint[5] as to curse or swear; she will no more desire to shine at balls and assemblies or make a figure amongst those that are most finely dressed than she will desire to dance upon a rope to please spectators. She will know that the one is as far from the wisdom and excellency of the Christian spirit as the other.

It was this general intention that made the primitive Christians such eminent instances of piety, that made the goodly fellowship of the Saints and all the glorious army of martyrs and confessors. And if you will here stop and ask yourself why you are not as pious as the primitive Christians were, your own heart will tell you that it is neither through ignorance nor inability, but purely because you never thoroughly intended it. You observe the same Sunday worship that they did; and you are strict in it because it is your full intention to be so. And when you as fully intend to be like them in their ordinary common life, when you intend to please God in all your actions, you will find it as possible as to be strictly exact in the service of the church. And when you have this intention to please God in all your actions as the happiest and best thing in the world, you will find in you as great an aversion to everything that is vain and impertinent in common life, whether of business or pleasure, as you now have to anything that is profane. You will be as fearful of living in any foolish way, either of spending your time or your fortune, as you are now fearful of neglecting the public worship.

Now who that wants this general sincere intention can be reckoned a Christian? And yet if it was amongst Christians, it would change the whole face of the world; true piety and exemplary holiness would be as common and visible as buying and selling or any trade in life.

Let a clergyman but be thus pious and he will converse as if he had been brought up by an Apostle, he will no more think and talk of noble preferment than of noble eating or a glorious chariot. He will no more complain of the frowns of the world or a small cure[6] or the want of a patron than he will complain of the want of a laced coat or a running[7] horse. Let him but intend to please God in all his actions as the happiest and best thing in the world, and then he will know that there is nothing noble in a clergyman but a burning zeal for the salvation of souls, nor anything poor in his profession but idleness and a worldly spirit.

Again, let a tradesman but have this intention and it will make him a saint in his shop; his everyday business will be a course of wise and reasonable actions made holy to God by being done in obedience to His will and pleasure. He will buy and sell and labor and travel, because by so doing he can do some good to himself and others. But then, as nothing can please God but what is wise and reasonable and holy, so he will neither buy, nor sell, nor labor in any other manner, nor to any other end, but such as may be shown to be wise and reasonable and holy. He will therefore consider not what arts, or methods, or application will soonest make him richer and greater than his brethren, or remove him from a shop to a life of state and pleasure; but he will consider what arts, what methods, what application can make worldly business most acceptable to God and make a life of trade a life of holiness, devotion, and piety. This will be the temper and spirit of every tradesman; he cannot stop short of these degrees of piety whenever it is his intention to please God in all his actions, as the best and happiest thing in the world.

And on the other hand, whoever is not of this spirit and temper in his trade and profession and does not carry it on only so far as is best subservient to a wise and holy and heavenly life, it is certain that he has not this intention; and yet without it, who can be shown to be a follower of Jesus Christ?

Again, let the gentleman of birth and fortune but have this intention and you will see how it will carry him from every appearance of evil to every instance of piety and goodness.

He cannot live by chance or as humor and fancy carries him because he knows that nothing can please God but a wise and regular course of life. He cannot live in idleness and indulgence, in sports and gaming, in pleasures and intemperance, in vain expenses and high living, because these things cannot be turned into means of piety and holiness, or made so many parts of a wise and religious life.

As he thus removes from all appearance of evil, so he hastens and aspires after every instance of goodness. He does not ask what is allowable and pardonable, but what is commendable and praiseworthy. He does not ask whether God will forgive the folly of our lives, the madness of our pleasures, the vanity of our expenses, the richness of our equipage, and the careless consumption of our time; but he asks whether God is pleased with these things, or whether these are the appointed ways of gaining his favor. He does not inquire whether it be pardonable to hoard up money, to adorn ourselves with diamonds and gild our chariots, whilst the widow and the orphan, the sick and the prisoner, want to be relieved; but he asks whether God has required these things at our hands, whether we shall be called to account at the last day for the neglect of them, because it is not his intent to live in such ways as, for ought we know, God may perhaps pardon, but to be diligent in such ways, as we know, that God will infallibly reward.

He will not therefore look at the lives of Christians, to learn how he ought to spend his estate, but he will look into the scriptures and make every doctrine, parable, precept, or instruction that relates to rich men a law to himself in the use of his estate.

He will have nothing to do with costly apparel because the rich man in the gospel was clothed with purple and fine linen. He denies himself the pleasures and indulgences which his estate could procure because our blessed Savior saith, "Woe unto you that are rich, for ye have received your consolation." He will have but one rule for charity, and that will be to spend all that he can that way because the Judge of quick and dead hath said that all that is so given, is given to him.

He will have no hospitable table for the rich and wealthy to come and feast with him in good eating and drinking because our blessed Lord saith, "When thou makest a dinner, call not thy friends, nor thy brethren, neither thy kinsmen, nor thy rich neighbors, lest they also bid thee again, and a recompense be made thee. But when thou makest a feast, call the poor, the maimed, the lame, the blind, and thou shalt be blessed. For they cannot recompense thee, for thou shalt be recompensed at the resurrection of the just" (Luke 14:12-14).

He will waste no money in gilded roofs or costly furniture. He will not be carried from pleasure to pleasure in expensive state and equipage because an inspired Apostle hath said that "all that is in the world, the lust of the flesh, the lust of the eyes, and the pride of life, is not of the Father, but is of the world."

Let not anyone look upon this as an imaginary description of charity that looks fine in the notion but cannot be put in practice. For it is so far from being an imaginary impracticable form of life that it has been practiced by great numbers of Christians in former ages who were glad to turn their whole estates into a constant course of charity. And it is so far from being impossible now that if we can find any Christians that sincerely intend to please God in all their actions as the best and happiest thing in the world, whether they be young or old, single or married, men or women, if they have but this intention, it will be impossible for them to do otherwise. This one principle will infallibly carry them to this height of charity, and they will find themselves unable to stop short of it.

For how is it possible for a man that intends to please God in the use of his money, and intends it because he judges it to be his greatest happiness, how is it possible for such a one in such a state of mind to bury his money in needless impertinent finery, in covering himself or his horses with gold, whilst there are any works of piety and charity to be done with it, or any ways of spending it well?

This is as strictly impossible as for a man that intends to please God in his words to go into company on purpose to swear and lie.

For as all waste and unreasonable expense is done designedly and with deliberation, so no one can be guilty of it whose constant intention is to please God in the use of his money.

I have chosen to explain this matter by appealing to this intention because it makes the case so plain, and because everyone that has a mind may see it in the clearest light and feel it in the strongest manner, only by looking into his own heart. For it is as easy for every person to know whether he intends to please God in all his actions as for any servant to know whether this be his intention toward his master. Everyone also can as easily tell how he lays out his money and whether he considers how to please God in it, as he can tell where his estate is and whether it be in money or land. So that here is no plea left for ignorance or frailty; as to this matter, everybody is in the light, and everybody has power. And no one can fail but he that is not so much a Christian as to intend to please God in the use of his estate.

You see two persons, one is regular in public′ and private prayer, the other is not. Now the reason of this difference is not this, that one has strength and power to observe prayer, and the other has not; but the reason is this, that one intends to please God in the duties of devotion, and the other has no intention about it. Now the case is the same in the right or wrong use of our time and money. You see one person throwing away his time in sleep and idleness, in visiting and diversions, and his money in the most vain and unreasonable expenses. You see another careful of every day, dividing his hours by rules of reason and religion and spending all his money in works of charity; now the difference is not owing to this, that one has strength and power to do thus, and the other has not; but it is owing to this, that one intends to please God in the right use of all his time and all his money, and the other has no intention about it.

Here therefore let us judge ourselves sincerely, let us not vainly content ourselves with the common disorders of our lives, the vanity of our expenses, the folly of our diversions, the pride of our habits, the idleness of our lives, and the wasting of our time, fancying that these are such imperfections as we fall into through the unavoidable weakness and frailty of our natures; but let us be assured that these disorders of our common life are owing to this, that we have not so much Christianity as to intend to please God in all the actions of our life, as the best and happiest thing in the world. So that we must not look upon ourselves in a state of common and pardonable imperfection, but in such a state as wants the first and most fundamental principle of Christianity, viz., an intention to please God in all our actions.

And if anyone was to ask himself how it comes to pass that there are any degrees of sobriety which he neglects, any practices of humility which he wants, any method of charity which he does not follow, any rules of redeeming time which he does not observe, his own heart will tell him that it is because he never intended to be so exact in those duties. For whenever we fully intend it, it is as possible to conform to all this regularity of life as 'tis possible for a man to observe times of prayer.

So that the fault does not lie here, that we desire to be good and perfect, but through the weakness of our nature fall short of it; but it is because we have not piety enough to intend to be as good as we can or to please God in all the actions of our life. This we see is plainly the case of him that spends his time in sports, when he should be at church; it is not his want of power, but his want of intention or desire to be there.

And the case is plainly the same in every other folly of human life. She that spends her time and money in the unreasonable ways and fashions of the world does not do so because she wants power to be wise and religious in the management of her time and money, but because she has no intention or desire of being so. When she feels this intention, she will find it as possible to act up to it as to be strictly sober and chaste, because it is her care and desire to be so.

This doctrine does not suppose that we have no need of divine grace, or that it is in our own power to make ourselves perfect. It only supposes that through the want of a sincere intention of pleasing God in all our actions we fall into such irregularities of life as by the ordinary means of grace we should have power to avoid.

And that we have not that perfection which our present state of grace makes us capable of because we don't so much as intend to have it.

It only teaches us that the reason why you see no real mortification or self-denial, no eminent charity, no profound humility, no heavenly affection, no true contempt of the world, no Christian meekness, no sincere zeal, no eminent piety in the common lives of Christians is this, because they don't so much as intend to be exact and exemplary in these virtues.

NOTES

4. Estates: resources and possessions.
5. Patch or paint: that is, apply cosmetics.
6. A small cure: an unprofitable "living," that is, a parish which provides only a meager income.
7. Running: racing.

Chapter 3

Of the great danger and folly of not intending to be as eminent and exemplary as we can in the practice of all Christian virtues.

Although the goodness of God and his rich mercies in Christ Jesus are a sufficient assurance to us that he will be merciful to our unavoidable weaknesses and infirmities, that is, to such failings as are the effects of ignorance or surprise, yet we have no reason to expect the same mercy toward those sins which we have lived in through a want of intention to avoid them.

For instance, the case of a common swearer who dies in that guilt seems to have no title to the divine mercy for this reason, because he can no more plead any weakness or infirmity in his excuse than the man that hid his talent in the earth could plead his want of strength to keep it out of the earth.

But now if this be right reasoning in the case of a common swearer, that his sin is not to be reckoned a pardonable frailty because he has no weakness to plead in its excuse, why then do we not carry this way of reasoning to its true extent? Why don't we as much condemn every other error of life that has no more weakness to plead in its excuse than common swearing?

For if this be so bad a thing, because it might be avoided if we did but sincerely intend it, must not then all other erroneous ways of life be very guilty if we live in them, not through weakness and inability, but because we never sincerely intended to avoid them?

For instance, you perhaps have made no progress in the most important Christian virtues, you have scarce gone halfway in humility and charity; now if your failure in these duties is purely owing to your want of intention of performing them in any true degree, have you not then as little to plead for yourself and are you not as much without all excuse as the common swearer?

Why, therefore, don't you press these things home upon your conscience? Why do you not think it as dangerous for you to live in such defects as are in your power to amend, as 'tis dangerous for a common swearer to live in the breach of that duty which it is in his power to observe? Is not negligence and a want of a sincere intention as blamable in one case as in another?

You, it may be, are as far from Christian perfection as the common swearer is from keeping the third commandment; are you not therefore as much condemned by the doctrines of the gospel as the swearer is by the third commandment?

You perhaps will say that all people fall short of the perfection of the gospel, and therefore you are content with your failings. But this is saying nothing to the purpose. For the question is not whether gospel perfection can be fully attained, but whether you come as near it as a sincere intention and careful diligence can carry you. Whether you are not in a much lower state than you might be, if you sincerely intended and carefully labored to advance yourself in all Christian virtues.

If you are as forward in the Christian life as your best endeavors can make you, then you may justly hope that your imperfections will not be laid to your charge; but if your defects in piety, humility, and charity are owing to your negligence and want of sincere intention to be as eminent as you can in these virtues, then you leave yourself as much without excuse as he that lives in the sin of swearing through the want of a sincere intention to depart from it.

The salvation of our souls is set forth in scripture as a thing of difficulty that requires all our diligence, that is to be worked out with fear and trembling.

We are told that "strait is the gate, and narrow is the way that leadeth unto life, and few there be that find it," that "many are called, but few are chosen." And that many will miss of their salvation who seem to have taken some pains to obtain it. As in these words, "Strive to enter in at the strait gate, for many I say unto you will seek to enter in, and shall not be able."

Here our blessed Lord commands us to strive to enter in because many will fail who only seek to enter. By which we are plainly taught that religion is a state of labor and striving, and that many will fail of their salvation, not because they took no pains or care about it, but because they did not take pains and care enough; they only sought, but did not strive to enter in.

Every Christian, therefore, should as well examine his life by these doctrines as by the commandments. For these doctrines are as plain marks of our condition as the commandments are plain marks of our duty.

For if salvation is only given to those who strive for it, then it is as reasonable for me to consider whether my course of life be a course of striving to obtain it as to consider whether I am keeping any of the commandments.

If my religion is only a formal compliance with those modes of worship that are in fashion where I live; if it costs me no pains or trouble; if it lays me under no rules and restraints; if I have no careful thoughts and sober reflections about it, is it not great weakness to think that I am striving to enter in at the strait gate?

If I am seeking everything that can delight my senses and regale my appetites, spending my time and fortune in pleasures, in diversions and worldly enjoyments, a stranger to watchings, fastings, prayers, and mortifications, how can it be said that I am working out my salvation with fear and trembling?

If there is nothing in my life and conversation that shows me to be different from Jews and heathens, if I use the world and worldly enjoyments as the generality of people now do and in all ages have done, why should I think that I am amongst those few who are walking in the narrow way to heaven?

And yet if the way is narrow, if none can walk in it but those that strive, is it not as necessary for me to consider whether the way I am in be narrow enough or the labor I take be a sufficient striving as to consider whether I sufficiently observe the second or third commandment?

The sum of this matter is this. From the above-mentioned and many other passages of scripture, it seems plain that our salvation depends upon the sincerity and perfection of our endeavors to obtain it.

Weak and imperfect men shall, notwithstanding their frailties and defects, be received as having pleased God if they have done their utmost to please Him.

The rewards of charity, piety, and humility will be given to those whose lives have been a careful labor to exercise these virtues in as high a degree as they could.

We cannot offer to God the service of angels; we cannot obey Him as man in a state of perfection could; but fallen men can do their best, and this is the perfection that is required of us; it is only the perfection of our best endeavors, a careful labor to be as perfect as we can.

But if we stop short of this, for ought we know we stop short of the mercy of God and leave ourselves nothing to plead from the terms of the gospel. For God has there made no promises of mercy to the slothful and negligent. His mercy is only offered to our frail and imperfect but best endeavors to practice all manner of righteousness.

As the law to angels is angelical righteousness, as the law to perfect beings is strict perfection, so the law to our imperfect natures is the best obedience that our frail nature is able to perform.

The measure of our love to God seems in justice to be the measure of our love of every virtue. We are to love and practice it with all our heart, with all our soul, with all our mind, and with all our strength. And when we cease to live with this regard to virtue, we live below our nature, and instead of being able to plead our infirmities, we stand chargeable with negligence.

It is for this reason that we are exhorted to work out our salvation with fear and trembling; because unless our heart and passions are eagerly bent upon the work of our salvation; unless holy fears animate our endeavors and keep our consciences strict and tender about every part of our duty, constantly examining how we live and how fit we are to die, we shall in all probability fall into a state of negligence and sit down in such a course of life as will never carry us to the rewards of Heaven.

And he that considers that a just God can only make such allowances as are suitable to His justice, that our works are all to be examined by fire, will find that fear and trembling are proper tempers for those that are drawing near so great a trial.

And indeed there is no probability that anyone should do all the duty that is expected from him, or make that progress in piety which the holiness and justice of God requires of him, but he that is constantly afraid of falling short of it.

Now this is not intended to possess people's minds with a scrupulous anxiety and discontent in the service of God, but to fill them with a just fear of living in sloth and idleness and in the neglect of such virtues as they will want at the day of judgment.

It is to excite them to an earnest examination of their lives, to such zeal and care and concern after Christian perfection as they use in any matter that has gained their heart and affections.

It is only desiring them to be so apprehensive of their state, so humble in the opinion of themselves, so earnest after higher degrees of piety, and so fearful of falling short of happiness as the great Apostle St. Paul was when he thus wrote to the Philippians: "Not as though I had already attained, either were already perfect, . . . but this one thing I do, forgetting those things which are behind, and reaching forth unto those things which are before: I press toward the mark for the prize of the high calling of God in Christ Jesus." And then he adds, "Let us therefore, as many as are perfect, be thus minded."

But now, if the Apostle thought it necessary for those who were in his state of perfection to be thus minded, that is, thus laboring, pressing, and aspiring after some degrees of holiness to which they were not then arrived, surely it is much more necessary for us, who are born in the dregs of time and laboring under great imperfections, to be thus minded, that is, thus earnest and striving after such degrees of a holy and divine life as we have not yet attained.

The best way for anyone to know how much he ought to aspire after holiness is to consider not how much will make his present life easy, but to ask himself how much he thinks will make him easy at the hour of death.

Now any man that dares be so serious as to put this question to himself will be forced to answer that at death everyone will wish that he had been as perfect as human nature can be.

Is not this therefore sufficient to put us not only upon wishing but laboring after all that perfection, which we shall then lament the want of? Is it not excessive folly to be content with such a course of piety as we already know cannot content us, at a time when we shall so want it as to have nothing else to comfort us? How can we carry a severer condemnation against ourselves than to believe that at the hour of death we shall want the virtues of the Saints and wish that we had been amongst the first servants of God, and yet take no methods of arriving at their height of piety whilst we are alive?

Though this is an absurdity that we can easily pass over at present, whilst the health of our bodies, the passions of our minds, the noise and hurry and pleasures and business of the world, lead us on with eyes that see not and ears that hear not, yet at death it will set itself before us in a dreadful magnitude, it will haunt us like a dismal ghost, and our conscience will never let us take our eyes from it.

We see in worldly matters what a torment self-condemnation is, and how hardly a man is able to forgive himself when he has brought himself into any calamity or disgrace, purely by his own folly. The affliction is made doubly tormenting because he is forced to charge it all upon himself as his own act and deed, against the nature and reason of things and contrary to the advice of all his friends.

Now by this we may in some degree guess how terrible the pain of that self-condemnation will be when a man shall find himself in the miseries of death, under the severity of a self-condemning conscience, charging all his distress upon his own folly and madness, against the sense and reason of his own mind, against all the doctrines and precepts of religion, and contrary to all the instructions, calls, and warnings, both of God and man.

Penitens was a busy, notable tradesman, and very prosperous in his dealings, but died in the thirty-fifth year of his age.

A little before his death, when the doctors had given him over,[8] some of his neighbors came one evening to see him, at which time he spake thus to them.

I see, says he, my friends, the tender concern you have for me by the grief that appears in your countenances, and I know the thoughts that you now have about me. You think how melancholy a case it is to see so young a man, and in such flourishing business, delivered up to death. And perhaps, had I visited any of you in my condition, I should have had the same thoughts of you.

But now, my friends, my thoughts are no more like your thoughts than my condition is like yours.

It is no trouble to me now to think that I am to die young, or before I have raised an estate.[9]

These things are now sunk into such mere nothings that I have no name little enough to call them by. For if in a few days or hours, I am to leave this carcase to be buried in the earth, and to find myself either forever happy in the favor of God, or eternally separated from all light and peace, can any words sufficiently express the littleness of everything else?

Is there any dream like the dream of life which amuses us with the neglect and disregard of these things? Is there any folly like the folly of our manly state which is too wise and busy to be at leisure for these reflections?

When we consider death as a misery, we only think of it as a miserable separation from the enjoyments of this life. We seldom mourn over an old man that dies rich, but we lament the young that are taken away in the progress of their fortune. You yourselves look upon me with pity, not that I am going unprepared to meet the Judge of quick and dead, but that I am to leave a prosperous trade in the flower of my life.

This is the wisdom of our manly thoughts. And yet what folly of the silliest children is so great as this?

For what is there miserable or dreadful in death, but the consequences of it? When a man is dead, what does anything signify to him, but the state he is then in?

Our poor friend Lepidus died, you know, as he was dressing himself for a feast; do you think it is now part of his trouble that he did not live till that entertainment was over? Feasts and business and pleasures and enjoyments seem great things to us whilst we think of nothing else; but as soon as we add death to them, they all sink into an equal littleness; and the soul that is separated from the body no more laments the loss of business than the losing of a feast.

If I am now going into the joys of God, could there be any reason to grieve that this happened to me before I was forty years of age? Could it be a sad thing to go to Heaven before I had made a few more bargains, or stood a little longer behind a counter?

And if I am to go amongst lost spirits, could there be any reason to be content that this did not happen to me till I was old and full of riches?

If good angels were ready to receive my soul, could it be any grief to me that I was dying upon a poor bed in a garret?

And if God had delivered me up to evil spirits, to be dragged by them to places of torments, could it be any comfort to me that they found me upon a bed of state?

When you are as near death as I am, you will know that all the different states of life, whether of youth or age, riches or poverty, greatness or meanness, signify no more to you than whether you die in a poor or stately apartment.[10]

The greatness of those things which follow death makes all that goes before it sink into nothing.

Now that judgment is the next thing that I look for, and everlasting happiness or misery is come so near me, all the enjoyments and prosperities of life seem as vain and insignificant, and to have no more to do with my happiness than the clothes that I wore before I could speak.

But, my friends, how am I surprised that I have not always had these thoughts? For what is there in the terrors of death, in the vanities of life, or the necessities of piety, but what I might have as easily and fully seen in any part of my life?

What a strange thing is it that a little health or the poor business of a shop should keep us so senseless of these great things that are coming so fast upon us!

Just as you came into my chamber, I was thinking with myself what numbers of souls there are now in the world in my condition at this very time, surprised with a summons to the other world; some taken from their shops and farms, others from their sports and pleasures, these at suits at law, those at gaming tables, some on the road, others at their own firesides, and all seized at an hour when they thought nothing of it, frighted at the approach of death, confounded at the vanity of all their labors, designs, and projects, astonished at the folly of their past lives and not knowing which way to turn their thoughts to find any comfort. Their consciences flying in their faces, bringing all their sins to their remembrance, tormenting them with deepest convictions of their own folly, presenting them with the sight of the angry Judge, the worm that never dies, the fire that is never quenched, the gates of Hell, the powers of darkness, and the bitter pains of eternal death.

Oh my friends! bless God that you are not of this number, that you have time and strength to employ yourselves in such works of piety as may bring you peace at the last.

And take this along with you, that there is nothing but a life of great piety, or a death of great stupidity, that can keep off these apprehensions.

Had I now a thousand worlds, I would give them all for one year more, that I might present unto God one year of such devotion and good works as I never before so much as intended.

You perhaps, when you consider that I have lived free from scandal and debauchery and in the communion of the church, wonder to see me so full of remorse and self-condemnation at the approach of death.

But alas! what a poor thing is it to have lived only free from murder, theft, and adultery, which is all that I can say of myself.

You know indeed that I have never been reckoned a sot, but you are at the same time witnesses and have been frequent companions of my intemperance, sensuality, and great indulgence. And if I am now going to a judgment where nothing will be rewarded but good works, I may well be concerned that though I am no sot, yet I have no Christian sobriety to plead for me.

It is true, I have lived in the communion of the church and generally frequented its worship and service on Sundays when I was neither too idle, or not otherwise disposed of by my business and pleasures. But then my conformity to the public worship has been rather a thing of course than any real intention of doing that which the service of the church supposes; had it not been so, I had been oftener at church, more devout when there, and more fearful of ever neglecting it.

But the thing that now surprises me above all wonders is this, that I never had so much as a general intention of living up to the piety of the gospel. This never so much as entered into my head or my heart. I never once in my life considered whether I was living as the laws of religion direct, or whether my way of life was such as would procure me the mercy of God at this hour.

And can it be thought that I have kept the gospel terms of salvation without ever so much as intending in any serious and deliberate manner either to know them, or keep them? Can it be thought that I have pleased God with such a life as He requires, though I have lived without ever considering what He requires, or how much I have performed? How easy a thing would salvation be, if it could fall into my careless hands, who have never had so much serious thoughts about it, as about any one common bargain that I have made?

In the business of life I have used prudence and reflection, I have done everything by rules and methods. I have been glad to converse with men of experience and judgment to find out the reasons why some fail, and others succeed in any business. I have taken no step in trade but with great care and caution, considering every advantage or danger that attended it. I have always had my eye upon the main end of business and have studied all the ways and means of being a gainer by all that I undertook.

But what is the reason that I have brought none of these tempers to religion? What is the reason that I, who have so often talked of the necessity of rules and methods and diligence in worldly business, have all this while never once thought of any rules or methods or managements to carry me on in a life of piety?

Do you think anything can astonish and confound a dying man like this? What pain do you think a man must feel when his conscience lays all this folly to his charge, when it shall show him how regular, exact, and wise he has been in small matters that are passed away like a dream and how stupid and senseless he has lived, without any reflection, without any rules, in things of such eternal moment as no heart can sufficiently conceive them!

Had I only my frailties and imperfections to lament at this time, I should lie here humbly trusting in the mercies of God. But alas! how can I call a general disregard and a thorough neglect of all religious improvement a frailty or imperfection, when it was as much in my power to have been exact, and careful, and diligent in a course of piety as in the business of my trade?

I could have called in as many helps, have practiced as many rules, and been taught as many certain methods of holy living as of thriving in my shop, had I but so intended and desired it.

Oh my friends! A careless life, unconcerned and unattentive to the duties of religion is so without all excuse, so unworthy of the mercy of God, such a shame to the sense and reason of our minds that I can hardly conceive a greater punishment than for a man to be thrown into the state that I am in, to reflect upon it.

Penitens was here going on, but had his mouth stopped by a convulsion, which never suffered him to speak any more. He lay convulsed about twelve hours, and then gave up the ghost.

Now if every reader would imagine this Penitens to have been some particular acquaintance or relation of his and fancy that he saw and heard all that is here described, that he stood by his bedside when his poor friend lay in such distress and agony, lamenting the folly of his past life, it would in all probability teach him such wisdom as never entered into his heart before. If to this, he should consider how often he himself might have been surprised in the same state of negligence and made an example to the rest of the world, this double reflection both upon the distress of his friend and the goodness of that God who had preserved him from it would in all likelihood soften his heart into holy tempers and make him turn the remainder of his life into a regular course of piety.

This therefore being so useful a meditation, I shall here leave the reader, as, I hope, seriously engaged in it.

NOTES

8. Given him over: that is, given him up to die.
9. Raised an estate: that is, become rich or well endowed with property.
10. Apartment: chamber or room.

Chapter 4

We can please God in no state or employment of life but by intending and devoting it all to His honor and glory.

Having in the first chapter stated the general nature of devotion and shown that it implies not any form of prayer but a certain form of life that is offered to God not at any particular times or places, but everywhere and in everything, I shall now descend to some particulars and show how we are to devote our labor and employment, our time and fortunes, unto God.

As a good Christian should consider every place as holy because God is there, so he should look upon every part of his life as a matter of holiness because it is to be offered unto God.

The profession of a clergyman is a holy profession because it is a ministration in holy things, an attendance at the altar. But worldly business is to be made holy unto the Lord by being done as a service to Him and in conformity to His divine will.

For as all men and all things in the world as truly belong unto God as any places, things, or persons that are devoted to divine service, so all things are to be used, and all persons are to act in their several states and employments, for the glory of God.

Men of worldly business therefore must not look upon themselves as at liberty to live to themselves, to sacrifice to their own humors and tempers because their employment is of a worldly nature. But they must consider that as the world and all worldly professions as truly belong to God as persons and things that are devoted to the altar, so it is as much the duty of men in worldly business to live wholly unto God as 'tis the duty of those who are devoted to divine service.

As the whole world is God's, so the whole world is to act for

God. As all men have the same relation to God, as all men have all their powers and faculties from God, so all men are obliged to act for God with all their powers and faculties.

As all things are God's, so all things are to be used and regarded as the things of God. For men to abuse things on earth and live to themselves is the same rebellion against God as for angels to abuse things in Heaven, because God is just the same Lord of all on earth as He is the Lord of all in Heaven.

Things may and must differ in their use, but yet they are all to be used according to the will of God.

Men may and must differ in their employments, but yet they must all act for the same ends, as dutiful servants of God in the right and pious performance of their several callings.

Clergymen must live wholly unto God in one particular way, that is, in the exercise of holy office, in the ministration of prayers and sacraments, and a zealous distribution of spiritual goods.

But men of other employments are in their particular ways as much obliged to act as the servants of God and live wholly unto Him in their several callings.

This is the only difference between clergymen and people of other callings.

When it can be shown that men might be vain, covetous, sensual, worldly minded, or proud in the exercise of their worldly business, then it will be allowable for clergymen to indulge the same tempers in their sacred profession. For though these tempers are most odious and most criminal in clergymen, who besides their baptismal vow have a second time devoted themselves to God to be His servants, not in the common offices of human life, but in the spiritual service of the most holy sacred things, and who are therefore to keep themselves as separate and different from the common life of other men as a church or an altar is to be kept separate from houses and tables of common use. Yet as all Christians are by their baptism devoted to God and made professors of holiness, so are they all in their several callings to live as holy and heavenly persons, doing everything in their common life only in such a manner as it may be received by God as a service done to Him. For things spiritual and temporal, sacred and common, must like men and angels, like heaven and earth, all conspire in the glory of God.

As there is but one God and Father of us all, whose glory gives light and life to everything that lives, whose presence fills all places, whose power supports all beings, whose providence ruleth all events, so everything that lives whether in Heaven or earth, whether they be thrones or principalities, men or angels, they must all with one spirit live wholly to the praise and glory of this one God and Father of them all. Angels as angels in their heavenly ministrations, but men as men, women as women, bishops as bishops, priests as priests, and deacons as deacons, some with things spiritual, and some with things temporal, offering to God the daily sacrifice of a reasonable life, wise actions, purity of heart, and heavenly affections.

This is the common business of all persons in this world. It is not left to any women in the world to trifle away their time in the follies and impertinencies of a fashionable life, nor to any men to resign themselves up to worldly cares and concerns; it is not left to the rich to gratify their passions in the indulgencies and pride of life, nor to the poor to vex and torment their hearts with the poverty of their state; but men and women, rich and poor, must with bishops and priests walk before God in the same wise and holy spirit, in the same denial of all vain tempers and in the same discipline and care of their souls, not only because they have all the same rational nature and are servants of the same God, but because they all want the same holiness to make them fit for the same happiness to which they are all called. It is therefore absolutely necessary for all Christians, whether men or women, to consider themselves as persons that are devoted to holiness, and so order their common ways of life by such rules of reason and piety as may turn it into continual service unto almighty God.

Now to make our labor or employment an acceptable service unto God, we must carry it on with the same spirit and temper that is required in giving of alms, or any work of piety. For, if "whether we eat or drink, or whatsoever we do, we must do all to the glory of God" (1 Cor. 10:31); if "we are to use this world as if we used it not"; if "we are to present our bodies a living sacrifice, holy, acceptable to God" (Rom. 12:1); if "we are to live by faith, and not by sight," and to "have our conversation in heaven"; then it is necessary that the common way of our life in every state be made to glorify God by such tempers as make our prayers and adorations acceptable to him. For if we are worldly or earthly minded in our employments, if they are carried on with vain desires and covetous tempers only to satisfy ourselves, we can no more be said to live to the glory of God than gluttons and drunkards can be said to eat and drink to the glory of God.

As the glory of God is one and the same thing, so whatever we do suitable to it must be done with one and the same spirit. That same state and temper of mind which makes our alms and devotions acceptable must also make our labor or employment a proper offering unto God. If a man labors to be rich and pursues his business that he may raise himself to a state of figure and glory in the world, he is no longer serving God in his employment; he is acting under other masters and has no more title to a reward from God than he that gives alms that he may be seen, or prays that he may be heard of men. For vain and earthly desires are no more allowable in our employments than in our alms and devotions. For these tempers of worldly pride and vainglory are not only evil when they mix with our good works, but they have the same evil nature and make us odious to God when they enter into the common business of our employment. If it were allowable to indulge covetous or vain passions in our worldly employments, it would then be allowable to be vainglorious in our devotions. But as our alms and devotions are not an acceptable service but when they proceed from a heart truly devoted to God, so our common employment cannot be reckoned a service to Him but when it is performed with the same temper and piety of heart.

Most of the employments of life are in their own nature lawful, and all those that are so may be made a substantial part of our duty to God if we engage in them only so far, and for such ends, as are suitable to beings that are to live above the world. This is the only measure of our application to any worldly business, let it be what it will, where it will, it must have no more of our hands, our hearts, or our time than is consistent with a hearty, daily, careful preparation of ourselves for another life. For as all Christians, as such, have renounced this world to prepare themselves by daily devotion and universal holiness for an eternal state of quite another nature, they must look upon worldly employments as upon worldly wants and bodily infirmities, things not to be desired, but only to be endured and suffered till death and the resurrection has carried us to an eternal state of real happiness.

Now he that does not look at the things of this life in this degree of littleness cannot be said either to feel or believe the greatest truths of Christianity. For if he thinks anything great or important in human business, can he be said to feel or believe those scriptures which represent this life and the greatest things of life as bubbles, vapors, dreams, and shadows?

If he thinks figure and show and worldly glory to be any proper happiness of a Christian, how can he be said to feel or believe this doctrine, "Blessed are ye when men shall hate you, and when they shall separate you from their company, and shall reproach you, and cast out your name as evil for the son of man's sake"? For surely if there was any real happiness in figure and show and worldly glory, if these things deserved our thoughts and care, it could not be matter of the highest joy when we are torn from them by persecutions and sufferings. If, therefore, a man will so live as to show that he feels and believes the most fundamental doctrines of Christianity, he must live above the world. This is the temper that must enable him to do the business of life and yet live wholly unto God and to go through some worldly employment with a heavenly mind. And it is as necessary that people live in their employments with this temper as it is necessary that their employment itself be lawful.

The husbandman that tilleth the ground is employed in an honest business that is necessary in life and very capable of being made an acceptable service unto God. But if he labors and toils, not to serve any reasonable ends of life, but in order to have his plough made of silver and to have his horses harnessed in gold, the honesty of his employment is lost as to him, and his labor becomes his folly.

A tradesman may justly think that it is agreeable to the will of God for him to sell such things as are innocent and useful in life, such as help both himself and others to a reasonable support and enable them to assist those that want to be assisted. But if instead of this, he trades only with regard to himself without any other rule than that of his own temper, if it be his chief end in it to grow rich that he may live in figure and indulgence and be able to retire from business to idleness and luxury, his trade, as to him, loses all its innocency[11] and is so far from being an acceptable service to God that it is only a more plausible course of covetousness, self-love, and ambition. For such a one turns the necessities of employment into pride and covetousness, just as the sot and epicure turn the necessities of eating and drinking into gluttony and drunkenness. Now he that is up early and late, that sweats and labors for these ends, that he may be some time or other rich and live in pleasure and indulgence, lives no more to the glory of God than he that plays and games for the same ends. For though there is a great difference between trading and gaming, yet most of that difference is lost when men once trade with the same desires and tempers and for the same ends that others game. Charity and fine dressing are things very different, but if men give alms for the same reasons that others dress fine, only to be seen and admired, charity is then but like the vanity of fine clothes. In like manner, if the same motives make some people painful and industrious in their trades which make others constant at gaming, such pains is but like the pains of gaming.

Calidus has traded above thirty years in the greatest city of the kingdom; he has been so many years constantly increasing his trade and his fortune. Every hour of the day is with him an hour of business; and though he eats and drinks very heartily, yet every meal seems to be in a hurry, and he would say grace if he had time. Calidus ends every day at the tavern but has not leisure to be there till near nine o'clock. He is always forced to drink a good hearty glass to drive thoughts of business out of his head and make his spirits drowsy enough for sleep. He does business all the time that he is rising, and has settled several matters before he can get to his counting room. His prayers are a short ejaculation or two, which he never misses in stormy tempestuous weather because he has always something or other at sea. Calidus will tell you with great pleasure that he has been in this hurry for so many years and that it must have killed him long ago, but that it has been a rule with him to get out of the town every Saturday and make the Sunday a day of quiet and good refreshment in the country.

He is now so rich that he would leave off his business and amuse his old age with building and furnishing a fine house in the country, but that he is afraid he should grow melancholy if he was to quit his business. He will tell you with great gravity that it is a dangerous thing for a man that has been used to get money ever to leave it off. If thoughts of religion happen at any time to steal into his head, Calidus contents himself with thinking that he never was a friend to heretics and infidels, that he has always been civil to the minister of his parish, and very often given something to the charity schools.

Now this way of life is at such a distance from all the doctrines and discipline of Christianity that no one can live in it through ignorance or frailty. Calidus can no more imagine that he is born again of the spirit, that he is in Christ a new creature, that he lives here as a stranger and pilgrim, setting his affections upon things above, and laying up treasures in heaven (John 3:5; 1 Pet. 2:11; Col. 3:2). He can no more imagine this than he can think that he has been all his life an Apostle, working miracles and preaching the gospel.

It must also be owned that the generality of trading people, especially in great towns, are too much like Calidus. You see them all the week buried in business, unable to think of anything else, and then spending the Sunday in idleness and refreshment, in wandering into the country, in such visits and jovial meetings as make it often the worst day of the week.

Now they do not live thus because they cannot support themselves with less care and application to business, but they live thus because they want to grow rich in their trades and to maintain their families in some such figure and degree of finery as a reasonable Christian life has no occasion for. Take away but this temper and then people of all trades will find themselves at leisure to live every day like Christians, to be careful of every duty of the gospel, to live in a visible course of religion, and be every day strict observers both of private and public prayer.

Now the only way to do this is for people to consider their trade as something that they are obliged to devote to the glory of God, something that they are to do only in such a manner as that they may make it a duty to Him. Nothing can be right in business that is not under these rules. The Apostle commands servants to be obedient to their masters in singleness of heart as unto Christ. Not with eye service as men pleasers, but as the servants of Christ, doing the will of God from the heart. With good will doing service as unto the Lord, and not to men (Eph. 6:5; Col. 3:22, 23).

This passage sufficiently shows that all Christians are to live wholly unto God in every state and condition, doing the work of their common calling in such a manner and for such ends as to make it a part of their devotion or service to God. For certainly if poor slaves are not to comply with their business as men pleasers, if they are to look wholly unto God in all their actions and serve in singleness of heart as unto the Lord, surely men of other employments and conditions must be as much obliged to go through their business with the same singleness of heart, not as pleasing the vanity of their own minds, not as gratifying their own selfish, worldly passions, but as the servants of God in all that they have to do. For surely no one will say that a slave is to devote his state of life unto God and make the will of God the sole rule and end of his service, but that a tradesman need not act with the same spirit of devotion in his business. For this is as absurd as to make it necessary for one man to be more just or faithful than another.

It is therefore absolutely certain that no Christian is to enter any further into business, nor for any other ends than such as he can in singleness of heart offer unto God as a reasonable service. For the Son of God has redeemed us for this only end, that we should by a life of reason and piety live to the glory of God; this is the only rule and measure for every order and state of life. Without this rule the most lawful employment becomes a sinful state of life.

Take away this from the life of a clergyman, and his holy profession serves only to expose him to a greater damnation. Take away this from tradesmen, and shops are but so many houses of greediness and filthy lucre. Take away this from gentlemen, and the course of their life becomes a course of sensuality, pride, and wantonness. Take away this rule from our tables, and all falls into gluttony and drunkenness. Take away this measure from our dress and habits, and all is turned into such paint and glitter and ridiculous ornaments as are a real shame to the wearer. Take away this from the use of our fortunes, and you will find people sparing in nothing but charity. Take away this from our diversions, and you will find no sports too silly nor any entertainments too vain and corrupt to be the pleasure of Christians.

If therefore we desire to live unto God, it is necessary to bring our whole life under this law, to make His glory the sole rule and measure of our acting in every employment of life. For there is no other true devotion but this of living devoted to God in the common business of our lives.

So that men must not content themselves with the lawfulness of their employments, but must consider whether they use them as they are to use everything, as strangers and pilgrims that are baptized into the Resurrection of Jesus Christ, that are to follow Him in a wise and heavenly course of life in the mortification of all worldly desires, and in purifying and preparing their souls for the blessed enjoyment of God (Col. 3:1; 1 Pet. 2:11; Eph. 5:26, 27).

For to be vain, or proud, or covetous, or ambitious in the common course of our business is as contrary to these holy tempers of Christianity as cheating and dishonesty.

If a glutton was to say in excuse of his gluttony that he only eats such things as it is lawful to eat, he would make as good an excuse for himself as the greedy, covetous, ambitious tradesman that should say he only deals in lawful business. For as a Christian is not only required to be honest, but to be of a Christian spirit and make his life an exercise of humility, repentance, and heavenly affection, so all tempers that are contrary to these are as contrary to Christianity as cheating is contrary to honesty.

So that the matter plainly comes to this, all irregular tempers in trade and business are but like irregular tempers in eating and drinking.

Proud views and vain desires in our worldly employments are as truly vices and corruptions as hypocrisy in prayer or vanity in alms. And there can be no reason given why vanity in our alms should make us odious to God, but what will prove any other kind of pride to be equally odious. He that labors and toils in a calling that he may make a figure in the world and draw the eyes of people upon the splendor of his condition is as far from the pious humility of a Christian as he that gives alms that he may be seen of men. For the reason why pride and vanity in our prayers and alms renders them an unacceptable service to God is not because there is anything particular in prayers and alms that cannot allow of pride, but because pride is in no respect nor in anything made for man; it destroys the piety of everything that it touches, and renders every action that it governs incapable of being offered unto God.

So that if we could so divide ourselves as to be humble in some respects and proud in others, such humility would be of no service to us because God requires us as truly to be humble in all our actions and designs as to be true and honest in all our actions and designs.

And as a man is not honest and true because he is so to a great many people or upon several occasions, but because truth and honesty is the measure of all his dealings with everybody, so the case is the same in humility or any other temper; it must be the general ruling habit of our minds and extend itself to all our actions and designs before it can be imputed to us.

We indeed sometimes talk as if a man might be humble in some things and proud in others, humble in his dress but proud of his learning, humble in his person, but proud in his views and designs. But though this may pass in common discourse, where few things are said according to strict truth, it cannot be allowed when we examine into the nature of our actions.

It is very possible for a man that lives by cheating to be very punctual in paying for what he buys; but then everyone is assured that he does not do so out of any principle of true honesty.

In like manner it is very possible for a man that is proud of his estate, ambitious in his views, or vain of his learning to disregard his dress and person in such a manner as a truly humble man would do; but to suppose that he does so out of a true principle of religious humility is full as absurd as to suppose that a cheat pays for what he buys out of a principle of religious honesty.

As therefore all kinds of dishonesty destroy our pretences to an honest principle of mind, so all kinds of pride destroy our pretences to a humble spirit.

No one wonders that those prayers and alms which proceed from pride and ostentation are odious to God; but yet it is as easy to show that pride is as pardonable there as anywhere else.

If we could suppose that God rejects pride in our prayers and alms but bears with pride in our dress, our persons, or estates, it would be the same thing as to suppose that God condemns falsehood in some actions, but allows it in others. For pride in one thing differs from pride in another thing as the robbing of one man differs from the robbing of another.

Again, if pride and ostentation is so odious that it destroys the merit and worth of the most reasonable actions, surely it must be equally odious in those actions which are only founded in the weakness and infirmity of our nature. As thus, alms are commanded by God as excellent in themselves, as true instances of a divine temper, but clothes are only allowed to cover our shame; surely therefore it must at least be as odious a degree of pride to be vain in our clothes as to be vain in our alms.

Again, we are commanded to pray without ceasing as a means of rendering our souls more exalted and divine, but we are forbidden to lay up treasures upon earth; and can we think that it is not as bad to be vain of those treasures which we are forbidden to lay up as to be vain of those prayers which we are commanded to make.

Women are required to have their heads covered and to adorn themselves with shamefacedness; if therefore they are vain in those things which are expressly forbidden, if they patch and paint that part which can only be adorned by shamefacedness, surely they have as much to repent of for such a pride as they have whose pride is the motive to their prayers and charity (1 Cor. 11:13; 1 Tim. 2:9). This must be granted, unless we will say that it is more pardonable to glory in our shame than to glory in our virtue.

All these instances are only to show us the great necessity of such a regular and uniform piety as extends itself to all the actions of our common life.

That we must eat and drink and dress and discourse according to the sobriety of the Christian spirit, engage in no employments but such as we can truly devote unto God, nor pursue them any further than so far as conduces to the reasonable ends of a holy devout life.

That we must be honest, not only on particular occasions and in such instances as are applauded in the world, easy to be performed and free from danger or loss, but from such a living principle of justice as makes us love truth and integrity in all its instances, follow it through all dangers and against all opposition, as knowing that the more we pay for any truth, the better is our bargain and that then our integrity becomes a pearl when we have parted with all to keep it.

That we must be humble, not only in such instances as are expected in the world or suitable to our tempers or confined to particular occasions, but in such a humility of spirit as renders us meek and lowly in the whole course of our lives as shows itself in our dress, our person, our conversation, our enjoyment of the world, the tranquillity of our minds, patience under injuries, submission to superiors, and condescensions to those that are below us, and in all the outward actions of our lives.

That we must devote not only times and places to prayer, but be everywhere in the spirit of devotion, with hearts always set toward Heaven, looking up to God in all our actions, and doing everything as His servants, living in the world as in a holy temple of God, and always worshipping Him though not with our lips, yet with the thankfulness of our hearts, the holiness of our actions, and the pious and charitable use of all His gifts. That we must not only send up petitions and thoughts now and then to Heaven, but must go through all our worldly business with a heavenly spirit as members of Christ's mystical body, that with new hearts and new minds are to turn an earthly life into a preparation for a life of greatness and glory in the Kingdom of Heaven.

Now the only way to arrive at this piety of spirit is to bring all your actions to the same rule as your devotions and alms. You very well know what it is that makes the piety of your alms or devotions; now the same rules, the same regard to God, must render everything else that you do a fit and acceptable service unto God.

Enough, I hope, has been said to show you the necessity of thus introducing religion into all the actions of your common life, and of living and acting with the same regard to God in all that you do as in your prayers and alms.

Eating is one of the lowest actions of our lives, it is common to us with mere animals, yet we see that the piety of all ages of the world has turned this ordinary action of an animal life into a piety to God by making every meal to begin and end with devotion.

We see yet some remains of this custom in most Christian

families, some such little formality as shows you that people used to call upon God at the beginning and end of their meals. But indeed, it is now generally so performed as to look more like a mockery upon devotion than any solemn application of the mind unto God. In one house you may perhaps see the head of the family just pulling off his hat, in another half getting up from his seat; another shall, it may be, proceed so far as to make as if he said something; but, however, these little attempts are the remains of some devotion that was formerly used at such times and are proofs that religion has formerly belonged to this part of common life.

But to such a pass are we now come that though the custom is yet preserved, yet we can hardly bear with him that seems to perform it with any degree of seriousness, and look upon it as a sign of a fanatical temper if a man has not done as soon as he begins.

I would not be thought to plead for the necessity of long prayers at these times; but thus much I think may be said, that if prayer is proper at these times, we ought to oblige ourselves to use such a form of words as should show that we solemnly appeal to God for such graces and blessings as are then proper to the occasion. Otherwise, the mock ceremony, instead of blessing our victuals, does but accustom us to trifle with devotion and give us a habit of being unaffected with our prayers.

If every head of a family was, at the return of every meal, to oblige himself to make a solemn adoration of God in such a decent manner as becomes a devout mind, it would be very likely to teach him that swearing, sensuality, gluttony, and loose discourse were very improper at those meals which were to begin and end with devotion.

And if in these days of general corruption this part of devotion is fallen into a mock ceremony, it must be imputed to this cause that sensuality and intemperance have got too great a power over us to suffer us to add any devotion to our meals. But thus much must be said, that when we are as pious as Jews and heathens of all ages have been, we shall think it proper to pray at the beginning and end of our meals.

I have appealed to this pious custom of all ages of the world as a proof of the reasonableness of the doctrine of this and the foregoing chapters, that is, as a proof that religion is to be the rule and measure of all the actions of ordinary life. For surely, if we are not to eat but under such rules of devotion, it must plainly appear that whatever else we do must in its proper way be done with the same regard to the glory of God, and agreeably to the principles of a devout and pious mind.

NOTES

11. Innocency: innocence, an older form of the word.

Chapter 5

Persons that are free from the necessity of labor and employments are to consider themselves as devoted to God in a higher degree.

Great parts of the world are free from the necessities of labor and employments and have their time and fortunes in their own disposal.

But as no one is to live in his employment according to his own humor, or for such ends as please his own fancy, but is to do all his business in such a manner as to make it a service unto God, so those who have no particular employment are so far from being left at greater liberty to live to themselves, to pursue their own humors and spend their time and fortunes as they please, that they are under greater obligations of living wholly unto God in all their actions.

The freedom of their state lays them under a greater necessity of always choosing and doing the best things.

They are those of whom much will be required because much is given unto them.

A slave can only live unto God in one particular way, that is, by religious patience and submission in his state of slavery.

But all ways of holy living, all instances, and all kinds of virtue lie open to those who are masters of themselves, their time, and their fortune.

It is as much the duty, therefore, of such persons to make a wise use of their liberty, to devote themselves to all kinds of virtue, to aspire after everything that is holy and pious, to endeavor to be eminent in all good works, and to please God in the highest and most perfect manner; it is as much their duty to be thus wise in the conduct of themselves and thus extensive in their endeavors after holiness as it is the duty of a slave to be resigned unto God in his state of slavery.

You are no laborer or tradesman, you are neither merchant, nor soldier; consider yourself, therefore, as placed in a state in some degree like that of good angels, who are sent into the world as ministering spirits for the general good of mankind, to assist, protect, and minister for them who shall be heirs of salvation.

For the more you are free from the common necessities of men, the more you are to imitate the higher perfections of angels.

Had you, Serena, been obliged by the necessities of life to wash clothes for your maintenance or to wait upon some mistress that demanded all your labor, it would then be your duty to serve and glorify God by such humility, obedience, and faithfulness as might adorn that state of life.

It would then be recommended to your care to improve that one talent to its greatest height. That when the time came that mankind were to be rewarded for their labors by the great Judge of quick and dead, you might be received with a "well done, good and faithful servant, enter thou into the joy of thy Lord" (Matt. 25:21).

But as God has given you five talents, as he has placed you above the necessities of life, as he has left you in the hands of yourself in the happy liberty of choosing the most exalted ways of virtue, as he has enriched you with many gifts of fortune and left you nothing to do but to make the best use of variety of blessings, to make the most of a short life, to study your own perfection, the honor of God, and the good of your neighbor, so it is now your duty to imitate the greatest servants of God, to inquire how the most eminent Saints have lived, to study all the arts and methods of perfection, and to set no bounds to your love and gratitude to the bountiful author of so many blessings.

It is now your duty to turn your five talents into five more, and to consider how your time and leisure and health and fortune may be made so many happy means of purifying your own soul, improving your fellow creatures in the ways of virtue, and of carrying you at last to the greatest heights of eternal glory.

As you have no mistress to serve, so let your own soul be the object of your daily care and attendance. Be sorry for its impurities, its spots and imperfections, and study all the holy arts of restoring it to its natural and primitive purity.

Delight in its service, and beg of God to adorn it with every grace and perfection.

Nourish it with good works, give it peace in solitude, get it strength in prayer, make it wise with reading, enlighten it by meditation, make it tender with love, sweeten it with humility, humble it with penance, enliven it with Psalms and hymns, and comfort it with frequent reflections upon future glory. Keep it in the presence of God and teach it to imitate those guardian angels, which though they attend on human affairs and the lowest of mankind, yet always behold the face of our Father which is in Heaven (Matt. 18:10).

This, Serena, is your profession. For as sure as God is one God, so sure is it that he has but one command to all mankind, whether they be bond or free, rich or poor, and that is, to act up to the excellency of that nature which he has given them, to live by reason, to walk in the light of religion, to use everything as wisdom directs, to glorify God in all His gifts and dedicate every condition of life to His service.

This is the one common command of God to all mankind. If you have an employment, you are to be thus reasonable and pious and holy in the exercise of it; if you have time and a fortune in your own power, you are obliged to be thus reasonable and holy and pious in the use of all your time and all your fortune.

The right religious use of everything and every talent is the indispensable duty of every being that is capable of knowing right and wrong.

For the reason why we are to do anything as unto God and with regard to our duty and relation to Him is the same reason why we are to do everything as unto God, and with regard to our duty and relation to Him.

That which is a reason for our being wise and holy in the discharge of all our business is the same reason for our being wise and holy in the use of all our money.

As we have always the same natures and are everywhere the servants of the same God, as every place is equally full of His presence, and everything is equally His gift, so we must always act according to the reason of our nature; we must do everything as the servants of God; we must live in every place, as in His presence; we must use everything, as that ought to be used which belongs to God.

Either this piety and wisdom and devotion is to go through every way of life and to extend to the use of everything, or it is to go through no part of life.

If we might forget ourselves, or forget God, if we might disregard our reason and live by humor and fancy in anything, or at any time, or in any place, it would be as lawful to do the same in everything, at every time, and every place.

If therefore some people fancy that they must be grave and solemn at church, but may be silly and frantic at home; that they must live by some rule on the Sunday, but may spend other days by chance; that they must have some times of prayer, but may waste the rest of their time as they please; that they must give some money in charity, but may squander away the rest as they have a mind; such people have not enough considered the nature of religion or the true reasons of piety. For he that upon principles of reason can tell why it is good to be wise and heavenly minded at church can tell that it's always desirable to have the same tempers in all other places. He that truly knows why he should spend any time well knows that it is never allowable to throw any time away. He that rightly understands the reasonableness and excellency of charity will know that it can never be excusable to waste any of our money in pride and folly, or in any needless expenses.

For every argument that shows the wisdom and excellency of charity proves the wisdom of spending all our fortune well. Every argument that proves the wisdom and reasonableness of having times of prayer shows the wisdom and reasonableness of losing none of our time.

If anyone could show that we need not always act as in the divine presence, that we need not consider and use everything as the gift of God, that we need not always live by reason and make religion the rule of all our actions, the same arguments would show that we need never act as in the presence of God nor make religion and reason the measure of any of our actions. If therefore we are to live unto God at any time, or in any place, we are to live unto Him at all times and all places. If we are to use anything as the gift of

God, we are to use everything as His gift. If we are to do anything by strict rules of reason and piety, we are to do everything in the same manner. Because reason and wisdom and piety are as much the best things at all times and in all places, as they are the best things at any time or in any place.

If it is our glory and happiness to have a rational nature that is endued with wisdom and reason, that is capable of imitating the divine nature, then it must be our glory and happiness to improve our reason and wisdom, to act up to the excellency of our rational nature, and to imitate God in all our actions to the utmost of our power. They therefore who confine religion to times and places and some little rules of retirement, who think that it is being too strict and rigid to introduce religion into common life and make it give laws to all their actions and ways of living, they who think thus not only mistake, but they mistake the whole nature of religion. For surely they mistake the whole nature of religion who can think any part of their life is made more easy for being free from it. They may well be said to mistake the whole nature of wisdom who don't think it desirable to be always wise. He has not learnt the nature of piety who thinks it too much to be pious in all his actions. He does not sufficiently understand what reason is who does not earnestly desire to live in everything according to it.

If we had a religion that consisted in absurd superstitions, that had no regard to the perfection of our nature, people might well be glad to have some part of their life excused from it. But as the religion of the gospel is only the refinement and exaltation of our best faculties, as it only requires a life of the highest reason, as it only requires us to use this world as in reason it ought to be used, to live in such tempers as are the glory of intelligent beings, to walk in such wisdom as exalts our nature, and to practice such piety as will raise us to God, who can think it grievous to live always in the spirit of such a religion, to have every part of his life full of it, but he that would think it much more grievous to be as the angels of God in Heaven?

Further, as God is one and the same being, always acting like Himself and suitably to His own nature, so it is the duty of every being that He has created to live according to the nature that He has given it, and always to act like itself.

It is therefore an immutable law of God that all rational beings should act reasonably in all their actions, not at this time, or in that place, or upon this occasion, or in the use of some particular thing, but at all times, in all places, at all occasions, and in the use of all things. This is a law that is as unchangeable as God and can no more cease to be than God can cease to be a God of wisdom and order.

When therefore any being that is endued with reason does an unreasonable thing at any time or in any place or in the use of anything, it sins against the great law of its nature, abuses itself, and sins against God the author of that nature.

They therefore who plead for indulgences and vanities for any foolish fashions, customs, and humors of the world, for the misuse of our time or money, plead for a rebellion against our nature, for a rebellion against God who has given us reason for no other end than to make it the rule and measure of all our ways of life.

When therefore you are guilty of any folly or extravagance or indulge any vain temper, don't consider it as a small matter because it may seem so if compared to some other sins; but consider it as it is acting contrary to your nature, and then you will see that there is nothing small that is unreasonable. Because all unreasonable ways are contrary to the nature of all rational beings, whether men or angels. Neither of which can be any longer agreeable to God than so far as they act according to the reason and excellence of their nature.

The infirmities of human life make such food and raiment necessary for us, as angels do not want; but then it is no more allowable for us to turn these necessities into follies and indulge ourselves in the luxury of food or the vanities of dress than it is allowable for angels to act below the dignity of their proper state. For a reasonable life and a wise use of our proper condition is as much the duty of all men as it is the duty of all angels and intelligent beings. These are not speculative flights or imaginary notions, but are plain and undeniable laws that are founded in the nature of rational beings, who as such are obliged to live by reason and glorify God by a continual right use of their several talents and faculties. So that though men are not angels, yet they may know for what ends and by what rules men are to live and act by considering the state and perfection of angels. Our blessed Savior has plainly turned our thoughts this way by making this petition a constant part of all our prayers, "Thy will be done on earth, as it is in heaven." A plain proof that the obedience of men is to imitate the obedience of angels, and that rational beings on earth are to live unto God as rational beings in Heaven live unto him.

When therefore you would represent to your mind how Christians ought to live unto God and in what degrees of wisdom and holiness they ought to use the things of this life, you must not look at the world, but you must look up to God and the society of angels and think what wisdom and holiness is fit to prepare you for such a state of glory. You must look to all the highest precepts of the gospel, you must examine yourself by the Spirit of Christ, you must think how the wisest men in the world have lived, you must think how departed souls would live if they were again to act the short part of human life, you must think what degrees of wisdom and holiness you will wish for when you are leaving the world.

Now all this is not overstraining the matter, or proposing to ourselves any needless perfection. It is but barely complying with the Apostle's advice where he says, "Finally, brethren, whatsoever things are true, whatsoever things are just, whatsoever things are pure, whatsoever things are of good report; if there be any virtue, and if there be any praise, think on these things" (Phil. 4:8). For no one can come near the doctrine of this passage but he that proposes to himself to do everything in this life as the servant of God, to live by reason in everything that he does, and to make the wisdom and holiness of the gospel the rule and measure of his desiring and using every gift of God.

Chapter 6

Containing the great obligations and the great advantages of making a wise and religious use of our estates and fortunes.

As the holiness of Christianity consecrates all states and employments of life unto God, as it requires us to aspire after a universal obedience, doing and using everything as the servants of God, so are we more especially obliged to observe this religious exactness in the use of our estates and fortunes.

The reason of this would appear very plain if we were only to consider that our estate is as much the gift of God as our eyes or our hands, and is no more to be buried or thrown away at pleasure than we are to put out our eyes or throw away our limbs as we please.

But besides this consideration, there are several other great and important reasons why we should be religiously exact in the use of our estates.

First, because the manner of using our money or spending our estate enters so far into the business of every day and makes so great a part of our common life that our common life must be much of the same nature as our common way of spending our estate. If reason and religion govern us in this, then reason and religion hath got great hold of us; but if humor, pride, and fancy are the measures of our spending our estate, then humor, pride, and fancy will have the direction of the greatest part of our life.

Secondly, another great reason for devoting all our estate to right uses is this, because it is capable of being used to the most excellent purposes and is so great a means of doing good. If we waste it, we don't waste a trifle that signifies little, but we waste that which might be made as eyes to the blind, as a husband to the widow, as a father to the orphan. We waste that which not only enables us to minister worldly comforts to those that are in distress, but that which might purchase for ourselves everlasting treasures in Heaven. So that if we part with our money in foolish ways, we part with a great power of comforting our fellow creatures and of making ourselves forever blessed.

If there be nothing so glorious as doing good, if there is nothing that makes us so like to God, then nothing can be so glorious in the use of our money as to use it all in works of love and goodness, making ourselves friends and fathers and benefactors to all our fellow creatures, imitating the divine love and turning all our power into acts of generosity, care, and kindness, to such as are in need of it.

If a man had eyes and hands and feet that he could give to those that wanted them, if he should either lock them up in a chest or please himself with some needless or ridiculous use of them instead of giving them to his brethren that were blind and lame, would we not justly reckon him an inhuman wretch? If he should rather choose to amuse himself with furnishing his house with those things than to entitle himself to an eternal reward by giving them to those that wanted eyes and hands, might we not justly reckon him mad?

Now money has very much the nature of eyes and feet; if we either lock it up in chests, or waste it in needless and ridiculous expenses upon ourselves whilst the poor and the distressed want it for their necessary uses, if we consume it in the ridiculous ornaments of apparel whilst others are starving in nakedness, we are not far from the cruelty of him that chooses rather to adorn his house with the hands and eyes than to give them to those that want them. If we choose to indulge ourselves in such expensive enjoyments as have no real use in them, such as satisfy no real want, rather than to entitle ourselves to an eternal reward by disposing of our money well, we are guilty of his madness that rather chooses to lock up eyes and hands than to make himself for ever blessed by giving them to those that want them.

For after we have satisfied our own sober and reasonable wants, all the rest of our money is but like spare eyes or hands; it is something that we cannot keep to ourselves without being foolish in the use of it, something that can only be used well by giving it to those that want it.

Thirdly, if we waste our money, we are not only guilty of wasting a talent which God has given us, we are not only guilty of making that useless which is so powerful a means of doing good, but we do ourselves this further harm, that we turn this useful talent into a powerful means of corrupting ourselves; because so far as it is spent wrong, so far it is spent in the support of some wrong temper, in gratifying some vain and unreasonable desires, in conforming to those fashions and pride of the world, which as Christians and reasonable men we are obliged to renounce.

As wit and fine parts cannot be trifled away and only lost, but will expose those that have them into greater follies if they are not strictly devoted to piety, so money if it is not used strictly according to reason and religion cannot only be trifled away but it will betray people into greater follies and make them live a more silly and extravagant life than they could have done without it. If, therefore, you don't spend your money in doing good to others, you must spend it to the hurt of yourself. You will act like a man that should refuse to give that as a cordial to a sick friend, though he could not drink it himself without inflaming his blood. For this is the case of superfluous money; if you give it to those that want it, it is a cordial; if you spend it upon yourself in something that you do not want, it only inflames and disorders your mind, and makes you worse than you would be without it.

Consider again the forementioned comparison; if the man that would not make a right use of spare eyes and hands should be continually trying to use them himself spoil his own eyes and hands, we might justly accuse him of still greater madness.

Now this is truly the case of riches spent upon ourselves in vain and needless expenses; in trying to use them where they have no real use, nor we any real want, we only use them to our great hurt, in creating unreasonable desires, in nourishing ill tempers, in indulging our passions and supporting a worldly, vain turn of mind. For high eating and drinking, fine clothes and fine houses, state and equipage, gay pleasures and diversions, do all of them naturally hurt and disorder our hearts; they are the food and nourishments of all the folly and weakness of our nature, and are certain means to make us vain and worldly in our tempers. They are all of them the support of something that ought not to be supported; they are contrary to that sobriety and piety of heart which relishes divine things; they are like so many weights upon our minds, that make us less able and less inclined to raise up our thoughts and affections to the things that are above.

So that money thus spent is not merely wasted or lost, but it is spent to bad purposes and miserable effects, to the corruption and disorder of our hearts, and to the making us less able to live up to the sublime doctrines of the gospel. It is but like keeping money from the poor, to buy poison for ourselves.

For so much as is spent in the vanity of dress may be reckoned so much laid out to fix vanity in our minds. So much as is laid out for idleness and indulgence may be reckoned so much given to render our hearts dull and sensual. So much as is spent in state and equipage may be reckoned so much spent to dazzle your own eyes, and render you the idol of your own imagination. And so in everything, when you go from reasonable wants, you only support some unreasonable temper, some turn of mind, which every good Christian is called upon to renounce.

So that on all accounts, whether we consider our fortune as a talent and trust from God, or the great good that it enables us to do, or the great harm that it does to ourselves if idly spent, on all these great accounts it appears that it is absolutely necessary to make reason and religion the strict rule of using all our fortune.

Every exhortation in scripture to be wise and reasonable, satisfying only such wants as God would have satisfied; every exhortation to be spiritual and heavenly, pressing after a glorious change of our nature; every exhortation to love our neighbor as ourselves, to love all mankind as God has loved them, is a command to be strictly religious in the use of our money. For none of these tempers can be complied with unless we be wise and reasonable, spiritual and heavenly, exercising a brotherly love, a godlike charity in the use of all our fortune. These tempers, and this use of our worldly goods, is so much the doctrine of all the New Testament that you can't read a chapter without being taught something of it. I shall only produce one remarkable passage of scripture which is sufficient to justify all that I have said concerning this religious use of all our fortune.

"When the Son of man shall come in His glory, and the holy

Angels with Him, then shall He sit upon the throne of His glory. And before Him shall be gathered all nations; and He shall separate them one from another, as a shepherd divideth the sheep from the goats; and He shall set the sheep on His right hand, but the goats on the left. Then shall the King say unto them on His right hand, come ye blessed of my Father, inherit the kingdom prepared for you from the foundation of the world. For I was an hungered, and ye gave me meat; I was thirsty, and ye gave me drink: I was a stranger and ye took me in; naked, and ye clothed me: I was sick, and ye visited me; I was in prison, and ye came unto me. . . . Then shall He say unto them on the left hand, depart from me, ye cursed, into everlasting fire, prepared for the devil and his angels, for I was an hungered, and ye gave me no meat; I was thirsty, and ye gave me no drink: I was a stranger and ye took me not in; naked, and ye clothed me not; sick, and in prison, and ye visited me not. These shall go away into everlasting punishment, but the righteous into life eternal."

I have quoted this passage at length because, if one looks at the way of the world, one would hardly think that Christians had ever read this part of scripture. For what is there in the lives of Christians that looks as if their salvation depended upon these good works? And yet the necessity of them is here asserted in the highest manner, and pressed upon us by a lively description of the glory and terrors of the day of judgment.

Some people, even of those who may be reckoned virtuous Christians, look upon this text only as a general recommendation of occasional works of charity, whereas it shows the necessity not only of occasional charities now and then, but the necessity of such an entire charitable life as is a continual exercise of all such works of charity as we are able to perform.

You own that you have no title to salvation if you have neglected these good works because such persons as have neglected them are at the last day to be placed on the left hand, and banished with a "depart ye cursed." There is, therefore, no salvation but in the performance of these good works. Who is it, therefore, that may be said to have performed these good works? Is it he that has sometime assisted a prisoner, or relieved the poor or sick? This would be as absurd as to say that he had performed the duties of devotion who had sometime said his prayers. Is it therefore he that has several times done these works of charity? This can no more be said than he can be said to be the truly just man who had done acts of justice several times. What is the rule therefore, or measure of performing these good works? How shall a man trust that he performs them as he ought?

Now the rule is very plain and easy and such as is common to every other virtue or good temper, as well as to charity. Who is the humble, or meek, or devout, or just, or faithful man? Is it he that has several times done acts of humility, meekness, devotion, justice, or fidelity? No. But it is he that lives in the habitual exercise of these virtues. In like manner, he only can be said to have performed these works of charity who lives in the habitual exercise of them to the utmost of his power. He only has performed the duty of divine love who loves God with all his heart, and with all his mind, and with all his strength. And he only has performed the duty of these good works who has done them with all his heart, and with all his mind, and with all his strength. For there is no other measure of our doing good than our power of doing it.

The Apostle St. Peter puts this question to our blessed Savior, "Lord, how oft shall my brother sin against me, and I forgive him? 'till seven times?" Jesus saith unto him, "I say not unto thee, until seven times; but until seventy times seven" (Matt. 18:21-22). Not as if after this number of offences a man might then cease to forgive; but the expression of seventy times seven is to show us that we are not to bound our forgiveness by any number of offences, but are to continue forgiving the most-repeated offences against us. Thus our Savior saith in another place, "If he trespass against thee seven times in a day, and seven times in a day turn again to thee, saying, I repent, thou shalt forgive him" (Luke 17:4). If, therefore, a man ceases to forgive his brother because he has forgiven him often already, if he excuses himself from forgiving this man because he has forgiven several others, such a one breaks this law of Christ concerning the forgiving one's brother.

Now the rule of forgiving is also the rule of giving; you are not to give or do good to seven, but to seventy times seven. You are not to cease from giving because you have given often to the same person, or to other persons, but must look upon yourself as much obliged to continue relieving those that continue in wants, as you was obliged to relieve them once or twice. Had it not been in your power, you had been excused from relieving any person once; but if it is in your power to relieve people often, it is as much your duty to do it often as it is the duty of others to do it but seldom because they are but seldom able. He that is not ready to forgive every brother as often as he wants to be forgiven does not forgive like a disciple of Christ. And he that is not ready to give to every brother that wants to have something given him does not give like a disciple of Christ. For it is as necessary to give to seventy times seven, to live in the continual exercise of all good works to the utmost of our power, as it is necessary to forgive until seventy times seven, and live in the habitual exercise of this forgiving temper toward all that want it.

And the reason of all this is very plain because there is the same goodness, the same excellency, and the same necessity of being thus charitable at one time as at another. It is as much the best use of our money to be always doing good with it as it is the best use of it at any particular time, so that that which is a reason for charitable action is as good a reason for a charitable life. That which is a reason for forgiving one offence is the same reason for forgiving all offences. For such charity has nothing to recommend it today but what will be the same recommendation of it tomorrow; and you cannot neglect it at one time without being guilty of the same sin as if you neglected it at another time.

As sure, therefore, as these works of charity are necessary to salvation, so sure is it that we are to do them to the utmost of our power, not today or tomorrow, but through the whole course of our life. If therefore it be our duty at any time to deny ourselves any needless expenses, to be moderate and frugal, that we may have to give to those that want, it is as much our duty to do so at all times that we may be further able to do more good. For if it is at any time a sin to prefer needless vain expense to works of charity, it is so at all times, because charity as much excels all needless and vain expenses at one time as at another. So that if it is ever necessary to our salvation to take care of these works of charity and to see that we make ourselves in some degree capable of doing them, it is as necessary to our salvation to take care to make ourselves as capable as we can be of performing them in all the parts of our life.

Either therefore you must so far renounce your Christianity as to say that you need never perform any of these good works, or you must own that you are to perform them all your life in as high a degree as you are able. There is no middle way to be taken, any more than there is a middle way betwixt pride and humility or temperance and intemperance. If you do not strive to fulfill all charitable works, if you neglect any of them that are in your power and deny assistance to those that want what you can give, let it be when it will or where it will, you number yourself amongst those that want Christian charity, because it is as much your duty to do good with all that you have and to live in the continual exercise of good works as it is your duty to be temperate in all that you eat and drink.

Hence also appears the necessity of renouncing all those foolish and unreasonable expenses which the pride and folly of mankind has made so common and fashionable in the world. For if it is necessary to do good works as far as you are able, it must be as necessary to renounce those needless ways of spending money which render you unable to do works of charity.

You must therefore no more conform to these ways of the world than you must conform to the vices of the world; you must no more spend with those that idly waste their money as their own humor leads them than you must drink with the drunken, or indulge yourself with the epicure,[12] because a course of such expenses is no more consistent with a life of charity than excess in drinking is consistent with a life of sobriety. When therefore anyone tells you of the lawfulness of expensive apparel, or the innocency[13] of pleasing yourself with costly satisfactions, only imagine that the same person was to tell you that you need not do works of charity, that Christ does not require you to do good unto your poor brethren as unto Him, and then you will see the wickedness of such advice; for to tell you that you may live in such expenses as make it impossible for you to live in the exercise of good works is the same thing as telling you that you need not have any care about such good works themselves.

NOTES
12. Epicure: a kind of implied personification, meant to designate one who gives himself up totally to sensual pleasures and gluttony.
13. Excellency: that is, excellence.

Chapter 7

How the imprudent use of an estate corrupts all the
tempers of the mind and fills the heart with poor and
ridiculous passions through the whole course of life,
represented in the character of Flavia.

It has already been observed that a prudent and religious care
is to be used in the manner of spending our money or estate because
the manner of spending our estate makes so great a part of our
common life and is so much the business of every day, that according as we are wise or imprudent in this respect, the whole course of
our lives will be rendered either very wise, or very full of folly.

Persons that are well affected to religion, that receive instructions of piety with pleasure and satisfaction, often wonder how it
comes to pass that they make no greater progress in that religion
which they so much admire.

Now the reason of it is this. It is because religion lives only in
their head, but something else has possession of their hearts; and
therefore they continue from year to year mere admirers and prais-
ers of piety without ever coming up to the reality and perfection of
its precepts.

If it be asked why religion does not get possession of their
hearts, the reason is this. It is not because they live in gross sins or
debaucheries, for their regard to religion preserves them from such
disorders.

But it is because their hearts are constantly employed, perverted, and kept in a wrong state by the indiscreet use of such
things as are lawful to be used.

The use and enjoyment of their estates is lawful, and therefore
it never comes into their heads to imagine any great danger from
that quarter. They never reflect that there is a vain and imprudent

use of their estates, which though it does not destroy like gross sins, yet so disorders the heart and supports it in such sensuality and dullness, such pride and vanity, as makes it incapable of receiving the life and spirit of piety.

For our souls may receive an infinite hurt and be rendered incapable of all virtue, merely by the use of innocent and lawful things.

What is more innocent than rest and retirement? And yet what more dangerous than sloth and idleness? What is more lawful than eating and drinking? And yet what more destructive of all virtue, what more fruitful of all vice, than sensuality and indulgence?

How lawful and praiseworthy is the care of a family? And yet how certainly are many people rendered incapable of all virtue by a worldly and solicitous temper?

Now it is for want of religious exactness in the use of these innocent and lawful things that religion cannot get possession of our hearts. And it is in the right and prudent management of ourselves, as to these things, that all the art of holy living chiefly consists.

Gross sins are plainly seen and easily avoided by persons that profess religion. But the indiscreet and dangerous use of innocent and lawful things, as it does not shock and offend our consciences, so it is difficult to make people at all sensible of the danger of it.

A gentleman that expends all his estate in sports, and a woman that lays out all her fortune upon herself, can hardly be persuaded that the spirit of religion cannot subsist in such a way of life.

These persons, as has been observed, may live free from debaucheries, they may be friends of religion, so far as to praise and speak well of it and admire it in their imaginations; but it cannot govern their hearts and be the spirit of their actions till they change their way of life and let religion give laws to the use and spending of their estates.

For a woman that loves dress, that thinks no expense too great to bestow upon the adorning of her person, cannot stop there. For that temper draws a thousand other follies along with it and will render the whole course of her life, her business, her conversation, her hopes, her fears, her taste, her pleasures and diversions, all suitable to it.

Flavia and Miranda are two maiden sisters that have each of

them two hundred pounds a year. They buried their parents twenty years ago, and have since that time spent their estate as they pleased.

Flavia has been the wonder of all her friends for her excellent management in making so surprising a figure in so moderate a fortune. Several ladies that have twice her fortune are not able to be always so genteel and so constant at all places of pleasure and expense. She has everything that is in the fashion, and is in every place where there is any diversion. Flavia is very orthodox, she talks warmly against heretics and schismatics, is generally at church, and often at the Sacrament. She once commended a sermon that was against the pride and vanity of dress, and thought it was very just against Lucinda, whom she takes to be a great deal finer than she need to be. If anyone asks Flavia to do something in charity, if she likes the person who makes the proposal or happens to be in a right temper, she will toss him half a crown or a crown, and tell him if he knew what a long milliner's bill she had just received he would think it a great deal for her to give. A quarter of a year after this, she hears a sermon upon the necessity of charity; she thinks the man preaches well, that it is a very proper subject, that people want much to be put in mind of it; but she applies nothing to herself because she remembers that she gave a crown some time ago when she could so ill spare it.

As for poor people themselves, she will admit of no complaints from them; she is very positive they are all cheats and liars and will say anything to get relief, and therefore it must be a sin to encourage them in their evil ways.

You would think Flavia had the tenderest conscience in the world if you was to see how scrupulous and apprehensive she is of the guilt and danger of giving amiss.

She buys all books of wit and humor, and has made an expensive collection of all our English poets. For she says, one cannot have a true taste of any of them without being very conversant with them all.

She will sometimes read a book of piety if it is a short one, if it is much commended for style and language, and she can tell where to borrow it.

Flavia is very idle, and yet very fond of fine work. This makes her often sit working in bed until noon, and be told many a long story before she is up, so that I need not tell you that her morning devotions are not always rightly performed.

Flavia would be a miracle of piety if she was but half so careful of her soul as she is of her body. The rising of a pimple in her face, the sting of a gnat, will make her keep her room two or three days, and she thinks they are very rash people that don't take care of things in time. This makes her so overcareful of her health that she never thinks she is well enough, and so overindulgent that she never can be really well. So that it costs her a great deal in sleeping draughts and waking draughts, in spirits for the head, in drops for the nerves, in cordials for the stomach, and in saffron for her tea.

If you visit Flavia on the Sunday, you will always meet good company, you will know what is doing in the world, you will hear the last lampoon, be told who wrote it and who is meant by every name that is in it. You will hear what plays were acted that week, which is the finest song in the opera, who was intolerable at the last assembly, and what games are most in fashion. Flavia thinks they are atheists that play at cards on the Sunday, but she will tell you the nicety of all the games, what cards she held, how she played them, and the history of all that happened at play as soon as she comes from church. If you would know who is rude and ill natured, who is vain and foppish, who lives too high, and who is in debt; if you would know what is the quarrel at a certain house, or who and who are in love; if you would know how late Belinda comes home at night, what clothes she has bought, how she loves compliments, and what a long story she told at such a place; if you would know how cross Lucius is to his wife, what ill-natured things he says to her when nobody hears him; if you would know how they hate one another in their hearts, though they appear so kind in public, you must visit Flavia on the Sunday. But still she has so great a regard for the holiness of the Sunday that she has turned a poor old widow out of her house as a profane wretch for having been found once mending her clothes on the Sunday night.

Thus lives Flavia; and if she lives ten years longer, she will have spent about fifteen hundred and sixty Sundays after this manner. She will have wore[14] about two hundred different suits of clothes. Out of this thirty years of her life, fifteen of them will have been disposed of in bed; and of the remaining fifteen, about four-teen of them will have been consumed in eating, drinking, dressing, visiting, conversation, reading and hearing plays and romances, at operas, assemblies, balls, and diversions. For you may reckon all the time that she is up thus spent, except about an hour and half that is disposed of at church most Sundays in the year. With great management, and under mighty rules of economy, she will have spent sixty hundred pounds upon herself, bating only some shil-lings, crowns, or half crowns that have gone from her in accidental charities.

I shall not take upon me to say that it is impossible for Flavia to be saved; but thus much must be said, that she has no grounds from scripture to think she is in the way of salvation. For her whole life is in direct opposition to all those tempers and practices which the gospel has made necessary to salvation.

If you was to hear her say that she had lived all her life like Anna the prophetess, who departed not from the temple, but served God with fastings and prayers night and day, you would look upon her as very extravagant; and yet this would be no greater an extravagance than for her to say that she had been striving to enter in at the strait gate, or making any one doctrine of the gospel a rule of her life.

She may as well say that she lived with our Savior when he was upon earth as that she has lived in imitation of Him, or made it any part of her care to live in such tempers as He required of all those that would be His disciples. She may as truly say that she has every day washed the Saints' feet as that she has lived in Christian humility and poverty of spirit, and as reasonably think that she has taught a charity school as that she has lived in works of charity. She has as much reason to think that she has been a sentinel in an army as that she has lived in watching and self-denial. And it may as fairly be said that she lived by the labor of her hands as that she had given all diligence to make her calling and election sure.

And here it is to be well observed that the poor, vain turn of mind, the irreligion, the folly and vanity of this whole life of Flavia is all owing to the manner of using her estate. It is this that has formed her spirit, that has given life to every idle temper, that has supported every trifling passion and kept her from all thoughts of a prudent, useful, and devout life.

When her parents died, she had no thought about her two hundred pounds a year, but that she had so much money to do what she would with, to spend upon herself and purchase the pleasures and gratifications of all her passions.

And it is this setting out, this false judgment and indiscreet use of her fortune, that has filled her whole life with the same indiscretion, and kept her from thinking of what is right and wise and pious in everything else.

If you have seen her delighted in plays and romances, in scandal and backbiting, easily flattered and soon affronted; if you have seen her devoted to pleasures and diversions, a slave to every passion in its turn, nice[15] in everything that concerned her body or dress, careless of everything that might benefit her soul, always wanting some new entertainment and ready for every happy invention in show or dress, it was because she had purchased all these tempers with the yearly revenue of her fortune.

She might have been humble, serious, devout, a lover of good books, an admirer of prayer and retirement, careful of her time, diligent in good works, full of charity and the love of God, but that the imprudent use of her estate forced all the contrary tempers upon her.

And it was no wonder that she should turn her time, her mind, her health and strength to the same uses that she turned her fortune. It is owing to her being wrong in so great an article of life that you can see nothing wise, or reasonable, or pious in any other part of it.

Now though the irregular trifling spirit of this character belongs, I hope, but to few people, yet many may here learn some instruction from it and perhaps see something of their own spirit in it.

For as Flavia seems to be undone by the unreasonable use of her fortune, so the lowness of most people's virtue, the imperfections of their piety and the disorders of their passions is generally owing to their imprudent use and enjoyment of lawful and innocent things.

More people are kept from a true sense and taste of religion by a regular kind of sensuality and indulgence than by gross drunkenness. More men live, regardless of the great duties of piety, through too great a concern for worldly goods than through direct injustice.

This man would perhaps be devout, if he was not so great a virtuoso. Another is deaf to all the motives to piety by indulging an idle, slothful temper.

Could you cure this man of his great curiosity and inquisitive temper, or that of his false satisfaction and thirst after learning, you need do no more to make them both become men of great piety.

If this woman would make fewer visits, or that not be always talking, they would neither of them find it half so hard to be affected with religion.

For all these things are only little when they are compared to great sins; and though they are little in that respect, yet they are great, as they are impediments and hindrances of a pious spirit.

For as consideration is the only eye of the soul, as the truths of religion can be seen by nothing else, so whatever raises a levity of mind, a trifling spirit, renders the soul incapable of seeing, apprehending, and relishing the doctrines of piety.

Would we therefore make a real progress in religion, we must not only abhor gross and notorious sins, but we must regulate the innocent and lawful parts of our behavior and put the most common and allowed actions of life under the rules of discretion and piety.

NOTES

14. Wore: that is, worn.
15. Nice: fastidious.

Chapter 8

How the wise and pious use of an estate naturally carries us to great perfection in all the virtues of the Christian life, represented in the character of Miranda.

Any one pious regularity of any one part of our life is of great advantage, not only on its own account, but as it uses us to live by rule and think of the government of ourselves.

A man of business that has brought one part of his affairs under certain rules is in a fair way to take the same care of the rest.

So he that has brought any one part of his life under the rules of religion may thence be taught to extend the same order and regularity into other parts of his life.

If anyone is so wise as to think this time too precious to be disposed of by chance and left to be devoured by anything that happens in his way; if he lays himself under a necessity of observing how every day goes through his hands and obliges himself to a certain order of time in his business, his retirements, and devotions, it is hardly to be imagined how soon such a conduct would reform, improve, and perfect the whole course of his life.

He that once thus knows the value and reaps the advantage of a well-ordered time will not long be a stranger to the value of anything else that is of any real concern to him.

A rule that relates even to the smallest part of our life is of great benefit to us, merely as it is a rule.

For as the proverb saith, "He that has begun well, has half done," so he that has begun to live by rule has gone a great way toward the perfection of his life.

By rule must here be constantly understood a religious rule, observed upon a principle of duty to God.

For if a man should oblige himself to be moderate in his meals only in regard to his stomach, or abstain from drinking only to avoid the headache, or be moderate in his sleep through fear of a lethargy,[16] he might be exact in these rules without being at all the better man for them.

But when he is moderate and regular in any of these things out of a sense of Christian sobriety and self-denial, that he may offer unto God a more reasonable and holy life, then it is that the smallest rule of this kind is naturally the beginning of great piety.

For the smallest rule in these matters is of great benefit as it teaches us some part of the government of ourselves, as it keeps up a tenderness of mind, as it presents God often to our thoughts and brings a sense of religion into the ordinary actions of our common life.

If a man, whenever he was in company where anyone swore, talked lewdly, or spoke evil of his neighbor, should make it a rule to himself either gently to reprove him, or if that was not proper, then to leave the company as decently as he could, he would find that this little rule, like a little leaven hid in a great quantity of meal, would spread and extend itself through the whole form of his life.

If another should oblige himself to abstain on the Lord's Day from many innocent and lawful things, as traveling, visiting, common conversation, and discoursing upon worldly matters, as trade, news, and the like, if he should devote the day, besides the public worship, to greater retirement, reading, devotion, instruction, and works of charity, though it may seem but a small thing or a needless nicety to require a man to abstain from such things as may be done without sin, yet whoever would try the benefit of so little a rule would perhaps thereby find such a change made in his spirit, and such a taste of piety raised in his mind as he was an entire stranger to before.

It would be easy to show in many other instances how little and small matters are the first steps and natural beginnings of great perfection.

But the two things which of all others most want to be under a strict rule and which are the greatest blessings both to ourselves and others when they are rightly used are our time and our money. These talents are continual means and opportunities of doing good.

He that is piously strict and exact in the wise management of either of these cannot be long ignorant of the right use of the other. And he that is happy in the religious care and disposal of them both is already ascended several steps upon the ladder of Christian perfection.

Miranda (the sister of Flavia) is a sober reasonable Christian; as soon as she was mistress of her time and fortune, it was her first thought how she might best fulfill everything that God required of her in the use of them, and how she might make the best and happiest use of this short life. She depends upon the truth of what our blessed Lord hath said, "that there is but one thing needful," and therefore makes her whole life but one continual labor after it. She has but one reason for doing or not doing, for liking or not liking anything, and that is the will of God. She is not so weak as to pretend to add what is called the fine lady to the true Christian; Miranda thinks too well to be taken with the sound of such silly words; she has renounced the world to follow Christ in the exercise of humility, charity, devotion, abstinence, and heavenly affections, and that is Miranda's fine breeding.

Whilst she was under her mother, she was forced to be genteel, to live in ceremony, to sit up late at nights, to be in the folly of every fashion, and always visiting on Sundays, to go patched and loaded with a burden of finery[17] to the Holy Sacrament, to be in every polite conversation, to hear profaneness at the playhouse and wanton songs and love intrigues at the opera, to dance at public places, that fops and rakes might admire the fineness of her shape and the beauty of her motions. The remembrance of this way of life makes her exceeding careful to atone for it by a contrary behavior.

Miranda does not divide her duty between God, her neighbor, and herself; but she considers all as due to God, and so does everything in His name and for His sake. This makes her consider her fortune as the gift of God that is to be used as everything is that belongs to God, for the wise and reasonable ends of a Christian and holy life. Her fortune therefore is divided betwixt herself and several other poor people, and she has only her part of relief from it. She thinks it the same folly to indulge herself in needless vain expenses as to give to other people to spend in the same way. Therefore, as she will not give a poor man money to go see a puppet show, neither will she allow herself any to spend in the same manner, thinking it very proper to be as wise herself as she expects poor men should be. For is it a folly and a crime in a poor man, says Miranda, to waste what is given him in foolish trifles, whilst he wants meat, drink, and clothes?[18] And is it less folly, or a less crime in me to spend that money in silly diversions which might be so much better spent in imitation of the divine goodness, in works of kindness and charity toward my fellow creatures and fellow Christians? If a poor man's own necessities are a reason why he should not waste any of his money idly, surely the necessities of the poor, the excellency of charity, which is received as done to Christ Himself, is a much greater reason why no one should ever waste any of his money. For if he does so, he does not only do like the poor man, only waste that which is wanted for the most noble use, and which Christ Himself is ready to receive at his hands. And if we are angry at a poor man and look upon him as a wretch when he throws away that which should buy his own bread, how must we appear in the sight of God if we make a wanton idle use of that which should buy bread and clothes for the hungry and naked brethren, who are as near and dear to God as we are, and fellow heirs of the same state of future glory? This is the spirit of Miranda, and thus she uses the gifts of God; she is only one of a certain number of poor people that are relieved out of her fortune, and she only differs from them in the blessedness of giving.

Excepting her victuals, she never spent near ten pound a year upon herself. If you was to see her, you would wonder what poor body it was that was so surprisingly neat and clean. She has but one rule that she observes in her dress, to be always clean, and in the cheapest things. Everything about her resembles the purity of her soul, and she is always clean without because she is always pure within.

Every morning sees her early at her prayers, she rejoices in the beginning of every day because it begins all her pious rules of holy living and brings the fresh pleasure of repeating them. She seems to be as a guardian angel to those that dwell about her, with her watchings and prayers blessing the place where she dwells and making intercession with God for those that are asleep.

Her devotions have had some intervals and God has heard

several of her private prayers before the light is suffered to enter into her sister's room. Miranda does not know what it is to have a dull half day; the returns of her hours of prayer and her religious exercises come too often to let any considerable part of it lie heavy upon her hands.

When you see her at work, you see the same wisdom that governs all her other actions; she is either doing something that is necessary for herself or necessary for others who want to be assisted. There is scarce a poor family in the neighborhood but wears something or other that has had the labor of her hands. Her wise and pious mind neither wants the amusement, nor can bear with the folly of idle and impertinent work. She can admit of no such folly as this in the day because she is to answer for all her actions at night. When there is no wisdom to be observed in the employment of her hands, when there is no useful or charitable work to be done, Miranda will work no more. At her table she lives strictly by this rule of Holy Scripture, "Whether ye eat, or drink, or whatever ye do, do all to the glory of God." This makes her begin and end every meal as she begins and ends every day, with acts of devotion. She eats and drinks only for the sake of living, and with so regular an abstinence that every meal is an exercise of self-denial, and she humbles her body every time that she is forced to feed it. If Miranda was to run a race for her life, she would submit to a diet that was proper for it. But as the race which is set before her is a race of holiness, purity, and heavenly affection, which she is to finish in a corrupt, disordered body of earthly passions, so her everyday diet has only this one end, to make her body fitter for this spiritual race. She does not weigh her meat[19] in a pair of scales, but she weighs it in a much better balance; so much as gives a proper strength to her body and renders it able and willing to obey the soul, to join in Psalms and prayers, and lift up eyes and hands toward heaven with greater readiness, so much is Miranda's meal, so that Miranda will never have her eyes swell with fatness or pant under a heavy load of flesh 'till she has changed her religion.

The Holy Scriptures, especially of the New Testament, are her daily study; these she reads with a watchful attention, constantly casting an eye upon herself, and trying herself by every doctrine that is there. When she has the New Testament in her hand, she supposes herself at the feet of our Savior and His Apostles and makes everything that she learns of them so many laws of her life. She receives their sacred words with as much attention and reverence as if she saw their persons and knew that they were just come from Heaven, on purpose to teach her the way that leads to it.

She thinks that the trying of herself every day by the doctrines of scripture is the only possible way to be ready for her trial at the last day. She is sometimes afraid that she lays out too much money in books because she cannot forbear buying all practical books of any note, especially such as enter into the heart of religion and describe the inward holiness of the Christian life. But of all human writings, the lives of pious persons and eminent Saints are her greatest delight. In these she searches as for hidden treasure, hoping to find some secret of holy living, some uncommon degree of piety which she may make her own. By this means Miranda has her head and her heart so stored with all the principles of wisdom and holiness, she is so full of the one main business of life, that she finds it difficult to converse upon any other subject; and if you are in her company when she thinks it proper to talk, you must be made wiser and better, whether you will or no.

To relate her charity would be to relate the history of every day for twenty years; for so long has all her fortune been spent that way. She has set up near twenty poor tradesmen that had failed in their business, and saved as many from failing. She has educated several poor children that were picked up in the streets, and put them in a way of an honest employment. As soon as any laborer is confined at home with sickness, she sends him till he recovers twice the value of his wages, that he may have one part to give to his family as usual, and the other to provide things convenient for his sickness.

If a family seems too large to be supported by the labor of those that can work in it, she pays their rent and gives them something yearly toward their clothing. By this means there are several poor families that live in a comfortable manner, and are from year to year blessing her in their prayers.

If there is any poor man or woman that is more than ordinarily wicked and reprobate, Miranda has her eye upon them, she watches their time of need and adversity; and if she can discover that they are in any great straits or affliction, she gives them speedy relief. She has this care for this sort of people, because she once saved a very profligate person from being carried to prison, who immediately became a true penitent.

There is nothing in the character of Miranda more to be admired than this temper. For this tenderness of affection toward the most abandoned sinners is the highest instance of a divine and godlike soul.

Miranda once passed by a house where the man and his wife were cursing and swearing at one another in a most dreadful manner, and three children crying about them; this sight so much affected her compassionate mind that she went the next day and bought the three children, that they might not be ruined by living with such wicked parents; they now live with Miranda, are blessed with her care and prayers, and all the good works which she can do for them. They hear her talk, they see her live, they join with her in Psalms and prayers. The eldest of them has already converted his parents from their wicked life and shows a turn of mind so remarkably pious that Miranda intends him for holy orders, that being thus saved himself, he may be zealous in the salvation of souls, and do to other miserable objects as she has done to him.

Miranda is a constant relief to poor people in their misfortunes and accidents; there are sometimes little misfortunes that happen to them, which of themselves they could never be able to overcome. The death of a cow or a horse, or some little robbery, would keep them in distress all their lives. She does not suffer them to grieve under such accidents as these. She immediately gives them the full value of their loss and makes use of it as a means of raising their minds toward God.

She has a great tenderness for old people that are grown past their labor. The parish allowance to such people is very seldom a comfortable maintenance. For this reason, they are the constant objects of her care; she adds so much to their allowance as somewhat exceeds the wages they got when they were young. This she does to comfort the infirmities of their age, that being free from trouble and distress, they may serve God in peace and tranquillity of mind. She has generally a large number of this kind, who by her charities and exhortations to holiness spend their last days in great piety and devotion.

Miranda never wants[20] compassion, even to common beggars,

especially toward those that are old or sick, or full of sores, that want eyes or limbs. She hears their complaints with tenderness, gives them some proof of her kindness, and never rejects them with hard or reproachful language for fear of adding affliction to her fellow creatures.

If a poor old traveler tells her that he has neither strength, nor food, nor money left, she never bids him go to the place from whence he came, or tells him that she cannot relieve him because he may be a cheat, or she does not know him; but she relieves him for that reason because he is a stranger and unknown to her. For it is the most noble part of charity to be kind and tender to those whom we never saw before and perhaps never may see again in this life. "I was a stranger, and ye took me in," saith our blessed Savior; but who can perform this duty that will not relieve persons that are unknown to him?

Miranda considers that Lazarus was a common beggar, that he was the care of angels and carried into Abraham's bosom. She considers that our blessed Savior and His Apostles were kind to beggars, that they spoke comfortably to them, healed their diseases, and restored eyes and limbs to the lame and blind, that Peter said to the beggar that wanted an alms from him, "Silver and gold have I none, but such as I have give I thee; in the name of Jesus Christ of Nazareth, rise up and walk." Miranda, therefore, never treats beggars with disregard and aversion, but she imitates the kindness of our Savior and His Apostles toward them; and though she cannot, like them, work miracles for their relief, yet she relieves them with that power that she hath, and may say with the Apostle, "Such as I have give I thee, in the name of Jesus Christ."

It may be, says Miranda, that I may often give to those that do not deserve it, or that will make an ill use of my alms. But what then? Is not this the very goodness that is recommended to us in scripture, that by imitating of it we may be children of our Father which is in Heaven, "Who sendeth rain on the just, and on the unjust?" And shall I withhold a little money or food from my fellow creature, for fear he should not be good enough to receive it of me? Do I beg of God to deal with me, not according to my merit, but according to his own great goodness, and shall I be so absurd as to withhold my charity from a poor brother because he may perhaps not deserve it? Shall I use a measure toward him, which I pray God never to use toward me?

Besides, where has the scripture made merit the rule or measure of charity? On the contrary, the scripture saith, "If thy enemy hunger, feed him; if he thirst, give him drink."

Now this plainly teaches us that the merit of persons is to be no rule of our charity, but that we are to do acts of kindness to those that least of all deserve it. For if I am to love and do good to my worst enemies, if I am to be charitable to them notwithstanding all their spite and malice, surely merit is no measure of charity. If I am not to withhold my charity from such bad people and who are at the same time my enemies, surely I am not to deny alms to poor beggars whom I neither know to be bad people, nor any way my enemies.

You will perhaps say that by this means I encourage people to be beggars. But the same thoughtless objection may be made against all kinds of charities, for they may encourage people to depend upon them. The same may be said against forgiving our enemies, for it may encourage people to do us hurt. The same may be said even against the goodness of God, that by pouring His blessings on the evil and on the good, on the just and on the unjust, evil and unjust men are encouraged in their wicked ways. The same may be said against clothing the naked, or giving medicines to the sick, for that may encourage people to neglect themselves and be careless of their health. But when the love of God dwelleth in you, when it has enlarged your heart and filled you with bowels of mercy and compassion, you will make no more such objections as these.

When you are at any time turning away the poor, the old, the sick and helpless traveler, the lame, or the blind, ask yourself this question: do I sincerely wish these poor creatures may be as happy as Lazarus that was carried by angels into Abraham's bosom? Do I sincerely desire that God would make them fellow heirs with me in eternal glory? Now if you search into your soul, you will find that there is none of these motions there, that you are wishing nothing of this. For it is impossible for anyone heartily to wish a poor creature so great a happiness, and yet not have a heart to give him a small alms. For this reason, says Miranda, as far as I can, I give to all because I pray to God to forgive all; and I cannot refuse an alms to those whom I pray God to bless, whom I wish to be partakers of eternal glory, but am glad to show some degree of love to such as I hope will be the objects of the infinite love of God. And if, as our Savior has assured us, "It be more blessed to give than to receive," we ought to look upon those that ask our alms as so many friends and benefactors that come to do us a greater good than they can receive, that come to exalt our virtue, to be witnesses of our charity, to be monuments of our love, to be our advocates with God, to be to us in Christ's stead, to appear for us at the day of judgment, and to help us to a blessedness greater than our alms can bestow on them.

This is the spirit, and this is the life of the devout Miranda; and if she lives ten years longer, she will have spent sixty hundred pounds in charity, for that which she allows herself may fairly be reckoned amongst her alms.

When she dies, she must shine amongst apostles and saints and martyrs, she must stand amongst the first servants of God and be glorious amongst those that have fought the good fight and finished their course with joy.

NOTES

16. Lethargy: a pathological state of drowsiness or prolonged sleep.
17. Patched . . . finery: made up with cosmetics and wearing extravagantly fine and splendid clothes.
18. Is it . . . clothes?] corrected by the 2nd ed.; the 1st ed. reads: it is . . . clothes.
19. Meat: any food.
20. Wants: lacks.

Chapter 9

Containing some reflections upon the life of Miranda, and showing how it may and ought to be imitated by all her sex.

Now this life of Miranda, which I heartily recommend to the imitation of her sex, however contrary it may seem to the way and fashion of the world, is yet suitable to the true spirit and founded upon the plainest doctrines of Christianity.

To live as she does is as truly suitable to the gospel of Christ, as to be baptized or receive the Sacrament.

Her spirit is that which animated the Saints of former ages; and it is because they lived as she does that we now celebrate their memories and praise God for their examples.

There is nothing that is whimsical, trifling, or unreasonable in her character, but everything there described is a right and proper instance of a solid and real piety.

It is as easy to show that it is whimsical to go to church, or to say one's prayers, as that it is whimsical to observe any of these rules of life. For all Miranda's rules of living unto God, of spending her time and fortune, of eating, working, dressing, and conversing, are as substantial parts of reasonable and holy life as devotion and prayer.

For there is nothing to be said for the wisdom of sobriety, the wisdom of devotion, the wisdom of charity, or the wisdom of humility, but what is as good an argument for the wise and reasonable use of apparel.

Neither can anything be said against the folly of luxury, the folly of prodigality, the folly of ambition, of idleness, or indulgence, but what must be said against the folly of dress. For religion is as deeply concerned in the one as in the other.

If you may be vain in one thing, you may be vain in every-thing; for one kind of vanity only differs from another as one kind of intemperance differs from another.

If you spend your fortune in the needless vain finery of dress, you cannot condemn prodigality, or extravagance, or luxury, without condemning yourself.

If you fancy that it is your only folly, and that therefore there can be no great matter in it, you are like those that think they are only guilty of the folly of covetousness, or the folly of ambition. Now though some people may live so plausible a life as to appear chargeable with no other fault than that of covetousness or ambi-tion, yet the case is not as it appears, for covetousness or ambition cannot subsist in a heart that is in other respects rightly devoted to God.

In like manner, though some people may spend most that they have in needless expensive ornaments of dress and yet seem to be in every other respect truly pious, yet it is certainly false; for it is as impossible for a mind that is in a true state of religion to be vain in the use of clothes as to be vain in the use of alms or devotions. Now to convince you of this from your own reflections, let us suppose that some eminent Saint, as for instance, that the holy Virgin Mary was sent into the world to be again in a state of trial for a few years, and that you was going to her, to be edified by her great piety. Would you expect to find her dressed out and adorned in fine and expensive clothes? No. You would know in your own mind that it was as impossible as to find her learning to dance. Do but add *saint* or *holy* to any person, either man or woman, and your own mind tells you immediately that such a character cannot admit of the vanity of fine apparel. A Saint genteelly dressed is as great non-sense as an Apostle in an embroidered suit; everyone's own natural sense convinces him of the inconsistency of these things.

Now what is the reason that when you think of a Saint or eminent servant of God, you cannot admit of the vanity of apparel? Is it not because it is inconsistent with such a right state of heart, such true and exalted piety? And is not this therefore a demonstra-tion that where such vanity is admitted, there a right state of heart, true and exalted piety must needs be wanted? For as certainly as the holy Virgin Mary could not indulge herself, or conform to the vanity of the world in dress and figure, so certain is it that none can indulge themselves in this vanity but those who want her piety of heart; and consequently, it must be owned that all needless and expensive finery of dress is the effect of a disordered heart that is not governed by the true spirit of religion.

Covetousness is not a crime because there is any harm in gold or silver, but because it supposes a foolish and unreasonable state of mind that is fallen from its true good and sunk into such a poor and wretched satisfaction.

In like manner, the expensive finery of dress is not a crime because there is anything good or evil in clothes, but because the expensive ornaments of clothing shows a foolish and unreasonable state of heart that is fallen from right notions of human nature, that abuses the end of clothing and turns the necessities of life into so many instances of pride and folly.

All the world agree in condemning remarkable fops. Now what is the reason of it? Is it because there is anything sinful in their particular dress or affected manners? No. But it is because all people know that it shows the state of a man's mind and that it is impossible for so ridiculous an outside to have anything wise or reasonable or good within. And indeed to suppose a fop of great piety is as much nonsense as to suppose a coward of great courage. So that all the world agree in owning that the use and manner of clothes is a mark of the state of a man's mind, and consequently that it is a thing highly essential to religion. But then it should be well considered that as it is not only the sot that is guilty of intemperance, but everyone that transgresses the right and religious measures of eating and drinking, so it should be considered that it is not only the fop that is guilty of the vanity and abuse of dress, but everyone that departs from the reasonable and religious ends of clothing.

As therefore every argument against sottishness is as good an argument against all kinds of intemperance, so every argument against the vanity of fops is as good an argument against all vanity and abuse of dress. For they are all of the same kind and only differ as one degree of intemperance may differ from another. She that only paints a little may as justly accuse another because she paints a great deal as she that uses but a common finery of dress accuse another that is excessive in her finery.

For as in the matter of temperance there is no rule but the

sobriety that is according to the doctrines and spirit of our religion, so in the matter of apparel there is no rule.to be observed but such a right use of clothes as is strictly according to the doctrines and spirit of our religion. To pretend to make the way of the world our measure in these things is as weak and absurd as to make the way of the world the measure of our sobriety, abstinence, or humility. It is a pretence that is exceedingly absurd in the mouths of Christians who are to be so far from conforming to the fashions of this life that to have overcome the world is made an essential mark of Christianity.

This therefore is the way that you are to judge of the crime of vain apparel. You are to consider it as an offence against the proper use of clothes, as covetousness is an offence against the proper use of money; you are to consider it as an indulgence of proud and unreasonable tempers, as an offence against the humility and sobriety of the Christian spirit; you are to consider it as an offence against all those doctrines that require you to do all to the glory of God, that require you to make a right use of your talents; you are to consider it as an offence against all those texts of scripture that command you to love your neighbor as yourself, to feed the hungry, to clothe the naked, and do all works of charity that you are able, so that you must not deceive yourself with saying, Where can be the harm of clothes? For the covetous man might as well say, Where can be the harm of gold or silver? But you must consider that it is a great deal of harm to want that wise, and reasonable, and humble state of heart which is according to the spirit of religion, and which no one can have in the manner that he ought to have it who indulges himself either in the vanity of dress, or the desire of riches.

There is therefore nothing right in the use of clothes, or in the use of anything else in the world, but the plainness and simplicity of the gospel. Every other use of things (however polite and fashionable in the world) distracts and disorders the heart and is inconsistent with that inward state of piety, that purity of heart, that wisdom of mind and regularity of affection, which Christianity requireth.

If you would be a good Christian, there is but one way, you must live wholly unto God; and if you would live wholly unto God, you must live according to the wisdom that comes from God; you must act according to right judgments of the nature and value of things; you must live in the exercise of holy and heavenly affections and use all the gifts of God to His praise and glory.

Some persons perhaps, who admire the purity and perfection of this life of Miranda, may say, How can it be proposed as a common example? How can we who are married, or we who are under the direction of our parents, imitate such a life?

It is answered, Just as you may imitate the life of our blessed Savior and His Apostles. The circumstances of our Savior's life and the state and condition of His Apostles was more different from yours than that of Miranda's is; and yet their life, the purity and perfection of their behavior, is the common example that is proposed to all Christians.

It is their spirit, therefore, their piety, their love of God, that you are to imitate, and not the particular form of their life.

Act under God as they did, direct your common actions to that end which they did, glorify your proper state with such love of God, such charity to your neighbor, such humility and self-denial, as they did; and then, though you are only teaching your own children, and St. Paul is converting whole nations, yet you are following His steps and acting after His example.

Don't think therefore that you can't or need not be like Miranda because you are not in her state of life; for as the same spirit and temper would have made Miranda a Saint, though she had been forced to labor for a maintenance, so if you will but aspire after her spirit and temper, every form and condition of life will furnish you with sufficient means of employing it.

Miranda is what she is because she does everything in the name and with regard to her duty to God; and when you do the same, you will be exactly like her, though you are never so different from her in the outward state of your life.

You are married, you say; therefore, you have not your time and fortune in your power as she has.

It is very true; and therefore you cannot spend so much time, nor so much money in the manner that she does.

But now Miranda's perfection does not consist in this, that she spends so much time or so much money in such a manner, but that she is careful to make the best use of all that time and all that fortune which God has put into her hands. Do you therefore make the best use of all that time and money which is in your disposal, and then you are like Miranda.

If she has two hundred pounds a year, and you have only two mites, have you not the more reason to be exceeding exact in the wisest use of it? If she has a great deal of time, and you have but a little, ought you not to be the more watchful and circumspect, lest that little should be lost?

You say, if you was to imitate the cleanly plainness and cheapness of her dress, you should offend your husbands.

First, be very sure that this is true before you make it an excuse.

Secondly, if your husbands do really require you to patch your faces, to expose your breasts naked, and to be fine and expensive in all your apparel, then take these two resolutions:

First, to forbear from all this as soon as your husbands will permit you.

Secondly, to use your utmost endeavors to recommend yourselves to their affections by such solid virtues as may correct the vanity of their minds, and teach them to love you for such qualities as will make you amiable in the sight of God and His holy angels.

As to this doctrine concerning the plainness and modesty of dress, it may perhaps be thought by some to be sufficiently confuted by asking whether all persons are to be clothed in the same manner.

These questions are generally put by those who had rather perplex the plainest truths than be obliged to follow them.

Let it be supposed that I had recommended a universal plainness of diet. Is it not a thing sufficiently reasonable to be universally recommended? But would it thence follow that the nobleman and the laborer were to live upon the same food?

Suppose I had pressed a universal temperance, does not religion enough justify such a doctrine? But would it therefore follow that all people were to drink the same liquors and in the same quantity?

In like manner, though plainness and sobriety of dress is recommended to all, yet it does by no means follow that all are to be clothed in the same manner.

Now what is the particular rule with regard to temperance? How shall particular persons that use different liquors and in different quantities preserve their temperance?

Is not this the rule? Are they not to guard against indulgence, to make their use of liquors a matter of conscience, and allow of no refreshments but such as are consistent with the strictest rules of Christian sobriety?

Now transfer this rule to the matter of apparel, and all questions about it are answered.

Let everyone but guard against the vanity of dress, let them but make their use of clothes a matter of conscience, let them but desire to make the best use of their money, and then everyone has a rule that is sufficient to direct them in every state of life. This rule will no more let the great be vain in their dress than intemperate in their liquors, and yet will leave it as lawful to have some difference in their apparel as to have some difference in their drink.

But now will you say that you may use the finest, richest wines, when and as you please, that you may be as expensive in them as you have a mind because different liquors are allowed? If not, how can it be said that you may use clothes as you please and wear the richest things you can get because the bare difference of clothes is lawful?

For as the lawfulness of different liquors leaves no room nor any excuse for the smallest degrees of intemperance in drinking, so the lawfulness of different apparel leaves no room nor any excuse for the smallest degrees of vanity in dress.

To ask what is vanity in dress is no more a puzzling question than to ask what is intemperance in drinking. And though religion does not here state the particular measure for all individuals, yet it gives such general rules as are a sufficient direction in every state of life.

He that lets religion teach him that the end of drinking is only so far to refresh our spirits as to keep us in good health and make soul and body fitter for all the offices of a holy and pious life, and that he is to desire to glorify God by a right use of this liberty, will always know what intemperance is in his particular state.

So he that lets religion teach him that the end of clothing is only to hide our shame and nakedness and to secure our bodies from the injuries of weather, and that he is to desire to glorify God by a sober and wise use of this necessity, will always know what vanity of dress is in his particular state.

And he that thinks it a needless nicety to talk of the religious use of apparel has as much reason to think it a needless nicety to talk of the religious use of liquors. For luxury and indulgence in dress is as great an abuse as luxury and indulgence in eating and drinking. And there is no avoiding either of them but by making religion the strict measure of our allowance in both cases. And there is nothing in religion to excite a man to this pious exactness in one case, but what is as good a motive to the same exactness in the other.

Further, as all things that are lawful and not therefore expedient, so there are some things lawful in the use of liquors and apparel, which by abstaining from them for pious ends may be made means of great perfection.

Thus for instance, if a man should deny himself such use of liquors as is lawful, if he should refrain from such expense in his drink as might be allowed without sin; if he should do this, not only for the sake of a more pious self-denial, but that he might be able to relieve and refresh the helpless poor and sick.

If another should abstain from the use of that which is lawful in dress, if he should be more frugal and mean in his habit than the necessities of religion absolutely require; if he should do this not only as a means of a better humility, but that he may be more able to clothe other people, these persons might be said to do that which was highly suitable to the true spirit, though not absolutely required by the letter of the law of Christ.

For if those who give a cup of cold water to a disciple of Christ shall not lose their reward, how dear must they be to Christ who often give themselves water, that they may be able to give wine to the sick and languishing members of Christ's body!

But to return. All that has been here said to married women may serve for the same instruction to such as are still under the direction of their parents.

Now though the obedience which is due to parents does not

oblige them to carry their virtues no higher than their parents require them, yet their obedience requires them to submit to their direction in all things not contrary to the laws of God.

If therefore your parents require you to live more in the fashion and conversation of the world, or to be more expensive in your dress and person, or to dispose of your time otherwise than suits with your desires after greater perfection, you must submit and bear it as your cross till you are at liberty to follow the higher counsels of Christ and have it in your power to choose the best ways of raising your virtue to its greatest height.

Now although whilst you are in this state you may be obliged to forgo some means of improving your virtue, yet there are some others to be found in it that are not to be had in a life of more liberty.

For if in this state where obedience is so great a virtue, you comply in all things lawful out of a pious, tender sense of duty, then those things which you thus perform are, instead of being hindrances of your virtue, turned into means of improving it.

What you lose by being restrained from such things as you would choose to observe, you gain by that excellent virtue of obedience in humbly complying against your temper.

Now what is here granted is only in things lawful, and therefore the diversion of our English stage is here excepted, being elsewhere proved, as I think, to be absolutely unlawful.[21]

Thus much to show how persons under the direction of others may imitate the wise and pious life of Miranda.

But as for those who are altogether in their own hands, if the liberty of their state makes them covet the best gifts, if it carries them to choose the most excellent ways, if they having all in their own power should turn the whole form of their life into a regular exercise of the highest virtues, happy are they who have so learned Christ!

All persons cannot receive this saying. They that are able to receive it, let them receive it and bless that Spirit of God which has put such good motions into their hearts.

God may be served and glorified in every state of life. But as there are some states of life more desirable than others that more purify our natures, that more improve our virtues and dedicate us unto God in a higher manner, so those who are at liberty to choose for themselves seem to be called by God to be more eminently devoted to His service.

Ever since the beginning of Christianity, there hath been two orders, or ranks of people amongst good Christians.

The one that feared and served God in the common offices and business of a secular, worldly life.

The other renouncing the common business and common enjoyments of life, as riches, marriage, honors, and pleasures, devoted themselves to voluntary poverty, virginity, devotion, and retirement, that by this means they might live wholly unto God in the daily exercise of a divine and heavenly life.

This testimony I have from the famous ecclesiastical historian Eusebius, who lived at the time of the first general Council, when the faith of our Nicene Creed was established, when the church was in its greatest glory and purity, when its bishops were so many holy fathers and eminent Saints.

"Therefore," saith he, "there hath been instituted in the Church of Christ two ways, or manners of living. The one raised above the ordinary state of nature and common ways of living rejects wedlock, possessions, and worldly goods, and being wholly separate and removed from the ordinary conversation of common life, is appropriated and devoted solely to the worship and service of God, through an exceeding degree of heavenly love.

"They who are of this order of people seem dead to the life of this world, and having their bodies only upon earth are in their minds and contemplations dwelling in heaven. From whence, like so many heavenly inhabitants, they look down upon human life, making intercessions and oblations to Almighty God for the whole race of mankind. And this not with the blood of beasts, or the fat, or smoke, and burning of bodies, but with the highest exercises of true piety, with cleansed and purified hearts, and with an whole form of life strictly devoted to virtue. These are their sacrifices, which they continually offering unto God implore his mercy and favor for themselves and their fellow creatures.

"Christianity receives this as the perfect manner of life.

"The other is of a lower form, and suiting itself more to the condition of human nature, admits of chaste wedlock, the care of children and family, of trade and business, and goes through all the employments of life under a sense of piety and fear of God.

"Now they who have chosen this manner of life have their set times for retirement and spiritual exercises, and particular days are set apart for their hearing and learning the word of God. And this order of people are considered as in the second state of piety" (Eusebius, Dem. Evan. *l. 1. c. 8).*[22]

Thus this learned historian.

If therefore persons of either sex, moved with the life of Miranda and desirous of perfection, should unite themselves into little societies professing voluntary poverty, virginity, retirement, and devotion, living upon bare necessaries, that some might be relieved by their charities and all be blessed with their prayers and benefited by their example; or if for want of this, they should practice the same manner of life in as high a degree as they could by themselves, such persons would be so far from being chargeable with any superstition or blind devotion that they might be justly said to restore that piety which was the boast and glory of the church when its greatest Saints were alive.

Now as this learned historian observes that it was an exceeding great degree of heavenly love that carried these persons so much above the common ways of life to such an eminent state of holiness, so it is not to be wondered at that the religion of Jesus Christ should fill the hearts of many Christians with this high degree of love.

For a religion that opens such a scene of glory, that discovers things so infinitely above all the world, that so triumphs over death, that assures us of such mansions of bliss where we shall so soon be as the angels of God in heaven, what wonder is it if such a religion, such truths and expectations, should in some holy souls destroy all earthly desires and make the ardent love of heavenly things be the one continual passion of their hearts?

If the religion of Christians is founded upon the infinite humiliation, the cruel mockings and scourgings, the prodigious sufferings, the poor, persecuted life and painful death of a crucified Son of God, what wonder is it if many humble adorers of this profound mystery, many affectionate lovers of a crucified Lord, should renounce their share of worldly pleasures and give themselves up to a continual course of mortification and self-denial, that thus suffering with Christ here, they may reign with him hereafter?

If truth itself hath assured us that there is but one thing needful, what wonder is it that there should be some amongst Christians so full of faith as to believe this in the highest sense of the words, and to desire such a separation from the world that their care and attention to the one thing needful may not be interrupted?

If our blessed Lord hath said, "If thou wilt be perfect, go and sell that thou hast, and give to the poor, and thou shalt have treasure in heaven: And come and follow me," what wonder is it that there should be amongst Christians some such zealous followers of Christ, so intent upon heavenly treasure, so desirous of perfection, that they should renounce the enjoyment of their estates, choose a voluntary poverty, and relieve all the poor that they are able?

If the chosen vessel, St. Paul, hath said, "He that is unmarried careth for the things that belong to the Lord, how he may please the Lord: And that there is this difference also between a wife and a virgin; the unmarried woman careth for the things of the Lord, that she may be holy both in body and Spirit," what wonder is it if the purity and perfection of the virgin state hath been the praise and glory of the church in its first and purest ages?

That there hath always been some so desirous of pleasing God, so zealous after every degree of purity and perfection, so glad of every means of improving their virtue, that they have renounced the comforts and enjoyments of wedlock to trim their lamps, to purify their souls, and wait upon God in a state of perpetual virginity?

And if now in these our days we want examples of these several degrees of perfection, if neither clergy nor laity are enough of this spirit, if we are so far departed from it that a man seems, like St. Paul at Athens, a setter forth of strange doctrines when he recommends self-denial, renunciation of the world, regular devotion, retirement, virginity, and voluntary poverty, 'tis because we are fallen into an age where the love not only of many, but of most, is waxed cold.

I have made this little appeal to antiquity and quoted these few passages of scripture to support some uncommon practices in the life of Miranda, and to show that her highest rules of holy living, her devotion, self-denial, renunciation of the world, her charity, virginity, and voluntary poverty are founded in the sublimest counsels of Christ and His Apostles, suitable to the high expectations of another life, proper instances of a heavenly love, and all followed by the greatest Saints of the best and purest ages of the church.

"He that hath ears to hear, let him hear."

NOTES

21. Law is referring to his *Absolute Unlawfulness of the Stage-Enterment* (1726).
22. The reference is to Eusebius's *Demonstratio Evangelica*, or *Demonstration of the Gospel*.

Chapter 10

Showing how all orders and ranks of men and women of all ages are obliged to devote themselves unto God.

I have in the foregoing chapters gone through the several great instances of Christian devotion and shown that all the parts of our common life, our employments, our talents and gifts of fortune, are all to be made holy and acceptable unto God by a wise and religious use of everything, and by directing our actions and designs to such ends as are suitable to the honor and glory of God.

I shall now show that this regularity of devotion, this holiness of common life, this religious use of everything that we have, is a devotion that is the duty of all orders of Christian people.

Fulvius has had a learned education and taken his degrees in the university; he came from thence that he might be free from any rules of life. He takes no employment upon him, nor enters into any business because he thinks that every employment or business calls people to the careful performance and just discharge of its several duties. When he is grave, he will tell you that he did not enter into holy orders because he looks upon it to be a state that requires great holiness of life, and that it does not suit his temper to be so good. He will tell you that he never intends to marry because he cannot oblige himself to that regularity of life and good behavior, which he takes to be the duty of those that are at the head of a family. He refused to be godfather to his nephew because he will have no trust of any kind to answer for.

Fulvius thinks that he is conscientious in this conduct, and is therefore content with the most idle, impertinent, and careless life.

He has no religion, no devotion, no pretences to piety. He lives by no rules, and thinks all is very well because he is neither a priest, nor a father, nor a guardian, nor has any employment or family to look after.

But Fulvius, you are a rational creature, and as such are as much obliged to live according to reason and order as a priest is obliged to attend at the altar, or a guardian to be faithful to his trust; if you live contrary to reason, you don't commit a small crime, you don't break a small trust; but you break the law of your nature, you rebel against God who gave you that nature and put yourself amongst those whom the God of reason and order will punish as apostates and deserters.

Though you have no employment, yet as you are baptized into the profession of Christ's religion, you are as much obliged to live according to the holiness of the Christian spirit and perform all the promises made at your baptism as any man is obliged to be honest and faithful in his calling. If you abuse this great calling, you are not false in a small matter, but you abuse the precious blood of Christ; you crucify the Son of God afresh; you neglect the highest instances of divine goodness; you disgrace the church of God; you blemish the body of Christ; you abuse the means of grace and the promises of glory; and it will be more tolerable for Tyre and Sidon at the day of judgment than for you.

It is therefore great folly for anyone to think himself at liberty to live as he pleases because he is not in such a state of life as some others are. For if there is anything dreadful in the abuse of any trust, if there is anything to be feared for the neglect of any calling, there is nothing more to be feared than the wrong use of our reason, nor anything more to be dreaded than the neglect of our Christian calling which is not to serve the little uses of a short life, but to redeem souls unto God, to fill heaven with Saints, and finish a kingdom of eternal glory unto God.

No man therefore must think himself excused from the exactness of piety and morality because he has chosen to be idle and independent in the world; for the necessities of a reasonable and holy life are not founded in the several conditions and employments of this life, but in the immutable nature of God, and the nature of man. A man is not to be reasonable and holy because he is a priest or a father of a family; but he is to be a pious priest and a good father because piety and goodness are the laws of human nature.

Could any man please God without living according to reason and order, there would be nothing displeasing to God in an idle priest or a reprobate father. He therefore that abuses his reason is like him that abuses the priesthood; and he that neglects the holiness of the Christian life is as the man that disregards the most important trust.

If a man was to choose to put out his eyes rather than enjoy the light and see the works of God, if he should voluntarily kill himself by refusing to eat and drink, everyone would own that such a one was a rebel against God that justly deserved his highest indignation. You would not say that this was only sinful in a priest or a master of a family, but in every man as such.

Now wherein does the sinfulness of this behavior consist? Does it not consist in this, that he abuses his nature and refuses to act that part for which God had created him? But if this be true, then all persons that abuse their reason, that act a different part from that for which God created them, are like this man, rebels against God and on the same account subject to His wrath.

Let us suppose that this man instead of putting out his eyes had only employed them in looking at ridiculous things, or shut them up in sleep, that instead of starving himself to death by not eating at all, he should turn every meal into a feast and eat and drink like an epicure. Could he be said to have lived more to the glory of God? Could he any more be said to act the part for which God had created him than if he had put out his eyes and starved himself to death?

Now do but suppose a man acting unreasonably; do but suppose him extinguishing his reason instead of putting out his eyes, and living in a course of folly and impertinence instead of starving himself to death, and then you have found out as great a rebel against God.

For he that puts out his eyes or murders himself has only this guilt, that he abuses the powers that God has given him, that he refuses to act that part for which he was created and puts himself into a state that is contrary to the divine will. And surely this is the guilt of everyone that lives an unreasonable, unholy, and foolish life.

As therefore no particular state or private life is an excuse for the abuse of our bodies or self-murder, so no particular state or private life is an excuse for the abuse of our reason or the neglect of the holiness of the Christian religion. For surely it is as much the will of God that we should make the best use of our rational faculties, that we should conform to the purity and holiness of Christianity, as it is the will of God that we should use our eyes and eat and drink for the preservation of our lives.

Till therefore a man can show that he sincerely endeavors to live according to the will of God to be that which God requires him to be, till he can show that he is striving to live according to the holiness of the Christian religion, whosoever he be or wheresoever he be, he has all that to answer for that they have who refuse to live, who abuse the greatest trusts and neglect the highest calling in the world.

Everybody acknowledges that all orders of men are to be equally and exactly honest and faithful; there is no exception to be made in these duties for any private or particular state of life. Now if we would but attend to the reason and nature of things, if we would but consider the nature of God and the nature of man, we should find the same necessity for every other right use of our reason, for every grace or religious temper of the Christian life. We should find it as absurd to suppose that one man must be exact in piety and another need not as to suppose that one man must be exact in honesty but another need not. For Christian humility, sobriety, devotion, and piety are as great and necessary parts of a reasonable life as justice and honesty.

And on the other hand, pride, sensuality, and covetousness are as great disorders of the soul, are as high an abuse of our reason and as contrary to God, as cheating and dishonesty.

Theft and dishonesty seem indeed to vulgar eyes to be greater sins because they are so hurtful to civil society and are so severely punished by human laws.

But if we consider mankind in a higher view, as God's order or society of rational beings that are to glorify Him by the right use of their reason and by acting conformably to the order of their nature, we shall find that every temper that is equally contrary to reason and order, that opposes God's ends and designs and disorders the beauty and glory of the rational world, is equally sinful in man and equally odious to God. This would show us that the sin of sensuality is like the sin of dishonesty and renders us as great objects of the divine displeasure.

Again, if we consider mankind in a further view, as a redeemed order of fallen spirits that are baptized into a fellowship with the Son of God to be temples of the Holy Ghost; to live according to His holy inspirations; to offer to God the reasonable sacrifice of a humble, pious, and thankful life; to purify themselves from the disorders of their fall; to make a right use of the means of grace in order to be sons of eternal glory; if we look at mankind in this true light, then we shall find that all tempers that are contrary to this holy society, that are abuses of this infinite mercy, all actions that make us unlike to Christ, that disgrace His body, that abuse the means of grace and oppose our hopes of glory, have everything in them that can make us forever odious unto God. So that though pride and sensuality and other vices of the like kind do not hurt civil society as cheating and dishonesty do, yet they hurt that society and oppose those ends which are greater and more glorious in the eyes of God than all the societies that relate to this world.

Nothing therefore can be more false than to imagine that because we are private persons that have taken upon us no charge of employment of life, that therefore we may live more at large, indulge our appetites, and be less careful of the duties of piety and holiness; for it is as good an excuse for cheating and dishonesty, because he that abuses his reason, that indulges himself in lust and sensuality and neglects to act the wise and reasonable part of a true Christian, has everything in his life to render him hateful to God that is to be found in cheating and dishonesty.

If therefore you rather choose to be an idle epicure than to be unfaithful, if you rather choose to live in lust and sensuality than to injure your neighbor in his goods, you have made no better a provision for the favor of God than he that rather chooses to rob a house than to rob a church.

For the abusing of our own nature is as great a disobedience against God as the injuring our neighbor, and he that wants piety toward God has done as much to damn himself as he that wants honesty toward men. Every argument, therefore, that proves it necessary for all men in all stations of life to be truly honest proves it equally necessary for all men in all stations of life to be truly holy and pious and do all things in such a manner as is suitable to the glory of God.

Again, another argument to prove that all orders of men are obliged to be thus holy and devout in the common course of their lives, in the use of everything that they enjoy, may be taken from our obligation to prayer.

It is granted that prayer is a duty that belongs to all states[23] and conditions of men. Now if we inquire into the reason of this, why no state of life is to be excused from prayer, we shall find it as good a reason why every state of life is to be made a state of piety and holiness in all its parts.

For the reason why we are to pray unto God and praise Him with hymns and Psalms of thanksgiving is this, because we are to live wholly unto God and glorify Him all possible ways. It is not because the praises of words or forms of thanksgiving are more particularly parts of piety, or more the worship of God than other things, but it is because they are possible ways of expressing our dependence, our obedience and devotion to God. Now if this be the reason of verbal praises and thanksgivings to God, because we are to live unto God all possible ways, then it plainly follows that we are equally obliged to worship and glorify God in all other actions that can be turned into acts of piety and obedience to Him. And as actions are of much more significancy[24] than words, it must be a much more acceptable worship of God to glorify Him in all the actions of our common life than with any little form of words at any particular times.

Thus, if God is to be worshipped with forms of thanksgivings, he that makes it a rule to be content and thankful in every part and accident of his life because it comes from God praises God in a much higher manner than he that has some set time for singing of Psalms. He that dares not to say an ill-natured word or do an unreasonable thing because he considers God as everywhere present performs a better devotion than he that dares not miss the church. To live in the world as a stranger and a pilgrim, using all its enjoyments as if we used them not, making all our actions so many steps toward a better life, is offering a better sacrifice to God than any forms of holy and heavenly prayers.

To be humble in all our actions, to avoid every appearance of pride and vanity, to be meek and lowly in our words, actions, dress, behavior, and designs in imitation of our blessed Savior, is worshipping God in a higher manner than they who have only times to fall low on their knees in devotions. He that contents himself with necessaries that he may give the remainder to those that want it, that dares not to spend any money foolishly because he considers it as a talent from God which must be used according to his will, praises God with something that is more glorious than songs of praise.

He that has appointed times for the use of wise and pious prayers performs a proper instance of devotion; but he that allows himself no times, nor any places, nor any actions, but such as are strictly conformable to wisdom and holiness, worships the divine nature with the most true and substantial devotion. For who does not know that it is better to be pure and holy than to talk about purity and holiness? Nay, who does not know that a man is to be reckoned no further pure or holy or just than as he is pure and holy and just in the common course of his life? But if this be plain, then it is also plain that it is better to be holy than to have holy prayers.

Prayers therefore are so far from being a sufficient devotion that they are the smallest parts of it. We are to praise God with words and prayers because it is a possible way of glorifying God who has given us such faculties as may be so used. But then as words are but small things in themselves, as times of prayer are but little if compared with the rest of our lives, so that devotion which consists in times and forms of prayer is but a very small thing if compared to that devotion which is to appear in every other part and circumstance of our lives.

Again, as it is an easy thing to worship God with forms of words and to observe times of offering them unto Him, so it is the smallest kind of piety.

And on the other hand, as it is more difficult to worship God with our substance, to honor Him with the right use of our time, to offer to Him the continual sacrifice of self-denial and mortification; as it requires more piety to eat and drink only for such ends as may glorify God, to undertake no labor nor allow of any diversion but where we can act in the name of God; as it is more difficult to sacrifice all our corrupt tempers, correct all our passions, and make piety to God the rule and measure of all the actions of our common life, so the devotion of this kind is a much more acceptable service unto God than those words of devotion which we offer to Him either in the church or in our closet.

Every sober reader will easily perceive that I don't intend to lessen the true and great value of prayers, either public or private, but only to show him that they are certainly but a very slender part of devotion when compared to a devout life.

To see this in a yet clearer light, let us suppose a person to have appointed times for praising God with Psalms and hymns and to be strict in the observation of them; let it be supposed also that in his common life he is restless and uneasy, full of murmurings and complaints at everything, never pleased but by chance as his temper happens to carry him, but murmuring and repining at the very seasons and having something to dislike in everything that happens to him. Now can you conceive anything more absurd and unreasonable than such a character as this? Is such a one to be reckoned thankful to God because he has forms of praise which he offers to Him? Nay, is it not certain that such forms of praise must be so far from being an acceptable devotion to God that they must be abhorred as an abomination? Now the absurdity which you see in this instance is the same in any other part of our life; if our common life hath any contrariety to our prayers, it is the same abomination as songs of thanksgiving in the mouths of murmurers.

Bended knees, whilst you are clothed with pride; heavenly petitions, whilst you are hoarding up treasures upon earth; holy devotions, whilst you live in the follies of the world; prayers of meekness and charity, whilst your heart is the seat of spite and resentment; hours of prayer, whilst you give up days and years to idle diversions, impertinent visits, and foolish pleasures are as absurd, unacceptable service to God as forms of thanksgiving from a person that lives in repinings and discontent.

So that unless the common course of our lives be according to the common spirit of our prayers, our prayers are so far from being a real or sufficient degree of devotion that they become an empty lip-labor or, what is worse, a notorious hypocrisy.

Seeing therefore we are to make the spirit and temper of our prayers the common spirit and temper of our lives, this may serve to convince us that all orders of people are to labor and aspire after the same utmost perfection of the Christian life. For as all Christians are to use the same holy and heavenly devotions as they are all with the same earnestness to pray for the Spirit of God, so is it a sufficient proof that all orders of people are to the utmost of their power to make their life agreeable to that one spirit for which they are all to pray.

As certain therefore as the same holiness of prayers requires the same holiness of life, so certain is it that all Christians are called to the same holiness of life.

A soldier or a tradesman is not called to minister at the altar or preach the gospel; but every soldier or tradesman is as much obliged to be devout, humble, holy, and heavenly minded in all the parts of his common life as a clergyman is obliged to be zealous, faithful, and laborious in all the parts of his profession.

And all this for this one plain reason, because all people are to pray for the same holiness, wisdom, and divine tempers, and to make themselves as fit as they can for the same Heaven.

All men therefore, as men, have one and the same important business, to act up to the excellency of their rational nature, and to make reason and order the law of all their designs and actions. All Christians, as Christians, have one and the same calling, to live according to the excellency of the Christian spirit and to make the sublime precepts of the gospel the rule and measure of all their tempers in common life. The one thing needful to one is the one thing needful to all.

The merchant is no longer to hoard up treasures upon earth, the soldier is no longer to fight for glory, the great scholar is no longer to pride himself in the depths of science, but they must all with one spirit count all things but loss for the excellency of the knowledge of Christ Jesus.

The fine lady must teach her eyes to weep and be clothed with humility. The polite gentleman must exchange the gay thoughts of wit and fancy for a broken and a contrite heart. The man of quality must so far renounce the dignity of his birth as to think himself miserable till he is born again. Servants must consider their service as done unto God. Masters must consider their servants as their brethren in Christ that are to be treated as their fellow members of the mystical body of Christ.

Young ladies must either devote themselves to piety, prayer, self-denial, and all good works in a virgin state of life, or else marry to be holy, sober, and prudent in the care of a family, bringing up their children in piety, humility, and devotion and abounding in all other good works to the utmost of their state and capacity. They have no choice of anything else, but must devote themselves to God in one of these states. They may choose a married or a single life but it is not left to their choice whether they will make either state a state of holiness, humility, devotion, and all other duties of the Christian life. It is no more left in their power because they have fortunes or are born of rich parents to divide themselves betwixt God and the world or take such pleasures as their fortune will afford them than it is allowable for them to be sometimes chaste and modest and sometimes not.

They are not to consider how much religion may secure them a fair character or how they may add devotion to an impertinent, vain, and giddy life, but must look into the spirit and temper of their prayers, into the nature and end of Christianity, and then they will find that whether married or unmarried they have but one business upon their hands, to be wise and pious and holy, not in little modes and forms of worship but in the whole turn of their minds, in the whole form of all their behavior and in the daily course of their common life.

Young gentlemen must consider what our blessed Savior said to the young gentleman in the gospel; He bid him sell all that he had and give to the poor. Now though this text should not oblige all people to sell all, yet it certainly obliges all kinds of people to employ all their estates in such wise and reasonable and charitable ways as may sufficiently show that all that they have is devoted to God and that no part of it is kept from the poor, to be spent in needless, vain, and foolish expenses.

If therefore young gentlemen propose to themselves a life of pleasure and indulgence, if they spend their estates in high living, in luxury and intemperance, in state and equipage, in pleasures and diversions, in sports and gaming, and such like wanton gratifications of their foolish passions, they have as much reason to look upon themselves to be angels as to be disciples of Christ.

Let them be assured that it is the one only business of a Christian gentleman to distinguish himself by good works, to be eminent in the most sublime virtues of the gospel, to bear with the ignorance and weakness of the vulgar, to be a friend and patron to all that dwell about him, to live in the utmost heights of wisdom and holiness and show through the whole course of his life a true religious greatness of mind. They must aspire after such a gentility as they might have learnt from seeing the blessed Jesus, and show no other spirit of a gentleman but such as they might have got by living with the holy Apostles. They must learn to love God with all their heart, with all their soul, and with all their strength, and their neighbor as themselves; and then they have all the greatness and distinction that they can have here and are fit for an eternal happiness in Heaven thereafter.

Thus in all orders and conditions either of men or women this is the one common holiness, which is to be the common life of all Christians.

The merchant is not to leave devotion to the clergyman, nor the clergyman to leave humility to the laborer; women of fortune are not to leave it to the poor of their sex to be discreet, chaste, keepers at home, to adorn themselves in modest apparel, shamefacedness, and sobriety, nor poor women leave it to the rich to attend at the worship and service of God. Great men must be eminent for true poverty of spirit, and people of a low and afflicted state must greatly rejoice in God.

The man of strength and power is to forgive and pray for his enemies, and the innocent sufferer that is chained in prison must with Paul and Silas at midnight sing praises to God. For God is to be glorified, holiness is to be practiced, and the spirit of religion is to be the common spirit of every Christian in every state and condition of life.

For the Son of God did not come from above to add an external form of worship to the several ways of life that are in the world, and so to leave people to live as they did before in such tempers and enjoyments as the fashion and spirit of the world approves. But as He came down from Heaven altogether divine and heavenly in His own nature, so it was to call mankind to a divine and heavenly life, to the highest change of their whole nature and temper, to be born again of the Holy Spirit, to walk in the wisdom and light and love of God and be like Him to the utmost of their power, to renounce all the most plausible ways of the world, whether of greatness, business, or pleasure, to a mortification of all their most agreeable passions, and to live in such wisdom and purity and holiness as might fit them to be glorious in the enjoyment of God to all eternity.

Whatever therefore is foolish, ridiculous, vain, or earthly, or sensual in the life of a Christian is something that ought not to be there; it is a spot and a defilement that must be washed away with tears of repentance. But if anything of this kind runs through the course of our whole life, if we allow ourselves in things that are either vain, foolish, or sensual, we renounce our profession.

For as sure as Jesus Christ was wisdom and holiness, as sure as He came to make us like Himself and to be baptized into His Spirit, so sure is it that none can be said to keep to their Christian profession but they who to the utmost of their power live a wise and holy and heavenly life. This and this alone is Christianity, a universal holiness in every part of life, a heavenly wisdom in all our actions, not conforming to the spirit and temper of the world, but turning all worldly enjoyments into means of piety and devotion to God.

But now if this devout state of heart, if these habits of inward holiness be true religion, then true religion is equally the duty and happiness of all orders of men; for there is nothing to recommend it to one that is not the same recommendation of it to all states of people.

If it be the happiness and glory of a bishop to live in this devout spirit, full of these holy tempers, doing everything as unto God, it is as much the glory and happiness of all men and women, whether young or old, to live in the same spirit. And whoever can find any reasons why an ancient bishop should be intent upon divine things, turning all his life into the highest exercises of piety, wisdom, and devotion, will find them so many reasons why he should to the utmost of his power do the same himself.

If you say that a bishop must be an eminent example of Christian holiness because of his high and sacred calling, you say right. But if you say that it is more to his advantage to be exemplary than it is yours, you greatly mistake. For there is nothing to make the highest degree of holiness desirable to a bishop but what makes them equally desirable to every young person of every family.

For an exalted piety, high devotion, and the religious use of everything is as much the glory and happiness of one state of life as it is of another.

Do but fancy in your mind what a spirit of piety you would have in the best bishop in the world, how you would have him love God, how you would have him imitate the life of our Savior and his Apostles, how you would have him live above the world, shining in all the instances of a heavenly life, and then you have found out that spirit which you ought to make the spirit of your own life.

I desire every reader to dwell a while upon this reflection and perhaps he will find more conviction from it than he imagines. Everyone can tell how good and pious he would have some people to be; everyone knows how wise and reasonable a thing it is in a bishop to be entirely above the world and be an eminent example of Christian perfection. As soon as you think of a wise and ancient bishop you fancy some exalted degree of piety, a living example of all those holy tempers which you find described in the gospel.

Now if you ask yourself what is the happiest thing for a young clergyman to do, you must be forced to answer that nothing can be so happy and glorious for him as to be like that excellent holy bishop.

If you go on and ask what is the happiest thing for any young gentleman or his sisters to do, the answer must be the same, that nothing can be so happy or glorious for them as to live in such habits of piety, in such exercises of a divine life as this good old bishop does. For everything that is great and glorious in religion is as much the true glory of every man or woman as it is the glory of any bishop. If high degrees of divine love, if fervent charity, if spotless purity, if heavenly affection, if constant mortification, if frequent devotion, be the best and happiest way of life for any Christian, it is so for every Christian.

Consider again, if you was to see a bishop in the whole course of his life, living below his character, conforming to all the foolish tempers of the world and governed by the same cares and fears which govern vain and worldly men, what would you think of him? Would you think that he was only guilty of a small mistake? No. You would condemn him as erring in that which is not only the most, but the only important matter that relates to him. Stay awhile in this consideration till your mind is fully convinced how miserable a mistake it is in a bishop to live a careless, worldly life.

Whilst you are thinking in this manner turn your thoughts toward some of your acquaintance, your brother or sister or any young person. Now if you see the common course of their lives to be not according to the doctrines of the gospel, if you see that their way of life cannot be said to be a sincere endeavor to enter in at the strait gate, you see something that you are to condemn in the same degree and for the same reasons. They don't commit a small mistake, but are wrong in that which is their all, and mistake their true happiness as much as that bishop does who neglects the high duties of his calling. Apply this reasoning to yourself; if you find yourself living an idle, indulgent, vain life, choosing rather to gratify your passions than to live up to the doctrines of Christianity and practice the plain precepts of our blessed Lord, you have all that blindness and unreasonableness to charge upon yourself that you can charge upon any irregular bishop.

For all the virtues of the Christian life, its perfect purity, its heavenly tempers, are as much the sole rule of your life as the sole rule of the life of a bishop. If you neglect these holy tempers, if you don't eagerly aspire after them, if you do not show yourself a visible example of them, you are as much fallen from your true happiness, you are as great an enemy to yourself and have made as bad a choice, as that bishop that chooses rather to enrich his family than to be like an Apostle. For there is no reason why you should think the highest holiness, the most heavenly tempers to be the duty and happiness of a bishop, but what is as good a reason why you should think the same tempers to be the duty and happiness of all Christians. And as the wisest bishop in the world is he who lives in the greatest heights of holiness, who is most exemplary in all the exercises of a divine life, so the wisest youth, the wisest woman, whether married or unmarried, is she that lives in the highest degrees of Christian holiness and all the exercises of a divine and heavenly life.

NOTES

23. States: sorts.
24. Significancy: having deep importance or significance.

Chapter 11

Showing how great devotion fills our lives with the greatest peace and happiness that can be enjoyed in this world.

Some people will perhaps object that all these rules of holy living unto God in all that we do are too great a restraint upon human life, that it will be made too anxious a state by thus introducing a regard to God in all our actions, and that, by depriving ourselves of so many seemingly innocent pleasures, we shall render our lives dull, uneasy, and melancholy.

To which it may be answered:

First, that these rules are prescribed for and will certainly procure a quite contrary end. That instead of making our lives dull and melancholy, they will render them full of content and strong satisfactions. That by these rules we only change the childish satisfactions of our vain and sickly passions for the solid enjoyments and real happiness of a sound mind.

Secondly, that as there is no foundation for comfort in the enjoyments of this life but in the assurance that a wise and good God governeth the world, so the more we find out God in everything, the more we apply to Him in every place, the more we look up to Him in all our actions, the more we conform to His will, the more we act according to His wisdom and imitate His goodness, by so much the more do we enjoy God, partake of the divine nature and heighten and increase all that is happy and comfortable in human life.

Thirdly, he that is endeavoring to subdue and root out of his mind all those passions of pride, envy, and ambition which religion opposes is doing more to make himself happy even in this life than he that is contriving means to indulge them.

For these passions are the causes of all the disquiets and vexations of human life. They are the dropsies and fevers of our minds, vexing them with false appetites and restless cravings after such things as we do not want, and spoiling our taste for those things which are our proper good.

Do but imagine that you somewhere or other saw a man that proposed reason as the rule of all his actions, that had no desires but after such things as nature wants and religion approves, that was as pure from all the motions of pride, envy, and covetousness as from thoughts of murder; that in this freedom from worldly passions he had a soul full of divine love, wishing and praying that all men may have what they want of worldly things and be partakers of eternal glory in the life to come.

Do but fancy a man living in this manner and your own conscience will immediately tell you that he is the happiest man in the world and that it is not in the power of the richest fancy to invent any higher happiness in the present state of life.

And on the other hand, if you suppose him to be in any degree less perfect, if you suppose him but subject to one foolish fondness or vain passion, your own conscience will again tell you that he so far lessens his own happiness and robs himself of the true enjoyment of his other virtues. So true is it that the more we live by the rules of religion, the more peaceful and happy do we render our lives.

Again, as it thus appears that real happiness is only to be had from the greatest degrees of piety, the greatest denials of our passions, and the strictest rules of religion, so the same truth will appear from a consideration of human misery. If we look into the world and view the disquiets and troubles of human life, we shall find that they are all owing to our violent and irreligious passions.

Now all trouble and uneasiness is founded in the want of something or other. Would we therefore know the true cause of our troubles and disquiets, we must find out the cause of our wants, because that which creates and increaseth our wants does in the same degree create and increase our trouble and disquiets.

God Almighty has sent us into the world with very few wants. Meat and drink and clothing are the only things necessary in life, and as these are only our present needs, so the present world is well furnished to supply these needs.

If a man had half the world in his power he can make no more of it than this; as he wants it only to support an animal life, so is it unable to do anything else for him or to afford him any other happiness.

This is the state of man, born with few wants and into a large world very capable of supplying them. So that one would reasonably suppose that men should pass their lives in content and thankfulness to God, at least that they should be free from violent disquiets and vexations, as being placed in a world that has more than enough to relieve all their wants.

But if to all this we add that this short life, thus furnished with all that we want in it, is only a short passage to eternal glory where we shall be clothed with the brightness of angels and enter into the joys of God, we might still more reasonably expect that human life should be a state of peace and joy and delight in God. Thus it would certainly be if reason had its full power over us.

But alas, though God and nature and reason make human life thus free from wants and so full of happiness, yet our passions, in rebellion against God, against nature and reason, create a new world of evils and fill human life with imaginary wants and vain disquiets.

The man of pride has a thousand wants which only his own pride has created, and these render him as full of trouble as if God had created him with a thousand appetites without creating anything that was proper to satisfy them. Envy and ambition have also their endless wants which disquiet the souls of men, and by their contradictory motions render them as foolishly miserable as those that want to fly and creep at the same time.

Let but any complaining, disquieted man tell you the ground of his uneasiness and you will plainly see that he is the author of his own torment, that he is vexing himself at some imaginary evil which will cease to torment him as soon as he is content to be that which God and nature and reason require him to be.

If you should see a man passing his days in disquiet because he could not walk upon the water or catch birds as they fly by him, you would readily confess that such a one might thank himself for such uneasiness. But now if you look into all the most tormenting disquiets of life you will find them all thus absurd, where people are only tormented by their own folly and vexing themselves at such things as no more concern them nor are any more their proper good than walking upon the water or catching birds.

What can you conceive more silly and extravagant than to suppose a man racking his brains and studying night and day how to fly, wandering from his own house and home, wearying himself with climbing upon every ascent, cringing and courting everybody he meets to lift him up from the ground, bruising himself with continual falls and at last breaking his neck? And all this from an imagination that it would be glorious to have the eyes of people gazing up at him, and mighty happy to eat and drink and sleep at the top of the highest trees in the kingdom. Would you not readily own that such a one was only disquieted by his own folly?

If you ask what it signifies to suppose such silly creatures as these as are nowhere to be found in human life, it may be answered that wherever you see an ambitious man, there you see this vain and senseless flyer.

Again, if you should see a man that had a large pond of water, yet living in continual thirst, not suffering himself to drink half a draught for fear of lessening his pond, if you should see him wasting his time and strength in fetching more water to his pond, always thirsty yet always carrying a bucket of water in his hand, watching early and late to catch the drops of rain, gaping after every cloud and running greedily into every mire and mud in hopes of water and always studying how to make every ditch empty itself into his pond; if you should see him grow gray and old in these anxious labors and at last end a careful, thirsty life by falling into his own pond, would you not say that such a one was not only the author of all his own disquiets, but was foolish enough to be reckoned amongst idiots and madmen? But yet foolish and absurd as this character is, it does not represent half the follies and absurd disquiets of the covetous man.

I could now easily proceed to show the same effects of all our other passions, and make it plainly appear that all our miseries, vexations, and complaints are entirely of our own making and that in the same absurd manner as in these instances of the covetous and ambitious man. Look where you will, you will see all worldly vexations but like the vexation of him that was always in mire and mud in search of water to drink when he had more at home than was sufficient for a hundred horses.

Celia is always telling you how provoked she is, what intolerable shocking things happen to her, what monstrous usage she suffers, and what vexations she meets with everywhere. She tells you that her patience is quite worn out and there is no bearing the behavior of people. Every assembly that she is at sends her home provoked; something or other has been said or done that no reasonable, well-bred person ought to bear. Poor people that want her charity are sent away with hasty answers not because she has not a heart to part with any money, but because she is too full of some trouble of her own to attend to the complaints of others. Celia has no business upon her hands but to receive the income of a plentiful fortune; but yet by the doleful turn of her mind, you would be apt to think that she had neither food nor lodging. If you see her look more pale than ordinary, if her lips tremble when she speaks to you, it is because she is just come from a visit where Lupus took no notice at all of her but talked all the time to Lucinda, who has not half her fortune. When cross accidents have so disordered her spirits that she is forced to send for the doctor to make her able to eat, she tells him, in great anger at providence, that she never was well since she was born and that she envies every beggar that she sees in health.

This is the disquiet life of Celia, who has nothing to torment her but her own spirit.

If you could inspire her with Christian humility, you need do no more to make her as happy as any person in the world. This virtue would make her thankful to God for half so much health as she has had, and help her to enjoy more for the time to come. This virtue would keep off tremblings of the spirits and loss of appetite, and her blood would need nothing else to sweeten it.

I have just touched upon these absurd characters for no other end but to convince you in the plainest manner that the strictest rules of religion are so far from rendering a life dull, anxious, and uncomfortable (as is above objected) that on the contrary all the miseries, vexations, and complaints that are in the world are all owing to the want of religion, being directly caused by those absurd passions which religion teaches us to deny.

For all the wants which disturb human life, which make us uneasy to ourselves, quarrelsome with others, and unthankful to God, which weary us in vain labors and foolish anxieties, which carry us from project to project, from place to place in a poor pursuit of we don't know what, are the wants which neither God, nor nature, nor reason hath subjected us to, but are solely infused into us by pride, envy, ambition, and covetousness.

So far therefore as you reduce your desires to such things as nature and reason require, so far as you regulate all the motions of your heart by the strict rules of religion, so far you remove yourself from that infinity of wants and vexations which torment every heart that is left to itself.

Most people indeed confess that religion preserves us from a great many evils and helps us in many respects to a more happy enjoyment of ourselves; but then they imagine that this is only true of such a moderate share of religion as only gently restrains us from the excesses of our passions. They suppose that the strict rules and restraints of an exalted piety are such contradictions to our nature as must needs make our lives dull and uncomfortable.

Although the weakness of this objection sufficiently appears from what hath been already said, yet I shall add one word more to it.

This objection supposes that religion moderately practiced adds much to the happiness of life, but that such heights of piety as the perfection of religion requireth have a contrary effect.

It supposes therefore that it is happy to be kept from the excesses of envy, but unhappy to be kept from other degrees of envy. That it is happy to be delivered from a boundless ambition, but unhappy to be without a more moderate ambition. It supposes also that the happiness of life consists in a mixture of virtue and vice, a mixture of ambition and humility, charity and envy, heavenly affection and covetousness. All which is as absurd as to suppose that it is happy to be free from excessive pains, but unhappy to be without more moderate pains, or that the happiness of health consisted in being partly sick and partly well.

For if humility be the peace and rest of the soul, then no one has so much happiness from humility as he that is the most humble. If excessive envy is a torment of the soul, he most perfectly extinguishes every spark of envy. If there is any peace and joy in doing any action according to the will of God, he that brings the most of his actions to this rule does most of all increase the peace and joy of his life.

And thus it is in every virtue; if you act up to every degree of it, the more happiness you have from it. And so of every vice: If you only abate its excesses, you do but little for yourself; but if you reject it in all degrees, then you feel the true ease and joy of a reformed mind.

As for example: If religion only restrains the excesses of revenge but lets the spirit still live within you in lesser instances, your religion may have made your life a little more outwardly decent but not made you at all happier or easier in yourself. But if you have once sacrificed all thoughts of revenge in obedience to God, and are resolved to return good for evil at all times that you may render yourself more like to God and fitter for his mercy in the kingdom of love and glory, this is a height of virtue that will make you feel its happiness.

Secondly, as to those satisfactions and enjoyments which an exalted piety requireth us to deny ourselves, this deprives us of no real comfort of life.

For, first, piety requires us to renounce no ways of life where we can act reasonably and offer what we do to the glory of God. All ways of life, all satisfactions and enjoyments that are within these bounds, are no way denied us by the strictest rules of piety. Whatever you can do or enjoy as in the presence of God as His servant, as His rational creature, that has received reason and knowledge from Him, all that you can perform conformably to a rational nature and the will of God, all this is allowed by the laws of piety. And will you think that your life will be uncomfortable unless you may displease God, be a fool and mad, and act contrary to that reason and wisdom which he has implanted in you?

And as for those satisfactions which we dare not offer to a holy God, which are only invented by the folly and corruption of the world, which inflame our passions and sink our souls into grossness and sensuality and render us incapable of the divine favor either here or hereafter, surely it can be no uncomfortable state of life to be rescued by religion from such self-murder and to be rendered capable of eternal happiness.

Let us suppose a person destitute of that knowledge which we have from our senses placed somewhere alone by himself, in the midst of a variety of things which he did not know how to use, that he has by him bread, wine, water, golden dust, iron chains, gravel, garments, fire, etc. Let it be supposed that he has no knowledge of the right use of these things, nor any direction from his senses how to quench his thirst, or satisfy his hunger, or make any use of the things about him. Let it be supposed that in his drought he puts golden dust into his eyes; when his eyes smart, he puts wine into his ears; that in his hunger, he puts gravel in his mouth; that in pain, he loads himself with the iron chains; that feeling cold, he puts his feet in the water; that being frighted at the fire, he runs away from it; that being weary, he makes a seat of his bread. Let it be supposed that through his ignorance of the right use of the things that are about him, he will vainly torment himself whilst he lives and at last die, blinded with dust, choked with gravel, and loaded with irons. Let it be supposed that some good being came to him and showed him the nature and use of all the things that were about him and gave him such strict rules of using them as would certainly, if observed, make him the happier for all that he had, and deliver him from the pains of hunger, and thirst, and cold.

Now could you with any reason affirm that those strict rules of using those things that were about him had rendered that poor man's life dull and uncomfortable?

Now this is in some measure a representation of the strict rules of religion; they only relieve our ignorance, save us from tormenting ourselves, and teach us to use everything about us to our proper advantage.

Man is placed in a world full of variety of things; his ignorance makes him use many of them as absurdly as the man that put dust in his eyes to relieve his thirst, or put on chains to remove pain.

Religion therefore here comes in to his relief and gives him strict rules of using everything that is about him, that by so using them suitably to his own nature and the nature of the things, he may have always the pleasure of receiving a right benefit from them. It shows him what is strictly right in meat, and drink, and clothes, and that he has nothing else to expect from the things of this world but to satisfy such wants of his own, and then to extend his assistance to all his brethren, that as far as he is able, he may help all his fellow creatures to the same benefit from the world that he hath.

It tells him that this world is incapable of giving him any other happiness and that all endeavors to be happy in heaps of money, or acres of land, in fine clothes, rich beds, stately equipage, and show and splendor are only vain endeavors, ignorant attempts after impossibilities, these things being no more able to give the least degree of happiness than dust in the eyes can cure thirst, or gravel in the mouth satisfy hunger, but like dust and gravel misapplied will only serve to render him more unhappy by such an ignorant misuse of them.

It tells him that although this world can do no more for him than satisfy these wants of the body, yet that there is a much greater good prepared for man than eating, drinking, and dressing, that it is yet invisible to his eyes, being too glorious for the apprehension of flesh and blood, but reserved for him to enter upon as soon as this short life is over, where, in a new body formed to an angelic likeness, he shall dwell in the light and glory of God to all eternity.

It tells him that this state of glory will be given to all those that make a right use of the things of this present world, who do not blind themselves with golden dust, or eat gravel, or groan under loads of iron of their own putting on, but use bread, water, wine, and garments for such ends as are according to nature and reason, and who with faith and thankfulness worship the kind giver of all that they enjoy here and hope for hereafter.

Now can anyone say that the strictest rules of such a religion as this debar us of any of the comforts of life? Might it not as justly be said of those rules that only hindered a man from choking himself with gravel? For the strictness of these rules only consists in the exactness of their rectitude.

Who would complain of the severe strictness of a law that without any exception forbade the putting of dust into our eyes? Who could think it too rigid, that there were no abatements? Now this is the strictness of religion, it requires nothing of us strictly or without abatements, but where every degree of the thing is wrong, where every indulgence does us some hurt.

If religion forbids all instances of revenge without any exception, 'tis because all revenge is of the nature of poison, and though we don't take so much as to put an end to life, yet if we take any at all, it corrupts the whole mass of blood and makes it difficult to be restored to our former health.

If religion commands a universal charity, to love our neighbor as ourselves, to forgive and pray for all our enemies without any reserve, 'tis because all degrees of love are degrees of happiness that strengthen and support the divine life of the soul and are as necessary to its health and happiness as proper food is necessary to the health and happiness of the body.

If religion has laws against laying up treasures upon earth and commands us to be content with food and raiment, 'tis because every other use of the world is abusing it to our own vexation and turning all its conveniencies into snares and traps to destroy us. 'Tis because this plainness and simplicity of life secures us from the cares and pains of restless pride and envy and makes it easier to keep that strait road that will carry us to eternal life.

If religion saith, "Sell that thou hast, and give to the poor," 'tis because there is no other natural or reasonable use of our riches, no other way of making ourselves happier for them, 'tis because it is as strictly right to give others that which we do not want ourselves as 'tis right to use so much as our own wants require. For if a man has more food than his own nature requires, how base and unreasonable is it to invent foolish ways wasting it and make sport for his own full belly, rather than let his fellow creatures have the same comfort from food which he hath had. It is so far therefore from being a hard law of religion to make this use of our riches that a reasonable man would rejoice in that religion which teaches him to be happier in that which he keeps for himself, which teaches him to make spare food and raiment be greater blessings to him than that which feeds and clothes his own body.

If religion requires us sometimes to fast and deny our natural appetites, 'tis to lessen that struggle and war that is our nature; 'tis to render our bodies fitter instruments of purity and more obedient to the good motions of divine grace; 'tis to dry up the springs of our passions that war against the soul, to cool the flame of our blood, and render the mind more capable of divine meditations. So that although these abstinences give some pain to the body, yet they so lessen the power of bodily appetites and passions and so increase our taste of spiritual joys that even these severities of religion, when practiced with discretion, add much to the comfortable enjoyment of our lives.

If religion calleth us to a life of watching and prayer, 'tis because we live amongst a crowd of enemies and are always in need of the assistance of God. If we are to confess and bewail our sins, 'tis because such confessions relieve the mind and restore it to ease, as burdens and weights taken off the shoulders relieve the body and make it easier to itself. If we are to be frequent and fervent in holy petitions, 'tis to keep us steady in the sight of our true good and that we may never want the happiness of a lively faith, a joyful hope, and well-grounded trust in God. If we are to pray often, 'tis that we may be often happy in such secret joys as only prayer can give, in such communications of the divine presence as will fill our minds with all the happiness that beings not in Heaven are capable of.

Was there anything in the world more worth our care, was there any exercise of the mind or any conversation with men that turned more to our advantage than this intercourse with God, we should not be called to such a continuance in prayer. But if a man considers what it is that he leaves when he retires to devotion, he will find it no small happiness to be so often relieved from doing nothing, or nothing to the purpose, from dull idleness, unprofitable labor, or vain conversation. If he considers that all that is in the world and all that is doing in it is only for the body and bodily enjoyments, he will have reason to rejoice at those hours of prayer which carry him to higher consolations, which raise him above these poor concerns, which open to his mind a scene of greater things and accustom his soul to the hope and expectation of them.

If religion commands us to live wholly unto God and to do all to His glory, 'tis because every other way is living wholly against ourselves and will end in our own shame and confusion of face.

As everything is dark that God does not enlighten, as everything is senseless that has not its share of knowledge from him, as nothing lives but by partaking of life from him, as nothing exists but because he commands it to be, so there is no glory or greatness but what is the glory or greatness of God.

We indeed may talk of human glory as we may talk of human life or human knowledge; but as we are sure that human life implies nothing of our own but a dependent living in God or enjoying so much life in God, so human glory, whenever we find it, must be only so much glory as we enjoy in the glory of God.

This is the state of all creatures, whether men or angels; as they make not themselves, so they enjoy nothing from themselves; if they are great, it must be only as great receivers of the gifts of God; their power can only be so much of the divine power acting in them; their wisdom can be only so much of the divine wisdom shining within them, and their light and glory only so much of the light and glory of God shining upon them.

As they are not men or angels because they had a mind to be so themselves but because the will of God formed them to be what they are, so they cannot enjoy this or that happiness of men or angels because they have a mind to it but because it is the will of God that such things be the happiness of men, and such things the happiness of angels. But now if God be thus all in all, if His will is thus the measure of all things and all natures, if nothing can be done but by His power, if nothing can be seen but by a light from Him, if we have nothing to fear but from His justice, if we have nothing to hope for but from His goodness, if this is the nature of man thus helpless in himself, if this is the state of all creatures, as well those in Heaven as those on earth, if they are nothing, can do nothing, can suffer no pain nor feel any happiness but so far and in such degrees as the power of God does all this, if this be the state of things, then how can we have the least glimpse of joy or comfort, how can we have any peaceful enjoyment of ourselves but by living wholly unto that God, using and doing everything conformably to His will? A life thus devoted unto God, looking wholly unto Him in all our actions and doing all things suitably to His glory, is so far from being dull and uncomfortable that it creates new comforts in everything that we do.

On the contrary, would you see how happy they are who live according to their own wills, who cannot submit to the dull and melancholy business of a life devoted unto God, look at the man in the parable to whom his Lord had given one talent.

He could not bear the thoughts of using his talent according to the will of him from whom he had it, and therefore he chose to make himself happier in a way of his own. "Lord," says he, "I knew thee, that thou art an hard man, reaping where thou hadst not sown, and gathering where thou hadst not strawed.[25] and I was afraid, and went and hid thy talent in the earth. Lo there thou hast that is thine."

His Lord having convicted him out of his own mouth dispatches him with this sentence, "Cast the unprofitable servant into outer darkness; there shall be weeping, and gnashing of teeth" (Matt. 25:30).

Here you see how happy this man made himself by not acting wholly according to his Lord's will. It was, according to his own account, a happiness of murmuring and discontent; I knew thee, says he, that thou wast a hard man. It was a happiness of fears and apprehensions; I was, says he, afraid. It was a happiness of vain labors and fruitless travails. I went, says he, and hid thy talent; and after having been a while the sport of foolish passions, tormenting fears, and fruitless labors, he is rewarded with darkness, eternal weeping, and gnashing of teeth.

Now this is the happiness of all those who look upon a strict and exalted piety, that is, a right use of their talent, to be a dull and melancholy state of life.

They may live a while free from the restraints and directions of religion, but instead thereof they must be under the absurd government of their passions. They must, like the man in the parable, live in murmurings and discontents, in fears and apprehensions. They may avoid the labor of doing good, of spending their time devoutly, of laying up treasures in heaven, of clothing the naked, of visiting the sick; but then they must, like this man, have labors and pains in vain that tend to no use or advantage, that do no good either to themselves or others; they must travail, and labor, and work, and dig to hide their talent in the earth. They must, like him at their Lord's coming, be convicted out of their own mouths, be accused by their own hearts, and have everything that they have said and thought of religion be made to show the justice of their condemnation to eternal darkness, weeping and gnashing of teeth.

This is the purchase that they make who avoid the strictness and perfection of religion in order to live happily.

On the other hand, would you see a short description of the happiness of a life rightly employed, wholly devoted to God, you must look at the man in the parable to whom his Lord had given five talents. "Lord," says he, "thou deliveredst unto me five talents: behold I have gained besides them five talents more. His Lord said unto him, well done thou good and faithful servant; thou hast been faithful over a few things, I will make thee ruler over many things; enter thou into the joy of thy Lord."

Here you see a life that is wholly intent upon the improvement of the talents, that is devoted wholly unto God, is a state of happiness, prosperous labors, and glorious success. Here are not, as in the former case, any uneasy passions, murmurings, vain fears, and fruitless labors. The man is not toiling and digging in the earth for no end or advantage, but his pious labors prosper in his hands, his happiness increases upon him, the blessing of five becomes the blessing of ten talents, and he is received with a "well done good and faithful servant, enter thou into the joy of thy Lord."

Now as the case of these men in the parable left nothing else to their choice but either to be happy in using their gifts to the glory of the Lord or miserable by using them according to their own humors and fancies, so the state of Christianity leaves us no other choice.

All that we have, all that we are, all that we enjoy, are only so many talents from God. If we use them to the ends of a pious and holy life, our five talents will become ten and our labors will carry us into the joy of our Lord; but if we abuse them to the gratifications of our own pride and vanity, we shall live here in vain labors and foolish anxieties, shunning religion as a melancholy thing, accusing our Lord as a hard master, and then fall into everlasting misery.

We may for a while amuse ourselves with names, and sounds, and shadows of happiness; we may talk of this or that greatness and dignity; but if we desire real happiness, we have no other possible way to it but by improving our talents by so holily and piously using the powers and faculties of men in this present state that we may be happy and glorious in the powers and faculties of angels in the world to come.

How ignorant therefore are they of the nature of religion, of the nature of man, and the nature of God who think a life of strict piety and devotion to God to be a dull uncomfortable state when it's so plain and certain that there is neither comfort or joy to be found in anything else.

NOTES

25. Strawed: strewed, or strewn, that is, scattered. Law follows the usage of the King James or "Authorized Version" of the parable of the talents (Matthew 25:14-30).

Chapter 12

The happiness of a life wholly devoted unto God further proved from the vanity, the sensuality, and the ridiculous, poor enjoyments which they are forced to take up with who live according to their own humors. This represented in various characters.

We may still see more of the happiness of a life devoted unto God by considering the poor contrivances for happiness and the contemptible ways of life which they are thrown into who are not under the directions of a strict piety but seeking after happiness by other methods.

If one looks at their lives who live by no rule but their own humors and fancies; if one sees but what it is which they call joy, and greatness, and happiness; if one sees how they rejoice, and repent, change and fly from one delusion to another, one shall find great reason to rejoice that God hath appointed a straight and narrow way that leadeth unto life, and that we are not left to the folly of our own minds or forced to take up with such shadows of joy and happiness as the weakness and folly of the world has invented. I say *invented* because those things which make up the joy and happiness of the world are mere inventions which have no foundation in nature and reason, are no way the proper good or happiness of man, no way perfect either his body, or his mind, or carry him to his true end.

As for instance, when a man proposes to be happy in ways of ambition by raising himself to some imaginary heights above other people, this is truly an invention of happiness which has no foundation in nature, but is as mere a cheat of our own making as if a man should intend to make himself happy by climbing up a ladder.

If a woman seeks for happiness from fine clothes or spots upon her face, from jewels and rich clothes, this is as merely an invention of happiness as contrary to nature and reason as if she should propose to make herself happy by painting a post and putting the same finery upon it. It is in this respect that I call these joys and happiness of the world mere inventions of happiness, because neither God nor nature nor reason hath appointed them as such; but whatever appears joyful, or great, or happy in them is entirely created or invented by the blindness and vanity of our own minds.

And it is on these inventions of happiness that I desire you to cast your eye, that you may thence learn how great a good religion is which delivers you from such a multitude of follies and vain pursuits, as are the torment and vexation of minds that wander from their true happiness in God.

Look at Flatus and learn how miserable they are who are left to the folly of their own passions.

Flatus is rich and in health yet always uneasy and always searching after happiness. Every time you visit him you find some new project in his head, he is eager upon it as something that is more worth his while and will do more for him than anything that is already past. Every new thing so seizes him that if you was to take him from it, he would think himself quite undone. His sanguine temper and strong passions promise him so much happiness in everything that he is always cheated, and is satisfied with nothing.

At his first setting out in life, fine clothes was his delight, his inquiry was only after the best tailors and peruke[26] makers, and he had no thoughts of excelling in anything but dress. He spared no expense, but carried every nicety to its greatest height. But this happiness not answering his expectations, he left off his brocades, put on a plain coat, railed at fops and beaux, and gave himself up to gaming with great eagerness.

This new pleasure satisfied him for some time, he envied no other way of life. But being by the fate of play drawn into a duel where he narrowly escaped his death, he left off the dice and sought for happiness no longer amongst the gamesters.

The next thing that seized his wandering imagination was the diversions of the town, and for more than a twelvemonth, you heard him talk of nothing but ladies, drawing rooms, birthnights, plays, balls, and assemblies. But growing sick of these, he had recourse to hard drinking. Here he had many a merry night, and met with stronger joys than any he had felt before. Here he had thoughts of setting up his staff and looking out no further; but unluckily falling into a fever, he grew angry at all strong liquors and took his leave of the happiness of being drunk.

The next attempt after happiness carried him into the field; for two or three years nothing was so happy as hunting. He entered upon it with all his soul, and leaped more hedges and ditches than had ever been known in so short a time. You never saw him but in a green coat; he was the envy of all that blow the horn, and always spoke to his dogs in great propriety of language. If you met him at home in a bad day, you would hear him blow his horn and be entertained with the surprising accidents of the last noble chase. No sooner had Flatus outdone all the world in the breed and education of his dogs, built new kennels, new stables, and bought a new hunting seat, but he immediately got sight of another happiness, hated the senseless noise and hurry of hunting, gave away his dogs, and was for some time after deep in the pleasures of building.

Now he invents new kinds of dovecotes, and has such contrivances in his barns and stables as were never seen before. He wonders at the dullness of the old builders, is wholly bent upon the improvement of architecture, and will hardly hang a door in the ordinary way. He tells his friends that he never was so delighted in anything in his life, that he has more happiness amongst his brick and mortar than ever he had at court, and that he is contriving how to have some little matter to do that way as long as he lives.

The next year he leaves his house unfinished, complains to everybody of masons and carpenters, and devotes himself wholly to the happiness of riding about. After this, you can never see him but on horseback, and so highly delighted with this new way of life that he would tell you, give him but his horse and a clean country to ride in and you might take all the rest to yourself. A variety of new saddles and bridles and a great change of horses added much to the pleasure of this new way of life. But however, having after some time tired both himself and his horses, the happiest thing he could think of next was to go abroad and visit foreign countries; and there indeed happiness exceeded his imagination, and he was only uneasy that he had begun so fine a life no sooner. The next month he returned home, unable to bear any longer the impertinence of foreigners.

After this, he was a great student for one whole year; he was up early and late at his Italian grammar that he might have the happiness of understanding the opera whenever he should hear one and not be like those unreasonable people that are pleased with they don't know what.

Flatus is very ill-natured, or otherwise, just as his affairs happen to be when you visit him; if you find him when some project is almost worn out, you will find a peevish ill-bred man, but if you had seen him just as he entered upon his riding regimen, or begun to excel in sounding of the horn, you had been saluted with great civility.

Flatus is now at a full stand and is doing what he never did in his life before: He is reasoning and reflecting with himself. He loses several days in considering which of his cast-off ways of life he should try again.

But here a new project comes into his relief. He is now living upon herbs, and running about the country to get himself into as good wind as any running footman[27] in the kingdom.

I have been thus circumstantial in so many foolish particulars of this kind of life because I hope that every particular folly that you here see will naturally turn itself into an argument for the wisdom and happiness of a religious life.

If I could lay before you a particular account of all the circumstances of terror and distress that daily attend a life at sea, the more particular I was in the account, the more I should make you feel and rejoice in the happiness of living upon the land.

In like manner, the more I enumerate the follies, anxieties, delusions, and restless desires which go through every part of a life devoted to human passions and worldly enjoyments, the more you must be affected with that peace and rest and solid content which religion gives to the souls of men.

If you but just cast your eye upon a madman or a fool, it perhaps signifies little or nothing to you; but if you was to attend them for some days and observe the lamentable madness and stupidity of all their actions, this would be an affecting sight and would make you often bless yourself for the enjoyment of your reason and senses.

Just so, if you are only told in the gross of the folly and madness of a life devoted to the world, it makes little or no impression upon you; but if you are shown how such people live every day, if you see the continual folly and madness of all their particular actions and designs, this would be an affecting sight and make you bless God for having given you a greater happiness to aspire after.

So that characters of this kind, the more folly and ridicule they have in them, provided that they be but natural, are most useful to correct our minds, and therefore are nowhere more proper than in books of devotion and practical piety. And as in several cases we best learn the nature of things by looking at that which is contrary to them, so perhaps we best apprehend the excellency of wisdom by contemplating the wild extravagancies of folly.

I shall therefore continue this method a little further and endeavor to recommend the happiness of piety to you by showing you in some other instances how miserably and poorly they live who live without it.

But you will perhaps say that the ridiculous, restless life of Flatus is not the common state of those who resign themselves up to live by their own humors[28] and neglect the strict rules of religion, and that therefore it is not so great an argument of the happiness of a religious life as I would make it.

I answer that I am afraid it is one of the most general characters in life, and that few people can read it without seeing something in it that belongs to themselves. For where shall we find that wise and happy man who has not been eagerly pursuing different appearances of happiness, sometimes thinking it was here and sometimes there?

And if people were to divide their lives into particular stages and ask themselves what they were pursuing, or what it was which they had chiefly in view when they were twenty years old, what at twenty-five, what at thirty, what at forty, what at fifty, and so on, till they were brought to their last bed, numbers of people would find that they had liked, and disliked, and pursued as many different appearances of happiness as are to be seen in the life of Flatus.

And thus it must necessarily be more or less with all those who propose any other happiness than that which arises from a strict and regular piety.

But secondly, let it be granted that the generality of people are not of such restless, fickle tempers as Flatus; the difference then is only this—Flatus is continually changing and trying something new, but others are content with some one state: They don't leave gaming, and then fall to hunting. But they have so much steadiness in their tempers that some seek after no other happiness but that of heaping up riches; others grow old in the sports of the field; others are content to drink themselves to death without the least inquiry after any other happiness.

Now is there anything more happy or reasonable in such a life as this than in the life of Flatus? Is it not as great and desirable, as wise and happy, to be constantly changing from one thing to another as to be nothing else but a gatherer of money, a hunter, a gamester, or a drunkard all your life?

Shall religion be looked upon as a burden, as a dull and melancholy state, for calling men from such happiness as this to live according to the laws of God, to labor after the perfection of their nature and prepare themselves for an endless state of joy and glory in the presence of God?

But turn your eyes now another way and let the trifling joys, the gewgaw happiness, of Feliciana teach you how wise they are, what delusion they escape, whose hearts and hopes are fixed upon a happiness in God.

If you was to live with Feliciana but one-half year, you would see all the happiness that she is to have as long as she lives. She has no more to come but the poor repetition of that which could never have pleased once but through a littleness of mind and want of thought.

She is to be again dressed fine and keep her visiting day. She is again to change the color of her clothes, again to have a new head, and again put patches on her face. She is again to see who acts best at the playhouse and who sings finest at the opera. She is again to make ten visits in a day, and be ten times in a day trying to talk artfully, easily, and politely about nothing.

She is to be again delighted with some new fashion and again angry at the change of some old one. She is to be again at cards and gaming at midnight, and again in bed at noon. She is to be again pleased with hypocritical compliments, and again disturbed at imaginary affronts. She is to be again pleased with her good luck at gaming, and again tormented with the loss of her money. She is again to prepare herself for a birthnight, and again see the town full of good company. She is again to hear the cabals and intrigues of the town, again to have secret intelligence of private amours, and early notice of marriages, quarrels, and partings.

If you see her come out of her chariot more briskly than usual, converse with more spirit, and seem fuller of joy than she was last week, it is because there is some surprising new dress or new diversion just come to town.

These are all the substantial and regular parts of Feliciana's happiness, and she never knew a pleasant day in her life but it was owing to some one or more of these things.

It is for this happiness that she has always been deaf to the reasonings of religion, that her heart has been too gay and cheerful to consider what is right or wrong in regard to eternity, or to listen to the sound of such dull words as wisdom, piety, and devotion.

It is for fear of losing some of this happiness that she dares not meditate on the immortality of her soul, consider her relation to God, or turn her thoughts toward those joys which make Saints and angels infinitely happy in the presence and glory of God.

But now let it here be observed that as poor a round of happiness as this appears, yet most women that avoid the restraints of religion for a gay life must be content with very small parts of it. As they have not Feliciana's fortune and figure in the world, so they must give away the comforts of a pious life for a very small part of her happiness.

And if you look into the world and observe the lives of those women, whom no arguments can persuade to live wholly unto God in a wise and pious employment of themselves, you will find most of them to be such as lose all the comforts of religion without gaining the tenth part of Feliciana's happiness. They are such as spend their time and fortunes only in mimicking the pleasures of richer people, and rather look and long after than enjoy those delusions, which are only to be purchased by considerable fortunes.

But if a woman of high birth and great fortune, having read the gospel, should rather wish to be an underservant in some pious family where wisdom, piety, and great devotion directed all the actions of every day, if she should rather wish this than to live at the top of Feliciana's happiness, I should think her neither mad nor melancholy, but that she judged as rightly of the spirit of the gospel as if she had rather wished to be poor Lazarus at the gate than to be the rich man clothed in purple and fine linen and faring sumptuously every day.

But to proceed. Would you know what a happiness it is to be governed by the wisdom of religion and be devoted to the joys and hopes of a pious life, look at the poor condition of Succus whose greatest happiness is a good night's rest in bed and a good meal when he is up. When he talks of happiness, it is always in such expressions as shows you that he has only his bed and his dinner in his thoughts.

This regard to his meals and repose makes Succus order all the rest of his time with relation to them. He will undertake no business that may hurry his spirits or break in upon his hours of eating and rest. If he reads, it shall only be for half an hour because that is sufficient to amuse the spirits, and he will read something that may make him laugh, as rendering the body fitter for its food and rest. Or if he has at any time a mind to indulge a grave thought, he always has recourse to a useful treatise upon the ancient cookery. Succus is an enemy to all party matters, having made it an observation that there is as good eating amongst the Whigs as the Tories.

He talks coolly and moderately upon all subjects, and is as fearful of falling into a passion as of catching cold, being very positive that they are both equally injurious to the stomach. If ever you see him more hot than ordinary, it is upon some provoking occasion when the dispute about cookery runs very high, or in the defence of some beloved dish which has often made him happy. But he has been so long upon these subjects, is so well acquainted with all that can be said on both sides, and has so often answered all objections that he generally decides the matter with great gravity.

Succus is very loyal, and as soon as ever he likes any wine, he drinks the king's health with all his heart. Nothing could put rebellious thoughts into his head unless he should live to see a proclamation against eating of pheasants' eggs.

All the hours that are not devoted either to repose or nourishment are looked upon by Succus as waste or spare time. For this reason he lodges near a coffee house and a tavern, that when he rises in the morning he may be near the news, and when he parts at night he may not have far to bed. In the morning you always see him in the same place in the coffee room, and if he seems more attentively engaged than ordinary, it is because some criminal is broke out of Newgate, or some lady was robbed last night but they can't tell where. When he has learnt all that he can, he goes home to settle the matter with the barber's boy that comes to shave him.

The next waste-time that lies upon his hands is from dinner to supper. And if melancholy thoughts ever come into his head, it is at this time when he is often left to himself for an hour or more, and that after the greatest pleasure he knows is just over. He is afraid to sleep because he has heard it is not healthful at that time, so that he is forced to refuse so welcome a guest.

But here he is soon relieved by a settled method of playing at cards till it is time to think of some little nice matter for supper.

After this, Succus takes his glass, talks of the excellency of the English constitution, and praises that minister the most who keeps the best table.

On a Sunday night you may sometimes hear him condemning the iniquity of the town rakes, and the bitterest thing that he says against them is this, that he verily believes some of them are so abandoned as not to have a regular meal or a sound night's sleep in a week.

At eleven Succus bids all good night, and parts in great friendship. He is presently in bed and sleeps till it is time to go to the coffee house next morning.

If you was to live with Succus for a twelvemonth, this is all that you would see in his life except a few curses and oaths that he uses as occasion offers.

And now I cannot help making this reflection: That as I believe the most likely means in the world to inspire a person with true piety was to have seen the example of some eminent professor of religion,[29] so the next thing that is likely to fill one with the same zeal is to see the folly, the baseness, and poor satisfactions of a life destitute of religion. As the one excites us to love and admire the wisdom and greatness of religion, so the other may make us fearful of living without it.

For who can help blessing God for the means of grace and for the hope of glory when he sees what variety of folly they sink into who live without it? Who would not heartily engage in all the labors and exercises of a pious life, be steadfast, immovable, and always abounding in the work of the Lord, when he sees what dull sensuality, what poor views, what gross enjoyments they are left to who seek for happiness in other ways?

So that whether we consider the greatness of religion or the littleness of all other things and the meanness of all other enjoyments, there is nothing to be found in the whole nature of things for a thoughtful mind to rest upon but a happiness in the hopes of religion.

Consider now with yourself how unreasonably it is pretended that a life of strict piety must be a dull and anxious state. For can it with any reason be said that the duties and restraints of religion must render our lives heavy and melancholy when they only deprive us of such happiness as has been here laid before you?

Must it be tedious and tiresome to live in the continual exercise of charity, devotion, and temperance, to act wisely and virtuously, to do good to the utmost of your power, to imitate the divine perfections and prepare yourself for the enjoyment of God? Must it be dull and tiresome to be delivered from blindness and vanity, from false hopes and vain fears, to improve in holiness, to feel the comforts of conscience in all your actions, to know that God is your friend, that all must work for your good, that neither life nor death, neither men nor devils can do you any harm, but that all your sufferings and doings that are offered unto God, all your watchings and prayers and labors of love and charity, all your improvements are in a short time to be rewarded with everlasting glory in the presence of God; must such a state as this be dull and tiresome for want of such happiness as Flatus or Feliciana enjoys?

Now if this cannot be said, then there is no happiness or pleasure lost by being strictly pious, nor has the devout man anything to envy in any other state of life. For all the art and contrivance in the world without religion cannot make more of human life, or carry its happiness to any greater height than Flatus or Feliciana have done.

The finest wit, the greatest genius upon earth, if not governed by religion, must be as foolish and low and vain in his methods of happiness as the poor Succus.

If you was to see a man dully endeavoring all his life to satisfy his thirst by holding up one and the same empty cup to his mouth, you would certainly despise his ignorance.

But if you should see others of brighter parts and finer understandings ridiculing the dull satisfaction of one cup and thinking to satisfy their own thirst by a variety of gilt and golden empty cups, would you think that these were ever the wiser, or happier, or better employed for their finer parts?

Now this is all the difference that you can see in the happiness of this life.

The dull and heavy soul may be content with one empty appearance of happiness and be continually trying to hold one and the same empty cup to his mouth all his life. But then let the wit, the great scholar, the fine genius, the great statesman, the polite gentleman, lay all their heads together and they can only show you more and various empty appearances of happiness; give them all the world into their hands, let them cut and carve as they please, they can only make a greater variety of empty cups.

So that if you don't think it hard to be deprived of the pleasures of gluttony for the sake of religion, you have no reason to think it hard to be restrained from any other worldly pleasure. For search as deep and look as far as you will, there is nothing here to be found that is nobler or greater than high eating and drinking unless you look for it in the wisdom and laws of religion.

And if all that is in the world are only so many empty cups, what does it signify which you take, or how many you take, or how many you have?

If you would but use[30] yourself to such meditations as these to reflect upon the vanity of all orders of life without piety, to consider how all the ways of the world are only so many different ways of error, blindness, and mistake, you would soon find your heart made wiser and better by it. These meditations would awaken your soul into a zealous desire of that solid happiness which is only to be found in recourse to God.

Examples of great piety are not now common in the world; it may not be your happiness to live within sight of any, or to have your virtue inflamed by their light and fervor. But the misery and folly of worldly men is what meets your eyes in every place, and you need not look far to see how poorly, how vainly men dream away their lives for want of religious wisdom.

This is the reason that I have laid before you so many characters of the vanity of a worldly life, to teach you to make a benefit of the corruption of the age, and that you may be made wise though not by the sight of what piety is, yet by seeing what misery and folly reigns where piety is not.

If you would turn your mind to such reflections as these, your own observation would carry this instruction much further, and all your conversation and acquaintance with the world would be a daily conviction to you of the necessity of seeking some greater happiness than all the poor enjoyments of this world can give.

To meditate upon the perfection of the divine attributes, to contemplate the glories of heaven, to consider the joys of Saints and angels living forever in the brightness and glory of the divine presence, these are the meditations of souls advanced in piety, and not so suited to every capacity.

But to see and consider the emptiness and error of all worldly happiness, to see the grossness of sensuality, the poorness of pride, the stupidity of covetousness, the vanity of dress, the delusion of honor, the blindness of our passions, the uncertainty of our lives, and the shortness of all worldly projects; these are meditations that are suited to all capacities, fitted to strike all minds; they require no depth of thought or sublime speculation, but are forced upon us by all our senses and taught us by almost everything that we see and hear.

This is that wisdom that crieth, and putteth forth her voice in the streets (Prov. 8:1), that standeth at all our doors, that appealeth to all our senses, teaching us in everything and everywhere by all that we see and all that we hear, by births and burials, by sickness and health, by life and death, by pains and poverty, by misery and vanity, and by all the changes and chances of life, that there is nothing else for man to look after, no other end in nature for him to drive at, but a happiness which is only to be found in the hopes and expectations of religion.

NOTES

26. Peruke: a wig.
27. Running footman: a servant employed to run ahead of his master's carriage.
28. Humors: whims or fancies.
29. Professor of religion: that is, one who professes religion.
30. Use: accustom or be occupied with.

Chapter 13

That not only a life of vanity or sensuality, but even the most regular kind of life that is not governed by great devotion sufficiently shows its miseries, its wants, and emptiness to the eyes of all the world. This represented in various characters.

It is a very remarkable saying of our Lord and Savior to His Disciples in these words: "Blessed are your eyes, for they see, and your ears, for they hear." They teach us two things: First, that the dullness and heaviness of men's minds with regard to spiritual matters is so great that it may justly be compared to the want of eyes and ears.

Secondly, that God has so filled everything and every place with motives and arguments for a godly life that they who are but so blessed, so happy as to use their eyes and their ears must needs be affected with them.

Now though this was in a more especial manner the case of those whose senses were witnesses of the life and miracles and doctrines of our blessed Lord, yet is it as truly the case of all Christians at this time. For the reasons of religion, the calls to piety, are so written and engraved upon everything, and present themselves so strongly and so constantly to all our senses in everything that we meet, that they can only be disregarded by eyes that see not and ears that hear not.

What greater motive to a religious life than the vanity, the poorness of all worldly enjoyments? And yet who can help seeing and feeling this every day of his life?

What greater call to look toward God than the pains, the sickness, the crosses and vexations of this life, and yet whose eyes and ears are not witnesses of them?

What miracles could more strongly appeal to our senses, or what message from heaven speak louder to us than the daily dying and departure of our fellow creatures does?

So that the one thing needful, or the great end of life, is not left to be discovered by fine reasoning and deep reflections, but is pressed upon us in the plainest manner, by the experience of all our senses, by everything that we meet with in life.

Let us but intend to see and hear, and then the whole world becomes a book of wisdom and instruction to us. All that is regular in the order of nature, all that is accidental in the course of things, all the mistakes and disappointments that happen to ourselves, all the miseries and errors that we see in other people, become so many plain lessons of advice to us, teaching us with as much assurance as an angel from Heaven that we can no ways raise ourselves to any true happiness but by turning all our thoughts, our wishes, and endeavors after the happiness of another life.

It is this right use of the world that I would lead you into by directing you to turn your eyes upon every shape of human folly, that you may thence draw fresh arguments and motives of living to the best and greatest purposes of your creation.

And if you would but carry this intention about you, of profiting by the follies of the world and of learning the greatness of religion from the littleness and vanity of every other way of life, if, I say, you would but carry this intention in your mind, you would find every day, every place, and every person, a fresh proof of their wisdom who choose to live wholly unto God. You would then often return home the wiser, the better, and the more strengthened in religion by everything that has fallen in your way.

Octavius is a learned, ingenious man, well versed in most parts of literature, and no stranger to any kingdom in Europe. The other day, being just recovered from a lingering fever, he took upon him to talk thus to his friends.

My glass, says he, is almost run out; and your eyes see how many marks of age and death I bear about me. But I plainly feel myself sinking away faster than any standers-by imagine. I fully believe that one year more will conclude my reckoning.

The attention of his friends was much raised by such a declaration, expecting to hear something truly excellent from so learned a man who had but a year longer to live, when Octavius proceeded in this manner. For these reasons, says he, my friends, I have left off all taverns; the wine of those places is not good enough for me in this decay of nature. I must now be nice in what I drink; I can't pretend to do as I have done, and therefore am resolved to furnish my own cellar with a little of the very best though it cost me ever so much.

I must also tell you, my friends, that age forces a man to be wise in many other respects and makes us change many of our opinions and practices.

You know how much I have liked a large acquaintance; I now condemn it as an error. Three or four cheerful, diverting companions is all that I now desire because I find that in my present infirmities, if I am left alone or to grave company, I am not so easy to myself.

A few days after Octavius had made this declaration to his friends, he relapsed into his former illness, was committed to a nurse who closed his eyes before his fresh parcel of wine came in.

Young Eugenius, who was present at this discourse, went home a new man, with full resolutions of devoting himself wholly unto God.

I never, says Eugenius, was so deeply affected with the wisdom and importance of religion as when I saw how poorly and meanly the learned Octavius was to leave the world through the want of it.

How often had I envied his great learning, his skill in languages, his knowledge of antiquity, his address[31] and fine manner of expressing himself upon all subjects! But when I saw how poorly it all ended, what was to be the last year of such a life, and how foolishly the master of all these accomplishments was then forced to talk for want of being acquainted with the joys and expectations of piety, I was thoroughly convinced that there was nothing to be envied or desired but a life of true piety, nor anything so poor and comfortless as a death without it.

Now as the young Eugenius was thus edified and instructed in the present case, so if you are so happy as to have anything of his thoughtful temper, you will meet with variety of instruction of this kind; you will find that arguments for the wisdom and happiness of a strict piety offer themselves in all places and appeal to all your senses in the plainest manner.

You will find that all the world preaches to an attentive mind, and that if you have but ears to hear, almost everything you meet teaches you some lesson of wisdom. But now if to these admonitions and instructions which we receive from our senses from an experience of the state of human life, if to these we add the lights of religion, those great truths which the Son of God has taught us, it will be then as much past all doubt that there is but one happiness for man as that there is but one God.

For since religion teaches us that our souls are immortal, that piety and devotion will carry them to an eternal enjoyment of God, and that carnal, worldly tempers will sink them into an everlasting misery with damned spirits, what gross nonsense and stupidity is it to give the name of joy or happiness to anything but that which carries us to this joy and happiness in God?

Was all to die with our bodies, there might be some pretence for those different sorts of happiness that are now so much talked of; but since our *all* begins at the death of our bodies, since all men are to be immortal either in misery or happiness in a world entirely different from this, since they are all hastening hence at all uncertainties as fast as death can cut them down, some in sickness, some in health, some sleeping, some waking, some at midnight, others at cock-crowing, and all at hours that they know not of, is it not certain that no man can exceed another in joy and happiness but so far as he exceeds him in those virtues which fit him for a happy death?

Cognatus is a sober, regular clergyman of good repute in the world, and well esteemed in his parish. All his parishioners say he is an honest man and very notable at making a bargain. The farmers listen to him with great attention when he talks of the properest time of selling corn.

He has been for twenty years a diligent observer of markets, and has raised a considerable fortune by good management.

Cognatus is very orthodox and full of esteem for our English Liturgy;[32] and if he has not prayers on Wednesdays and Fridays, 'tis because his predecessor had not used the parish to any such custom.

As he cannot serve both his livings himself, so he makes it matter of conscience to keep a sober curate upon one of them, whom he hires to take care of all the souls in the parish at as cheap a rate as a sober man can be procured.

Cognatus has been very prosperous all his time, but still he has had the uneasiness and vexations that they have who are deep in worldly business. Taxes, losses, crosses, bad mortgages, bad tenants, and the hardness of the times are frequent subjects of his conversation, and a good or a bad season has a great effect upon his spirits.

Cognatus has no other end in growing rich but that he may leave a considerable fortune to a niece whom he has politely educated in expensive finery by what he has saved out of the tithes of two livings.[33]

The neighbors look upon Cognatus as a happy clergyman because they see him (as they call it) in good circumstances; and some of them intend to dedicate their own sons to the church because they see how well it has succeeded with Cognatus whose father was but an ordinary man.

But now, if Cognatus, when he first entered into holy orders, had perceived how absurd a thing it is to grow rich by the gospel, if he had proposed to himself the example of some primitive father, if he had had the piety of the great St. Austin in his eye who durst not enrich any of his relations out of the revenue of the church, if instead of twenty years care to lay up treasures upon earth, he had distributed the income of every year in the most Christian acts of charity and compassion; if instead of tempting his niece to be proud, and providing her with such ornaments as the Apostle forbids, he had clothed, comforted, and assisted numbers of widows, orphans, and distressed, who were all to appear for him at the last day; if instead of the cares and anxieties of bad bonds, troublesome mortgages, and ill bargains, he had had the constant comfort of knowing that his treasure was securely laid up where neither moth corrupteth, nor thieves break through and steal, could it with any reason be said that he had mistaken the spirit and dignity of his order or lessened any of that happiness which is to be found in his sacred employment?

If instead of rejoicing in the happiness of a second living, he had thought it as unbecoming the office of a clergyman to traffic for gain in holy things as to open a shop; if he had thought it better to recommend some honest labor to his niece than to support her in idleness by the labors of a curate (better that she should want fine clothes and a rich husband than that cures of souls should be farmed about,[34] and brother clergymen not suffered to live by those altars at which they serve); if this had been the spirit of Cognatus, could it with any reason be said that these rules of religion, this strictness of piety, had robbed Cognatus of any real happiness? Could it be said that a life thus governed by the spirit of the gospel must be dull and melancholy if compared to that of raising a fortune for a niece?

Now as this cannot be said in the present case, so in every other kind of life, if you enter into the particulars of it, you will find that however easy and prosperous it may seem, yet you cannot add piety to any part of it without adding so much of a better joy and happiness to it.

Look now at that condition of life which draws the envy of all eyes.

Negotius is a temperate, honest man. He served his time under a master of great trade, but has by his own management made it a more considerable business than ever it was before. For thirty years last past, he has wrote fifty or sixty letters in a week and is busy in corresponding with all parts of Europe. The general good of trade seems to Negotius to be the general good of life; whomsoever he admires, whatever he commends or condemns either in church or state, is admired, commended, or condemned with some regard to trade.

As money is continually pouring in upon him, so he often lets it go in various kinds of expense and generosity, and sometimes in ways of charity. Negotius is always ready to join in any public contribution. If a purse is making at any place where he happens to be, whether it be to buy a plate for a horse race, or to redeem a prisoner out of jail, you are always sure of having something from him.

He has given a fine ring of bells[35] to a church in the country; and there is much expectation that he will sometime or other make a more beautiful front to the market house than has yet been seen in

181

any place. For it is the generous spirit of Negotius to do nothing in a mean way.

If you ask what it is that has secured Negotius from all scandalous vices, it is the same thing that has kept him from all strictness of devotion, it is his great business. He has always had too many important things in his head, his thoughts have been too much employed to suffer him to fall either into any courses of rakery, or to feel the necessity of an inward, solid piety.

For this reason he hears of the pleasures of debauchery and the pleasures of piety with the same indifferency, and has no more desire of living in the one than in the other because neither of them consist with that turn of mind and multiplicity of business which are his happiness.

If Negotius was asked what it is which he drives at in life, he would be as much at a loss for an answer as if he was asked what any other person is thinking of. For though he always seems to himself to know what he is doing and has many things in his head which are the motives of his actions, yet he cannot tell you of any one general end of life that he has chosen with deliberation as being truly worthy of all his labor and pains.

He has several confused notions in his head which have been a long time there, such as these, viz., that it is something great to have more business than other people, to have more dealings upon his hands than a hundred of the same profession, to grow continually richer and richer and to raise an immense fortune before he dies. The thing that seems to give Negotius the greatest life and spirit and to be most in his thoughts is an expectation that he has, that he shall die richer than any of his business ever did.

The generality of people when they think of happiness think upon Negotius, in whose life every instance of happiness is supposed to meet: sober, prudent, rich, prosperous, generous, and charitable.

Let us now therefore look at this condition in another, but truer light.

Let it be supposed that this same Negotius was a painful, laborious man, every day deep in variety of affairs, that he neither drank nor debauched but was sober and regular in his business. Let it be supposed that he grew old in this course of trading, and that the end and design of all this labor, and care, and application to business was only this, that he might die possessed of more than a hundred thousand pair of boots and spurs and as many greatcoats.

Let it be supposed that the sober part of the world say of him when he is dead that he was a great and happy man, a thorough master of business, and had acquired a hundred thousand pair of boots and spurs when he died.

Now if this was really the case, I believe it would be readily granted that a life of such business was as poor and ridiculous as any that can be invented. But it would puzzle anyone to show that a man that has spent all his time and thoughts in business and hurry that he might die, as it is said, worth a hundred thousand pounds is any whit wiser than he who has taken the same pains to have as many pairs of boots and spurs when he leaves the world.

For if the temper and state of our souls be our whole state, if the only end of life be to die as free from sin and as exalted in virtue as we can, if naked as we came, so naked are we to return and to stand a trial before Christ and His holy angels for everlasting happiness or misery, what can it possibly signify what a man had or had not in this world? What can it signify what you call those things which a man has left behind him, whether you call them his or anyone's else, whether you call them a hundred thousand pounds or a hundred thousand pair of boots and spurs? I say, call them; for the things signify no more to him than the names.

Now it is easy to see the folly of a life thus spent, to furnish a man with such a number of boots and spurs. But yet there needs no better faculty of seeing, no finer understanding to see the folly of a life spent in making a man a possessor of ten towns before he dies.

For if when he has got all his towns, or all his boots, his soul is to go to its own place amongst separate spirits and his body be laid by in a coffin till the last trumpet calls him to judgment; where the inquiry will be, how humbly, how devoutly, how purely, how meekly, how piously, how charitably, how heavenly we have spoken, thought, and acted whilst we were in the body; how can we say that he who has worn out his life in raising a hundred thousand pounds has acted wiser for himself than he who has had the same care to procure a hundred thousand of anything else?

But further: Let it now be supposed that Negotius, when he

first entered into business, happening to read the gospel with attention and eyes open, found that he had a much greater business upon his hands than that to which he had served an apprenticeship, that there were things which belong to man of much more importance than all that our eyes can see, so glorious as to deserve all our thoughts, so dangerous as to need all our care, and so certain as never to deceive the faithful laborer.

Let it be supposed that from reading this book he had discovered that his soul was more to him than his body, that it was better to grow in the virtues of the soul than to have a large body or a full purse, that it was better to be fit for Heaven than to have variety of fine houses upon the earth, that it was better to secure an everlasting happiness than to have plenty of things which he cannot keep, better to live in habits of humility, piety, devotion, charity, and self-denial than to die unprepared for judgment, better to be most like our Savior or some eminent Saint than to excel all the tradesmen in the world in business and bulk of fortune.

Let it be supposed that Negotius believing these things to be true entirely devoted himself to God at his first setting out in the world, resolving to pursue his business no further than was consistent with great devotion, humility, and self-denial, and for no other ends but to provide himself with a sober subsistence, and to do all the good that he could to the souls and bodies of his fellow creatures.

Let it therefore be supposed that instead of the continual hurry of business he was frequent in his retirements and a strict observer of all the hours of prayer; that instead or restless desires after more riches, his soul had been full of the love of God and heavenly affection, constantly watching against worldly tempers, and always aspiring after divine grace; that instead of worldly cares and contrivances, he was busy in fortifying his soul against all approaches of sin; that instead of costly show and expensive generosity of a splendid life, he loved and exercised all instances of humility and lowliness; that instead of great treats and full tables, his house only furnished a sober refreshment to those that wanted it.

Let it be supposed that his contentment kept him free from all kinds of envy, that his piety made him thankful to God in all crosses and disappointments, that his charity kept him from being rich by a continual distribution to all objects of compassion.

Now had this been the Christian spirit of Negotius, can anyone say that he had lost the true joy and happiness of life by thus conforming to the spirit and living up to the hopes of the gospel?

Can it be said that a life made exemplary by such virtues as these which keep Heaven always in our sight, which both delight and exalt the soul here and prepare it for the presence of God hereafter, must be poor and dull if compared to that of heaping up riches which can neither stay with us, nor we with them?

It would be endless to multiply examples of this kind to show you how little is lost and how much is gained by introducing a strict and exact piety into every condition of human life.

I shall now therefore leave it to your own meditation to carry this way of thinking further, hoping that you are enough directed by what is here said to convince yourself that a true and exalted piety is so far from rendering any life dull and tiresome that it is the only joy and happiness of every condition in the world.

Imagine to yourself some person in a consumption or any other lingering distemper that was incurable.

If you was to see such a man wholly intent upon doing everything in the spirit of religion, making the wisest use of all his time, fortune, and abilities; if he was for carrying every duty of piety to its greatest height, and striving to have all the advantage that could be had from the remainder of his life; if he avoided all business but such as was necessary; if he was averse to all the follies and vanities of the world, had no taste for finery and show, but sought for all his comfort in the hopes and expectations of religion, you would certainly commend his prudence, you would say that he had taken the right method to make himself as joyful and happy as anyone can be in a state of such infirmity.

On the other hand, if you should see the same person with trembling hands, short breath, thin jaws, and hollow eyes wholly intent upon business and bargains as long as he could speak, if you should see him pleased with fine clothes when he could scarce stand to be dressed, and laying out his money in horses and dogs rather than purchase the prayers of the poor for his soul which was so soon to be separated from his body, you would certainly condemn him as a weak and silly man.

Now as it is easy to see the reasonableness, the wisdom and

happiness of a religious spirit in a consumptive man, so if you pursue the same way of thinking, you will as easily perceive the same wisdom and happiness of a pious temper in every other state of life.

For how soon will every man that is in health be in the state of him that is in a consumption? How soon will he want all the same comforts and satisfactions of religion which every dying man wants?

And if it be wise and happy to live piously because we have not above a year to live, is it not being more wise and making ourselves more happy because we may have more years to come? If one year of piety before we die is so desirable, is not more years of piety much more desirable?

If a man had five fixed years to live, he could not possibly think at all without intending to make the best use of them all. When he saw his stay so short in this world, he must needs think that this was not a world for him; and when he saw how near he was to another world that was eternal, he must surely think it very necessary to be very diligent in preparing himself for it.

Now as reasonable as piety appears in such a circumstance of life, it is yet more reasonable in every circumstance of life to every thinking man.

For who but a madman can reckon that he has five years certain to come?

And if it be reasonable and necessary to deny our worldly tempers and live wholly unto God because we are certain that we are to die at the end of five years, surely it must be much more reasonable and necessary for us to live in the same spirit because we have no certainty that we shall live five weeks.

Again, if we were to add twenty years to the five, which is in all probability more than will be added to the lives of many people who are at man's estate, what a poor thing is this! How small a difference is there between five and twenty-five years?

It is said that a day is with God as a thousand years, and a thousand years as one day because in regard to His eternity, this difference is as nothing.

Now as we are all created to be eternal, to live in an endless succession of ages upon ages, where thousands and millions of thousands of years will have no proportion to our everlasting life in

God, so with regard to this eternal state, which is our real state, twenty-five years is as poor a pittance as twenty-five days.

Now we can never make any true judgment of time as it relates to us without considering the true state of our duration. If we are temporary beings, then a little time may justly be called a great deal in relation to us; but if we are eternal beings, then the difference of a few years is as nothing.

If we were to suppose three different sorts of rational beings, all of different but fixed duration, one sort that lived certainly only a month, the other a year, and the third a hundred years, now if these beings were to meet together and talk about time, they must talk in a very different language; half an hour to those that were to live but a month must be a very different thing to what it is to those who are to live a hundred years.

As therefore time is thus different a thing with regard to the state of those who enjoy it, so if we would know what time is with regard to ourselves, we must consider our state.

Now since our eternal state is as certainly ours as our present state, since we are as certainly to live forever as we now live at all, it is plain that we cannot judge of the value of any particular time as to us, but by comparing it to that eternal duration for which we are created.

If you would know what five years signify to a being that was to live a hundred, you must compare five to a hundred and see what proportion it bears to it, and then you will judge right.

So if you would know what twenty years signify to a son of Adam, you must compare it not to a million of ages, but to an eternal duration to which no number of millions bears any proportion, and then you will judge right by finding it nothing.

Consider therefore this: How would you condemn the folly of a man that should lose his share of future glory for the sake of being rich, or great, or praised, or delighted in any enjoyment, only one poor day before he was to die!

But if the time will come when a number of years will seem less to everyone than a day does now, what a condemnation must it then be if eternal happiness should appear to be lost for something less than the enjoyment of a day!

Why does a day seem a trifle to us now? It is because we have years to set against it. It is the duration of years that makes it appear as nothing.

What a trifle therefore must the years of a man's age appear when they are forced to be set against eternity, when there shall be nothing but eternity to compare them with!

Now this will be the case of every man as soon as he is out of the body; he will be forced to forget the distinctions of days and years and to measure time, not by the course of the sun, but by setting it against eternity.

As the fixed stars by reason of our being placed at such distance from them appear but as so many points, so when we placed in eternity shall look back upon all time, it will all appear but as a moment.

Then a luxury, an indulgence, a prosperity, a greatness of fifty years will seem to everyone that looks back upon it as the same poor short enjoyment as if he had been snatched away in his first sin.

These few reflections upon time are only to show how poorly they think, how miserably they judge, who are less careful of an eternal state because they may be at some years' distance from it than they would be if they knew they were within a few weeks of it.

NOTES

31. Address: adroitness and comportment.
32. English Liturgy: that is, the Book of Common Prayer.
33. Tithes . . . livings: revenues derived from the parish.
34. Farmed about: contracted out.
35. Ring of bells: set of bells for the church tower.

Chapter 14

Concerning that part of devotion which relates to times and hours of prayer. Of daily early prayer in the morning. How we are to improve our forms of prayer, and how to increase the spirit of devotion.

Having in the foregoing chapters shown the necessity of a devout spirit or habit of mind in every part of our common life, in the discharge of all our business, in the use of all the gifts of God, I come now to consider that part of devotion which relates to times and hours of prayer.

I take it for granted that every Christian that is in health is up early in the morning; for it is much more reasonable to suppose a person up early because he is a Christian than because he is a laborer, or a tradesman, or a servant, or has business that wants him.

We naturally conceive some abhorrence of a man that is in bed when he should be at his labor or in his shop. We can't tell how to think anything good of him who is such a slave to drowsiness as to neglect his business for it.

Let this therefore teach us to conceive how odious we must appear in the sight of Heaven if we are in bed shut up in sleep and darkness, when we should be praising God, and are such slaves to drowsiness as to neglect our devotions for it.

For if he is to be blamed as a slothful drone that rather chooses the lazy indulgence of sleep than to perform his proper share of worldly business, how much more is he to be reproached that had rather lie folded up in a bed than be raising up his heart to God in acts of praise and adoration?

Prayer is the nearest approach to God and the highest enjoyment of Him that we are capable of in this life.

It is the noblest exercise of the soul, the most exalted use of our best faculties, and the highest imitation of the blessed inhabitants of Heaven.

When our hearts are full of God, sending up holy desires to the throne of grace, we are then in our highest state, we are upon the utmost heights of human greatness; we are not before kings and princes, but in the presence and audience of the Lord of all the world, and can be no higher till death is swallowed up in glory.

On the other hand, sleep is the poorest, dullest refreshment of the body that is so far from being intended as an enjoyment that we are forced to receive it either in a state of insensibility or in the folly of dreams.

Sleep is such a dull, stupid state of existence that even amongst mere animals we despise them most which are most drowsy.

He therefore that chooses to enlarge the slothful indulgence of sleep rather than be early at his devotions to God chooses the dullest refreshment of the body before the highest, noblest employment of the soul; he chooses that state which is a reproach to mere animals rather than that exercise which is the glory of angels.

You will perhaps say, though you rise late yet you are always careful of your devotions when you are up.

It may be so. But what then? Is it well done of you to rise late because you pray when you are up? Is it pardonable to waste great part of the day in bed because some time after you say your prayers?

It is as much your duty to rise to pray, as to pray when you are risen. And if you are late at your prayers, you offer to God the prayers of an idle, slothful worshipper that rises to prayer as idle servants rise to their labor.

Further, if you fancy that you are careful of your devotions when you are up though it be your custom to rise late, you deceive yourself, for you cannot perform your devotions as you ought. For he that cannot deny himself this drowsy indulgence but must pass away good part of the morning in it is no more prepared for prayer when he is up than he is prepared for fasting, abstinence, or any other self-denial. He may indeed more easily read over a form of prayer than he can perform these duties; but he is no more disposed to enter into the true spirit of prayer than he is disposed to fasting. For sleep thus indulged gives a softness and idleness to all our tempers, and makes us unable to relish anything but what suits with an idle state of mind and gratifies our natural tempers as sleep does. So that a person that is a slave to this idleness is in the same temper when he is up, and though he is not asleep yet he is under the effects of it; and everything that is idle, indulgent, or sensual pleases him for the same reason that sleep pleases him; and on the other hand, everything that requires care, or trouble, or self-denial is hateful to him for the same reason that he hates to rise. He that places any happiness in this morning indulgence would be glad to have all the day made happy in the same manner, though not with sleep yet with such enjoyments as gratify and indulge the body in the same manner that sleep does, or at least with such as come as near to it as they can. The remembrance of a warm bed is in his mind all the day, and he is glad when he is not one of those that sit starving in a church.

Now you don't imagine that such a one can truly mortify that body which he thus indulges; yet you might as well think this as that he can truly perform his devotions, or live in such a drowsy state of indulgence and yet relish the joys of a spiritual life.

For surely, no one will pretend to say that he knows and feels the true happiness of prayer who does not think it worth his while to be early at it.

It is not possible in nature for an epicure to be truly devout; he must renounce this habit of sensuality before he can relish the happiness of devotion.

Now he that turns sleep into an idle indulgence does as much to corrupt and disorder his soul, to make it a slave to bodily appetites and keep it incapable of all devout and heavenly tempers, as he that turns the necessities of eating into a course of indulgence.

A person that eats and drinks too much does not feel such effects from it as those do who live in notorious instances of gluttony and intemperance; but yet his course of indulgence, though it be not scandalous in the eyes of the world nor such as torments his own conscience, is a great and constant hindrance to his improvement in virtue; it gives him eyes that see not and ears that hear not; it creates a sensuality in the soul, increases the power of bodily passions, and makes him incapable of entering into the true spirit of religion.

Now this is the case of those who waste their time in sleep; it does not disorder their lives or wound their consciences as notorious acts of intemperance do; but like any other more moderate course of indulgence, it silently and by smaller degrees wears away the spirit of religion and sinks the soul into a state of dullness and sensuality.

If you consider devotion only as a time of so much prayer, you may perhaps perform it though you live in this daily indulgence. But if you consider it as a state of the heart, as a lively fervor of the soul that is deeply affected with a sense of its own misery and infirmities and desiring the Spirit of God more than all things in the world, you will find that the spirit of indulgence and the spirit of prayer cannot subsist together. Mortification of all kinds is the very life and soul of piety, but he that has not so small a degree of it as to be able to be early at his prayers can have no reason to think that he has taken up his cross and is following Christ.

What conquest has he got over himself? What right hand has he cut off? What trials is he prepared for? What sacrifice is he ready to offer unto God who cannot be so cruel to himself as to rise to prayer at such time as the drudging part of the world are content to rise to their labor?

Some people will not scruple to tell you that they indulge themselves in sleep because they have nothing to do, and that if they had either business or pleasure to rise to, they would not lose so much of their time in sleep. But such people must be told that they mistake the matter, that they have a great deal of business to do, they have a hardened heart to change, they have the whole spirit of religion to seek.

You must not therefore consider how small a crime it is to rise late, but you must consider how great a misery it is to want the spirit of religion, to have a heart not rightly affected with prayer, and to live in such softness and idleness as makes you incapable of the most fundamental duties of a truly Christian and spiritual life.

This is the right way of judging of the crime of wasting great part of your time in bed.

You must not consider the thing barely in itself but what it proceeds from, what virtues it shows to be wanting, what vices it naturally strengthens. For every habit of this kind discovers the state of the soul and plainly shows the whole turn of your mind.

If our blessed Lord used to pray early before day, if He spent whole nights in prayer, if the devout Anna was day and night in the temple, if St. Paul and Silas at midnight sang praises unto God, if the primitive Christians for several hundred years, besides their hours of prayer in the daytime, met publicly in the churches at midnight to join in Psalms and prayers, is it not certain that these practices showed the state of their heart? Are they not so many plain proofs of the whole turn of their minds?

And if you live in a contrary state, wasting great part of every day in sleep, thinking any time soon enough to be at your prayers, is it not equally certain that this practice as much shows the state of your heart and the whole turn of your mind?

So that if this indulgence is your way of life, you have as much reason to believe yourself destitute of the true spirit of devotion as you have to believe the Apostles and Saints of the primitive church were truly devout. For as their way of life was a demonstration of their devotion, so a contrary way of life is as strong a proof of a want of devotion.

When you read the scriptures, you see a religion that is all life and spirit and joy in God, that supposes our souls risen from earthly desires and bodily indulgences to prepare for another body, another world, and other enjoyments. You see Christians represented as temples of the Holy Ghost, as children of the day, as candidates for an eternal crown, as watchful virgins that have their lamps always burning in expectation of the bridegroom. But can he be thought to have this joy in God, this care of eternity, this watchful spirit, who has not zeal enough to rise to his prayers?

When you look into the writings and lives of the first Christians, you see the same spirit that you see in the scriptures. All is reality, life, and action. Watching and prayers, self-denial and mortification, was the common business of their lives.

From that time to this, there has been no person like them eminent for piety who has not like them been eminent for self-denial and mortification. This is the only royal way that leads to a kingdom.

But how far are you from this way of life, or rather how contrary to it, if instead of imitating their austerity and mortification, you can't so much as renounce so poor an indulgence as to be able to rise to your prayers? If self-denials and bodily sufferings, if watchings and fastings, will be marks of glory at the day of judgment, where must we hide our heads that have slumbered away our time in sloth and softness?

You perhaps now find some pretences to excuse yourself from that severity of fasting and self-denial which the first Christians practiced. You fancy that human nature is grown weaker and that the difference of climates may make it not possible for you to observe their methods of self-denial and austerity in these colder countries.

But all this is but pretence; for the change is not in the outward state of things but in the inward state of our minds. When there is the same spirit in us that there was in the Apostles and primitive Christians, when we feel the weight of religion as they did, when we have their faith and hope, we shall take up our cross and deny ourselves and live in such methods of mortification as they did.

Had St. Paul lived in a cold country, had he had a constitution made weak with a sickly stomach and often infirmities, he would have done as he advised Timothy, he would have mixed a little wine with his water.

But still he would have lived in a state of self-denial and mortification. He would have given this same account of himself: "I therefore so ran, not as uncertainly, so fight I, not as one that beateth the air; but I keep under my body, and bring it unto subjection, lest that by any means, when I have preached to others, I myself should be a castaway."

After all, let it now be supposed that you imagine there is no necessity for you to be so sober and vigilant, so fearful of yourself, so watchful over your passions, so apprehensive of danger, so careful of your salvation as the Apostles were. Let it be supposed that you imagine that you want less self-denial and mortification to subdue your bodies and purify your souls than they wanted, that you need not have your loins girt and your lamps burning as they had, will you therefore live in a quite contrary state? Will you make your life as constant a course of softness and indulgence as theirs was of strictness and self-denial?

If therefore you should think that you have time sufficient both for prayer and other duties though you rise late, yet let me persuade you to rise early as an instance of self-denial. It is so small a one that if you cannot comply with it, you have no reason to think yourself capable of any other.

If I was to desire you not to study the gratifications of your palate in the niceties of meats[36] and drinks, I would not insist much upon the crime of wasting your money in such a way, though it be a great one; but I would desire you to renounce such a way of life because it supports you in such a state of sensuality and indulgence as renders you incapable of relishing the most essential doctrines of religion.

For the same reason, I don't insist much on the crime of wasting so much of your time in sleep, though it be a great one; but I desire you to renounce this indulgence because it gives a softness and idleness to your soul, and is so contrary to that lively, zealous, watchful, self-denying spirit which was not only the Spirit of Christ and His Apostles, the spirit of all the Saints and martyrs which have ever been amongst men, but must be the spirit of all those who would not sink in the common corruption of the world.

Here therefore we must fix our charge against this practice; we must blame it not as having this or that particular evil, but as a general habit that extends itself through our whole spirit and supports a state of mind that is wholly wrong.

It is contrary to piety, not as accidental slips and mistakes in life are contrary to it, but in such a manner as an ill habit of body is contrary to health.

On the other hand, if you was to rise early every morning as an instance of self-denial, as a method of renouncing indulgence, as a means of redeeming your time and fitting your spirit for prayer, you would find mighty advantages from it. This method, though it seems such a small circumstance of life, would in all probability be a means of great piety. It would keep it constantly in your head that softness and idleness were to be avoided, that self-denial was a part of Christianity. It would teach you to exercise power over yourself and make you able by degrees to renounce other pleasures and tempers that war against the soul.

This one rule would teach you to think of others; it would dispose your mind to exactness, and be very likely to bring the remaining part of the day under rules of prudence and devotion.

But above all, one certain benefit from this method you will be sure of having; it will best fit and prepare you for the reception of the Holy Spirit. When you thus begin the day in the spirit of religion, renouncing sleep because you are to renounce softness and redeem your time, this disposition, as it puts your heart into a good state, so it will procure the assistance of the Holy Spirit; what is so planted and watered will certainly have an increase from God. You will then speak from your heart, your soul will be awake, your prayers will refresh you like meat and drink, you will feel what you say and begin to know what Saints and holy men have meant by fervors of devotion.

He that is thus prepared for prayer, who rises with these dispositions, is in a very different state from him who has no rules of this kind, who rises by chance as he happens to be weary of his bed, or is able to sleep no longer. If such a one prays only with his mouth, if his heart feels nothing of that which he says, if his prayers are only things of course, if they are a lifeless form of words which he only repeats because they are soon said, there is nothing to be wondered at in all this; for such dispositions are the natural effect of such a state of life.

Hoping therefore that you are now enough convinced of the necessity of rising early to your prayers, I shall proceed to lay before you a method of daily prayer.

I don't take upon me to prescribe to you the use of any particular forms of prayer, but only to show you the necessity of praying at such times, and in such a manner.

You will here find some helps how to furnish yourself with such forms of prayer as shall be useful to you. And if you are such a proficient in the spirit of devotion that your heart is always ready to pray in its own language, in this case I press no necessity of borrowed forms.

For though I think a form of prayer very necessary and expedient for public worship, yet if anyone can find a better way of raising his heart unto God in private than by prepared forms of prayer, I have nothing to object against it, my design being only to assist and direct such as stand in need of assistance.

Thus much, I believe, is certain, that the generality of Christians ought to use forms of prayer at all the regular times of prayer. It seems right for everyone to begin with a form of prayer; and if in the midst of his devotions he finds his heart ready to break forth into new and higher strains of devotion, he should leave his form for a while and follow those fervors of his heart till it again wants the assistance of his usual petitions.

This seems to be the true liberty of private devotion; it should be under the direction of some form but not so tied down to it but that it may be free to take such new expressions as its present fervors happen to furnish it with, which sometimes are more affecting and carry the soul more powerfully to God than any expressions that were ever used before.

All people that have ever made any reflections upon what passes in their own hearts must know that they are mighty changeable in regard to devotion. Sometimes our hearts are so awakened, have such strong apprehensions of the divine presence, are so full of deep compunction for our sins, that we cannot confess them in any language but that of tears.

Sometimes the light of God's countenance shines so bright upon us, we see so far into the invisible world, we are so affected with the wonders of the love and goodness of God that our hearts worship and adore in a language higher than that of words, and we feel transports of devotion which only can be felt.

On the other hand, sometimes we are so sunk into our bodies, so dull and unaffected with that which concerns our souls, that our hearts are as much too low for our prayers; we cannot keep pace with our forms of confession, or feel half of that in our hearts which we have in our mouths; we thank and praise God with forms of words, but our hearts have little or no share in them.

It is therefore highly necessary to provide against this inconstancy of our hearts by having at hand such forms of prayer as may best suit us when our hearts are in their best state, and also be most likely to raise and stir them up when they are sunk into dullness. For as words have a power of affecting our hearts on all occasions, as the same thing differently expressed has different effects upon our minds, so it is reasonable that we should make this advantage of language and provide ourselves with such forms of expressions as are most likely to move and enliven our souls and fill them with sentiments suitable to them.

The first thing that you are to do when you are upon your knees is to shut your eyes and with a short silence let your soul place itself in the presence of God; that is, you are to use this or some other better method to separate yourself from all common thoughts and make your heart as sensible as you can of the divine presence.

Now if this recollection of spirit is necessary, as who can say it is not, then how poorly must they perform their devotions who are always in a hurry, who begin them in haste, and hardly allow themselves time to repeat their very form with any gravity or attention? Theirs is properly saying prayers instead of praying.

To proceed: If you was to use yourself (as far as you can) to pray always in the same place, if you was to reserve that place for devotion and not allow yourself to do anything common in it, if you was never to be there yourself but in times of devotion, if any little room, or, if that cannot be, if any particular part of a room was thus used, this kind of consecration of it as a place holy unto God would have an effect upon your mind and dispose you to such tempers as would very much assist your devotion. For by having a place thus sacred in your room, it would in some measure resemble a chapel or house of God. This would dispose you to be always in the spirit of religion when you was there, and fill you with wise and holy thoughts when you was by yourself. Your own apartment would raise in your mind such sentiments as you have when you stand near an altar, and you would be afraid of thinking or doing anything that was foolish near that place which is the place of prayer and holy intercourse with God.

When you begin your petitions, use such various expressions of the attributes of God as may make you most sensible of the greatness and power of the divine nature.

Begin therefore in words like these: "O Being of all beings, Fountain of all light and glory, gracious Father of men and angels, whose universal Spirit is everywhere present giving life, and light, and joy to all angels in heaven, and all creatures upon earth," etc.

For these representations of the divine attributes which show us in some degree the majesty and greatness of God are an excellent means of raising our hearts into lively acts of worship and adoration.

What is the reason that most people are so much affected with this petition in the Burial Service of our church, "Yet, O Lord God most holy, O Lord most mighty, O holy and most merciful Savior, deliver us not into the bitter pains of eternal death"? It is because the joining together so many great expressions gives such a description of the greatness of the divine majesty as naturally affects every sensible mind.

Although, therefore, prayer does not consist in fine words or studied expressions, yet as words speak to the soul, as they have a certain power of raising thoughts in the soul, so those words which speak of God in the highest manner, which most fully express the power and presence of God, which raise thoughts in the soul most suitable to the greatness and providence of God, are the most useful and most edifying in our prayers.

When you direct any of your petitions to our blessed Lord, let it be in some expressions of this kind: "O Savior of the world, God of God, Light of Light, Thou that art the Brightness of Thy Father's Glory and the express Image of His Person, Thou that art the Alpha and Omega, the Beginning and End of all things, Thou that hast destroyed the power of the Devil, that hast overcome death, Thou that art entered into the Holy of Holies, that sittest at the right hand of the Father, that art high above all thrones and principalities, that makest intercession for all the world, Thou that art the Judge of the quick and dead, Thou that wilt speedily come down in Thy Father's glory to reward all men according to their works, be Thou my light and my peace," etc.

For such representations, which describe so many characters of our Savior's nature and power, are not only proper acts of adoration but will, if they are repeated with any attention, fill our hearts with the highest fervors of true devotion.

Again, if you ask any particular grace of our blessed Lord, let it be in some manner like this:

"O holy Jesus, Son of the most high God, Thou that wast scourged at a pillar, stretched and nailed upon a cross for the sins of the world, unite me to Thy cross, and fill my soul with Thy holy, humble, and suffering spirit. O Fountain of mercy, Thou that didst save the thief upon the cross, save me from the guilt of a sinful life; Thou that didst cast seven devils out of Mary Magdalene, cast out of my heart all evil thoughts and wicked tempers. O Giver of life, Thou that didst raise Lazarus from the dead, raise up my soul from the death and darkness of sin. Thou that didst give to Thy Apostles power over unclean spirits, give me power over my own heart. Thou that didst appear unto Thy Disciples when the doors were shut, do Thou appear unto me in the secret apartment of my heart. Thou that didst cleanse the lepers, heal the sick, and give sight to the blind, cleanse my heart, heal the disorders of my soul, and fill me with heavenly light."

Now these kind of appeals have a double advantage. First, as they are so many proper acts of our faith whereby we not only show our belief of the miracles of Christ, but turn them at the same time into so many instances of worship and adoration.

Secondly, as they strengthen and increase the faith of our prayers by presenting to our minds so many instances of that power and goodness which we call upon for our own assistance.

Again, in order to fill your prayers with excellent strains of devotion, it may be of use to you to observe this further rule:

When at any time, either in reading the scripture or any book of piety, you meet with a passage that more than ordinarily affects your mind and seems as it were to give your heart a new motion toward God, you should try to turn it into the form of a petition, and then give it a place in your prayers.

By this means, you would be often improving your prayers and storing yourself with proper forms of making the desires of your heart unto God.

At all the stated hours of prayer, it will be of great benefit to you to have something fixed and something at liberty in your devotions.

You should have some fixed subject which is constantly to be the chief matter of your prayer at that particular time, and yet have liberty to add such other petitions as your condition may then require.

For instance, as the morning is to you the beginning of a new life, as God has then given you a new enjoyment of yourself and a fresh entrance into the world, it is highly proper that your first devotions should be a praise and thanksgiving to God, as for a new creation; and that you should offer and devote body and soul, all that you are and all that you have, to His service and glory.

Receive therefore every day as a resurrection from death, as a new enjoyment of life; meet every rising sun with such sentiments of God's goodness as if you had seen it and all things new created upon your account; and under the sense of so great a blessing, let your joyful heart praise and magnify so good and glorious a Creator.

Let therefore praise and thanksgiving and oblation of yourself unto God be always the fixed and certain subject of your first prayers in the morning, and then take the liberty of adding such other devotions as the accidental difference of your state or the accidental difference of your heart shall then make most needful and expedient for you.

For one of the greatest benefits of private devotion consists in rightly adapting our prayers to these two conditions, the difference of our state, and the difference of our hearts.

By the difference of our state is meant the difference of our external state or condition as of sickness, health, pains, losses, disappointments, troubles, particular mercies or judgments from God, all sorts of kindnesses, injuries or reproaches from other people.

Now as these are great parts of our state of life, as they make great difference in it by continually changing, so our devotion will be made doubly beneficial to us when it watches to receive and sanctify all these changes of our state and turns them all into so many occasions of a more particular application to God of such thanksgivings, such resignation, such petitions, as our present state more especially requires.

And he that makes every change in his state a reason of presenting unto God some particular petitions suitable to that change will soon find that he has taken an excellent means not only of praying with fervor, but of living as he prays.

The next condition to which we are always to adapt some part of our prayers is the difference of our hearts, by which is meant the different state of the tempers of our hearts, as of love, joy, peace, tranquillity, dullness and dryness of spirit, anxiety, discontent, motions of envy and ambition, dark and disconsolate thoughts, resentments, fretfulness, and peevish tempers.

Now as these tempers through the weakness of our nature will have their succession more or less even in pious minds, so we should constantly make the present state of our heart the reason of some particular application to God.

If we are in the delightful calm of sweet and easy passions, of love and joy in God, we should then offer the grateful tribute of thanksgiving to God for the possession of so much happiness, thankfully owning and acknowleding Him as the bountiful giver of it all.

If on the other hand we feel ourselves laden with heavy passions, with dullness of spirit, anxiety, and uneasiness, we must then look up to God in acts of humility, confessing our unworthiness, opening our troubles to Him, beseeching Him in His good time to lessen the weight of our infirmities, and to deliver us from such passions as oppose the purity and perfection of our souls.

Now by thus watching and attending to the present state of our hearts and suiting some of our petitions exactly to their wants, we shall not only be well acquainted with the disorders of our souls, but also be well exercised in the method of curing them.

By this prudent and wise application of our prayers, we shall get all the relief from them that is possible; and the very changeableness of our hearts will prove a means of exercising a greater variety of holy tempers.

Now by all that has here been said you will easily perceive that persons careful of the greatest benefit of prayer ought to have a great share in the forming and composing their own devotions.

As to that part of their prayers which is always fixed to one certain subject, in that they may use the help of forms composed by other persons, but in that part of their prayers which they are always to suit to the present state of their life and the present state of their heart, there they must let the sense of their own condition help them to such kinds of petition, thanksgiving, or resignation as their present state more especially requires.

Happy are they who have this business and employment upon their hands!

And now, if people of leisure, whether men or women, who are so much at a loss how to dispose of their time, who are forced into poor contrivances, idle visits, and ridiculous diversions merely to get rid of hours that hang heavily upon their hands, if such were to appoint some certain spaces of their time to the study of devotion, searching after all the means and helps to attain a devout spirit, if they were to collect the best forms of devotion, to use themselves to transcribe the finest passages of scripture prayers, if they were to collect the devotions, confessions, petitions, praises, resignations, and thanksgivings which are scattered up and down in the Psalms and range them under proper heads as so much proper fuel for the flame of their own devotion, if their minds were often thus employed, sometimes meditating upon them, sometimes getting them by heart and making them as habitual as their own thoughts, how fervently would they pray who came thus prepared to prayer?

And how much better would it be to make this benefit of leisure time than to be dully and idly lost in the poor impertinencies of a playing, visiting, wandering life?

How much better would it be to be thus furnished with hymns and anthems of the Saints, and teach their souls to ascend to God than to corrupt, bewilder, and confound their hearts with the wild fancies, the lustful thoughts of lewd poets?

Now though people of leisure seem called more particularly to this study of devotion, yet persons of much business or labor must not think themselves excused from this or some better method of improving their devotion.

For the greater their business is, the more need they have of some such method as this to prevent its power over their hearts, to secure them from sinking into worldly tempers and preserve a sense and taste of heavenly things in their minds. And a little time regularly and constantly employed to any one use or end will do great things and produce mighty effects.

And it is for want of considering devotion in this light, as something that is to be nursed and cherished with care, as something that is to be made part of our business, that is to be improved with care and contrivance, by art and method and a diligent use of the best helps; it is for want of considering it in this light that so many people are so little benefited by it and live and die strangers to that spirit of devotion which by a prudent use of proper means they might have enjoyed in a high degree.

For though the spirit of devotion is the gift of God and not attainable by any mere power of our own, yet is it mostly given and never withheld from those who, by a wise and diligent use of proper means, prepare themselves for the reception of it.

And it is amazing to see how eagerly men employ their parts,[37] their sagacity, time, study, application, and exercise, how all helps are called to their assistance when anything is intended and desired in worldly matters, and how dull, negligent, and unimproved they are, how little they use their parts, sagacity, and abilities to raise and increase their devotion!

Mundanus is a man of excellent parts and clear apprehension. He is well advanced in age, and has made a great figure in business. Every part of trade and business that has fallen in his way has had some improvement from him, and he is always contriving to carry every method of doing anything well to its greatest height. Mundanus aims at the greatest perfection in everything. The soundness and strength of his mind and his just way of thinking upon things makes him intent upon removing all imperfections.

He can tell you all the defects and errors in all the common methods whether of trade, building, or improving land, or manufactures. The clearness and strength of his understanding, which he is constantly improving by continual exercise in these matters by often digesting his thoughts in writing and trying everything every way, has rendered him a great master of most concerns in human life.

Thus has Mundanus gone on, increasing his knowledge and judgment, as fast as his years came upon him.

The one only thing which has not fallen under his improvement, nor received any benefit from his judicious mind, is his devotion. This is just in the same poor state it was when he was only six years of age; and the old man prays now in that little form of words which his mother used to hear him repeat night and morning.

This Mundanus, that hardly ever saw the poorest utensil or ever took the meanest trifle into his hand without considering how it might be made or used to better advantage, has gone all his life long praying in the same manner as when he was a child without ever considering how much better or oftener he might pray, without considering how improvable the spirit of devotion is, how many helps a wise and reasonable man may call to his assistance, and how necessary it is that our prayers should be enlarged, varied, and suited to the particular state and condition of our lives.

If Mundanus sees a book of devotion, he passes it by as he does a spelling book because he remembers that he learned to pray so many years ago under his mother when he learnt to spell.

Now how poor and pitiable is the conduct of this man of sense who has so much judgment and understanding in everything, but that which is the whole wisdom of man?

And how miserably do many people more or less imitate this conduct?

All which seems to be owing to a strange infatuated state of negligence which keeps people from considering what devotion is. For if they did but once proceed so far as to reflect about it, or ask themselves any questions concerning it, they would soon see that the spirit of devotion was like any other sense or understanding that is only to be improved by study, care, application, and the use of such means and helps as are necessary to make a man a proficient in any art or science.

Classicus is a man of learning and well versed in all the best authors of antiquity. He has read them so much that he has entered into their spirit and can very ingeniously imitate the manner of any of them. All their thoughts are his thoughts, and he can express himself in their language. He is so great a friend to this improvement of the mind that if he lights of† a young scholar, he never fails to advise him concerning his studies.

Classicus tells his young man he must not think that he has done enough when he has only learnt languages, but that he must be daily conversant with the best authors, read them again and again, catch their spirit by living with them, and that there is no other way of becoming like them, or of making himself a man of taste and judgment.

How wise might Classicus have been and how much good might he have done in the world if he had but thought as justly of devotion as he does of learning?

He never, indeed, says anything shocking or offensive about devotion because he never thinks or talks about it. It suffers nothing from him but neglect and disregard.

The two Testaments would not have had so much as a place

---

†Lights of: chances upon or meets

amongst his books but that they are both to be had in Greek.

Classicus thinks that he sufficiently shows his regard for the holy scripture when he tells you that he has no other books of piety besides them.

It is very well, Classicus, that you prefer the Bible to all other books of piety; he has no judgment that is not thus far of your opinion.

But if you will have no other book of piety besides the Bible because it is the best, how comes it, Classicus, that you don't content yourself with one of the best books amongst the Greeks and Romans? How comes it that you are so greedy and eager after all of them? How comes it that you think the knowledge of one is a necessary help to the knowledge of the other? How comes it that you are so earnest, so laborious, so expensive of your time and money to restore broken periods and scraps of the ancients?

How comes it that you read so many commentators upon Cicero, Horace, and Homer, and not one upon the gospel? How comes it that you love to read a man? How comes it[38] that your love of Cicero and Ovid makes you love to read an author that writes like them, and yet your esteem for the gospel gives you no desire, nay, prevents your reading such books as breathe the very spirit of the gospel?

How comes it that you tell your young scholar he must not content himself with barely understanding his authors, but must be continually reading them all as the only means of entering into their spirit and forming his own judgment according to them?

Why then must the Bible lie alone in your study? Is not the spirit of the Saints, the piety of the holy followers of Jesus Christ, as good and necessary a means of entering into the spirit and taste of the gospel as the reading of the ancients is of entering into the spirit of antiquity?

Is the spirit of poetry only to be got by much reading of poets and orators? And is not the spirit of devotion to be got in the same way, by frequent reading the holy thoughts and pious strains of devout men?

Is your young poet to search after every line that may give new wings to his fancy or direct his imagination? And is it not as reasonable for him who desires to improve in the divine life, that is, in the heavenly things, to search after every strain of devotion that may move, kindle, and inflame the holy ardor of his soul?

Do you advise your orator to translate the best orations, to commit much of them to memory, to be frequently exercising his talent in this manner that habits of thinking and speaking justly may be formed in his mind? And is there not the same benefit and advantage to be made by books of devotion? Should not a man use them in the same way, that habits of devotion and aspiring to God in holy thoughts may be well formed in his soul?

Now the reason why Classicus does not think and judge thus reasonably of devotion is owing to his never thinking of it in any other manner than as the repeating a form of words. It never in his life entered into his head to think of devotion as a state of the heart, as an improvable talent of the mind, as a temper that is to grow and increase like our reason and judgment, and to be formed in us by such a regular diligent use of proper means as are necessary to form any other wise habit of mind.

And it is for want of this that he has been content all his life with the bare letter of prayer and eagerly bent upon entering into the spirit of heathen poets and orators.

And it is much to be lamented that numbers of scholars are more or less chargeable with this excessive folly, so negligent of improving their devotion and so desirous of other poor accomplishments as if they thought it a nobler talent to be able to write an epigram in the turn of Martial than to live and think and pray to God in the spirit of St. Austin.

And yet to correct this temper and fill a man with a quite contrary spirit, there seems to be no more required than the bare belief of the truth of Christianity.

And if you was to ask Mundanus and Classicus or any man of business or learning whether piety is not the highest perfection of man, or devotion the greatest attainment in the world, they must both be forced to answer in the affirmative or else give up the truth of the gospel.

For to set any accomplishment against devotion, or to think anything or all things in the world bear any proportion to its excellency, is the same absurdity in a Christian as it would be in a philosopher to prefer a meal's meat to the greatest improvement in knowledge.

For as philosophy professes purely the search and inquiry after knowledge, so Christianity supposes, intends, desires, and aims at nothing else but the raising fallen man to a divine life, to such habits of holiness, such degrees of devotion as may fit him to enter amongst the holy inhabitants of the Kingdom of Heaven.

He that does not believe this of Christianity may be reckoned an infidel, and he that believes thus much has faith enough to give him a right judgment of the value of things to support him in a sound mind and enable him to conquer all the temptations which the world shall lay in his way.

To conclude this chapter. Devotion is nothing else but right apprehensions and right affections toward God.

All practices therefore that heighten and improve our true apprehensions of God, all ways of life that tend to nourish, raise, and fix our affections upon him, are to be reckoned so many helps and means to fill us with devotion.

As prayer is the proper fuel of this holy flame, so we must use all our care and contrivance to give prayer its full power, as by alms, self-denial, frequent retirements and holy readings, composing forms for ourselves or using the best we can get, adding length of time and observing hours of prayer, changing, improving, and suiting our devotions to the condition of our lives and the state of our hearts.

Those who have most leisure seem more especially called to a more eminent observance of these holy rules of a devout life. And they who by the necessity of their state and not through their own choice have but little time to employ thus must make the best use of that little they have.

For this is the certain way of making devotion produce a devout life.

NOTES

36. Meats: foods, generally.
37. Parts: wits, intellectual ability.
38. That you love to read a man? How comes it] the 3nd ed. omits.

Chapter 15

Of chanting or singing of Psalms in our private devotions. Of the excellency and benefit of this kind of devotion. Of the great effects in hath upon our hearts. Of the means of performing it in the best manner.

You have seen in the foregoing chapter what means and methods you are to use to raise and improve your devotion, how early you are to begin your prayers and what is to be the subject of your first devotions in the morning.

There is one thing still remaining that you must be required to observe not only as fit and proper to be done, but as such as cannot be neglected without great prejudice to your devotions. And that is to begin all your prayers with a Psalm.

This is so right, is so beneficial to devotion, has so much effect upon our hearts, that it may be insisted upon as a common rule for all persons.

I don't mean that you should read over a Psalm, but that you should chant or sing one of those Psalms which we commonly call the reading Psalms. For singing is as much the proper use of a Psalm as devout supplication is the proper use of a form of prayer. And a Psalm only read is very much like a prayer that is only looked over.

Now the method of chanting a Psalm such as is used in the colleges in the universities and in some churches is such as all persons are capable of. The change of the voice in thus chanting of a Psalm is so small and natural that everybody is able to do it, and yet sufficient to raise and keep up the gladness of our hearts.

You are therefore to consider this chanting of a Psalm as a necessary beginning of your devotions, as something that is to awaken all that is good and holy within you, that is to call your spirits to their proper duty, to set you in your best posture toward heaven, and tune all the powers of your soul to worship and adoration.

For there is nothing that so clears a way for your prayers, nothing that so disperses dullness of heart, nothing that so purifies the soul from poor and little passions, nothing that so opens heaven or carries your heart so near it as these songs of praise.

They create a sense and delight in God, they awaken holy desires, they teach you how to ask, and they prevail with God to give. They kindle a holy flame, they turn your heart into an altar, your prayers into incense, and carry them as a sweet-smelling savor to the throne of grace.

The difference between singing and reading a Psalm will easily be understood if you consider the difference between reading and singing a common song that you like. Whilst you only read it, you only like it, and that is all; but as soon as you sing it, then you enjoy it, you feel the delight of it, it has got hold of you, your passions keep pace with it, and you feel the same spirit within you that there seems to be in the words.

If you was to tell a person that has such a song that he need not sing it, that it was sufficient to peruse it, he would wonder what you mean and would think you as absurd as if you was to tell him that he should only look at his food, to see whether it was good but need not eat it; for a song of praise not sung is very like any other good thing not made use of.

You will perhaps say that singing is a particular talent that belongs only to particular people, and that you have neither voice nor ear to make any music.

If you had said that singing is a general talent and that people differ in that as they do in all other things, you had said something much truer.

For how vastly do people differ in the talent of thinking, which is not only common to all men but seems to be the very essence of human nature? How readily do some people reason upon everything, and how hardly do others reason upon anything? How clearly do some people discourse upon the most abstruse matters, and how confusedly do others talk upon the plainest subjects?

Yet no one desires to be excused from thought, or reason, or discourse because he has not these talents as some people have them.

But it is full as just for a person to think himself excused from thinking upon God, from reasoning about his duty to Him, or discoursing about the means of salvation because he has not these talents in any fine degree; this is full as just as for a person to think himself excused from singing the praises of God because he has not a fine ear or a musical voice.

For as it is speaking, and not graceful speaking, that is a required part of prayer, as it is bowing, and not genteel bowing, that is a proper part of adoration, so it is singing, and not artful fine singing that is a required way of praising God.

If a person was to forbear praying because he had an odd tone in his voice, he would have as good an excuse as he has that forbears from singing Psalms because he has but little management of his voice. And as a man's speaking his prayers though in an odd tone may yet sufficiently answer all the ends of his own devotion, so a man's singing of a Psalm though not in a very musical way may yet sufficiently answer all the ends of rejoicing in and praising God.

Secondly, this objection might be of some weight if you was desired to sing to entertain other people, but is not to be admitted in the present case where you are only required to sing the praises of God as a part of your own private devotion.

If a person that has a very ill voice and a bad way of speaking was desired to be the mouth of a congregation, it would be a very proper excuse for him to say that he had not a voice or a way of speaking that was proper for prayer. But he would be very absurd if for the same reason he should neglect his own private devotions.

Now this is exactly the case of singing Psalms; you may not have the talent of singing so as to be able to entertain other people, and therefore it is reasonable to excuse yourself from it; but if for that reason you should excuse yourself from this way of praising God, you would be guilty of a great absurdity, because singing is no more required for the music that is made by it than prayer is required for the fine words that it contains, but as it is the natural and proper expression of a heart rejoicing in God.

Our blessed Savior and His Apostles sung a hymn; but it may reasonably be supposed that they rather rejoiced in God than made fine music.

Do but so live that your heart may truly rejoice in God, that it may feel itself affected with the praises of God, and then you will find that this state of your heart will neither want a voice nor ear to find a tune for a Psalm. Everyone at some time or other finds himself able to sing in some degree; there are some times and occasions of joy that make all people ready to express their sense of it in some sort of harmony. The joy that they feel forces them to let their voice have a part in it.

He therefore that saith he wants a voice or an ear to sing a Psalm mistakes the case; he wants that spirit that really rejoices in God; the dullness is in his heart and not in his ear; and when his heart feels a true joy in God, when it has a full relish of what is expressed in the Psalms, he will find it very pleasant to make the motions of his voice express the motions of his heart.

Singing, indeed, as it is improved into an art, as it signifies the running of the voice through such or such a compass of notes and keeping time with a studied variety of changes, is not natural nor the effect of any natural state of the mind, so in this sense it is not common to all people, any more than those antic and invented motions which make fine dancing are common to all people.

But singing, as it signifies a motion of the voice suitable to the motions of the heart and the changing of its tone according to the meaning of the words which we utter, is as natural and common to all men as it is to speak high when they threaten in anger, or to speak low when they are dejected and ask for a pardon.

All men therefore are singers in the same manner as all men think, speak, laugh, and lament. For singing is no more an invention than grief or joy are inventions.

Every state of the heart naturally puts the body into some state that is suitable to it and is proper to show it to other people. If a man is angry or disdainful, no one need instruct him how to express these passions by the tone of his voice. The state of his heart disposes him to a proper use of his voice.

If therefore there are but few singers of divine songs, if people want to be exhorted to this part of devotion, it is because there are but few whose hearts are raised to that height of piety as to feel any motions of joy and delight in the praises of God.

Imagine to yourself that you had been with Moses when he was led through the Red Sea, that you had seen the waters divide themselves and stand on a heap on both sides, that you had seen them held up till you had passed through, then let fall upon your enemies. Do you think that you should then have wanted a voice or an ear to have sung with Moses, "The Lord is my strength, and my song, and he is become my salvation," etc.? I know, your own heart tells you, that all people must have been singers upon such an occasion. Let this therefore teach you that it is the heart that tunes a voice to sing the praises of God, and that if you can't sing these same words now with joy, it is because you are not so affected with the salvation of the world by Jesus Christ as the Jews were, or you yourself would have been with their deliverance at the Red Sea.

That it is the state of the heart that disposes us to rejoice in any particular kind of singing may be easily proved from variety of observations upon human nature. An old debauchee may, according to the language of the world, have neither voice nor ear if you only sing a Psalm or a song in praise of virtue to him; but yet if in some easy tune you sing something that celebrates his former debauches, he will then, though he has no teeth in his head, show you that he has both a voice and an ear to join in such music. You then awaken his heart and he as naturally sings to such words as he laughs when he is pleased. And this will be the case in every song that touches the heart; if you celebrate the ruling passion of any man's heart, you put his voice in tune to join with you.

Thus if you can find a man whose ruling temper is devotion, whose heart is full of God, his voice will rejoice in those songs of praise which glorify that God that is the joy of his heart, though he has neither voice nor ear for other music. Would you therefore delightfully perform this part of devotion, it is not so necessary to learn a tune or practice upon notes as to prepare your heart; for as our blessed Lord saith, out of the heart proceed evil thoughts, murders, etc., so it is equally true that out of the heart proceed holy joys, thanksgiving, and praise. If you can once say with David, "My heart is fixed, O God, my heart is fixed," it will be very easy and natural to add, as he did, "I will sing and give praise," etc.

Secondly, let us now consider another reason for this kind of devotion. As singing is a natural effect of joy in the heart, so it has also a natural power of rendering the heart joyful.

The soul and body are so united that they have each of them

power over one another in their actions. Certain thoughts and sentiments in the soul produce such and such motions or actions in the body; and on the other hand, certain motions and actions of the body have the same power of raising such and such thoughts and sentiments in the soul. So that as singing is the natural effect of joy in the mind, so it is as truly a natural cause of raising joy in the mind.

As devotion of the heart naturally breaks out into outward acts of prayer, so outward acts of prayer are natural means of raising the devotion of the heart.

It is thus in all states and tempers of the mind. As the inward state of the mind produces outward actions suitable to it, so those outward actions have the like power of raising an inward state of mind suitable to them.

As anger produces angry words, so angry words increase anger.

So that if we barely consider human nature, we shall find that singing or chanting the Psalms is as proper and necessary to raise our hearts to a delight in God as prayer is proper and necessary to excite in us the spirit of devotion. Every reason for one is in all respects as strong a reason for the other.

If therefore you would know the reason and necessity of singing Psalms, you must consider the reason and necessity of praising and rejoicing in God because singing of Psalms is as much the true exercise and support of this spirit of thanksgiving as prayer is the true exercise and support of the spirit of devotion. And you may as well think that you can be devout as you ought without the use of prayer as that you can rejoice in God as you ought without the practice of singing of Psalms. Because this singing is as much the natural language of praise and thanksgiving as prayer is the natural language of devotion.

The union of soul and body is not a mixture of their substances as we see bodies united and mixed together but consists solely in the mutual power that they have of acting upon one another.

If two persons were in such a state of dependence upon one another that neither of them could act, or move, or think, or feel, or suffer, or desire anything without putting the other into the same condition, one might properly say that they were in a state of strict union although their substances were not united together.

Now this is the union of the soul and body; the substance of the

ERRATA

Some of the notes in this edition are incorrect. They are listed below in correct form:

A SERIOUS CALL TO A DEVOUT AND HOLY LIFE

13. Innocency: innocence, an older form of the word.
59. Significancy: significance, as on p. 139. Cf. Law's use of innocency (p. 80 and p. 103), indifferency (p. 226), and excellency (p. 249).

THE SPIRIT OF LOVE

1. See *Spirit of Love*. Second Part, p. 177 (Law's note).
4. See *Spirit of Love*. Second Part, p. 60 (Law's note).
9. Law lumps together these rationalist thinkers, ignoring their differences; but he means to object to that theory, particularly espoused by Locke, which maintained that the human mind at birth is a blank tablet (or tabula rasa) upon which ideas and experiences are subsequently imprinted. There can thus be no sure and undeviating metaphysical position for those who lack a knowledge of the "ground of nature" (a traditional mystical term for the place in the soul that has special contact with God). Cf. Theophilus's discussion of the Ten Commandments as "an outward imitation of that which was inwardly in man" (p. 406, below), by which he implies the theory of innate ideas which Locke denied.
10. Seven properties of nature: see the Introduction, p. 371 and Law's explanation that follows.
11. See *The Way to Divine Knowledge*, p. 196 (Law's note). Vulgar: common or ordinary.
14. Law particularly answered the Deists in some of earlier and polemical works. See the Introduction, p. 366 and p. 382, below.
16. See *The Spirit of Love*, Second Part, p. 53 (Law's note).
17. Law is referring to his *An Appeal To all that Doubt, or Disbelieve The Truths of the Gospel, whether They Be Deists, Arians, Socinians, Or Nominal Christians* (1740), and to his other works with a common theme, such as *A Demonstration of the Gross and Fundamental Errors of a late Book, called A Plain Account of the Nature and End of the Sacrament of the Lord's Supper* (1737); *The Grounds and Reason of Christian Regeneration* (1739); *The Spirit of Prayer* (1749), referred to below (p. 394).
27. See *Way to Divine Knowledge*, p. 200 to the end; *Spirit of Love*, First Part, p. 21 to the end (Law's note).
28. According to your name: "Theogenes" is a Greek name signifying "born of God," while Theophilus means "lover of God," and Eusebius, the third participant in these holy conversations means "one who is reverent and pious." This last figure appears also in *A Serious Call*, the name as well of the great ecclesiastical historian and scholar (c. 260-c. 340) whom Law quotes (see above, p. 130).
37. Earthy: As above (cf. p. 377 and n. 15), Law uses "earthy" to express the state of being bound to, contained within, and made up by the element earth.
41. See *Way To Divine Knowledge*, p. 199, etc.; *Spirit of Love*, p. 21, etc. (Law's note).

exercise our souls, but we must practice and exercise our bodies to all such outward actions as are conformable to these inward tempers.

If we would truly prostrate our souls before God, we must use our bodies to postures of lowliness; if we desire true fervors of devotion, we must make prayer the frequent labor of our lips. If we would banish all pride and passion from our hearts, we must force ourselves to all outward actions of patience and meekness. If we would feel inward motions of joy and delight in God, we must practice all the outward acts of it and make our voices call upon our hearts.

Now therefore, you may plainly see the reason and necessity of singing of Psalms; it is because outward actions are necessary to support inward tempers, and therefore the outward act of joy is necessary to raise and support the inward joy of the mind.

If any people were to leave off prayer because they seldom find the motions of their hearts answering the words which they speak, you would charge them with great absurdity. You would think it very reasonable that they should continue their prayers and be strict in observing all times of prayer as the most likely means of removing the dullness and indevotion of their hearts.

Now this is very much the case as to singing of Psalms; people often sing without finding any inward joy suitable to the words which they speak; therefore they are careless of it, or wholly neglect it, not considering that they act as absurdly as he that should neglect prayer because his heart was not enough affected with it. For it is certain that this singing is as much the natural means of raising motions of joy in the mind as prayer is the natural means of raising devotion.

I have been the longer upon this head because of its great importance to true religion. For there is no state of mind so holy, so excellent, and so truly perfect as that of thankfulness to God; and consequently nothing is of more importance in religion than that which exercises and improves this habit of mind.

A dull, uneasy, complaining spirit, which is sometimes the spirit of those that seem careful of religion, is yet of all tempers the most contrary to religion, for it disowns that God which it pretends to adore. For he sufficiently disowns God who does not adore Him as a Being of infinite goodness.

If a man does[39] not believe that all the world is as God's family

217

where nothing happens by chance but all is guided and directed by the care and providence of a Being that is all love and goodness to all His creatures, if a man do not believe this from his heart, he cannot be said truly to believe in God. And yet he that has this faith has faith enough to overcome the world, and always be thankful to God. For he that believes that everything happens to him for the best cannot possibly complain for the want of something that is better.

If therefore you live in murmurings and complaints, accusing all the accidents of life, it is not because you are a weak, infirm creature, but it is because you want the first principle of religion, a right belief in God. For as thankfulness is an express acknowledgment of the goodness of God toward you, so repinings and complaints are as plain accusations of God's want of goodness toward you.

On the other hand, would you know who is the greatest saint in the world? It is not he who prays most or fasts most; it is not he who gives most alms or is most eminent for temperance, chastity, or justice; but it is he who is always thankful to God, who wills everything that God willeth, who receives everything as an instance of God's goodness and has a heart always ready to praise God for it.

All prayer and devotion, fastings and repentance, meditation and retirement, all sacraments and ordinances, are but so many means to render the soul thus divine and conformable to the will of God and to fill it with thankfulness and praise for everything that comes from God. This is the perfection of all virtues; and all virtues that do not tend to it or proceed from it are but so many false ornaments of a soul not converted unto God.

You need not therefore now wonder that I lay so much stress upon singing a Psalm at all your devotions since you see it is to form your spirit to such joy and thankfulness to God as is the highest perfection of a divine and holy life.

If anyone would tell you the shortest, surest way to all happiness and all perfection, he must tell you to make it a rule to yourself to thank and praise God for everything that happens to you. For it is certain that whatever seeming calamity happens to you, if you thank and praise God for it, you turn it into a blessing. Could you therefore work miracles, you could not do more for yourself than by this thankful spirit, for it heals with a word speaking, and turns all that it touches into happiness.

If therefore you would be so true to your eternal interest as to propose this thankfulness as the end of all your religion, if you would but settle it in your mind that this was the state that you was to aim at by all your devotions, you would then have something plain and visible to walk by in all your actions, you would then easily see the effect of your improvement in piety. For so far as you renounce all selfish tempers and motions of your own will and seek for no other happiness but in the thankful reception of everything that happens to you, so far you may be safely reckoned to have advanced in piety.

And although this be the highest temper that you can aim at, though it be the noblest sacrifice that the greatest Saint can offer unto God, yet is it not tied to any time, or place, or great occasion but is always in your power and may be the exercise of every day. For the common events of every day are sufficient to discover and exercise this temper and may plainly show you how far you are governed in all your actions by this thankful spirit.

And for this reason I exhort you to this method in your devotion, that every day may be made a day of thanksgiving and that the spirit of murmur and discontent may be unable to enter into the heart, which is so often employed in singing praises of God.

It may perhaps after all be objected that although the great benefit and excellent effects of this practice are very apparent, yet it seems not altogether so fit for private devotions since it can hardly be performed without making our devotions public to other people and seems also liable to the charge of sounding a trumpet at our prayers.

It is therefore answered, first, that great numbers of people have it in their power to be as private as they please; such persons therefore are excluded from this excuse, which however it may be so to others, is none to them. Therefore, let such take the benefit of this excellent devotion.

Secondly, numbers of people are by the necessity of their state, as servants, apprentices, prisoners, and families in small houses, forced to be continually in the presence or sight of somebody or other.

Now are such persons to neglect their prayers because they cannot pray without being seen? Are they not rather obliged to be more exact in them, that others may not be witnesses of their neglect and so corrupted by their example?

Now what is here said of devotion may surely be said of this chanting a Psalm, which is only a part of devotion.

The rule is this: Don't pray that you may be seen of men, but if your confinement obliges you to be always in the sight of others, be more afraid of being seen to neglect than of being seen to have recourse to prayer.

Thirdly, the short of the matter is this. Either people can use such privacy in this practice as to have no hearers, or they cannot. If they can, then this objection vanishes as to them. And if they cannot, they should consider their confinement and the necessities of their state as the confinement of a prison, and then they have an excellent pattern to follow; they may imitate St. Paul and Silas who sang praises to God in prison, though we are expressly told that the prisoners heard them. They therefore did not refrain from this kind of devotion for fear of being heard by others. If therefore anyone is in the same necessity, either in prison or out of prison, what can he do better than to follow this example?

I cannot pass by this place of scripture without desiring the pious reader to observe how strongly we are here called upon to this use of Psalms, and what a mighty recommendation of it the practice of these two great Saints is.

In this their great distress, in prison, in chains, under the soreness of stripes, in the horror of night, the divinest, holiest thing they could do was to sing praises unto God.

And shall we after this need any exhortation to this holy practice? Shall we let the day pass without such thanksgivings as they would not neglect in the night? Shall a prison, chains, and darkness furnish them with songs of praise, and shall we have no singings in our closets?

Further, let it also be observed that while these two holy men were thus employed in the most exalted part of devotion, doing that on earth which angels do in heaven, that "the foundations of the prison were shaken, all the doors were opened, and everyone's bands were loosed" (Acts 16:26).

And shall we now ask for motives to this divine exercise, when instead of arguments we have here such miracles to convince us of its mighty power with God?

Could God by a voice from heaven more expressly call us to

these songs of praise than by thus showing us how he hears, delivers, and rewards those that use them?

But this by the way. I now return to the objection in hand, and answer fourthly, that the privacy of our prayers is not destroyed by our having but by our seeking witnesses of them.

If therefore nobody hears you but those you cannot separate yourself from, you are as much in secret, and your Father who seeth in secret will as truly reward your secrecy as if you was seen by him alone.

Fifthly, private prayer, as it is opposed to prayer in public, does not suppose that no one is to have any witness of it. For husbands and wives, brothers and sisters, parents and children, masters and servants, tutors and pupils, are to be witnesses to one another of such devotion as may truly and properly be called private. It is far from being a duty to conceal such devotion from such near relations.

In all these cases, therefore, where such relations sometimes pray together in private and sometimes apart by themselves, the chanting of a Psalm can have nothing objected against it.

Our blessed Lord commands us when we fast to anoint our heads and wash our faces that we appear not unto men to fast, but unto our Father which is in secret.

But this only means that we must not make public ostentation to the world of our fasting.

For if no one was to fast in private or could be said to fast in private but he that had no witnesses of it, no one could keep a private fast but he that lived by himself. For every family must know who fasts in it. Therefore the privacy of fasting does not suppose such a privacy as excludes everybody from knowing it, but such a privacy as does not seek to be known abroad.

Cornelius the devout centurion, of whom the scripture saith that he gave much and prayed to God always, saith unto St. Peter, "Four days ago I was fasting until this hour" (Acts 10:30).

Now that this fasting was sufficiently private and acceptable to God appears from the vision of an angel with which the holy man was blessed at that time.

But that it was not so private as to be entirely unknown to others appears as from the relation of it here, so from what is said in another place, that he "called two of his household servants, and a devout soldier of them that waited upon him continually" (Acts 10:7). So that Cornelius his fasting was so far from being unknown to his family that the soldiers and they of his household were made devout themselves by continually waiting upon him, that is, by seeing and partaking of his good works.

The whole of the matter is this. Great part of the world can be as private as they please; therefore let them use this excellent devotion between God and themselves.

As therefore the privacy or excellency of fasting is not destroyed by being known to some particular persons, neither would the privacy or excellency of your devotions be hurt, though by chanting a Psalm you should be heard by some of your family.[40]

Another great part of the world must and ought to have witnesses of several of their devotions; let them therefore not neglect the use of a Psalm at such times as it ought to be known to those with whom they live that they do not neglect their prayers. For surely there can be no harm in being known to be singing a Psalm at such times as it ought to be known that you are at your prayers.

And if at other times you desire to be in such secrecy at your devotions as to have nobody suspect it and for that reason forbear your Psalm, I have nothing to object against it, provided that at the known hours of prayer you never omit this practice.

For who would not be often doing that in the day which St. Paul and Silas would not neglect in the middle of the night? And if when you are thus singing it should come into your head how the prison shaked and the doors opened when St. Paul sang, it would do your devotion no harm.

Lastly, seeing our imaginations have great power over our hearts and can mightily affect us with their representations, it would be of great use to you if at the beginning of your devotions you was to imagine to yourself some such representations as might heat and warm your heart into a temper suitable to those prayers that you are then about to offer unto God.

As thus, before you begin your Psalm of praise and rejoicing in God, make this use of your imagination.

Be still and imagine to yourself that you saw the heavens open and the glorious choirs of cherubims and seraphims about the throne of God. Imagine that you hear the music of those angelic voices that cease not day and night to sing the glories of Him that is, and was, and is to come.

Help your imagination with such passages of scripture as these: "I beheld, and lo in heaven a great multitude which no man could number, of all nations, and kindreds, and people, and tongues, standing before the throne, and before the lamb, clothed with white robes, and palms in their hands. And they cried with a loud voice, Salvation to our God which sitteth upon the throne, and unto the lamb. And all the angels stood round about the throne, and fell before the throne on their faces, and worshipped God, saying, Amen: Blessing, and glory, and wisdom, and thanksgiving, and honor, and power, and strength be unto God, for ever and ever. Amen" (Rev. 7:9-12).

Think upon this till your imagination has carried you above the clouds, till it has placed you amongst those heavenly beings, and made you long to bear a part in their eternal music.

If you will but use yourself to this method and let your imagination dwell upon such representations as these, you will soon find it to be an excellent means of raising the spirit of devotion within you.

Always therefore begin your Psalm or song of praise with these imaginations; and at every verse of it, imagine yourself amongst those heavenly companions, that your voice is added to theirs, and that angels join with you and you with them, and that you with a poor and low voice are singing that on earth which they are singing in heaven.

Again, sometimes imagine that you had been one of those that joined with our blessed Savior when He sung a hymn. Strive to imagine to yourself with what majesty He looked; fancy that you had stood close by Him surrounded with His glory. Think how your heart would have been inflamed, what ecstasies of joy you would have then felt when singing with the Son of God. Think again and again with what joy and devotion you would then have sung had this been really your happy state, and what a punishment you should have thought it to have been then silent; and let this teach you how to be affected with Psalms and hymns of thanksgiving.

Again, sometimes imagine to yourself that you saw holy David with his hands upon his harp and his eyes fixed upon heaven, calling in transport upon all the creation, sun and moon, light and darkness, day and night, men and angels, to join with his rapturous soul in praising the Lord of Heaven.

Dwell upon this imagination till you think you are singing with this divine musician, and let such a companion teach you to exalt your heart unto God in the following Psalm, which you may use constantly first in the morning.

Psalm 145: "I will magnify thee, O God my king: and I will praise thy name for ever and ever," etc.

These following Psalms, as the 34th, 96th, 103rd, 111th, 146th, 147th, are such as wonderfully set forth the glory of God; and therefore you may keep to any one of them at any particular hour, as you like. Or you may take the finest parts of any Psalms, and so adding them together may make them fitter for your own devotion.

NOTES

39. If a man does not . . . if a man do not: With the shift from "does" to "do," Law means to indicate a change from a hypothetical statement to a conditional one, from the indicative to the subjunctive mood.

40. In the 2nd ed., this paragraph is transposed with the previous one.

Chapter 16

Recommending devotions at nine o'clock in the morning, called in scripture the third hour of the day. The subject of these prayers is humility.

I am now come to another hour of prayer which in scripture is called the third hour of the day, but according to our way of numbering the hours, it is called the ninth hour of the morning.

The devout Christian must at this time look upon himself as called upon by God to renew his acts of prayer and address himself again to the throne of grace.

There is indeed no express command in scripture to repeat our devotions at this hour. But then it is to be considered also that neither is there any express command to begin and end the day with prayer. So that if that be looked upon as a reason for neglecting devotion at this hour, it may as well be urged as a reason for neglecting devotion both at the beginning and end of the day.

But if the practice of the Saints in all ages of the world, if the customs of the pious Jews and primitive Christians be of any force with us, we have authority enough to persuade us to make this hour a constant season of devotion.

The scriptures show us how this hour was consecrated to devotion both by Jews and Christians, so that if we desire to number ourselves amongst those whose hearts were devoted unto God, we must not let this hour pass without presenting us to Him in some solemnities of devotion. And besides this authority for this practice, the reasonableness of it is sufficient to invite us to the observance of it.

For if you was up at a good time in the morning, your first devotions will have been at proper distance from this hour; you will have been long enough at other business to make it proper for you to return to this greatest of all business, the raising your soul and affections[41] unto God.

But if you have risen so late as to be hardly able to begin your first devotions at this hour, which is proper for your second, you may thence learn that the indulging yourself in the morning sleep is no small matter since it sets you so far back in your devotions and robs you of those graces and blessings which are obtained by frequent prayers.

For if prayer has power with God, if it looses the bands[42] of sin, if it purifies the soul, reforms our hearts, and draws down the aids of divine grace, how can that be reckoned a small matter which robs us of an hour of prayer?

Imagine yourself somewhere placed in the air as a spectator of all that passes in the world, and that you saw in one view the devotions which all Christian people offer unto God every day. Imagine that you saw some piously dividing the day and night as the primitive Christians did, and calling upon God at all those times that Saints and martyrs received their gifts and graces from God.

Imagine that you saw others living without any rules as to times and frequency of prayer, and only at their devotions sooner or later as sleep and laziness happens to permit them.

Now if you was to see this as God sees it, how do you suppose you should be affected with this sight? What judgment do you imagine you should pass upon these different sorts of people? Could you think that those who were thus exact in their rules of devotion got nothing by their exactness? Could you think that their prayers were received just in the same manner and procured them no more blessings than theirs do who prefer laziness and indulgence to times and rules of devotion?

Could you take the one to be as true servants of God as the other? Could you imagine that those who were thus different in their lives would find no difference in their states after death? Could you think it a matter of indifferency[43] to which of these people you were most like?

If not, let it be now your care to join yourself to that number of devout people, to that society of Saints, amongst whom you desire to be found when you leave the world.

And although the bare number and repetition of our prayers is of little value, yet since prayer rightly and attentively performed is the most natural means of amending and purifying our hearts, since importunity and frequency in prayer is as much pressed upon us by scripture as prayer itself, we may be sure that when we are frequent and importunate in our prayers we are taking the best means of obtaining the highest benefits of a devout life.

And on the other hand, they who through negligence, laziness, or any other indulgence render themselves either unable or unin-clined to observe rules and hours of devotion, we may be sure that they deprive themselves of those graces and blessings which an exact and fervent devotion procures from God.

Now as this frequency of prayer is founded in the doctrines of scripture and recommended to us by the practice of the true wor-shippers of God, so we ought not to think ourselves excused from it but where we can show that we are spending our time in such business as is more acceptable to God than these returns of prayer.

Least of all must we imagine that dullness, negligence, in-dulgence, or diversions can be any pardonable excuses for our not observing an exact and frequent method of devotion.

If you are of a devout spirit, you will rejoice at these returns of prayer which keep your soul in an holy enjoyment of God, which change your passions into divine love and fill your heart with stronger joys and consolations than you can possibly meet with in anything else.

And if you are not of a devout spirit, then you are moreover obliged to this frequency of prayer to train and exercise your heart into a true sense and feeling of devotion.

Now seeing the holy spirit of the Christian religion and the example of the Saints of all ages calls upon you thus to divide the day into hours of prayer, so it will be highly beneficial to you to make a right choice of those matters which are to be the subject of your prayers, and to keep every hour of prayer appropriated to some particular subject which you may alter or enlarge, according as the state you are in requires.

By this means, you will have an opportunity of being large and particular in all the parts of any virtue or grace which you then make the subject of your prayers. And by asking for it in all its parts, and making it the substance of a whole prayer once every day, you will soon find a mighty change in your heart, and that you cannot thus constantly pray for all the parts of any virtue every day of your life and yet live the rest of the day contrary to it.

If a worldly minded man was to pray every day against all the instances of a worldly temper, if he should make a large description of the temptations of covetousness and desire God to assist him to reject them all and to disappoint him in all covetous designs, he would find his conscience so much awakened that he would be forced either to forsake such prayers or to forsake a worldly life.

The same will hold true in any other instance. And if we ask and have not, 'tis because we ask amiss, because we ask in cold and general forms, such as only name the virtues without describing their particular parts, such as are not enough particular to our condition and therefore make no change in our hearts, whereas when a man enumerates all the parts of any virtue in his prayers, his conscience is thereby awakened, and he is frighted at seeing how far short he is of it. And this stirs him up to an ardor in devotion when he sees how much he wants of that virtue which he is praying for.

I have in the last chapter laid before you the excellency of praise and thanksgiving and recommended that as the subject of your first devotions in the morning.

And because a humble state of soul is the very state of religion, because humility is the life and soul of piety, the foundation and support of every virtue and good work, the best guard and security of all holy affections, I shall recommend humility to you as highly proper to be made the constant subject of your devotions at this third hour of the day, earnestly desiring you to think no day safe or likely to end well in which you have not thus early put yourself in this posture of humility and called upon God to carry you through the day in the exercise of a meek and lowly spirit.

This virtue is so essential to the right state of our souls that there is no pretending to a reasonable or pious life without it. We may as well think to see without eyes or live without breath as to live in the spirit of religion without the spirit of humility.

And although it is thus the soul and essence of all religious duties, yet is it, generally speaking, the least understood, the least regarded, the least intended, the least desired and sought after, of all other virtues amongst all sorts of Christians.

No people have more occasion to be afraid of the approaches of pride than those who have made some advances in a pious life. For pride can grow as well upon our virtues as our vices, and steals upon us on all occasions.

Every good thought that we have, every good action that we do, lays us open to pride and exposes us [44] to the assaults of vanity and self-satisfaction.

It is not only the beauty of our persons, the gifts of fortune, our natural talents, and the distinctions of life, but even our devotions and alms, our fastings and humiliations, expose us to fresh and strong temptations of this evil spirit.

And it is for this reason that I so earnestly advise every devout person to begin every day in this exercise of humility that he may go on in safety under the protection of this good guide and not fall a sacrifice to his own progress in those virtues which are to save mankind from destruction.

Humility does not consist in having a worse opinion of ourselves than we deserve, or in abasing ourselves lower than we really are. But as all virtue is founded in truth, so humility is founded in a true and just sense of our weakness, misery, and sin. He that rightly feels and lives in this sense of his condition lives in humility.

The weakness of our state appears from our inability to do anything as of ourselves. In our natural state we are entirely without any power; we are indeed active beings, but can only act by a power that is every moment lent us from God.

We have no more power of our own to move a hand or stir a foot than to move the sun or stop the clouds.

When we speak a word, we feel no more power in ourselves to do it than we feel ourselves able to raise the dead. For we act no more within our own power or by our own strength when we speak a word or make a sound than the Apostles acted within their own power or by their own strength when a word from their mouth cast out devils and cured diseases.

As it was solely the power of God that enabled them to speak to such purposes, so it is solely the power of God that enables us to speak at all.

We indeed find that we can speak, as we find that we are alive; but the actual exercise of speaking is no more in our own power than the actual enjoyment of life.

This is the dependent, helpless poverty of our state, which is a great reason for humility. For since we neither are nor can do anything of ourselves, to be proud of anything that we are, or of anything that we can do, and to ascribe glory to ourselves for these things as our own ornaments has the guilt both of stealing and lying. It has the guilt of stealing, as it gives to ourselves those things which only belong to God. It has the guilt of lying, as it is the denying the truth of our state and pretending to be something that we are not.

Secondly, another argument for humility is founded in the misery of our condition.

Now the misery of our condition appears in this, that we use these borrowed powers of our nature to the torment and vexation of ourselves and our fellow creatures.

God Almighty has entrusted us with the use of reason, and we use it to the disorder and corruption of our nature. We reason ourselves into all kinds of folly and misery, and make our lives the sport of foolish and extravagant passions, seeking after imaginary happiness in all kinds of shapes, creating to ourselves a thousand wants, amusing our hearts with false hopes and fears, using the world worse than irrational animals, envying, vexing, and torment-ing one another with restless passions and unreasonable contentions.

Let any man but look back upon his own life and see what use he has made of his reason, how little he has consulted it, and how less he has followed it. What foolish passions, what vain thoughts, what needless labors, what extravagant projects, have taken up the greatest part of his life. How foolish he has been in his words and conversation, how seldom he has done well with judgment, and how often he has been kept from doing ill by accident; how seldom he has been able to please himself, and how often he has displeased others; how often he has changed his counsels, hated what he loved and loved what he hated; how often he has been enraged and transported at trifles, pleased and displeased with the very same things, and constantly changing from one vanity to another. Let a man but take this view of his own life, and he will see reason enough to confess that pride was not made for man.

Let him but consider that if the world knew all that of him which he knows of himself, if they saw what vanity and passions govern his inside and what secret tempers sully and corrupt his best actions, he would have no more pretence to be honored and admired for his goodness and wisdom than a rotten and distempered body to be loved and admired for its beauty and comeliness.

This is so true and so known to the hearts of almost all people that nothing would appear more dreadful to them than to have their hearts thus fully discovered to the eyes of all beholders.

And perhaps there are very few people in the world who would not rather choose to die than to have all their secret follies, the errors of their judgments, the vanity of their minds, the falseness of their pretences, the frequency of their vain and disorderly passions, their uneasiness, hatreds, envies, and vexations made known unto the world.

And shall pride be entertained in a heart thus conscious of its own miserable behavior?

Shall a creature in such a condition that he could not support himself under the shame of being known to the world in his real state, shall such a creature because his shame is only known to God, to holy angels, and his own conscience, shall he, in the sight of God and holy angels, dare to be vain and proud of himself?

Thirdly, if to this we add the shame and guilt of sin, we shall find a still greater reason for humility.

No creature that had lived in innocence would have thereby got any pretence for self-honor and esteem because as a creature all that it is, or has, or does is from God; and therefore the honor of all that belongs to it is only due to God.

But if a creature that is a sinner and under the displeasure of the great governor of all the world and deserving nothing from him but pains and punishments for the shameful abuse of his powers, if such a creature pretends to self-glory for anything that he is or does, he can only be said to glory in his shame.

Now how monstrous and shameful the nature of sin is, is sufficiently apparent from that great atonement that is necessary to cleanse us from the guilt of it.

Nothing less has been required to take away the guilt of our sins than the sufferings and death of the Son of God. Had He not taken our nature upon Him, our nature had been forever separated from God and incapable of ever appearing before Him.

And is there any room for pride or self-glory whilst we are partakers of such a nature as this?

Have our sins rendered us so abominable and odious to Him that made us that He could not so much as receive our prayers or admit our repentance 'till the Son of God made Himself man and became a suffering advocate for our whole race, and can we in this state pretend to high thoughts of ourselves? Shall we presume to take delight in our own worth who are not worthy so much as to ask pardon for our sins without the mediation and intercession of the Son of God?

Thus deep is the foundation of humility laid in these deplorable circumstances of our condition, which show that it is as great an offence against truth and the reason of things for a man in this state of things to lay claim to any degrees of glory as to pretend to the honor of creating himself. If man will boast of anything as his own, he must boast of his misery and sin, for there is nothing else but this that is his own property. Turn your eyes toward heaven and fancy that you saw what is doing there, that you saw cherubims and seraphims and all the glorious inhabitants of that place all united in one work, not seeking glory from one another, not laboring their own advancement, not contemplating their own perfections, not singing their own praises, not valuing themselves and despising others, but all employed in one and the same work, all happy in one and the same joy, "casting down their crowns before the throne of God, giving glory, and honor, and power to him alone" (Rev. 4:10, 11).

Then turn your eyes to the fallen world and consider how unreasonable and odious it must be for such poor worms, such miserable sinners to take delight in their own fancied glories whilst the highest and most glorious sons of heaven seek for no other greatness and honor but that of ascribing all honor and greatness and glory to God alone.

Pride is only the disorder of the fallen world, it has no place amongst other beings; it can only subsist where ignorance and sensuality, lies and falsehood, lusts and impurity, reign.

Let a man, when he is most delighted with his own figure, look upon a crucifix and contemplate our blessed Lord stretched out and nailed upon a cross, and then let him consider how absurd it must be for a heart full of pride and vanity to pray to God through the sufferings of such a meek and crucified Savior.

These are the reflections that you are often to meditate upon, that you may thereby be disposed to walk before God and man in such a spirit of humility as becomes the weak, miserable, sinful state of all that are descended from fallen Adam.

When you have by such general reflections as these convinced your mind of the reasonableness of humility, you must not content yourself with this as if you was therefore humble because your mind acknowledges the reasonableness of humility, and declares against pride. But you must immediately enter yourself into the practice of this virtue like a young beginner that has all of it to learn, that can learn but little at a time, and with great difficulty. You must consider that you have not only this virtue to learn, but that you must be content to proceed as a learner in it all your time, endeavoring after greater degrees of it and practicing every day acts of humility, as you every day practice acts of devotion.

You would not imagine yourself to be devout because in your judgment you approved of prayers and often declared your mind in favor of devotion. Yet how many people imagine themselves humble enough for no other reason but because they often commend humility and make vehement declarations against pride?

Caecus is a rich man, of good birth[45] and very fine parts. He is fond of dress, curious in the smallest matters that can add any ornament to his person. He is haughty and imperious to all his inferiors, is very full of everything that he says, or does, and never imagines it possible for such a judgment as his to be mistaken. He can bear no contradiction, and discovers the weakness of your understanding as soon as ever you oppose him. He changes everything in his house, his habit, and his equipage as often as anything more elegant comes in his way. Caecus would have been very religious, but that he always thought he was so.

There is nothing so odious to Caecus as a proud man, and the misfortune is that in this he is so very quick-sighted that he discovers in almost everybody some strokes of vanity.

On the other hand, he is exceeding fond of humble and modest persons. Humility, says he, is so amiable a quality that it forces our esteem wherever we meet with it. There is no possibility of despising the meanest person that has it, or of esteeming the greatest man that wants it.

Caecus no more suspects himself to be proud than he suspects his want of sense. And the reason of it is because he always finds himself so in love with humility and so enraged at pride.

It is very true, Caecus, you speak sincerely when you say you love humility and abhor pride. You are no hypocrite, you speak the true sentiments of your mind; but then take this along with you, Caecus, that you only love humility and hate pride in other people. You never once in your life thought of any other humility or of any other pride than that which you have seen in other people.

The case of Caecus is a common case; many people live in all the instances of pride and indulge every vanity that can enter into their minds, and yet never suspect themselves to be governed by pride and vanity because they know how much they dislike proud people, and how mightily they are pleased with humility and modesty wherever they find them.

All their speeches in favor of humility and all their railings against pride are looked upon as so many true exercises and effects of their own humble spirit.

Whereas in truth these are so far from being proper acts or proofs of humility that they are great arguments of the want of it.

For the fuller of pride anyone is himself, the more impatient will he be at the smallest instances of it in other people. And the less humility anyone has in his own mind, the more will he demand and be delighted with it in other people.

You must therefore act by a quite contrary measure and reckon yourself only so far humble as you impose every instance of humility upon yourself and never call for it in other people. So far an enemy to pride as you never spare it in yourself, nor ever censure it in other persons.

Now in order to do this, you need only consider that pride and humility signify nothing to you, but so far as they are your own, that they do you neither good nor harm but as they are the tempers of your own heart.

Now in order to begin and set out well in the practice of humility, you must take it for granted that you are proud that you have all your life been more or less infected with this unreasonable temper.

You should believe also that it is your greatest weakness that your heart is most subject to it, that it is so constantly stealing upon you that you have reason to watch and suspect its approaches in all your actions.

For this is what most people, especially new beginners in a pious life, may with great truth think of themselves.

For there is no one vice that is more deeply rooted in our nature or that receives such constant nourishment from almost everything that we think or do. There being hardly anything in the world that we want or use or any action or duty of life, but pride finds some means or other to take hold of it. So that at what time soever we begin to offer ourselves to God, we can hardly be surer of anything than that we have a great deal of pride to repent of.

If therefore you find it disagreeable to your mind to entertain this opinion of yourself, and that you cannot put yourself amongst those that want to be cured of pride, you may be as sure as if an angel from heaven had told you that you have not only much, but all your humility to seek.

For you can have no greater sign of a more confirmed pride than when you think that you are humble enough. He that thinks he loves God enough shows himself to be an entire stranger to that holy passion, so he that thinks he has humility enough shows that he is not so much as a beginner in the practice of true humility.

NOTES

41. Affections: one's whole emotional and mental inclinations.

42. Bands: that is, bonds, originally a phonetic variant of bonds. Bands in Law's time carried something of the sense of the material by which one was bound, or banded (cf. "bandaged").

43. Indifferency: indifference, or being of no consequence one way or the other, implying a kind of impartiality.

44. Us] corrected by the 2nd ed., omitted by the 1st ed.

45. Birth] corrected by the 2nd ed.; the 1st ed. reads: breeding.

Chapter 17

Showing how difficult the practice of humility is made by the general spirit and temper of the world. How Christianity requireth us to live contrary to the world.

Every person when he first applies himself to the exercise of this virtue of humility must, as I said before, consider himself as a learner, that is to learn something that is contrary to former tempers and habits of mind, and which can only be got by daily and constant practice.

He has not only as much to do as he that has some new art or science to learn, but he has also a great deal to unlearn. He is to forget and lay aside his own spirit, which has been a long while fixing and forming itself; he must forget and depart from abundance of passions and opinions which the fashion, and vogue, and spirit of the world has made natural to him.

He must lay aside his own spirit because as we are born in sin, so in pride, which is as natural to us as self-love and continually springs from it. And this is one reason why Christianity is so often represented as a new birth and a new spirit.

He must lay aside the opinions and passions which he has received from the world because the vogue and fashion of the world, by which we have been carried away as in a torrent before we could pass right judgments of the value of things, is in many respects contrary to humility, so that we must unlearn what the spirit of the world has taught us before we can be governed by the spirit of humility.

The Devil is called in scripture the prince of this world because he has great power in it, because many of its rules and principles are invented by this evil spirit, the father of all lies and falsehood, to separate us from God and prevent our return to happiness.

Now according to the spirit and vogue of this world whose corrupt air we have all breathed, there are many things that pass for great and honorable and most desirable which yet are so far from being so that the true greatness and honor of our nature consists in the not desiring them.

To abound in wealth, to have fine houses and rich clothes, to be attended with splendor and equipage, to be beautiful in our persons, to have titles of dignity, to be above our fellow creatures, to command the bows and obeisance of other people, to be looked on with admiration, to overcome our enemies with power, to subdue all that oppose us, to set out ourselves in as much splendor as we can, to live highly and magnificently, to eat and drink and delight ourselves in the most costly manner, these are the great, the honorable, the desirable things to which the spirit of the world turns the eyes of all people. And many a man is afraid of standing still and not engaging in the pursuit of these things, lest the same world should take him for a fool.

The history of the gospel is chiefly the history of Christ's conquest over this spirit of the world. And the number of true Christians is only the number of those who, following the Spirit of Christ, have lived contrary to this spirit of the world.

"If any man hath not the Spirit of Christ, he is none of His." Again, "Whosoever is born of God, overcometh the world. Set your affections on things above, and not on things on the earth; for ye are dead, and your life is hid with Christ in God." This is the language of the whole New Testament. This is the mark of Christianity; you are to be dead, that is, dead to the spirit and temper of the world, and live a new life in the Spirit of Jesus Christ.

But notwithstanding the clearness and plainness of these doctrines which thus renounce the world, yet great part of Christians live and die slaves to the customs and temper of the world.

How many people swell with pride and vanity for such things as they would not know how to value at all, but that they are admired in the world?

Would a man take ten years more drudgery in business to add two horses more to his coach, but that he knows that the world most of all admires a coach and six? How fearful are many people of having their houses poorly furnished, or themselves meanly clothed for this only reason, lest the world should make no account of them and place them amongst low and mean people?

How often would a man have yielded to the haughtiness and ill nature of others and shown a submissive temper, but that he dares not pass for such a poor-spirited man in the opinion of the world?

Many a man would often drop a resentment and forgive an affront, but that he is afraid if he should, the world would not forgive him.

How many would practice Christian temperance and sobriety in its utmost perfection, were it not for the censure which the world passes upon such a life?

Others have frequent intentions of living up to the rules of Christian perfection which they are frighted from by considering what the world would say of them.

Thus do the impressions which we have received from living in the world enslave our minds that we dare not attempt to be eminent in the sight of God and holy angels for fear of being little in the eyes of the world.

From this quarter arises the greatest difficulty of humility because it cannot subsist in any mind but so far as it is dead to the world and has parted with all desires of enjoying its greatness and honors. So that in order to be truly humble, you must unlearn all those notions which you have been all your life learning from this corrupt spirit of the world.

You can make no stand against the assaults of pride, the meek affections of humility can have no place in your soul, till you stop the power of the world over you and resolve against a blind obedience to its laws.

And when you are once advanced thus far as to be able to stand still in the torrent of worldly fashions and opinions and examine the worth and value of things which are most admired and valued in the world, you have gone a great way in the gaining of your freedom and have laid a good foundation for the amendment of your heart.

For as great as the power of the world is, it is all built upon a blind obedience, and we need only open our eyes to get quit of its power.

Ask who you will, learned or unlearned, everyone seems to

know and confess that the general temper and spirit of the world is nothing else but humor, folly, and extravagance.

Who will not own that the wisdom of philosophy, the piety of religion, was always confined to a small number? And is not this expressly owning and confessing that the common spirit and temper of the world is neither according to the wisdom of philosophy nor the piety of religion?

The world therefore seems enough condemned even by itself to make it very easy for a thinking man to be of the same judgment.

And therefore I hope you will not think it a hard saying that in order to be humble you must withdraw your obedience from that vulgar spirit which gives laws to fops and coquettes, and form your judgments according to the wisdom of philosophy and the piety of religion. Who would be afraid of making such a change as this?

Again, to lessen your fear and regard to the opinion of the world, think how soon the world will disregard you and have no more thought or concern about you than about the poorest animal that died in a ditch.

Your friends, if they can, may bury you with some distinction and set up a monument to let posterity see that your dust lies under such a stone; and when that is done, all is done. Your place is filled up by another, the world is just in the same state it was, you are blotted out of its sight and as much forgotten by the world as if you had never belonged to it.

Think upon the rich, the great, and the learned persons that have made great figures and been high in the esteem of the world; many of them died in your time and yet they are sunk, and lost, and gone, and as much disregarded by the world as if they had been only so many bubbles of water.

Think again how many poor souls see Heaven lost, and lie now expecting a miserable eternity for their service and homage to a world that thinks itself every whit as well without them, and is just as merry as it was when they were in it.

Is it therefore worth your while to lose the smallest degree of virtue for the sake of pleasing so bad a master and so false a friend as the world is?

Is it worth your while to bow the knee to such an idol as this that so soon will have neither eyes, nor ears, nor a heart to regard you, instead of serving that great, and holy, and mighty God that will make all His servants partakers of His own eternity?

Will you let the fear of a false world that has no love for you keep you from the fear of that God who has only created you that He may love and bless you to all eternity?

Lastly, you must consider what behavior the profession of Christianity requireth of you with regard to the world.

Now this is plainly delivered in these words: "Who gave himself for our sins, that he might deliver us from this present evil world" (Gal. 1:4). Christianity therefore implieth a deliverance from this world; and he that professeth it, professeth to live contrary to everything and every temper that is peculiar to this evil world.

St. John declareth this opposition to the world in this manner, "They are of the world: therefore speak they of the world, and the world heareth them. We are of God" (1 John 4:5). This is the description of the followers of Christ; and it is proof enough that no people are to be reckoned Christians in reality who in their hearts and tempers belong to this world. "We know," saith the same Apostle, "that we are of God, and the whole world lieth in wickedness" (5:19). Christians therefore can no further know that they are of God than so far as they know they are not of the world; that is, that they don't live according to the ways and spirit of the world. For all the ways, and maxims, and politics, and tempers of the world lie in wickedness. And he is only of God, or born of God in Christ Jesus, who has overcome this world, that is, who has chosen to live by faith and govern his actions by the principles of a wisdom revealed from God by Christ Jesus.

St. Paul takes it for a certainty so well known to Christians that they are no longer to be considered as living in this world, that he thus argues from it, as from an undeniable principle, concerning the abolishing the rites of the Jewish law: "Wherefore if ye be dead with Christ from the rudiments of the world, why, as though living in the world, are ye subject to ordinances?" (Col. 2:20). Here could be no argument in this, but in the Apostle's taking it for undeniable that Christians knew that their profession required them to have done with all the tempers and passions of this world, to live as citizens of the new Jerusalem, and to have their conversation in Heaven.

Our blessed Lord Himself has fully determined this point in these words: "They are not of this world, as I am not of this world." This is the state of Christianity with regard to this world. If you are not thus out of and contrary to the world, you want the distinguishing mark of Christianity; you don't belong to Christ, but by being out of the world as he was out of it.

We may deceive ourselves, if we please, with vain and softening comments upon these words, but they are and will be understood in their first simplicity and plainness by everyone that reads them in the same spirit that our blessed Lord spoke them. And to understand them in any lower, less significant meaning is to let carnal wisdom explain away that doctrine by which itself was to be destroyed.

The Christian's great conquest over the world is all contained in the mystery of Christ upon the cross. It was there and from thence that He taught all Christians how they were to come out of and conquer the world and what they were to do in order to be His disciples. And all the doctrines, sacraments, and institutions of the gospel are only so many explications of the meaning and applications of the benefit of this great mystery.

And the state of Christianity implieth nothing else but an entire, absolute conformity to that Spirit which Christ showed in the mysterious sacrifice of Himself upon the cross.

Every man therefore is only so far a Christian as he partakes of this Spirit of Christ. It was this that made St. Paul so passionately express himself, "God forbid that I should glory, save in the cross of our Lord Jesus Christ." But why does he glory? Is it because Christ had suffered in his stead and had excused him from suffering? No, by no means. But it was because his Christian profession had called him to the honor of suffering with Christ, and of dying to the world under reproach and contempt as He had done upon the cross. For he immediately adds, "by whom the world is crucified unto me, and I unto the world" (Gal. 6:14). This you see was the reason of his glorying in the cross of Christ because it had called him to a like state of death and crucifixion to the world.

Thus was the cross of Christ in St. Paul's days the glory of

Christians, not as it signified their not being ashamed to own a Master that was crucified, but as it signified their glorying in a religion which was nothing else but a doctrine of the cross that called them to the same suffering spirit, the same sacrifice of themselves, the same renunciation of the world, the same humility and meekness, the same patient bearing of injuries, reproaches, and contempts, and the same dying to all the greatness, honors, and happiness of this world which Christ showed upon the cross.

To have a true idea of Christianity, we must not consider our blessed Lord as suffering in our stead, but as our representative acting in our name and with such particular merit as to make our joining with Him acceptable unto God.

He suffered and was a sacrifice to make our sufferings and sacrifice of ourselves fit to be received by God. And we are to suffer, to be crucified, to die and rise with Christ, or else His crucifixion, death, and Resurrection will profit us nothing.

The necessity of this conformity to all that Christ did and suffered upon our account is very plain from the whole tenor of scripture.

First, as to His sufferings, this is the only condition of our being saved by them, "if we suffer with Him, we shall also reign with Him."

Secondly, as to His crucifixion. "Knowing this, that our old man is crucified with Him," etc. (Rom. 6:6). Here you see Christ is not crucified in our stead; but unless our old man be really crucified with Him, the cross of Christ will profit us nothing.

Thirdly, as to the death of Christ, the condition is this: "If we be dead with Christ, we believe that we shall also live with Him." If therefore Christ be dead alone, if we are not dead with Him, we are as sure from this scripture that we shall not live with Him.

Lastly, as to the Resurrection of Christ, the scripture showeth us how we are to partake of the benefit of it: "If ye be risen with Christ, seek those things which are above, where Christ sitteth on the right hand of God" (Col. 3:1).

Thus you see how plainly the scripture sets forth our blessed Lord as our representative, acting and suffering in our name, binding and obliging us to conform to all that He did and suffered for us.

It was for this reason that the holy Jesus said of His Disciples and in them of all true believers, "They are not of this world, as I am not of this world." Because all true believers conforming to the sufferings, crucifixion, death, and Resurrection of Christ live no longer after the spirit and temper of this world, but their life is hid with Christ in God.

This is the state of separation from the world to which all orders of Christians are called. They must so far renounce all worldly tempers, be so far governed by the things of another life, as to show that they are truly and really crucified, dead, and risen with Christ. And it is as necessary for all Christians to conform to this great change of spirit, to be thus in Christ new creatures, as it was necessary that Christ should suffer, die, and rise again for our salvation.

How high the Christian life is placed above the ways of this world is wonderfully described by St. Paul in these words: "Wherefore henceforth know we no man after the flesh; yea, though we have known Christ after the flesh, yet henceforth know we him no more. Therefore if any man be in Christ, he is a new creature: old things are passed away; behold, all things are become new" (2 Cor. 5:16).

He that feels the force and spirit of these words can hardly bear any human interpretation of them. Henceforth, says he; that is, since the death and Resurrection of Christ, the state of Christianity is become so glorious a state that we don't even consider Christ Himself as in the flesh upon earth, but as a God of glory in Heaven; we know and consider ourselves not as men in the flesh, but as fellow members of a new society that are to have all our hearts, our tempers, and conversation in Heaven.

Thus it is that Christianity has placed us out of and above the world; and we fall from our calling as soon as we fall into the tempers of the world.

Now as it was the spirit of the world that nailed our blessed Lord to the cross, so every man that has the Spirit of Christ, that opposes the world as He did, will certainly be crucified by the world some way or other.

For Christianity still lives in the same world that Christ did; and these two will be utter enemies till the Kingdom of Darkness is entirely at an end.

Had you lived with our Savior as His true disciple, you had then been hated as he was; and if you now live in His Spirit, the world will be the same enemy to you now that it was to Him then.

"If ye were of the world," saith our blessed Lord, "the world would love its own; but because ye are not of the world, but I have chosen you out of the world, therefore the world hateth you" (John 15:19).

We are apt to lose the true meaning of these words by considering them only as a historical description of something that was the state of our Savior and His Disciples at that time. But this is reading the scripture as a dead letter; for they as exactly describe the state of true Christians at this and all other times, to the end of the world.

For as true Christianity is nothing else but the Spirit of Christ, so whether that Spirit appear in the person of Christ Himself, or His Apostles, or followers in any age, it is the same thing; whoever hath His Spirit will be hated, despised, and condemned by the world as He was.

For the world will always love its own, and none but its own: This is as certain and unchangeable as the contrariety betwixt light and darkness.

When the holy Jesus saith, "If the world hate you," he does not add by way of consolation that it may sometime or other cease its hatred, or that it will not always hate them; but He only gives this as a reason for their bearing it, "You know that it hated me before it hated you," signifying that it was He, that is His Spirit, that by reason of its contrariety to the world was then and always would be hated by it.

You will perhaps say that the world is now become Christian, at least that part of it where we live; and therefore the world is not now to be considered in that state of opposition to Christianity as when it was heathen.

It is granted, the world now professeth Christianity. But will anyone say that this Christian world is of the Spirit of Christ? Are its general tempers the tempers of Christ? Are the passions of sensuality, self-love, pride, covetousness, ambition, and vainglory less contrary to the spirit of the gospel now they are amongst Christians than when they were amongst heathens? Or will you say that the tempers and passions of the heathen world are lost and gone?

Consider, secondly, what you are to mean by the world. Now

244

this is fully described to our hands by St. John. "All that is in the world, the lust of the flesh, the lust of the eyes, and the pride of life," etc. (1 John 2:16). This is an exact and full description of the world. Now will you say that this world is become Christian? But if all this still subsists, then the same world is now in being, and the same enemy to Christianity that was in St. John's days.

It was this world that St. John condemned as being not of the Father; whether therefore it outwardly professeth or openly persecuteth Christianity, it is still in the same state of contrariety to the true spirit and holiness of the gospel.

And indeed the world by professing Christianity is so far from being a less dangerous enemy than it was before that it has by its favors destroyed more Christians than ever it did by the most violent persecution.

We must therefore be so far from considering the world as in a state of less enmity and opposition to Christianity than it was in the first times of the gospel that we must guard against it as a greater and more dangerous enemy than it was in those times.

It is a greater enemy because it has greater power over Christians by its favors, riches, honors, rewards, and protections than it had by the fire and fury of its persecutions.

It is a more dangerous enemy by having lost its appearance of enmity. Its outward profession of Christianity makes it no longer considered as an enemy, and therefore the generality of people are easily persuaded to resign themselves up to be governed and directed by it.

How many consciences are kept at quiet upon no other foundation but because they sin under the authority of the Christian world?

How many directions of the gospel lie by unregarded, and how unconcernedly do particular persons read them for no other reason but because they seem unregarded by the Christian world?

How many compliances do people make to the Christian world without any hesitation or remorse, which if they had been required of them only by heathens would have been refused as contrary to the holiness of Christianity?

Who could be content with seeing how contrary his life is to the gospel, but because he sees that he lives as the Christian world doth?

Who that reads the gospel would want to be persuaded of the

necessity of great self-denial, humility, and poverty of spirit, but that the authority of the world has banished this doctrine of the cross?

There is nothing, therefore, that a good Christian ought to be more suspicious of or more constantly guard against than the authority of the Christian world.

And all the passages of scripture which represent the world as contrary to Christianity, which require our separation from it as from a mammon of unrighteousness, a monster of iniquity, are all to be taken in the same strict sense in relation to the present world.

For the change that the world has undergone has only altered its methods but not lessened its power of destroying religion.

Christians had nothing to fear from the heathen world but the loss of their lives; but the world become a friend makes it difficult for them to save their religion.

Whilst pride, sensuality, covetousness, and ambition had only the authority of the heathen world, Christians were thereby made more intent upon the contrary virtues. But when pride, sensuality, covetousness, and ambition have the authority of the Christian world, then private Christians are in the utmost danger, not only of being shamed out of the practice, but of losing the very notion of the piety of the gospel.

There is therefore hardly any possibility of saving yourself from the present world but by considering it as the same wicked enemy to all true holiness as it is represented in the scriptures, and by assuring yourself that it is as dangerous to conform to its tempers and passions now it is Christian as when it was heathen.

For only ask yourself, is the piety, the humility, the sobriety of the Christian world, the piety, the humility, and sobriety of the Christian spirit? If not, how can you be more undone by any world than by conforming to that which is Christian?

Need a man do more to make his soul unfit for the mercy of God than by being greedy and ambitious of honor? Yet how can a man renounce this temper without renouncing the spirit and temper of the world in which you now live?

How can a man be made more incapable of the Spirit of Christ than by a wrong value for money, and yet how can he be more wrong in his value of it than by following the authority of the Christian world?

Nay, in every order and station of life, whether of learning or business, either in church or state, you cannot act up to the spirit of religion without renouncing the most general temper and behavior of those who are of the same order and business as yourself.

And though human prudence seems to talk mighty wisely about the necessity of avoiding particularities, yet he that dares not be so weak as to be particular will be often obliged to avoid the most substantial duties of Christian piety.

These reflections will, I hope, help you to break through those difficulties and resist those temptations which the authority and fashion of the world hath raised against the practice of Christian humility.

Chapter 18

Showing how the education which men generally receive in their youth makes the doctrines of humility
difficult to be practiced. The spirit of a better education represented in the character of Paternus.

Another difficulty in the practice of humility arises from our
education. We are all of us, for the most part, corruptly educated and
then committed to take our course in a corrupt world, so that it is no
wonder if examples of great piety are so seldom seen.

Great part of the world are undone by being born and bred in
families that have no religion, where they are made vicious and
irregular by being like those with whom they first lived.

But this is not the thing I now mean: The education that I here
intend is such as children generally receive from virtuous and sober
parents, and learned tutors and governors.

Had we continued perfect, as God created the first man,
perhaps the perfection of our nature had been a sufficient self-
instruction for everyone. But as sickness and diseases have created
the necessity of medicines and physicians, so the change and disorder of our rational nature has introduced the necessity of education
and tutors.

And as the only end of the physician is to restore nature to its
own state, so the only end of education is to restore our rational
nature to its proper state. Education therefore is to be considered as
reason borrowed at second hand which is, as far as it can, to supply
the loss of original perfection. And as physic may justly be called the
art of restoring health, so education should be considered in no other
light than as the art of recovering to man the use of his reason.

Now as the instruction of every art or science is founded upon
the discoveries, the wisdom, experience, and maxims of the several

great men that have labored in it so that human wisdom or right use of our reason, which young people should be called to by their education, is nothing[46] else but the best experience and finest reasonings of men that have devoted themselves to the study of wisdom and the improvement of human nature.

All, therefore, that great Saints and dying men, when the fullest of light and conviction and after the highest improvement of their reason, all that they have said of the necessity of piety, of the excellency of virtue, of their duty to God, of the emptiness of riches, of the vanity of the world, all the sentences, judgments, reasonings, and maxims of the wisest of philosophers when in their highest state of wisdom, should constitute the common lessons of instruction for youthful minds.

This is the only way to make the young and ignorant part of the world the better for the wisdom and knowledge of the wise and ancient.

An education which is not wholly intent upon this is as much beside the point as an art of physic that had little or no regard to the restoration of health.

The youths that attended upon Pythagoras, Socrates, Plato, and Epictetus were thus educated. Their everyday lessons and instructions were so many lectures upon the nature of man, his true end and the right use of his faculties, upon the immortality of the soul, its relation to God, the beauty of virtue and its agreeableness to the divine nature; upon the dignity of reason, the necessity of temperance, fortitude, and generosity, and the shame and folly of indulging our passions.

Now as Christianity has, as it were, new[47] created the moral and religious world and set everything that is reasonable, wise, holy, and desirable in its true point of light, so one would expect that the education of youth should be as much bettered and amended by Christianity as the faith and doctrines of religion are amended by it.

As it has introduced such a new state of things and so fully informed us of the nature of man, the ends of his creation, the state of his condition; as it has fixed all our goods and evils, taught us the means of purifying our souls, pleasing God, and becoming eternally happy; one might naturally suppose that every Christian country abounded with schools for the teaching, not only a few questions and answers of a catechism, but for the forming, training, and practicing youths in such an outward course of life as the highest precepts, the strictest rules, and the sublimest doctrines of Christianity require.

An education under Pythagoras or Socrates had no other end but to teach youth to think, judge, act, and follow such rules of life as Pythagoras and Socrates used.

And is it not as reasonable to suppose that a Christian education should have no other end but to teach youth how to think, and judge, and act, and live according to the strictest laws of Christianity?

At least one would suppose that in all Christian schools the teaching youth to begin their lives in the spirit of Christianity, in such severity of behavior, such abstinence, sobriety, humility, and devotion as Christianity requires, should not only be more, but a hundred times more regarded than any or all things else.

For our education should imitate our guardian angels, suggest nothing to our minds but what is wise and holy, help us to discover and subdue every vain passion of our hearts and every false judgment of our minds.

And it is as sober and reasonable to expect and require all this benefit of a Christian education as to require that physic should strengthen all that is right in our nature and remove that which is sickly and diseased.

But alas, our modern education is not of this kind.

The first temper that we try to awaken in children is pride, as dangerous a passion as that of lust. We stir them up to vain thoughts of themselves, and do everything we can to puff up their minds with a sense of their own abilities.

Whatever way of life we intend them for, we apply to the fire and vanity of their minds, and exhort them to everything from corrupt motives. We stir them up to action from principles of strife and ambition, from glory, envy, and a desire of distinction, that they may excel others and shine in the eyes of the world.

We repeat and inculcate these motives upon them till they think it a part of their duty to be proud, envious, and vainglorious of their own accomplishments.

And when we have taught them to scorn to be outdone by any, to bear no rival, to thirst after every instance of applause, to be content with nothing but the highest distinctions, then we begin to take comfort in them and promise the world some mighty things from youths of such a glorious spirit.

If children are intended for holy orders we set before them some eminent orator, whose fine preaching has made him the admiration of the age and carried him through all the dignities and preferments of the church.

We encourage them to have these honors in their eye and to expect the reward of their studies from them.

If the youth is intended for a trade, we bid him look at all the rich men of the same trade, and consider how many now are carried about in their stately coaches who began in the same low degree as he now does. We awaken his ambition and endeavor to give his mind a right turn by often telling him how very rich such and such a tradesman died.

If he is to be a lawyer then we set great counsellors, Lords Judges,[48] and chancellors before his eyes. We tell him what great fees and great applause attend fine pleading. We exhort him to take fire at these things, to raise a spirit of emulation in himself, and to be content with nothing less than the highest honors of the long robe.

That this is the nature of our best education is too plain to need any proof, and I believe there are few parents but would be glad to see these instructions daily given to their children.

And after all this we complain of the effects of pride, we wonder to see grown men acted and governed by ambition, envy, scorn, and a desire of glory, not considering that they were all the time of their youth called upon to all their action and industry upon the same principles.

You teach a child to scorn to be outdone, to thirst for distinction and applause, and is it any wonder that he continues to act all his life in the same manner?

Now if a youth is ever to be so far a Christian as to govern his heart by the doctrines of humility, I would fain know at what time he is to begin it, or if he is ever to begin it at all, why we train him up in tempers quite contrary to it?

How dry and poor must the doctrine of humility sound to a youth that has been spurred up to all his industry by ambition, envy, emulation, and a desire of glory and distinction? And if he is not to act by these principles when he is a man, why do we call him to act by them in his youth?

Envy is acknowledged by all people to be the most ungenerous, base, and wicked passion that can enter into the heart of man.

And is this a temper to be instilled, nourished, and established in the minds of young people?

I know it is said that it is not envy but emulation that is intended to be awakened in the minds of young men.

But this is vainly said. For when children are taught to bear no rival, and to scorn to be outdone by any of their age, they are plainly and directly taught to be envious. For it is impossible for anyone to have this scorn of being outdone and this contention with rivals without burning with envy against all those that seem to excel him or get any distinction from him. So that what children are taught is rank envy and only covered with a name of a less odious sound.

Secondly, if envy is thus confessedly bad and it be only emulation that is endeavored to be awakened in children, surely there ought to be great care taken that children may know the one from the other. That they may abominate the one as a great crime, whilst they give the other admission into their minds.

But if this were to be attempted, the fineness of the distinction betwixt envy and emulation would show that it was easier to divide them in words than to separate them in action.

For emulation, when it is defined in its best manner, is nothing else but a refinement upon envy, or rather the most plausible part of that black and venomous passion.

And though it is easy to separate them in the notion, yet the most acute philosopher that understands the art of distinguishing ever so well, if he gives himself up to emulation, will certainly find himself deep in envy.

For envy is not an original temper, but the natural, necessary, and unavoidable effect of emulation or a desire of glory.

So that he who establishes the one in the minds of people necessarily fixes the other there. And there is no other possible way of destroying envy but by destroying emulation or a desire of glory. For the one always rises and falls in proportion to the other.

I know it is said in defence of this method of education that ambition and a desire of glory are necessary to excite young people to industry, and that if we were to press upon them the doctrines of humility we should deject their minds and sink them into dullness and idleness.

But these people who say this don't consider that this reason, if it has any strength, is full as strong against pressing the doctrines of humility upon grown men lest we should deject their minds and sink them into dullness and idleness.

For who does not see that middle-aged men want as much the assistance of pride, ambition, and vainglory to spur them up to action and industry as children do? And it is very certain that the precepts of humility are more contrary to the designs of such men and more grievous to their minds when they are pressed upon them than they are to the minds of young persons.

This reason, therefore, that is given why children should not be trained up in the principles of true humility is as good a reason why the same humility should never be required of grown men.

Thirdly, let those people who think that children would be spoiled if they were not thus educated consider this.

Could they think that if any children had been educated by our blessed Lord or His holy Apostles that their minds would have been sunk into dullness and idleness?

Or could they think that such children would not have been trained up in the profoundest principles of a strict and true humility? Can they say that our blessed Lord, who was the meekest and humblest man that ever was on earth, was hindered by His humility from being the greatest example of worthy and glorious actions that ever were done by man?

Can they say that His Apostles, who lived in the humble spirit of their Master, did therefore cease to be laborious and active instruments of doing good to all the world?

A few such reflections as these are sufficient to expose all the poor pretences for an education in pride and ambition.

Paternus lived about two hundred years ago; he had but one son, whom he educated himself in his own house. As they were sitting together in the garden when the child was ten years old, Paternus thus began to him.

The little time that you have been in the world my child, you have spent wholly with me, and my love and tenderness to you has made you look upon me as your only friend and benefactor and the cause of all the comfort and pleasure that you enjoy. Your heart, I know, would be ready to break with grief if you thought this was the last day that I should live with you.

But, my child, though you now think yourself mighty happy because you have hold of my hand, you are now in the hands and under the tender care of a much greater Father and friend than I am, whose love to you is far greater than mine and from whom you receive such blessings as no mortal can give.

That God whom you have seen me daily worship, whom I daily call upon to bless both you and me and all mankind, whose wondrous acts are recorded in those scriptures which you constantly read; that God who created the heavens and the earth, who brought a flood upon the old world, who saved Noah in the Ark, who was the God of Abraham, Isaac, and Jacob, whom Job blessed and praised in the greatest afflictions, who delivered the Israelites out of the hands of the Egyptians, who was the protector of righteous Joseph, Moses, Joshua, and holy Daniel, who sent so many prophets into the world, who sent his Son Jesus Christ to redeem mankind; this God who has done all these great things, who has created so many millions of men, who lived and died before you was born, with whom the spirits of good men that are departed this life now live, whom infinite numbers of angels now worship in Heaven; this great God who is the Creator of worlds, of angels, and men, is your loving Father and friend, your good Creator and nourisher, from whom and not from me you received your being ten years ago at the time that I planted that little tender elm which you there see.

I myself am not half the age of this shady oak, under which we sit; many of our fathers have sat under its boughs. We have all of us called it ours in our turn, though it stands and drops its masters as it drops its leaves.

You see, my son, this wide and large firmament over our heads, where the sun and moon and all the stars appear in their turns. If you was to be carried up to any of these bodies at this vast distance from us, you would still discover others as much above you as the stars that you see here are above the earth. Were you to go up or down, east or west, north or south, you would find the same height without any top and the same depth without any bottom.

And yet my child, so great is God that all these bodies added together are but as a grain of sand in His sight. And yet you are as much the care of this great God and Father of all worlds and all spirits as if He had no son but you or there were no creature for Him to love and protect but you alone. He numbers the hairs of your head, watches over you sleeping and waking, and has preserved you from a thousand dangers which neither you nor I know anything of.

How poor my power is and how little I am able to do for you, you have often seen. Your late sickness has shown you how little I could do for you in that state, and the frequent pains of your head are plain proofs that I have no power to remove them.

I can bring you food and medicines but have no power to turn them into your relief and nourishment; it is God alone that can do this for you.

Therefore, my child, fear and worship and love God. Your eyes indeed cannot yet see Him, but everything you see are so many marks of His power and presence and He is nearer to you than anything that you can see.

Take Him for your Lord, and Father, and Friend; look up unto Him as the fountain and cause of all the good that you have received through my hands, and reverence me only as the bearer and minister of God's good things unto you. And He that blessed my father before I was born will bless you when I am dead.

Your youth and little mind is only yet acquainted with my family and therefore you think there is no happiness out of it.

But my child, you belong to a greater family than mine, you are a young member of the family of this almighty Father of all nations, who has created infinite orders of angels and numberless generations of men to be fellow members of one and the same society in Heaven.

You do well to reverence and obey my authority because God has given me power over you to bring you up in His fear and to do for you as the holy fathers recorded in scripture did for their children who are now in rest and peace with God.

I shall, in a short time, die and leave you to God and yourself, and if God forgiveth my sins I shall go to His Son Jesus Christ and

WILLIAM LAW

live amongst patriarchs and prophets, saints and martyrs, where I shall pray for you and hope for your safe arrival at the same place.

Therefore, my child, meditate on these great things and your soul will soon grow great and noble by so meditating upon them.

Let your thoughts often leave these gardens, these fields and farms, to contemplate upon God and Heaven, to consider upon angels and the spirits of good men living in light and glory.

As you have been used to look to me in all your actions and have been afraid to do anything unless you first knew my will, so let it now be a rule of your life to look up to God in all your actions, to do everything in His fear and to abstain from everything that is not according to His will.

Bear Him always in your mind, teach your thoughts to reverence Him in every place, for there is no place where He is not.

God keepeth a book of life wherein all the actions of all men are written; your name is there, my child, and when you die this book will be laid open before men and angels and according as your actions are there found, you will either be received to the happiness of those holy men who have died before you or be turned away amongst wicked spirits that are never to see God any more.

Never forget this book, my son; for it is written, it must be opened, you must see it and you must be tried by it. Strive, therefore, to fill it with your good deeds, that the handwriting of God may not appear against you.

God, my child, is all love and wisdom and goodness, and everything that He has made and every action that He does is the effect of them all. Therefore, you cannot please God, but so far as you strive to walk in love, wisdom, and goodness. As all wisdom, love, and goodness proceeds from God, so nothing but love, wisdom, and goodness can lead to God.

When you love that which God loves, you act with Him, you join yourself to Him, and when you love what He dislikes, then you oppose Him and separate yourself from Him. This is the true and the right way; think what God loves, and do you love it with all your heart.

First of all, my child, worship and adore God, think of Him magnificently, speak of Him reverently, magnify His providence,

256

adore His power, frequent His service, and pray unto Him frequently and constantly.

Next to this, love your neighbor, which is all mankind, with such tenderness and affection as you love yourself. Think how God loves all mankind, how merciful He is to them, how tender He is of them, how carefully He preserves them, and then strive to love the world as God loves it.

God would have all men to be happy; therefore do you will and desire the same. All men are great instances of divine love, therefore let all men be instances of your love.

But above all, my son, mark this: Never do anything through strife or envy or emulation or vainglory. Never do anything in order to excel other people, but in order to please God, and because it is His will that you should do everything in the best manner that you can.

For if it is once a pleasure to you to excel other people, it will by degrees be a pleasure to you to see other people not as good as yourself.

Banish therefore every thought of self-pride and self-distinction, and accustom yourself to rejoice in all the excellencies and perfections of your fellow creatures, and be as glad to see any of their good actions as your own.

For as God is as well pleased with their well doings as with yours, so you ought to desire that everything that is wise and holy and good may be performed in as high a manner by other people as by yourself.

Let this, therefore, be your only motive and spur to all good actions, honest industry, and business, to do everything in as perfect and excellent a manner as you can for this only reason, because it is pleasing to God, who desires your perfection and writes all your actions in a book. When I am dead, my son, you will be master of all my estate, which will be a great deal more than the necessities of one family require. Therefore, as you are to be charitable to the souls of men, and wish them the same happiness with you in Heaven, so be charitable to their bodies, and endeavor to make them as happy as you upon earth.

As God has created all things for the common good of all men, so let that part of them which is fallen to your share be employed as God would have all employed, for the common good of all.

Do good, my son, first of all to those that most deserve it, but remember to do good to all. The greatest sinners receive daily instances of God's goodness toward them; He nourishes and preserves them that they may repent and return to Him. Do you therefore imitate God and think no one too bad to receive your relief and kindness when you see that He wants it.

I am teaching you Latin and Greek, not that you should desire to be a great critic, a fine poet, or an eloquent orator. I would not have your heart feel any of these desires, for the desire of these accomplishments is a vanity of the mind and the masters of them are generally vain men. For the desire of anything that is not a real good lessens the application of the mind after that which is so.

But I teach you these languages that at proper times you may look into the history of past ages and learn the methods of God's providence over the world; that reading the writings of the ancient sages, you may see how wisdom and virtue have been the praises of great men of all ages, and fortify your mind by their wise sayings.

Let truth and plainness therefore be the only ornament of your language and study nothing but how to think of all things as they deserve, to choose everything that is best, to live according to reason and order, and to act in every part of your life in conformity to the will of God.

Study how to fill your heart full of the love of God and the love of your neighbor and then be content to be no deeper a scholar, no finer a gentleman, than these tempers will make you. As true religion is nothing else but simple nature governed by right reason, so it loves and requires great plainness and simplicity of life. Therefore, avoid all superfluous shows of finery and equipage and let your house be plainly furnished with moderate conveniences. Don't consider what your estate can afford but what right reason requires.

Let your dress be sober, clean, and modest, not to set out the beauty of your person but to declare the sobriety of your mind that your outward garb may resemble the inward plainness and simplicity of your heart. For it is highly reasonable that you should be one man, all of a piece, and appear outwardly such as you are inwardly.

As to your meat and drink, in them observe the highest rules of

Christian temperance and sobriety; consider your body only as the servant and minister of your soul; and only so nourish it as it may best perform a humble and obedient service to it.

But, my son, observe this as a most principal thing which I shall remember you of as long as I live with you.

Hate and despise all human glory, for it is nothing else but human folly. It is the greatest snare, and the greatest betrayer that you can possibly admit into your heart.

Love humility in all its instances, practice it in all its parts, for it is the noblest state of the soul of man; it will set your heart and affections right toward God and fill you with every temper that is tender and affectionate toward men.

Let every day, therefore, be a day of humility. Condescend to all the weakness and infirmities of your fellow creatures, cover their frailties, love their excellencies, encourage their prosperities, compassionate their distress, receive their friendship, overlook their unkindness, forgive their malice, be a servant of servants, and condescend to do the lowest offices to the lowest of mankind.

Aspire after nothing but your own purity and perfection and have no ambition but to do everything in so reasonable and religious a manner that you may be glad that God is everywhere present and sees and observes all your actions. The greatest trial of humility is a humble behavior toward your equals in age, estate, and condition of life. Therefore, be careful of all the motions of your heart toward these people. Let all your behavior toward them be governed by unfeigned love. Have no desire to put any of your equals below you, nor any anger at those that would put themselves above you. If they are proud, they are ill of a very bad distemper; let them therefore have your tender pity and perhaps your meekness may prove an occasion of their cure. But if your humility should do them no good it will, however, be the greatest good that you can do to yourself.

Remember that there is but one man in the world with whom you are to have perpetual contention and be always striving to exceed him, and that is yourself.

The time of practicing these precepts, my child, will soon be over with you; the world will soon slip through your hands, or rather you will soon slip through it. It seems but the other day since I received these same instructions from my dear father that I am now leaving with you. And the God that gave me ears to hear and a heart to receive what my father said unto me will, I hope, give you grace to love and follow the same instructions.

Thus did Paternus educate his son.

Can anyone now think that such an education as this would weaken and deject the minds of young people and deprive the world of any worthy and reasonable labors?

It is so far from that, that there is nothing so likely to ennoble and exalt the mind and prepare it for the most heroical exercise of all virtues.

For who will say that a love of God, a desire of pleasing Him, a love of our neighbor, a love of truth, of reason and virtue, a contemplation of eternity and the rewards of piety, are not stronger motives to great and good actions than a little uncertain popular praise?

On the other hand, there is nothing in reality that more weakens the mind and reduces it to meanness and slavery, nothing that makes it less master of its own actions or less capable of following reason, than a love of praise and honor.

For as praise and honor are often given to things and persons where they are not due as that is generally most praised and honored that most gratifies the humors, fashions, and vicious tempers of the world, so he that acts upon the desire of praise and applause must part with every other principle; he must say black is white, put bitter for sweet, and sweet for bitter, and do the meanest, basest things in order to be applauded.

For in a corrupt world as this is, worthy actions are only to be supported by their own worth, where instead of being praised and honored they are most often reproached and persecuted.

So that to educate children upon a motive of emulation or a desire of glory in a world where glory itself is false and most commonly given wrong is to destroy the natural integrity and fortitude of their minds and give them a bias which will oftener carry them to base and mean than great and worthy actions.

NOTES

46. Now . . . is nothing: The paragraph is an incomplete sentence, its sense being completed by the next statement of the following paragraph. "Now as the instruction" introduces a subordinate clause, but we must wait for "should constitute," the main verb of some lines later.

47. New: newly.

48. Lords Judges: high ranking and titled judges.

Chapter 19

Showing how the method of educating daughters makes it difficult for them to enter into the spirit of Christian humility. How miserably they are injured and abused by such an education. The spirit of a better education represented in the character of Eusebia.

That turn of mind which is taught and encouraged in the education of daughters makes it exceeding difficult for them to enter into such a sense and practice of humility as the spirit of Christianity requireth.

The right education of this sex is of the utmost importance to human life. There is nothing that is more desirable for the common good of all the world. For though women don't carry on the trade and business of the world, yet as they are mothers and mistresses of families that have for some time the care of the education of their children of both sorts, they are entrusted with that which is of the greatest consequence to human life. For this reason, good or bad women are likely to do as much good or harm in the world as good or bad men in the greatest business of life.

For as the health and strength or weakness of our bodies is very much owing to their methods of treating us when we were young, so the soundness or folly of our minds are not less owing to those first tempers and ways of thinking which we eagerly received from the love, tenderness, authority, and constant conversation of our mothers.

As we call our first language our mother tongue, so we may as justly call our first tempers our mother tempers; and perhaps it may be found more easy to forget the language than to part entirely with those tempers which we learnt in the nursery.

It is therefore much to be lamented that this sex, on whom so much depends, who have the first forming both of our bodies and our minds, are not only educated in pride but in the silliest and most contemptible part of it.

They are not indeed suffered to dispute with us the proud prizes of arts and sciences, of learning and eloquence, in which I have much suspicion they would often prove our superiors, but we turn them over to the study of beauty and dress and the whole world conspires to make them think of nothing else. Fathers and mothers, friends and relations, seem to have no other wish toward the little girl but that she may have a fair skin, a fine shape, dress well, and dance to admiration.

Now if a fondness for our persons, a desire of beauty, a love of dress, be a part of pride (as surely it is a most contemptible part of it), the first step toward a woman's humility seems to require a repentance of her education.

For it must be owned that, generally speaking, good parents are never more fond of their daughters than when they see them too fond of themselves and dressed in such a manner as is a great reproach to the gravity and sobriety of the Christian life.

And what makes this matter still more to be lamented is this, that women are not only spoiled by this education but we spoil that part of the world which would otherwise furnish most instances of an eminent and exalted piety.

For I believe it may be affirmed that for the most part there is a finer sense, a clearer mind, a readier apprehension, and gentler dispositions in that sex than in the other.

All which tempers, if they were truly improved by proper studies and sober methods of education, would in all probability carry them to greater heights of piety than are to be found amongst the generality of men.

For this reason I speak to this matter with so much openness and plainness, because it is much to be lamented that persons so naturally qualified to be great examples of piety should by an erroneous education be made poor and gaudy spectacles of the greatest vanity.

The church has formerly had eminent Saints in that sex, and it may reasonably be thought that it is purely owing to their poor and vain education that this honor of their sex is for the most part confined to former ages.

The corruption of the world indulges them in great vanity, and mankind seem to consider them in no other view than as so many painted idols that are to allure and gratify their passions, so that if many women are vain, light, gewgaw creatures, they have this to excuse themselves, that they are not only such as their education has made them, but such as the generality of the world allows them to be.

But then they should consider that the friends to their vanity are no friends of theirs. They should consider that they are to live for themselves, that they have as great a share in the rational nature as men have, that they have as much reason to pretend and as much necessity to aspire after the highest accomplishments of a Christian and solid virtue as the gravest and wisest amongst Christian philosophers.

They should consider that they are abused and injured and betrayed from their only perfection whenever they are taught that anything is an ornament in them that is not an ornament in the wisest amongst mankind.

It is generally said that women are naturally of little and vain minds, but this I look upon to be as false and unreasonable as to say that butchers are naturally cruel, for as their cruelty is not owing to their nature but to their way of life which has changed their nature, so whatever littleness and vanity is to be observed in the minds of women, it is like the cruelty of butchers, a temper that is wrought into them by that life which they are taught and accustomed to lead.

At least thus much must be said, that we cannot charge anything upon their nature till we take care that it is not perverted by their education.

And on the other hand, if it were true that they were thus naturally vain and light, then how much more blamable is that education which seems contrived to strengthen and increase this folly and weakness of their minds?

For if it were a virtue in a woman to be proud and vain in herself, we could hardly take better means to raise this passion in her than those that are now used in their education.

Matilda is a fine woman of good breeding, great sense, and much religion. She has three daughters that are educated by herself. She will not trust them with anyone else or at any school, for fear they should learn anything ill. She stays with the dancing master all the time he is with them because she will hear everything that is said to them. She has heard them read the scriptures so often that they can repeat great part of it without book; and there is scarce a good book of devotion but you may find it in their closets.[49]

Had Matilda lived in the first ages of Christianity, when it was practiced in the fullness and plainness of its doctrines, she had in all probability been one of its greatest Saints. But as she was born in corrupt times, where she wants examples of Christian perfection and hardly ever saw a piety higher than her own, so she has many defects and communicates them all to her daughters.

Matilda never was meanly dressed in her life, and nothing pleases her in dress but that which is very rich and beautiful to the eye.

Her daughters see her great zeal for religion, but then they see an equal earnestness for all sorts of finery. They see she is not negligent of her devotion but then they see her more careful to preserve her complexion and to prevent those changes which time and age threaten her with.

They are afraid to meet her if they have missed the church, but then they are more afraid to see her if they are not laced as straight as they can possibly be.

She often shows them her own picture, which was taken when their father fell in love with her. She tells them how distracted he was with passion at the first sight of her, and that she had never had so fine a complexion but for the diligence of her good mother, who took exceeding care of it.

Matilda is so intent upon all the arts of improving their dress that she has some new fancy almost every day and leaves no ornament untried, from the richest jewel to the poorest flower. She is so nice and critical in her judgment, so sensible of the smallest error, that the maid is often forced to dress and undress her daughters three or four times in a day before she can be satisfied with it.

As to the patching, she reserves that to herself, for, she says, if they are not stuck on with judgment, they are rather a prejudice than an advantage to the face.[50]

The children see so plainly the temper of their mother that they even affect to be more pleased with dress and to be more fond of every little ornament than they really are, merely to gain her favor.

They saw their eldest sister once brought to her tears, and her perverseness severely reprimanded, for presuming to say that she thought it was better to cover the neck than to go so far naked as the modern dress requires.

She stints them in their meals and is very scrupulous of what they eat and drink, and tells them how many fine shapes she has seen spoiled in her time for want of such care. If a pimple rises in their faces she is in a great fright and they themselves are as afraid to see her with it as if they had committed some great sin.

Whenever they begin to look too sanguine and heathful she calls in the assistance of the doctor, and if physic or illness will keep the complexion from inclining to coarse or ruddy she thinks them well employed.

By this means they are poor, pale, sickly, infirm creatures, vapored through want of spirits,[51] crying at the smallest accidents, swooning away at anything that frights them and hardly able to bear the weight of their best clothes.

The eldest daughter lived as long as she could under this discipline, and died in the twentieth year of her age.

When her body was opened, it appeared that her ribs had grown into her liver and that her other entrails were much hurt by being crushed together with her stays which her mother had ordered to be twitched so straight[52] that it often brought tears into her eyes whilst the maid was dressing her.

Her youngest daughter is run away with a gamester, a man of great beauty who in dressing and dancing has no superior.

Matilda says she should die with grief at this accident but that her conscience tells her she has contributed nothing to it herself. She appeals to their closets, to their books of devotion, to testify what care she has taken to establish her children in a life of solid piety and devotion.

Now though I don't intend to say that no daughters are brought up in a better way than this, for I hope there are many that are, yet thus much I believe may be said, that the much greater part of them are not brought up so well, or accustomed to so much religion as in the present instance.

Their minds are turned as much to the care of their beauty and dress and the indulgence of vain desires as in the present case, without having such rules of devotion to stand against it. So that if solid piety, humility, and a sober sense of themselves is much wanted in that sex, it is the plain and natural consequence of a vain and corrupt education.

And if they are often too ready to receive the first fops, beauxs, and fine dancers for their husbands, 'tis no wonder they should like that in men which they have been taught to admire in themselves.

And if they are often seen to lose that little religion they were taught in their youth, 'tis no more to be wondered at than to see a little flower choked and killed amongst rank weeds.

For personal pride and affectation, a delight in beauty and fondness of finery, are tempers that must either kill all religion in the soul or be themselves killed by it; they can no more thrive together than health and sickness.

Some people that judge hastily will perhaps here say that I am exercising too great a severity against the sex.

But more reasonable persons will easily observe that I entirely spare the sex and only arraign their education; that I not only spare them but plead their interest, assert their honor, set forth their perfections, commend their natural tempers, and only condemn that education which is so injurious to their interests, so debases their honor and deprives them of the benefit of their excellent natures and tempers.

Their education, I profess I cannot spare, but the only reason is because it is their greatest enemy, because it deprives the world of so many saints as might reasonably be expected from persons, so formed by their natural tempers to all goodness and tenderness, and so fitted by the clearness and brightness of their minds to contemplate, love, and admire everything that is holy, virtuous, and divine.

If it should here be said that I even charge too high upon their education and that they are not so much hurt by it as I imagine, it may be answered that though I don't pretend to state the exact degree of mischief that is done by it, yet its plain and natural tendency to do harm is sufficient to justify the most absolute condemnation of it.

But if anyone would know how generally women are hurt by this education, if he imagines there may be no personal pride or vain fondness of themselves in those that are patched and dressed out with so much glitter of art and ornament, let him only make the following experiment wherever he pleases.

Let him only acquaint any such woman with his opinion of her; I don't mean that he should tell her to her face or do it in any rude public manner; but let him contrive the most civil, secret, friendly way that he can think of, only to let her know his opinion, that he thinks she is neither handsome nor dresses well, nor becomes[53] her finery, and I dare say he will find there are but very few fine-dressed women that will like him never the worse for his bare opinion, though known to none but themselves, and that he will not be long without seeing the effects of her resentment.

But if such an experiment would show him that there are but few such women that could bear with his friendship after they knew he had such an opinion of them, surely it is time to complain of and accuse that education which so generally corrupts their hearts.

For though it is hard to judge of the hearts of people, yet where they declare their resentment and uneasiness at anything, there they pass the judgment upon themselves. If a woman can't forgive a man who thinks she has no beauty nor any ornament from her dress, there she infallibly discovers the state of her own heart and is condemned by her own and not another's judgment.

For we never are angry at others but when their opinions of us are contrary to that which we have of ourselves.

A man that makes no pretences to scholarship is never angry at those that don't take him to be a scholar, so if a woman had no opinion of her own person and dress she would never be angry at those who are of the same opinion with herself.

So that the general bad effects of this education are too much known to admit of any reasonable doubt.

But how possible it is to bring up daughters in a more excellent way, let the following character declare.

Eusebia is a pious widow, well born and well bred, and has a good estate for five daughters whom she brings up as one entrusted by God to fit five virgins for the Kingdom of Heaven. Her family has the same regulation as a religious house, and all its orders tend to the support of a constant regular devotion.

She, her daughters, and her maids meet together at all the hours of prayer in the day and chant Psalms and other devotions and spend the rest of their time in such good works and innocent diversions as render them fit to return to their Psalms and prayers.

She loves them as her spiritual children and they reverence her as their spiritual mother, with an affection far above that of the fondest friends.

She has divided part of her estate amongst them that everyone may be charitable out of their own stock, and each of them take it in their turns to provide for the poor and sick of the parish.

Eusebia brings them up to all kinds of labor that are proper for women, as sewing, knitting, spinning, and all other parts of house-wifery, not for their amusement, but that they may be serviceable to themselves and others, and be saved from those temptations which attend an idle life.

She tells them she had rather see them reduced to the necessity of maintaining themselves by their own work than to have riches to excuse themselves from labor. For though, says she, you may be able to assist the poor without your labor, yet by your labor you will be able to assist them more.

If Eusebia has lived as free from sin as it is possible for human nature, it is because she is always watching and guarding against all instances of pride. And if her virtues are stronger and higher than other people's, 'tis because they are all founded in a deep humility.

My children, says she, when your father died I was much pitied by my friends as having all the care of a family and the management of an estate fallen upon me.

But my own grief was founded upon another principle. I was grieved to see myself deprived of so faithful a friend, and that such an eminent example of Christian virtues should be taken from the eyes of his children before they were of an age to love and follow it.

But as to worldly cares which my friends thought so heavy upon me, they are most of them of our own making and fall away as soon as we know ourselves.

If a person in a dream is disturbed with strange appearances, his trouble is over as soon as he is awake and sees that it was the folly of a dream.

Now when a right knowledge of ourselves enters into our minds, it makes as great a change in all our thoughts and apprehensions as when we awake from the wanderings of a dream.

We acknowledge a man to be mad or melancholy who fancies himself to be glass, and so is afraid of stirring, or taking himself to be wax dare not let the sun shine upon him.

But, my children, there are things in the world which pass for wisdom, politeness, grandeur, happiness, and fine breeding, which show as great ignorance of ourselves and might as justly pass for thorough madness as when a man fancies himself to be glass or ice.

A woman that dares not appear in the world without fine clothes, that thinks it a happiness to have a face finely colored, to have a skin delicately fair, that had rather die than be reduced to poverty and be forced to work for a poor maintenance, is as ignorant of herself to the full as he that fancies himself to be glass.

For this reason, all my discourse with you has been to acquaint you with yourselves and to accustom you to such books and devotions as may best instruct you in this greatest of all knowledge.

You† would think it hard not to know the family into which you was born, what ancestors you were descended from, and what estate was to come to you. But, my children, you may know all this with exactness and yet be as ignorant of yourselves as he that takes himself to be wax.

For though you were all of you born of my body and bear your father's name, yet you are all of you pure spirits. I don't mean that you have not bodies that want meat and drink and sleep and clothing but that all that deserves to be called you is nothing else but spirit. A being spiritual and rational in its nature, that is as contrary to all fleshly or corporeal beings as life is contrary to death, that is made in the image of God to live forever, never to cease any more, but to enjoy life and reason and knowledge and happiness in the presence of God, and the society of angels and glorious spirits to all eternity.

Everything that you call yours besides this spirit is but like your clothing, something that is only to be used for awhile and then to end and die and wear away, and to signify no more to you than the clothing and bodies of other people.

But, my children, you are not only in this manner spirits but you are fallen spirits that began your life in a state of corruption and disorder, full of tempers and passions that blind and darken the reason of your mind and incline you to that which is hurtful.

---

†was . . . were: Law frequently writes "was" where we would prefer "were." Here he first thinks of "you" as being one group or unite influenced by "family," and he uses the singular "was;" but the "ancestors" of the next clause affects the choice of "where," even though in both instances the plural "you" is actually the subject of the verb.

Your bodies are not only poor and perishing like your clothes but they are like infected clothes that fill you with ill diseases and distempers which oppress the soul with sickly appetites and vain cravings.

So that all of us are like two beings that have, as it were, two hearts within us; with the one we see and taste and admire reason, purity and holiness; with the other we incline to pride and vanity and sensual delights.

This internal war we always feel within us more or less, and if you would know the one thing necessary to all the world, it is this; to preserve and perfect all that is rational, holy, and divine in our nature, and to mortify, remove, and destroy all that vanity, pride, and sensuality which springs from the corruption of our state.

Could you think, my children, when you look at the world and see what customs and fashions and pleasures and troubles and projects and tempers employ the hearts and time of mankind, that things were thus as I have told you?

But don't you be affected at these things. The world is in a great dream and but few people are awake in it.

We fancy that we fall into darkness when we die; but alas, we are most of us in the dark till then, and the eyes of our souls only then begin to see, when our bodily eyes are closing.

You see then your state, my children. You are to honor, improve, and perfect the spirit that is within you, you are to prepare it for the Kingdom of Heaven, to nourish it with the love of God and of virtue, to adorn it with good works, and to make it as holy and heavenly as you can. You are to preserve it from the errors and vanities of the world, to save it from the corruptions of the body, from those false delights and sensual tempers which the body tempts it with.

You are to nourish your spirits with pious readings and holy meditations, with watchings, fastings, and prayers, that you may taste and relish and desire that eternal state which is to begin when this life ends.

As to your bodies, you are to consider them as poor, perishing things that are sickly and corrupt at present and will soon drop into common dust. You are to watch over them as enemies that are always trying to tempt and betray you, and so never follow their advice and counsel; you are to consider them as the place and habitation of your souls, and so keep them pure and clean and decent; you are to consider them as the servants and instruments of action, and so give them food and rest and raiment, that they may be strong and healthful to do the duties of a charitable, useful, pious life.

Whilst you live thus you live like yourselves, and whenever you have less regard to your souls or more regard to your bodies than this comes to, whenever you are more intent upon adorning your persons than upon the perfecting of your souls, you are much more beside yourselves than he that had rather have a laced coat than a healthful body.

For this reason, my children, I have taught you nothing that was dangerous for you to learn; I have kept you from everything that might betray you into weakness and folly, or make you think anything fine but a fine mind, anything happy but the favor of God, or anything desirable but to do all the good you possibly can.

Instead of the vain, immodest entertainment of plays and operas, I have taught you to delight in visiting the sick and poor. What music and dancing and diversions are to many in the world, that prayers and devotions and Psalms are to you. Your hands have not been employed in plaiting the hair and adorning your persons, but in making clothes for the naked. You have not wasted your fortunes upon yourselves, but have added your labor to them for to do more good to other people.

Instead of forced shapes, patched faces, genteel airs, and affected motions, I have taught you to conceal your bodies with modest garments and let the world have nothing to view of you but the plainness, the sincerity, and humility of all your behavior.

You know, my children, the high perfection and the great rewards of virginity; you know how it frees from worldly cares and troubles and furnishes means and opportunities of higher advancements in a divine life; therefore, love and esteem and honor virginity. Bless God for all that glorious company of holy virgins that from the beginning of Christianity have, in the several ages of the church, renounced the cares and pleasures of matrimony to be perpetual examples of solitude, contemplation, and prayer.

But as everyone has their proper gift from God, as I look upon you all to be so many great blessings of a married state, so I leave it to your choice, either to do as I have done or to aspire after higher degrees of perfection in a virgin state of life.

I desire nothing, I press nothing upon you but to make the most of human life and to aspire after perfection in whatever state of life you choose.

Never, therefore, consider yourselves as persons that are to be seen, admired, and courted by men, but as poor sinners that are to save yourselves from the vanities and follies of a miserable world by humility, devotion, and self-denial. Learn to live for your own sakes and the service of God, and let nothing in the world be of any value with you but that which you can turn into a service to God and a means of your future happiness.

Consider often how powerfully you are called to a virtuous life and what great and glorious things God has done for you to make you in love with everything that can promote His glory.

Think upon the vanity and shortness of human life and let death and eternity be often in your minds, for these thoughts will strengthen and exalt your minds, make you wise and judicious and truly sensible of the littleness of all human things.

Think of the happiness of prophets and apostles, saints and martyrs, who are now rejoicing in the presence of God and see themselves possessors of eternal glory. And then think how desirable a thing it is to watch and pray and do good as they did, that when you die you may have your lot amongst them.

Whether married, therefore, or unmarried, consider yourselves as mothers and sisters, as friends and relations to all that want your assistance, and never allow yourselves to be idle whilst others are in want of anything that your hands can make for them.

This useful, charitable, humble employment of yourselves is what I recommend to you with great earnestness as being a substantial part of a wise and pious life. And besides the good you will thereby do to other people, every virtue of your own heart will be very much improved by it.

For next to reading, meditation, and prayer there is nothing that so secures our hearts from foolish passions, nothing that preserves so holy and wise a frame of mind, as some useful, humble employment of ourselves.

Never, therefore, consider your labor as an amusement, that is to get rid of your time, and so may be as trifling as you please; but consider it as something that is to be serviceable to yourselves and others, that is to serve some sober ends of life, to save and redeem your time and make it turn to your account when the works of all people shall be tried by fire.

When you was little I left you to little amusements to please yourselves in any things that were free from harm, but as you are now grown up to a knowledge of God and yourselves, as your minds are now acquainted with the worth and value of virtue and exalted with the great doctrines of religion, you are now to do nothing as children, but despise everything that is poor or vain and impertinent; you are now to make the labors of your hands suitable to the piety of your hearts, and employ yourselves for the same ends and with the same spirit as you watch and pray.

For if there is any good to be done by your labor, if you can possibly employ yourselves usefully to other people, how silly is it, how contrary to the wisdom of religion, to make that a mere amusement which might as easily be made an exercise of the greatest charity.

What would you think of the wisdom of him that should employ his time in distilling of waters and making liquors which nobody could use, merely to amuse himself with the variety of their color and clearness, when with less labor and expense he might satisfy the wants of those who have nothing to drink?

Yet he would be as wisely employed as those that are amusing themselves with such tedious works as they neither need nor hardly know how to use when they are finished, when with less labor and expense they might be doing as much good as he that is clothing the naked or visiting the sick.

Be glad, therefore, to know the wants of the poorest people and let your hands be employed in making such mean and ordinary things for them as their necessities require. By thus making your labor a gift and service to the poor, your ordinary work will be changed into a holy service and made as acceptable to God as your devotions.

And as charity is the greatest of all virtues, as it always was the chief temper of the greatest Saints, so nothing can make your own charity more amiable in the sight of God than this method of adding your labor to it.

The humility also of this employment will be as beneficial to you as the charity of it. It will keep you from all vain and proud thoughts of your own state and distinction in life, and from treating the poor as creatures of a different species. By accustoming yourselves to this labor and service for the poor as the representatives of Jesus Christ, you will soon find your heart softened into the greatest meekness and lowliness toward them. You will reverence their estate and condition, think it an honor to serve them, and never be so pleased with yourself as when you are most humbly employed in their service.

This will make you true disciples of your meek Lord and Master, who came into the world not to be ministered unto, but to minister; and though he was Lord of all and amongst the creatures of his own making, yet was amongst them as one that serveth.

Christianity has then had its most glorious effects upon your hearts when it has thus changed your spirit, removed all the pride of life from you, and made you delight in humbling yourselves beneath the lowest of all your fellow creatures.

Live therefore, my children, as you have begun your lives, in humble labor for the good of others, and let ceremonious visits and vain acquaintances have as little of your time as you possibly can. Contract no foolish friendships or vain fondnesses for particular persons, but love them most that most turn your love toward God and your compassion toward all the world.

But above all, avoid the conversation of fine-bred fops and beaux, and hate nothing more than the idle discourse, the flattery and compliments of that sort of men, for they are the shame of their own sex and ought to be the abhorrence of ours.

When you go abroad,[54] let humility, modesty, and a decent carriage[55] be all the state that you take upon you, and let tenderness, compassion, and a good nature be all the fine breeding that you show in any place.

If evil speaking, scandal, or backbiting be the conversation where you happen to be, keep your heart and your tongue to yourself, be as much grieved as if you was amongst cursing and swearing, and retire as soon as you can.

Though you intend to marry, yet let the time never come till you find a man that has those perfections which you have been laboring after yourselves, who is likely to be a friend to all your virtues and with whom it is better to live than to want the benefit of his example.

Love poverty and reverence poor people as for many reasons, so particularly for this, because our blessed Savior was one of the number and because you may make them all so many friends and advocates with God for you.

Visit and converse with them frequently; you will often find simplicity, innocence, patience, fortitude, and great piety amongst them, and where they are not so, your good example may amend them.

Rejoice at every opportunity of doing a humble action and exercising the meekness of your minds, whether it be, as the scripture expresses it, in washing the saints' feet, that is, in waiting upon and serving those that are below you, or in bearing with the haughtiness and ill manners of those that are your equals or above you. For there is nothing better than humility; it is the fruitful soil of all virtues and everything that is kind and good naturally grows from it.

Therefore, my children, pray for and practice humility and reject everything in dress or carriage or conversation that has any appearance of pride.

Strive to do everything that is praiseworthy, but do nothing in order to be praised, nor think of any reward for all your labors of love and virtue till Christ cometh with all His holy angels.

And above all, my children, have a care of vain and proud thoughts of your own virtues. For as soon as ever people live different from the common way of the world and despise its vanities, the Devil represents to their minds the height of their own perfections, and is content they should excel in good works provided that he can but make them proud of them.

Therefore, watch over your virtues with a jealous eye, and reject every vain thought as you would reject the most wicked imagination, and think what a loss it would be to you to have the fruit of all your good works devoured by the vanity of your own minds.

Never, therefore, allow yourselves to despise those who do not follow your rules of life, but force your hearts to love them and pray to God for them, and let humility be always whispering it into your ears that you yourselves will fall from those rules tomorrow if God should leave you to your own strength and wisdom.

When therefore you have spent days and weeks well, don't suffer your hearts to contemplate anything as your own, but give all the glory to the goodness of God, who has carried you through such rules of holy living as you were not able to observe by your own strength, and take care to begin the next day, not as proficients in virtue that can do great matters, but as poor beginners that want the daily assistance of God to save you from the grossest sins.

Your dear father was a humble, watchful, pious, wise man. Whilst his sickness would suffer him to talk with me, his discourse was chiefly about your education. He knew the benefits of humility, he saw the ruins which pride made in our sex, and therefore he conjured me with the tenderest expressions to renounce the fashionable ways of educating daughters in pride and softness, in the care of their beauty and dress, and to bring you all up in the plainest, simplest instances of a humble, holy, and industrious life.

He taught me an admirable rule of humility which he practiced all the days of his life, which was this: to let no morning pass without thinking upon some frailty and infirmity of our own that may put us to confusion, make us blush inwardly, and entertain a mean opinion of ourselves.

Think therefore, my children, that the soul of your good father who is now with God speaks to you through my mouth, and let the double desire of your father who is gone and I, who am with you, prevail upon you to love God, to study your own perfection, to practice humility, and with innocent labor and charity, to do all the good that you can to all your fellow creatures till God calls you to another life.

Thus did the pious widow educate her daughters.

The spirit of this education speaks so plainly for itself that I hope I need say nothing in its justification. If we could see it in life as well as read of it in books the world would soon find the happy effects of it.

A daughter thus educated would be a blessing to any family that she came into, a fit companion for a wise man, and make him happy in the government of his family and the education of his children.

And she that either was not inclined, or could not dispose of herself well in marriage, would know how to live to great and excellent ends in a state of virginity.

A very ordinary knowledge of the spirit of Christianity seems to be enough to convince us that no education can be of true advantage to young women but that which trains them up in humble industry, in great plainness of life, in exact modesty of dress, manners, and carriage, and in strict devotion. For what should a Christian woman be but a plain, unaffected, modest, humble creature, averse to everything in her dress and carriage that can draw the eyes of beholders or gratify the passions of lewd and amorous persons?

How great a stranger must he be to the gospel who does not know that it requires this to be the spirit of a pious woman?

Our blessed Savior saith "Whosoever looketh upon a woman to lust after her hath already committed adultery with her in his heart" (Matt. 5:28).

Need an education which turns women's minds to the arts and ornaments of dress and beauty be more strongly condemned than by these words? For surely if the eye is so easily and dangerously betrayed, every art and ornament is sufficiently condemned that naturally tends to betray it.

And how can a woman of piety more justly abhor and avoid anything than that which makes her person more a snare and temptation to other people? If lust and wanton eyes are the death of the soul, can any women think themselves innocent who, with naked breasts, patched faces, and every ornament of dress, invite the eye to offend?

And as there is no pretence for innocence in such a behavior, so neither can they tell how to set any bounds to their guilt. For as they can never know how much or how often they have occasioned sin in other people, so they can never know how much guilt will be placed to their own account.

This one would think should sufficiently deter every pious woman from everything that might render her the occasion of loose passions in other people.

St. Paul, speaking of a thing entirely innocent, reasons after this manner, "But take heed, lest by any means this liberty of yours become a stumbling-block to those that are weak. . . . And through thy knowledge thy weak brother perish, for whom Christ died. But when ye sin so against the brethren, and wound their weak conscience, ye sin against Christ. Wherefore, if meat make my brother to offend, I will eat no flesh while the world standeth, lest I make my brother to offend" (1 Cor. 8:9, 11-13).

Now if this is the spirit of Christianity, if it requires us to abstain from things thus lawful, innocent, and useful when there is any danger of betraying our weak brethren into any error thereby, surely it cannot be reckoned too nice or needless a point of conscience for women to avoid such things as are neither innocent nor useful but naturally tend to corrupt their own hearts and raise ill passions in other people.

Surely every woman of Christian piety ought to say, in the spirit of the Apostle, if patching and paint or any vain adorning of my person be a natural means of making weak, unwary eyes to offend, I will renounce all these arts as long as I live lest I should make my fellow creatures to offend.

I shall now leave this subject of humility, having said enough, as I hope, to recommend the necessity of making it the constant, chief subject of your devotion at this hour of prayer.

I have considered the nature and necessity of humility and its great importance to a religious life. I have shown you how many difficulties are formed against it from our natural tempers, the spirit of the world, and the common education of both sexes.

These considerations will, I hope, instruct you how to form your prayers for it to the best advantage, and teach you the necessity of letting no day pass without a serious earnest application to God for the whole spirit of humility, fervently beseeching him to fill every part of your soul with it to make it the ruling, constant habit of your mind, that you may not only feel it but feel all your other tempers arising from it, that you may have no thoughts, no desires, no designs but such as are the true fruits of a humble, meek, and lowly heart.

That you may always appear poor and little and mean in your own eyes and fully content that others should have the same opinion of you.

That the whole course of your life, your expense, your house, your dress, your manner of eating, drinking, conversing, and doing everything may be so many continual proofs of the true unfeigned humility of your heart.

That you may look for nothing, claim nothing, resent nothing; that you may go through all the actions and accidents of life calmly and quietly as in the presence of God, looking wholly unto Him, acting wholly for Him, neither seeking vain applause nor resenting neglects or affronts, but doing and receiving everything in the meek and lowly Spirit of our Lord and Savior Jesus Christ.

NOTES

49. Closets: small and private rooms.

50. Matilda regards "patching" as too important to leave to her daughters. The patch itself was usually a small piece of black silk worn on the face to conceal a blemish, or else to show off by contrast the fairness of the complexion.

51. Vapored . . . spirits: inclined to depression because of a lack of normal energy. Matilda will not allow the girls a proper diet for fear of their growing "coarse," that is, looking well fed and plump.

52. Twitched so straight: drawn tightly and made erect.

53. Becomes: is becoming to.

54. Abroad: out into the world.

55. Carriage: here signifying comportment or bearing.

Chapter 20

Recommending devotion at twelve o'clock, called in scripture the sixth hour of the day. This frequency of devotion equally desirable by all orders of people. Universal love is here recommended to be the subject of prayer at this hour. Of intercession as an act of universal love.

It will perhaps be thought by some people that these hours of prayer come too thick, that they can only be observed by people of great leisure and ought not to be pressed upon the generality of men who have the cares of families, trades, and employments, nor upon the gentry, whose state and figure in the world cannot admit of this frequency of devotion. And that it is only fit for monasteries and nunneries or such people as have no more to do in the world than they have.

To this it is answered:

First, that this method of devotion is not pressed upon any sort of people as absolutely necessary, but recommended to all people as the best, the happiest, and most perfect way of life.

And if a great and exemplary devotion is as much the greatest happiness and perfection of a merchant, a soldier, or a man of quality as it is the greatest happiness and perfection of the most retired contemplative life, then it is as proper to recommend it without any abatements to one order of men as to another, because happiness and perfection are of the same worth and value to all people.

The gentleman and tradesman may and must spend much of their time differently from the pious monk in the cloister or the contemplative hermit in the desert. But then, as the monk and hermit lose the ends of retirement unless they make it all serviceable to devotion, so the gentleman and merchant fail of the greatest ends of a social life, and live to their loss in the world unless devotion be their chief and governing temper.

It is certainly very honest and creditable for people to engage in trades and employments; it is reasonable for gentlemen to manage well their estates and families and take such recreations as are proper to their state. But then every gentleman and tradesman loses the greatest happiness of his creation, is robbed of something that is greater than all employments, distinctions, and pleasures of the world, if he does not live more to piety and devotion than to anything else in the world.

Here are therefore no excuses made for men of business and figure in the world. First, because it would be to excuse them from that which is the greatest end of living and be only finding so many reasons for making them less beneficial to themselves and less serviceable to God and the world.

Secondly, because most men of business and figure engage too far in worldly matters, much farther than the reasons of human life or the necessities of the world require.

Merchants and tradesmen, for instance, are generally ten times further engaged in business than they need, which is so far from being a reasonable excuse for their want of time for devotion that it is their crime and must be censured as a blamable instance of covetousness and ambition.

The gentry and people of figure either give themselves up to state employments or to the gratifications of their passions in a life of gaiety and debauchery; and if these things might be admitted as allowable avocations from devotion, devotion must be reckoned a poor circumstance of life.

Unless gentlemen can show that they have another God than the Father of our Lord Jesus Christ, another nature than that which is derived from Adam, another religion than the Christian, 'tis in vain to plead their state and dignity and pleasures as reasons for not preparing their souls for God by a strict and regular devotion.

For since piety and devotion are the common unchangeable means of saving all the souls in the world that shall be saved, there is nothing left for the gentleman, the soldier, and the tradesman but to take care that their several states be, by care and watchfulness, by meditation and prayer, made states of an exact and solid piety.

If a merchant, having forbore from too great business that he might quietly attend on the service of God, should therefore die worth twenty instead of fifty thousand pounds, could anyone say that he had mistaken his calling, or gone a loser out of the world?

If a gentleman should have killed fewer foxes, been less frequent at balls, gaming, and merry meetings, because stated parts of his time had been given to retirement, to meditation and devotion, could it be thought that when he left the world he would regret the loss of those hours that he had given to the care and improvement of his soul?

If a tradesman, by aspiring after Christian perfection and retiring himself often from his business should, instead of leaving his children fortunes to spend in luxury and idleness, leave them to live by their own honest labor, could it be said that he had made a wrong use of the world because he had shown his children that he had more regard to that which is eternal than to this which is so soon to be at an end?

Since, therefore, devotion is not only the best and most desirable practice in a cloister, but the best and most desirable practice of men, as men, and in every state of life, they that desire to be excused from it because they are men of figure and estates and business are no wiser than those that should desire to be excused from health and happiness because they were men of figure and estates.

I can't see why every gentleman, merchant, or soldier should not put these questions seriously to himself:

What is the best thing for me to intend and drive at in all my actions? How shall I do to make the most of human life? What ways shall I wish that I had taken when I am leaving the world?

Now to be thus wise and to make thus much use of our reason seems to be but a small and necessary piece of wisdom. For how can we pretend to sense and judgment if we dare not seriously consider and answer and govern our lives by that which such questions require of us?

Shall a nobleman think his birth too high a dignity to condescend to such questions as these? Or a tradesman think his business too great to take any care about himself?

Now here is desired no more devotion in anyone's life than the answering these few questions requires.

Any devotion that is not to the greater advantage of him that uses it than anything that he can do in the room of it, any devotion that does not procure an infinitely greater good than can be got by neglecting it, is freely yielded up; here is no demand of it.

But if people will live in so much ignorance as never to put these questions to themselves, but push on a blind life at all chances in quest of they don't know what nor why, without ever considering the worth or value or tendency of their actions, without considering what God, reason, eternity, and their own happiness require of them, it is for the honor of devotion that none can neglect it but those who are thus inconsiderate, who dare not inquire after that which is the best and most worthy of their choice.

It is true, Claudius, you are a man of figure and estate and are to act the part of such a station in human life; you are not called as Elijah was to be a prophet, or as St. Paul to be an Apostle.

But will you therefore not love yourself? Will you not seek and study your own happiness because you are not called to preach up the same things to other people?

You would think it very absurd for a man not to value his own health because he was not a physician, or the preservation of his limbs because he was not a bone-setter. Yet it is more absurd for you, Claudius, to neglect the improvement of your soul in piety because you are not an Apostle or a bishop.

Consider this text of scripture, "If ye live after the flesh, ye shall die; but if through the spirit ye do mortify the deeds of the body, ye shall live. For as many as are led by the Spirit of God, they are the sons of God" (Rom. 8:13, 14). Do you think that this scripture does not equally relate to all mankind? Can you find any exception here for men of figure and estates? Is not a spiritual and devout life here made the common condition on which all men are to become sons of God? Will you leave hours of prayer and rules of devotion to particular states of life when nothing but the same spirit of devotion can save you or any man from eternal death?

Consider again this text: "For we must all appear before the judgment seat of Christ, that everyone may receive the things done in his body, according to that he hath done, whether it be good or bad" (2 Cor. 5:10). Now if your estate would excuse you from appearing before this judgment seat, if your figure could protect you from receiving according to your works, there would be some pretence for leaving devotion to other people. But if you, who are now thus distinguished, must then appear naked amongst common souls, without any other distinction from others but such as your virtues or sins give you, does it not as much concern you as any prophet or Apostle to make the best provision for the best rewards at that great day?

Again, consider this doctrine of the Apostle: "For none of us," that is, of us Christians, "liveth to himself, and no man dieth to himself: for whether we live, we live unto the Lord; and whether we die, we die unto the Lord. For to this end Christ both died, and rose, and revived, that he might be Lord both of the dead and the living" (Rom. 14:7-9).

Now are you, Claudius, excepted out of the doctrine of this text? Will you, because of your condition, leave it to any particular sort of people to live and die unto Christ? If so, you must leave it to them to be redeemed by the death and Resurrection of Christ. For it is the express doctrine of the text that for this end Christ died and rose again, that none of us should live to himself. 'Tis not that priests or Apostles or monks or hermits should live no longer to themselves, but that none of us, that is, no Christian of what state soever, should live unto himself.

If, therefore, there be any instances of piety, any rules of devotion which you can neglect, and yet live as truly unto Christ as if you observed them, this text calls you to no such devotion. But if you forsake such devotion as you yourself know is expected from some particular sorts of people, such devotion as you know becomes people that live wholly unto Christ, that aspire after great piety; if you neglect such devotion for any worldly consideration that you may live more to your own temper and taste, more to the fashions and ways of the world, you forsake the terms on which all Christians are to receive the benefit of Christ's death and Resurrection. Observe further, how the same doctrine is taught by St. Peter: "As he which hath called you is holy, so be ye holy in all manner of conversation" (1 Pet. 1:15).

If therefore, Claudius, you are one of those that are here called, you see what it is that you are called to. It is not to have so much religion as suits with your temper, your business, or your pleasures, it is not to a particular sort of piety that may be sufficient for gentlemen of figure and estates, but it is, first, to be holy as He which hath called you is holy; secondly, it is to be thus holy in all manner of conversation; that is, to carry this spirit and degree of holiness into every part and through the whole form of your life.

And the reason the Apostle immediately gives why this spirit of holiness must be the common spirit of Christians as such is very affecting and such as equally calls upon all sorts of Christians. "Forasmuch as ye know," says he, "that ye were not redeemed with corruptible things, as silver and gold, from your vain conversation . . . but with the precious blood of Christ," etc.

As if he had said, forasmuch as ye know ye were made capable of this state of holiness, entered into a society with Christ, and made heirs of His glory, not by any human means, but by such a mysterious instance of love as infinitely exceeds everything that can be thought of in this world, since God has redeemed you to Himself and your own happiness at so great a price, how base and shameful must it be if you don't henceforth devote yourselves wholly to the glory of God and become holy, as He who hath called you is holy?

If therefore, Claudius, you consider your figure and estate, or if in the words of the text, you consider your gold and silver and the corruptible things of this life as any reason why you may live to your own humor and fancy, why you may neglect a life of strict piety and great devotion; if you think anything in the world can be an excuse for your not imitating the holiness of Christ in the whole course and form of your life, you make yourself as guilty as if you should neglect the holiness of Christianity for the sake of picking straws.

For the greatness of this new state of life to which we are called in Christ Jesus to be forever as the angels of God in Heaven, and the greatness of the price by which we are made capable of this state of glory, has turned everything that is worldly, temporal, and corruptible into an equal littleness, and made it as great baseness and folly, as great a contempt of the blood of Christ, to neglect any degrees of holiness because you are a man of some estate and quality, as it would be to neglect it because you had a fancy to pick straws.

Again, the same Apostle saith, "Know ye not, that your body is the temple of the Holy Ghost which is in you, and ye are not your own? For ye are bought with a price; therefore glorify God in your body, and in your spirit, which are God's" (1 Cor. 6:19, 20).

How poorly therefore, Claudius, have you read the scripture, how little do you know of Christianity, if you can yet talk of your estate and condition as a pretence for a freer kind of life?

Are you any more your own than he that has no estate or dignity in the world? Must mean and little people preserve their bodies as temples of the Holy Ghost by watching, fasting, and prayer, but may you indulge yours in idleness, in lusts and sensuality, because you have so much rent or such a title of distinction? How poor and ignorant are such thoughts as these?

And yet you must either think thus, or else acknowledge that the holiness of saints, prophets, and apostles is the holiness that you are to labor after with all the diligence and care that you can.

And if you leave it to others to live in such piety and devotion, in such self-denial, humility, and temperance as may render them able to glorify God in their body and in their spirit, you must leave it to them also to have the benefit of the blood of Christ.

Again, the Apostle saith, "You know how we exhorted, comforted, and charged every one of you, that you would walk worthy of God, who hath called you to His kingdom and glory" (1 Thess. 2:11, 12).

You perhaps, Claudius, have often heard these words without ever thinking how much they required of you. And yet you can't consider them without perceiving to what an eminent state of holiness they call you.

For how can the holiness of the Christian life be set before you in higher terms than when it is represented to you as walking worthy of God? Can you think of any abatements of virtue, any neglects of devotion, that are well consistent with a life that is to be made worthy of God? Can you suppose that any man walks in this manner but he that watches over all his steps, and considers how everything he does may be done in the spirit of holiness? And yet as high as these expressions carry this holiness, it is here plainly made the necessary holiness of all Christians. For the Apostle does not here exhort his fellow Apostles and Saints to this holiness, but he commands all Christians to endeavor after it. "We charged," says he, "everyone of you, that you would walk worthy of God, who hath called you to His kingdom and glory."

Again, St. Peter saith, "If any man speak, let him speak as the oracles of God; if any man minister, let him do it as of the ability that God giveth; that God in all things may be glorified in Jesus Christ" (1 Pet. 4:11).

Do you not here, Claudius, plainly perceive your high calling? Is he that speaketh to have such regard to his words that he appear to speak as by the direction of God? Is he that giveth to take care that he so giveth that what he disposeth of may appear to be a gift that he hath of God? And is all this to be done that God may be glorified in all things?

Must it not then be said, has any man nobility, dignity of state, or figure in the world? Let him so use his nobility or figure of life that it may appear he uses these as the gifts of God for the greater setting forth of His glory. Is there now, Claudius, anything forced or farfetched in this conclusion? Is it not the plain sense of the words that everything in life is to be made a matter of holiness unto God? If so, then your estate and dignity is so far from excusing you from great piety and holiness of life that it lays you under a greater necessity of living more to the glory of God, because you have more of His gifts that may be made serviceable to it.

For people therefore of figure or business or dignity in the world to leave great piety and eminent devotion to any particular orders of men or such as they think have little else to do in the world is to leave the Kingdom of God to them.

For it is the very end of Christianity to redeem all orders of men into one holy society, that rich and poor, high and low, masters and servants, may in one and the same spirit of piety become a "chosen generation, a royal priesthood, a holy nation, a peculiar people, that are to show forth the praises of Him, who hath called them out of darkness, into His marvellous light" (1 Pet. 2:9).

Thus much being said to show that great devotion and holiness is not to be left to any particular sort of people but to be the common spirit of all that desire to live up to the terms of common Christianity; I now proceed to consider the nature and necessity of universal love which is here recommended to be the subject of your devotion at this hour. You are here also called to intercession as the most proper exercise to raise and preserve that love.

By intercession is meant a praying to God and interceding with Him for our fellow creatures.

Our blessed Lord hath recommended His love to us as the

pattern and example of our love to one another. As, therefore, He is continually making intercession for us all, so ought we to intercede and pray for one another.

"A new commandment," saith He, "I give unto you, that ye love one another, as I have loved you. By this shall all men know that ye are my disciples, if ye love one another."

The newness of this precept did not consist in this, that men were commanded to love one another; for this was an old precept, both of the law of Moses and of nature. But it was new in this respect, that it was to imitate a new and till then unheard-of example of love; it was to love one another as Christ had loved us.

And if men are to know that we are disciples of Christ by thus loving one another according to His new example of love, then it is certain that if we are void of this love we make it as plainly known unto men that we are none of His disciples.

There is no principle of the heart that is more acceptable to God than a universal fervent love to all mankind, wishing and praying for their happiness, because there is no principle of the heart that makes us more like God, who is love and goodness itself and created all beings for their enjoyment of happiness.

The greatest idea that we can frame of God is when we conceive Him to be a Being of infinite love and goodness, using an infinite wisdom and power for the common good and happiness of all His creatures.

The highest notion, therefore, that we can form of man is when we conceive him as like to God in this respect as he can be, using all his finite faculties, whether of wisdom, power, or prayers, for the common good of all his fellow creatures, heartily desiring they may have all the happiness they are capable of and as many benefits and assistances from him as his state and condition in the world will permit him to give them.

And on the other hand, what a baseness and iniquity is there in all instances of hatred, envy, spite, and ill will, if we consider that every instance of them is so far acting in opposition to God and intending mischief and harm to those creatures which God favors, and protects, and preserves, in order to their happiness? An ill-natured man amongst God's creatures is the most perverse creature in the world, acting contrary to that love by which himself subsists and which alone gives subsistence to all that variety of beings that enjoy life in any part of the creation.

"Whatsoever ye would that men should do unto you, even so do unto them."

Now though this is a doctrine of strict justice, yet it is only a universal love that can comply with it. For as love is the measure of our acting toward ourselves, so we can never act in the same manner toward other people till we look upon them with that love with which we look upon ourselves.

As we have no degrees of spite or envy or ill will to ourselves, so we cannot be disposed toward others as we are toward ourselves till we universally renounce all instances of spite and envy and ill will even in the smallest degrees.

If we had any imperfection in our eyes that made us see any one thing wrong, for the same reason they would show us a hundred things wrong.

So if we have any temper of our hearts that makes us envious or spiteful or ill natured toward any one man, the same temper will make us envious and spiteful and ill natured toward a great many more.

If, therefore, we desire this divine virtue of love, we must exercise and practice our hearts in the love of all because it is not Christian love till it is the love of all.

If a man could keep this whole law of love and yet offend in one point, he would be guilty of all. For as one allowed instance of injustice destroys the justice of all our other actions, so one allowed instance of envy, spite, and ill will renders all our other acts of benevolence and affection nothing worth.

Acts of love that proceed not from a principle of universal love are but like acts of justice that proceed from a heart not disposed to universal justice.

A love which is not universal may indeed have tenderness and affection but it hath nothing of righteousness or piety in it; it is but humor, and temper, or interest, or such a love as publicans and heathens practice.

All particular envies and spites are as plain departures from the spirit of Christianity as any particular acts of injustice. For it is as much a law of Christ to treat everybody as your neighbor and to love your neighbor as yourself as 'tis a law of Christianity to abstain from theft.

Now the noblest motive to this universal tenderness and affection is founded in this doctrine, "God is love, and he that dwelleth in love, dwelleth in God."

Who, therefore, whose heart has any tendency toward God, would not aspire after this divine temper which so changes and exalts our nature into a union with Him?

How should we rejoice in the exercise and practice of this love which so often as we feel it is so often an assurance to us that God is in us, that we act according to His Spirit who is love itself? But we must observe that love has then only this mighty power of uniting us to God when it is so pure and universal as to imitate that love which God beareth to all His creatures.

God willeth the happiness of all beings though it is no happiness to Himself. Therefore we must desire the happiness of all beings though no happiness cometh to us from it.

God equally delighteth in the perfections of all His creatures; therefore, we should rejoice in those perfections wherever we see them and be glad to have other people perfect as ourselves.

As God forgiveth all and giveth grace to all, so we should forgive all those injuries and affronts which we receive from others and do all the good that we can to them.

God Almighty, besides His own great example of love, which ought to draw all His creatures after it, has so provided for us and made our happiness so common to us all that we have no occasion to envy or hate one another.

For we cannot stand in one another's way, or by enjoying any particular good, keep another from his full share of it.

As we cannot be happy but in the enjoyment of God, so we cannot rival or rob one another of this happiness.

And as to other things, the enjoyments and prosperities of this life, they are so little in themselves, so foreign to our happiness and, generally speaking, so contrary to that which they appear to be, that they are no foundation for envy or spite or hatred.

How silly would it be to envy a man that was drinking poison out of a golden cup? And yet who can say that he is acting wiser than thus when he is envying any instance of worldly greatness?

How many Saints has adversity sent to Heaven? And how many poor sinners has prosperity plunged into everlasting misery? A man seems then to be in the most glorious state when he has conquered, disgraced, and humbled his enemy, though it may be that same conquest has saved his adversary and undone himself.

This man had perhaps never been debauched but for his fortune and advancement; that had never been pious but through his poverty and disgrace.

She that is envied for her beauty may perchance owe all her misery to it, and another may be forever happy for having had no admirers of her person.

One man succeeds in everything and so loses all. Another meets with nothing but crosses and disappointments and thereby gains more than all the world is worth.

This clergyman may be undone by his being made a bishop, and that may save both himself and others by being fixed to his first poor vicarage.

How envied was Alexander when, conquering the world, he built towns, set up his statues, and left marks of his glory in so many kingdoms!

And how despised was the poor preacher St. Paul when he was beaten with rods! And yet how strangely was the world mistaken in their judgment! How much to be envied was St. Paul! How much to be pitied was Alexander!

These few reflections sufficiently show us that the different conditions of this life have nothing in them to excite our uneasy passions, nothing that can reasonably interrupt our love and affection to one another.

To proceed now to another motive to this universal love.

Our power of doing external acts of love and goodness is often very narrow and restrained. There are, it may be, but few people to whom we can contribute any worldly relief.

But though our outward means of doing good are often thus limited, yet if our hearts are but full of love and goodness we get, as it were, an infinite power because God will attribute to us those good works, those acts of love and tender charities, which we sincerely desired and would gladly have performed had it been in our power.

You cannot heal all the sick, relieve all the poor; you cannot comfort all in distress nor be a father to all the fatherless. You cannot, it may be, deliver many from their misfortunes or teach them to find comfort in God.

But if there is a love and tenderness in your heart that delights in these good works and excites you to do all that you can, if your love has no bounds but continually wishes and prays for the relief and happiness of all that are in distress, you will be received by God as a benefactor to those who have had nothing from you but your good will and tender affections.

You cannot build hospitals for the incurable; you cannot erect monasteries for the education of persons in holy solitude, continual prayer, and mortification; but if you join in your heart with those that do and thank God for their pious designs, if you are a friend to these great friends of mankind and rejoice in their eminent virtues, you will be received by God as a sharer of such good works as, though they had none of your hands, yet had all your heart.

This consideration surely is sufficient to make us look to and watch over our hearts with all diligence, to study the improvement of our inward tempers and aspire after every height and perfection of a loving, charitable, and benevolent mind.

And on the other hand, we may hence learn the great evil and mischief of all wrong turns of mind, of envy, spite, hatred, and ill will. For if the goodness of our hearts will entitle us to the reward of good actions which we never performed, it is certain that the badness of our hearts, our envy, ill nature, and hatred will bring us under the guilt of actions that we have never committed.

As he that lusteth after a woman shall be reckoned an adulterer, though he has only committed the crime in his heart, so the malicious, spiteful, ill-natured man that only secretly rejoices at evil shall be reckoned a murderer, though he has shed no blood.

Since, therefore, our hearts which are always naked and open to the eyes of God give such an exceeding extent and increase either to our virtues or vices, it is our best and greatest business to govern the motions of our hearts, to watch, correct, and improve the inward state and temper of our souls.

Now there is nothing that so much exalts our souls as this heavenly love. It cleanses and purifies like a holy fire and all ill tempers fall away before it. It makes room for all virtues, and carries them to their greatest height. Everything that is good and holy grows out of it and it becomes a continual source of all holy desires and pious practices.

By love, I don't mean any natural tenderness which is more or less in people according to their constitutions, but I mean a larger principle of the soul, founded in reason and piety, which makes us tender, kind, and benevolent to all our fellow creatures as creatures of God, and for His sake.

It is this love that loves all things in God as His creatures, as the images of His power, as the creatures of His goodness, as parts of His family, as members of His society, that becomes a holy principle of all great and good actions.

The love, therefore, of our neighbor is only a branch of our love to God. For when we love God with all our hearts, and with all our souls, and with all our strength, we shall necessarily love those beings that are so nearly related to God, that have everything from Him, and are created by Him to be objects of His own eternal love. If I hate or despise any one man in the world, I hate something that God cannot hate, and despise that which He loves.

And can I think that I love God with all my heart whilst I hate that which belongs only to God, which has no other master but Him, which bears His image, is part of His family and exists only by the continuance of His love toward it?

It was the impossibility of this that made St. John say, "That if any man saith he loveth God, and hateth his brother, he is a liar."

These reasons sufficiently show us that no love is holy or religious till it becomes universal.

For if religion requires me to love all persons as God's creatures that belong to Him, that bear His image, enjoy His protection and make parts of His family and household; if these are the great and necessary reasons why I should live in love and friendship with any one man in the world, they are the same great and necessary reasons why I should live in love and friendship with every man in the world, and consequently I offend against all these reasons and break through all these ties and obligations whenever I want love toward any one man. The sin therefore of hating or despising any one man is like the sin of hating all God's creation, and the necessity of loving any one man is the same necessity of loving every man in the world.

And though many people may appear to us ever so sinful, odious, or extravagant in their conduct, we must never look upon that as the least motive for any contempt or disregard of them, but look upon them with the greater compassion as being in the most pitiable condition that can be.

As it was the sins of the world that made the Son of God become a compassionate, suffering Advocate for all mankind, so no one is of the Spirit of Christ but he that has the utmost compassion for sinners. Nor is there any greater sign of your own perfection than when you find yourself all love and compassion toward them that are very weak and defective. And on the other hand, you have never less reason to be pleased with yourself than when you find yourself most angry and offended at the behavior of others. All sin is certainly to be hated and abhorred wherever it is, but then we must set ourselves against sin as we do against sickness and diseases, by showing ourselves tender and compassionate to the sick and diseased.

All other hatred of sin which does not fill the heart with the softest, tenderest affections toward persons miserable in it is the servant of sin at the same time that it seems to be hating it.

And there is no temper which even good men ought more carefully to watch and guard against than this. For it is a temper that lurks and hides itself under the cover of many virtues, and by being unsuspected does the more mischief.

A man naturally fancies that it is his own exceeding love of virtue that makes him not able to bear with those that want it. And when he abhors one man, despises another, and can't bear the name of a third, he supposes it all to be a proof of his own high sense of virtue and just hatred of sin.

And yet one would think that a man needed no other cure for this temper than this one reflection:

That if this had been the Spirit of the Son of God, if He had hated sin in this manner, there had been no redemption of the world; that if God had hated sinners in this manner day and night, the world itself had ceased long ago.

This, therefore, we may take for a certain rule, that the more we partake of the divine nature, the more improved we are ourselves, and the higher our sense of virtue is, the more we shall pity and compassionate those that want it. The sight of such people will then, instead of raising in us a haughty contempt or peevish indignation toward them, fill us with such bowels of compassion as when we see the miseries of a hospital.

That the follies, therefore, crimes, and ill behavior of our fellow creatures may not lessen that love and tenderness which we are to have for all mankind, we should often consider the reasons on which this duty of love is founded.

Now we are to love our neighbor, that is, all mankind, not because they are wise, holy, virtuous, or well behaved; for all mankind neither ever was, nor ever will be so; therefore, it is certain that the reason of our being obliged to love them cannot be founded in their virtue.

Again, if their virtue or goodness were the reason of our being obliged to love people, we should have no rule to proceed by because, though some people's virtues or vices are very notorious, yet generally speaking we are but very ill judges of the virtue and merit of other people.

Thirdly, we are sure that the virtue or merit of persons is not the reason of our being obliged to love them because we are commanded to pay the highest instances of love to our worst enemies; we are to love and bless and pray for those that most injuriously treat us. This therefore is demonstration that the merit of persons is not the reason on which our obligation to love them is founded.

Let us further consider what that love is which we owe to our neighbor. It is to love him as ourselves, that is, to have all those sentiments toward him which we have toward ourselves; to wish him everything that we may lawfully wish to ourselves, to be glad of every good and sorry for every evil that happens to him, and to be ready to do him all such acts of kindness as we are always ready to do to ourselves.

This love, therefore, you see, is nothing else but a love of benevolence; it requires nothing of us but such good wishes, tender affections, and such acts of kindness as we show to ourselves.

This is all the love that we owe to the best of men, and we are never to want any degree of this love to the worst or most unreasonable man in the world.

Now what is the reason why we are to love every man in this manner? It is answered that our obligation to love all men in this is founded upon many reasons.

First, upon a reason of equity, for if it is just to love ourselves in this manner, it must be unjust to deny any degree of this love to others, because every man is so exactly of the same nature and in the same condition as ourselves.

If, therefore, your own crimes and follies do not lessen your obligation to seek your own good and wish well to yourself, neither do the follies and crimes of your neighbor lessen your obligation to wish and seek the good of your neighbor.

Another reason for this love is founded in the authority of God who has commanded us to love every man as ourself.

Thirdly, we are obliged to this love in imitation of God's goodness, that we may be children of our Father which is in Heaven, who willeth the happiness of all His creatures and maketh His sun to rise on the evil and on the good.

Fourthly, our redemption by Jesus Christ calleth us to the exercise of this love, who came from Heaven and laid down His life out of love to the whole sinful world.

Fifthly, by the command of our Lord and Savior who has required us to love one another as He has loved us.

These are the great, perpetual reasons on which our obligation to love all mankind as ourselves is founded.

These reasons never vary or change, they always continue in their full force, and therefore equally oblige at all times and in regard to all persons.

God loves us, not because we are wise and good and holy, but in pity to us, because we want this happiness. He loves us in order to make us good. Our love, therefore, must take this course, not looking for or requiring the merit of our brethren but pitying their disorders and wishing them all the good that they want and are capable of receiving.

It appears now plainly from what has been said that the love which we owe to our brethren is only a love of benevolence. Secondly, that this duty of benevolence is founded upon such reasons as never vary or change, such as have no dependence upon the qualities of persons. From whence it follows that it is the same great sin to want this love to a bad man as to want it to a good man. Because he that denies any of this benevolence to a bad man offends against all the same reasons of love as he does that denies any benevolence to a good man, and consequently it is the same sin.

When, therefore, you let loose any ill-natured passion, either of hatred or contempt toward (as you suppose) an ill man, consider what you would think of another that was doing the same toward a good man and be assured that you are committing the same sin.

You will perhaps say, "How is it possible to love a good and a bad man in the same degree?"

Just as it's possible to be as just and faithful to a good man as to an evil man. Now are you in any difficulty about performing justice and faithfulness to a bad man? Are you in any doubts whether you need be so just and faithful to him as you need be to a good man? Now why is it that you are in no doubt about it? 'Tis because you know that justice and faithfulness are founded upon reasons that never vary or change, that have no dependence upon the merits of men but are founded in the nature of things in the laws of God and therefore are to be observed with an equal exactness toward good and bad men.

Now do but think thus justly of charity or love to your neighbor, that it is founded upon reasons that vary not, that have no dependence upon the merits of men, and then you will find it as possible to perform the same exact charity as the same exact justice to all men, whether good or bad.

You will perhaps further ask if you are not to have a particular esteem, veneration, and reverence for good men? It is answered, Yes. But then this high esteem and veneration is a thing very different from that love of benevolence which we owe to our neighbor.

The high esteem and veneration which you have for a man of eminent piety is no act of charity to him. It is not out of pity and compassion that you so reverence him but it is rather an act of charity to yourself that such esteem and veneration may excite you to follow his example.

You may and ought to love, like, and approve the life which the good man leads, but then this is only the loving of virtue wherever we see it. And we don't love virtue with the love of benevolence as anything that wants our good wishes, but as something that is our proper good.

The whole of the matter is this. The actions which you are to love, esteem, and admire are the actions of good and pious men, but the persons to whom you are to do all the good you can in all sorts of kindness and compassion are all persons whether good or bad.

This distinction betwixt love of benevolence and esteem or veneration is very plain and obvious. And you may perhaps still better see the plainness and necessity of it by this following instance.

No man is to have a high esteem or honor for his own accomplishments or behavior; yet every man is to love himself, that is, to wish well to himself; therefore, this distinction betwixt love and esteem is not only plain but very necessary to be observed.

Again, if you think it hardly possible to dislike the actions of unreasonable men and yet have a true love for them, consider this with relation to yourself.

It is very possible, I hope, for you not only to dislike but to detest and abhor a great many of your own past actions and to accuse yourself of great folly for them. But do you then lose any of those tender sentiments toward yourself which you used to have? Do you then cease to wish well to yourself? Is not the love of yourself as strong then as at any other time?

Now what is thus possible with relation to ourselves is in the same manner possible with relation to others. We may have the highest good wishes toward them, desiring for them every good that we desire for ourselves, and yet at the same time dislike their way of life.

To proceed: All that love which we may justly have for ourselves, we are in strict justice obliged to exercise toward all other men, and we offend against the great law of our nature and the greatest laws of God when our tempers toward others are different from those which we have toward ourselves. Now that self-love which is just and reasonable keeps us constantly tender, compassionate, and well affected toward ourselves. If therefore you don't feel these kind dispositions toward all other people, you may be assured that you are not in that state of charity which is the very life and soul of Christian piety.

You know how it hurts you to be made the jest and ridicule of other people; how it grieves you to be robbed of your reputation and deprived of the favorable opinion of your neighbors. If therefore you expose others to scorn and contempt in any degree, if it pleases you to see or hear of their frailties and infirmities, or if you are only loath to conceal their faults, you are so far from loving such people as yourself that you may be justly supposed to have as much hatred for them as you have love for yourself. For such tempers are as truly the proper fruits of hatred as the contrary tempers are the proper fruits of love.

And as it is a certain sign that you love yourself because you are tender of everything that concerns you, so it is as certain a sign that you hate your neighbor when you are pleased with anything that hurts him.

But now, if the want of a true and exact charity be so great a want that, as St. Paul saith, it renders our greatest virtues but empty sounds and tinkling cymbals, how highly does it concern us to study every art and practice every method of raising our souls to this state of charity? It is for this reason that you are here desired not to let this hour of prayer pass without a full and solemn supplication to God for all the instances of a universal love and benevolence to all mankind.

Such daily constant devotion being the only likely means of preserving you in such a state of love as is necessary to prove you to be a true follower of Jesus Christ.

Chapter 21

Of the necessity and benefit of intercession, considered as an exercise of universal love. How all orders of men are to pray and intercede with God for one another. How naturally such intercession amends and reforms the hearts of those that use it.

That intercession is a great and necessary part of Christian devotion is very evident from scripture.

The first followers of Christ seem to support all their love and to maintain all their intercourse and correspondence by mutual prayers for[56] one another.

St. Paul, whether he writes to churches or particular persons, shows his intercession to be perpetual for them that they are the constant subject of his prayers.

Thus to the Philippians, "I thank my God upon every remembrance of you. Always in every prayer of mine for you all, making request with joy" (Phil. 1:3, 4). Here we see not only a continual intercession but performed with so much gladness as shows that it was an exercise of love in which he highly rejoiced.

His devotion had also the same care for particular persons as appears by the following passage. "I thank my God, whom I serve from my forefathers, with a pure conscience, that without ceasing I have remembrance of thee in my prayers night and day" (2 Tim. 1:3). How holy an acquaintance and friendship was this, how worthy of persons that were raised above the world and related to one another as new members of a Kingdom of Heaven!

Apostles and great Saints did not only thus benefit and bless particular churches and private persons, but they themselves also received graces from God by the prayers of others. Thus saith St. Paul to the Corinthians, "You also helping together by prayer for us, that for the gift bestowed upon us by the means of many persons, thanks may be given by many on our behalf" (2 Cor. 1:11).

This was the ancient friendship of Christians, uniting and cementing their hearts, not by worldly considerations or human passions, but by the mutual communication of spiritual blessings, by prayers and thanksgivings to God for one another.

It was this holy intercession that raised Christians to such a state of mutual love as far exceeded all that had been praised and admired in human friendship. And when the same spirit of intercession is again in the world, when Christianity has the same power over the hearts of people that it then had, this holy friendship will be again in fashion and Christians will be again the wonder of the world for that exceeding love which they bear to one another.

For a frequent intercession with God, earnestly beseeching him to forgive the sins of all mankind, to bless them with his providence, enlighten them with his spirit, and bring them to everlasting happiness, is the divinest exercise that the heart of man can be engaged in.

Be daily therefore on your knees in a solemn, deliberate performance of this devotion, praying for others in such forms, with such length, importunity, and earnestness as you use for yourself; and you will find all little, ill-natured passions die away, your heart grow great and generous, delighting in the common happiness of others as you used only to delight in your own.

For he daily prays to God that all men may be happy in Heaven, takes the likeliest way to make him wish for and delight in their happiness on earth. And it is hardly possible for you to beseech and entreat God to make anyone happy in the highest enjoyments of his glory to all eternity, and yet be troubled to see him enjoy the much smaller gifts of God in this short and low state of human life.

For how strange and unnatural would it be to pray to God to grant health and a longer life to a sick man and at the same time to envy him the poor pleasure of agreeable medicines?

Yet this would be no more strange or unnatural than to pray to God that your neighbor may enjoy the highest degrees of His mercy and favor, and yet at the same time envy him the little credit and figure he hath amongst his fellow creatures.

When, therefore, you have once habituated your heart to a serious performance of this holy intercession you have done a great deal to render it incapable of spite and envy and to make it naturally delight in the happiness of all mankind.

This is the natural effect of a general intercession for all mankind. But the greatest benefits of it are then received when it descends to such particular instances as our state and condition in life more particularly require of us.

Though we are to treat all mankind as neighbors and brethren as any occasion offers, yet as we can only live in the actual society of a few and are by our state and condition more particularly related to some than others, so when our intercession is made an exercise of love and care for those amongst whom our lot is fallen, or who belong to us in a nearer relation, it then becomes the greatest benefit to ourselves and produces its best effects in our own hearts.

If therefore you should always change and alter your intercessions according as the needs and necessities of your neighbors or acquaintance seem to require, beseeching God to deliver them from such or such particular evils, or to grant them this or that particular gift or blessing, such intercessions, besides the great charity of them, would have a mighty effect upon your own heart as disposing you to every other good office and to the exercise of every other virtue toward such persons as have so often a place in your prayers.

This would make it pleasant to you to be courteous, civil, and condescending to all about you, and make you unable to say or do a rude or hard thing to those for whom you had used yourself to be so kind and compassionate in your prayers.

For there is nothing that makes us love a man so much as praying for him; and when you can once do this sincerely for any man, you have fitted your soul for the performance of everything that is kind and civil toward him. This will fill your heart with a generosity and tenderness that will give you a better and sweeter behavior than anything that is called fine breeding and good manners.

By considering yourself as an advocate with God for your neighbors and acquaintances, you would never find it hard to be at peace with them yourself. It would be easy to you to bear with and forgive those for whom you particularly implored the divine mercy and forgiveness.

Such prayers as these amongst neighbors and acquaintances would unite them to one another in the strongest bonds of love and tenderness. It would exalt and ennoble their souls and teach them to consider one another in a higher state as members of a spiritual society that are created for the enjoyment of the common blessings of God and fellow heirs of the same future glory.

And by being thus desirous that everyone should have their full share of the favors of God, they would not only be content but glad to see one another happy in the little enjoyments of this transitory life.

These would be the natural effects of such an intercession amongst people of the same town or neighborhood, or that were acquainted with one another's state and condition.

Ouranius is a holy priest, full of the spirit of the gospel, watching, laboring, and praying for a poor country village. Every soul in it is as dear to him as himself, and he loves them all as he loves himself because he prays for them all as often as he prays for himself.

If his whole life is one continual exercise of great zeal and labor, hardly ever satisfied with any degrees of care and watchfulness, 'tis because he has learned the great value of souls by so often appearing before God as an intercessor for them.

He never thinks he can love or do enough for his flock because he never considers them in any other view than as so many persons that, by receiving the gifts and graces of God, are to become his hope, his joy, and his crown of rejoicing.

He goes about his parish and visits everybody in it, but visits in the same spirit of piety that he preaches to them. He visits them to encourage their virtues, to assist them with his advice and counsel, to discover their manner of life and to know the state of their souls that he may intercede with God for them according to their particular necessities.

When Ouranius first entered into holy orders he had a haughtiness in his temper, a great contempt and disregard for all foolish and unreasonable people, but he has prayed away this spirit and has now the greatest tenderness for the most obstinate sinners, because he is always hoping that God will sooner or later hear those prayers that he makes for their repentance.

The rudeness, ill nature, or perverse behavior of any of his flock used at first to betray him into impatience, but it now raises no other passion in him than a desire of being upon his knees in prayer to God for them. Thus have his prayers for others altered and amended the state of his own heart.

It would strangely delight you to see with what spirit he converses, with what tenderness he reproves, with what affection he exhorts, and with what vigor he preaches, and 'tis all owing to this, because he reproves, exhorts, and preaches to those for whom he first prays to God.

This devotion softens his heart, enlightens his mind, sweetens his temper, and makes everything that comes from him instructive, amiable, and affecting.

At his first coming to his little village, it was as disagreeable to him as a prison and every day seemed too tedious to be endured in so retired a place. He thought his parish was too full of poor and mean people that were none of them fit for the conversation of a gentleman.

This put him upon a close application to his studies. He kept much at home, writ notes upon Homer and Plautus, and sometimes thought it hard to be called to pray by any poor body when he was just in the midst of one of Homer's battles.

This was his polite, or I may rather say, poor, ignorant turn of mind before devotion had got the government of his heart.

But now his days are so far from being tedious or his parish too great a retirement that he now only wants more time to do that variety of good which his soul thirsts after. The solitude of his little parish is become matter of great comfort to him because he hopes that God has placed him and his flock there to make it their way to Heaven.

He can now not only converse with, but gladly attend and wait upon the poorest kind of people. He is now daily watching over the weak and infirm, humbling himself to perverse, rude, ignorant people wherever he can find them, and is so far from desiring to be considered as a gentleman that he desires to be used as the servant of all; and in the spirit of his Lord and Master girds himself and is glad to kneel down and wash any of their feet.

He now thinks the poorest creature in his parish good enough and great enough to deserve the humblest attendances, the kindest friendships, the tenderest offices he can possibly show them.

He is so far now from wanting agreeable company that he thinks there is no better conversation in the world than to be talking with poor and mean people about the Kingdom of Heaven.

All these noble thoughts and divine sentiments are the effects of his great devotion; he presents everyone so often before God in his prayers that he never thinks he can esteem, reverence, or serve those enough for whom he implores so many mercies from God.

Ouranius is mightily affected with this passage of holy scripture, "the effectual, fervent prayer of a righteous man availeth much" (James 5:16).

This makes him practice all the arts of holy living and aspire after every instance of piety and righteousness that his prayers for his flock may have their full force and avail much with God.

For this reason he has sold a small estate that he had and has erected a charitable retirement for ancient, poor people to live in prayer and piety, that his prayers being assisted by such good works may pierce the clouds and bring down blessings upon those souls committed to his care.

Ouranius reads how God himself said unto Abimelech concerning Abraham, "He is a prophet; he shall pray for thee, and thou shalt live" (Gen. 20:7).

And again, how he said of Job, "And my servant Job shall pray for you; for him will I accept" (Job 42:8).

From these passages Ouranius justly concludes that the prayers of men eminent for holiness of life have an extraordinary power with God; that he grants to other people such pardons, reliefs, and blessings through their prayers as would not be granted to men of less piety and perfection. This makes Ouranius exceeding studious of Christian perfection, searching after every grace and holy temper, purifying his heart all manner of ways, fearful of every error and defect in his life lest his prayers for his flock should be less availing with God through his own defects in holiness.

This makes him careful of every temper of his heart, give alms of all that he hath, watch and fast, and mortify, and live according to the strictest rules of temperance, meekness, and humility that he may be in some degree like an Abraham or a Job in his parish and make such prayers for them as God will hear and accept.

These are the happy effects which a devout intercession hath produced in the life of Ouranius.

And if other people in their several stations were to imitate this example in such a manner as suited their particular state of life, they would certainly find the same happy effects from it.

If masters, for instance, were thus to remember their servants in their prayers, beseeching God to bless them and suiting their petitions to the particular wants and necessities of their servants, letting no day pass without a full performance of this part of devotion, the benefit would be as great to themselves as to their servants.

No way so likely as this to inspire them with a true sense of that power which they have in their hands to make them delight in doing good and becoming exemplary in all the parts of a wise and good master.

The presenting their servants so often before God, as equally related to God and entitled to the same expectations of Heaven as themselves, would naturally incline them to treat them, not only with such humanity as became fellow creatures, but with such tenderness, care, and generosity as became fellow heirs of the same glory. This devotion would make masters inclined to everything that was good toward their servants, be watchful of their behavior and as ready to require of them an exact observance of the duties of Christianity as of the duties of their service.

This would teach them to consider their servants as God's servants, to desire their perfection, to do nothing before them that might corrupt their minds, to impose no business upon them that should lessen their sense of religion or hinder them from their full share of devotion, both public and private. This praying for them would make them as glad to see their servants eminent in piety as themselves and contrive that they should have all the opportunities and encouragements, both to know and perform all the duties of the Christian life.

How natural would it be for such a master to perform every part of family devotion, to have constant prayers, to excuse no one's absence from them, to have the scriptures and books of piety often read amongst his servants, to take all opportunities of instructing them, of raising their minds to God and teaching them to do all their business as a service to God and upon the hopes and expectations of another life?

How natural would it be for such a one to pity their weakness and ignorance, to bear with the dullness of their understandings or the perverseness of their tempers, to reprove them with tenderness, exhort them with affection, as hoping that God would hear his prayers for them?

How impossible would it be for a master that thus interceded with God for his servants to use any unkind threatenings toward them, to damn and curse them as dogs and scoundrels and treat them only as the dregs of the creation.

This devotion would give them another spirit and make them consider how to make proper returns of care, kindness, and protection to those who had spent their strength and time in service and attendance upon them.

Now if gentlemen think it too low an employment for their state and dignity to exercise such a devotion as this for their servants, let them consider how far they are from the Spirit of Christ who made Himself not only an intercessor but a sacrifice for the whole race of sinful mankind.

Let them consider how miserable their greatness would be if the Son of God should think it as much below Him to pray for them as they do to pray for their fellow creatures.

Let them consider how far they are from that spirit which prays for its most unjust enemies if they have not kindness enough to pray for those by whose labors and service they live in ease themselves.

Again, if parents should thus make themselves advocates and intercessors with God for their children, constantly applying to Heaven in behalf of them, nothing would be more likely, not only to bless their children, but also to form and dispose their own minds to the performance of everything that was excellent and praiseworthy.

I don't suppose but that the generality of parents remember their children in their prayers and call upon God to bless them. But the thing here intended is not a general remembrance of them but a regular method of recommending all their particular needs and necessities unto God, and of praying for every such particular grace and virtue for them as their state and condition of life shall seem to require.

The state of parents is a holy state, in some degree like that of the priesthood, and calls upon them to bless their children with their prayers and sacrifices to God. Thus it was that holy Job watched over and blessed his children, he "sanctified them, he rose up early in the morning, and offered burnt offerings, according to the number of them all" (Job 1:5).

If parents, therefore, considering themselves in this light,

WILLIAM LAW

should be daily calling upon God in a solemn, deliberate manner, altering and extending their intercessions as the state and growth of their children required, such devotion would have a mighty influence upon the rest of their lives; it would make them very circumspect in the government of themselves, prudent and careful of everything they said or did lest their example should hinder that which they so constantly desired in their prayers.

If a father was daily making particular prayers to God that he would please to inspire his children with true piety, great humility, and strict temperance, what could be more likely to make the father himself become exemplary in these virtues? How naturally would he grow ashamed of wanting such virtues as he thought necessary for his children? So that his prayers for their piety would be a certain means of exalting his own to its greatest height.

If a father thus considered himself as an intercessor with God for his children to bless them with his prayers, what more likely means to make him aspire after every degree of holiness that he might thereby be fitter to obtain blessings from heaven for them? How would such thoughts make him avoid everything that was sinful and displeasing to God, lest when he prayed for his children God should reject his prayers?

How tenderly, how religiously would such a father converse with his children whom he considered as his little spiritual flock, whose virtues he was to form by his authority, nourish by his counsel, and prosper by his prayers to God for them?

How fearful would he be of all greedy and unjust ways of raising their fortune, of bringing them up in pride and indulgence or of making them too fond of the world lest he should thereby render them incapable of those graces which he was so often beseeching God to grant them?

These being the plain, natural, happy effects of this intercession, all parents, I hope, who have the real welfare of their children at heart, who desire to be their true friends and benefactors and to live amongst them in the spirit of wisdom and piety, will not neglect so great a means both of raising their own virtue and doing an eternal good to those who are so near and dear to them by the strongest ties of nature.

Lastly, if all people, when they feel the first approaches of resentment, envy, or contempt toward others, or if in all little disagreements and misunderstandings whatever, they should, instead of indulging their minds with little low reflections, have recourse at such times to a more particular and extraordinary intercession with God for such persons as had raised their envy, resentment, or discontent, this would be a certain way to prevent the growth of all uncharitable tempers.

If you was also to form your prayer or intercession at that time to the greatest degree of contrariety to that temper which you was then in, it would be an excellent means of raising your heart to the greatest state of perfection.

As for instance, when at any time you find in your heart motions of envy toward any person, whether on account of his riches, power, reputation, learning, or advancement, if you should immediately betake yourself at that time to your prayers and pray to God to bless and prosper him in that very thing which raised your envy, if you should express and repeat your petitions in the strongest terms, beseeching God to grant him all the happiness from the enjoyment of it that can possibly be received, you would soon find it to be the best antidote in the world to expel the venom of that poisonous passion.

This would be such a triumph over yourself, would so humble and reduce your heart into obedience and order, that the Devil would even be afraid of tempting you again in the same manner when he saw the temptation turned into so great a means of amending and reforming the state of your heart.

Again, if in any little difference or misunderstandings that you happened to have at any time with a relation, a neighbor, or anyone else, you should then pray for them in a more extraordinary manner than you ever did before, beseeching God to give them every grace and blessing and happiness you can think of, you would have taken the speediest method that can be of reconciling all differences and clearing up all misunderstandings. You would then think nothing too great to be forgiven, stay for no condescensions, need no mediation of a third person, but be glad to testify your love and good will to him who had so high a place in your secret prayers.

This would be the mighty power of such Christian devotion; it would remove all peevish passions, soften your heart into the most tender condescensions, and be the best arbitrator of all differences that happened betwixt you and any of your acquaintance.

The greatest resentments amongst friends and neighbors most often arise from poor punctilios and little mistakes in conduct. A certain sign that their friendship is merely human, not founded upon religious considerations or supported by such a course of mutual prayer for one another as the first Christians used.

For such devotion must necessarily either destroy such tempers or be itself destroyed by them.

You cannot possibly have any ill temper or show any unkind behavior to a man for whose welfare you are so much concerned as to be his advocate with God in private.

Hence we may also learn the odious nature and exceeding guilt of all spite, hatred, contempt, and angry passions; they are not to be considered as defects in good nature and sweetness of temper, not as failings in civility of manners or good breeding, but as such base tempers as are entirely inconsistent with the charity of intercession.

You think it a small matter to be peevish or ill natured to such or such a man, but you should consider whether it be a small matter to do that which you could not do if you had but so much charity as to be able to recommend him to God in your prayers.

You think it a small matter to ridicule one man and despise another, but you should consider whether it be a small matter to want that charity toward these people which Christians are not allowed to want toward their most inveterate enemies.

For be but as charitable to these men, do but bless and pray for them as you are obliged to bless and pray for your enemies, and then you will find that you have charity enough to make it impossible for you to treat them with any degree of scorn or contempt.

For you cannot possibly despise and ridicule that man whom your private prayers recommend to the love and favor of God.

When you despise and ridicule a man, it is with no other end but to make him ridiculous and contemptible in the eyes of other men, and in order to prevent their esteem of him. How, therefore, can it be possible for you sincerely to beseech God to bless that man with the honor of his love and favor whom you desire men to treat as worthy of their contempt?

Could you out of love to a neighbor desire your prince to honor him with every mark of his esteem and favor, and yet at the same time expose him to the scorn and derision of your own servants?

Yet this is as possible as to expose that man to the scorn and contempt of your fellow creatures whom you recommend to the favor of God in your secret prayers.

From these considerations we may plainly discover the reasonableness and justice of this doctrine of the gospel, "Whosoever shall say unto his brother, Racha, shall be in danger of the council; but whosoever shall say, Thou fool, shall be in danger of hell fire" (Matt. 5:22).

We are not, I suppose, to believe that every hasty word or unreasonable expression that slips from us by chance or surprise and is contrary to our intention and tempers is the great sin here signified.

But he that says "Racha" or "Thou fool" must chiefly mean him that allows himself in deliberate, designed acts of scorn and contempt toward his brother, and in that temper speaks to him and of him in reproachful language.

Now since it appears that these tempers are at the bottom the most rank uncharitableness, since no one can be guilty of them but because he has not charity enough to pray to God for his brother, it cannot be thought hard or rigorous justice that such tempers should endanger the salvation of Christians. For who would think it hard that a Christian cannot obtain the favor of God for himself unless he reverence and esteem his brother Christian as one that bears the image of God, as one for whom Christ died, as a member of Christ's body, as a member of that holy society on earth which is in union with that triumphant church in Heaven?

Yet all these considerations must be forgot, all these glorious privileges disregarded, before a man can treat him that has them as an object of scorn and contempt.

So that to scorn or despise a brother or, as our blessed Lord says, to call him "Racha," or "fool," must be looked upon as amongst the most odious, unjust, and guilty tempers that can be supported in the heart of a Christian, and justly excluding him from all his hopes in the salvation of Jesus Christ.

For to despise one for whom Christ died is to be as contrary to Christ as he that despises anything that Christ has said or done.

If a Christian that had lived with the holy Virgin Mary should, after the death of our Lord, have taken any occasion to treat her with contempt, you would certainly say that he had lost his piety toward our blessed Lord. For a true reverence for Christ must have forced him to treat her with respect, who was so nearly related to him.

I dare appeal to any man's mind whether it does not tell him that this relation of the Virgin Mary to our blessed Lord must have obliged all those that lived and conversed with her to treat her with great respect and esteem. Might not a man have justly dreaded the vengeance of God upon him for any scorn or contempt that he had shown to her?

Now if this be plain and obvious reasoning, if a contempt offered to the Virgin Mary must have been interpreted a contempt of Christ because of her near relation to him, then let the same reasoning show you the great impiety of despising any brother.

You cannot despise a brother without despising him that stands in a high relation to God, to his Son Jesus Christ, and to the Holy Trinity.

You would certainly think it a mighty impiety to treat a writing with great contempt that had been written by the finger of God, and can you think it a less impiety to condemn and vilify a brother who is not only the workmanship but the image of God?

You would justly think it great profaneness to condemn and trample upon an altar because it was appropriated to holy uses and had had the body of Christ so often placed upon it, and can you suppose it to be less profaneness to scorn and trample upon a brother who so belongs to God that his very body is to be considered as the "Temple of the Holy Ghost" (1 Cor. 6:15)?

Had you despised and ill treated the Virgin Mary, you had been chargeable with the impiety of despising her of whom Christ was born. And if you scorn and despise a brother you are chargeable with the impiety of despising him for whom Christ laid down his life.

And now if this scornful temper is founded upon a disregard of all these relations which every Christian bears to God and Christ and the Holy Trinity, can you wonder or think it hard that a Christian who thus allows himself to despise a brother should be in danger of hell fire?

Secondly, it must here be observed that though in these words, "Whosoever shall say, thou fool," etc., the great sin there condemned is an allowed temper of despising a brother, yet we are also to believe that all hasty expressions and words of contempt, though spoken by surprise or accident, are by this text condemned as great sins and notorious breaches of Christian charity.

They proceed from great want of Christian love and meekness, and call for great repentance. They are only little sins when compared with habits and settled tempers of treating a brother despitefully, and fall as directly under the condemnation of this text as the grossest habits of uncharitableness.

And the reason why we are always to apprehend great guilt and call ourselves to a strict repentance for these hasty expressions of anger and contempt is this: because they seldom are what they seem to be, that is, mere starts of temper that were occasioned purely by surprise or accident, but are much more our own proper acts than we generally imagine.

A man says a great many bitter things. He presently forgives himself because he supposes it was only the suddenness of the occasion or something accidental that carried him so far beyond himself.

But he should consider that perhaps the accident or surprise was not the occasion of his angry temper showing itself.

Now as this is, generally speaking, the case, as all haughty, angry language generally proceeds from some secret habits of pride in the heart, so people that are subject to it, though only now and then as accidents happen, have great reason to repent of more than their present behavior to charge themselves with greater guilt than accidental passion and to bring themselves to such penance and mortification as is proper to destroy habits of a haughty spirit.

And this may be the reason why the text looks no further than the outward language, why it only says "Whosoever shall say, Thou fool," because few can proceed so far as to the accidental use of haughty, disdainful language but they whose hearts are more or less possessed with habits and settled tempers of pride and haughtiness.

But to return. Intercession is not only the best arbitrator of all differences, the best promoter of true friendship, the best cure and preservative against all unkind tempers, all angry and haughty passions, but is also of great use to discover to us the true state of our own hearts.

There are many tempers which we think lawful and innocent which we never suspect of any harm, which, if they were to be tried by this devotion, would soon show us how we have deceived ourselves.

Susurrus is a pious, temperate, good man, remarkable for

abundance of excellent qualities. No one more constant at the service of the church, or whose heart is more affected with it. His charity is so great that he almost starves himself to be able to give greater alms to the poor.

Yet Susurrus had a prodigious failing along with these great virtues.

He had a mighty inclination to hear and discover all the defects and infirmities of all about him. You was welcome to tell him anything of anybody, provided that you did not do it in the style of an enemy. He never disliked an evil speaker but when his language was rough and passionate. If you would but whisper anything gently, though it was ever so bad in itself, Susurrus was ready to receive it.

When he visits, you generally hear him relating how sorry he is for the defects and failings of such a neighbor. He is always letting you know how tender he is of the reputation of his neighbor, how loath to say that which he is forced to say, and how gladly he would conceal it if it could be concealed.

Susurrus had such a tender, compassionate manner of relating things the most prejudicial to his neighbor that he even seemed, both to himself and others, to be exercising a Christian charity at the same time that he was indulging a whispering, evil-speaking temper.

Susurrus once whispered to a particular friend in great secrecy something too bad to be spoke of publicly. He ended with saying how glad he was that it had not yet took wind and that he had some hopes it might not be true, though the suspicions were very strong. His friend made him this reply:

You say, Susurrus, that you are glad it has not yet taken wind, and that you have some hopes it may not prove true. Go home therefore to your closet and pray to God for this man in such a manner, and with such earnestness, as you would pray for yourself on the like occasion.

Beseech God to interpose in his favor to save him from false accusers and bring all those to shame who by uncharitable whispers and secret stories wound him, like those that stab in the dark. And when you have made this prayer then you may, if you please, go tell the same secret to some other friend that you have told to me.

Susurrus was exceedingly affected with this rebuke and felt the force of it upon his conscience in as lively a manner as if he had seen the books opened at the day of judgment.

All other arguments might have been resisted, but it was impossible for Susurrus either to reject or to follow this advice without being equally self-condemned in the highest degree.

From that time to this he has constantly used himself to this method of intercession, and his heart is so entirely changed by it that he can now no more privately whisper anything to the prejudice of another than he can openly pray to God to do people hurt.

Whisperings and evil speakings now hurt his ears like oaths and curses, and he has appointed one day in the week to be a day of penance as long as he lives to humble himself before God in the sorrowful confession of his former guilt.

It may well be wondered how a man of so much piety as Susurrus could be so long deceived in himself as to live in such a state of scandal and evil speaking without suspecting himself to be guilty of it. But it was the tenderness and seeming compassion with which he heard and related everything that deceived both himself and others.

This was a falseness of heart which was only to be fully discovered by the true charity of intercession.

And if people of virtue who think as little harm of themselves as Susurrus did were often to try their spirit by such an intercession they would often find themselves to be such as they least of all suspected.

I have laid before you the many and great advantages of intercession. You have seen what a divine friendship it must needs beget amongst Christians, how dear it would render all relations and neighbors to one another, how it tends to make clergymen, masters, and parents exemplary and perfect in all the duties of their station, how certainly it destroys all envy, spite, and ill-natured passions, how speedily it reconciles all differences and with what a piercing light it discovers to a man the true state of his heart.

These considerations will, I hope, persuade you to make such intercession as is proper for your state, the constant, chief matter of your devotion at this hour of prayer.

NOTES
56. For: corrected by the 2nd ed.; the 1st ed. reads: with.

Chapter 22

Recommending devotion at three o'clock, called in scripture the ninth hour of the day. The subject of prayer at this hour is resignation to the divine pleasure. The nature and duty of conformity to the will of God in all our actions and designs.

I have recommended certain subjects to be made the fixed and chief matter of your devotions at all the hours of prayer that have been already considered.

As thanksgiving and oblation of yourself to God at your first prayers in the morning; at nine, the great virtue of Christian humility is to be the chief part of your petitions; at twelve, you are called upon to pray for all the graces of universal love and to raise it in your heart by such general and particular intercessions as your own state and relation to other people seem more particularly to require of you.

At this hour of the afternoon you are desired to consider the necessity of resignation and conformity to the will of God and to make this great virtue the principal matter of your prayers.

There is nothing wise or holy or just but the great will of God. This is as strictly true in the most rigid sense as to say that nothing is infinite and eternal but God.

No beings, therefore, whether in Heaven or on earth, can be wise or holy or just but so far as they conform to this will of God. It is conformity to this will that gives virtue and perfection to the highest services of angels in Heaven, and it is conformity to the same will that makes the ordinary actions of men on earth become an acceptable service unto God.

The whole nature of virtue consists in conforming, and the whole nature of vice in declining from the will of God. All God's creatures are created to fulfill His will; the sun and moon obey His will by the necessity of their nature; angels conform to His will by the perfection of their nature. If, therefore, you would show yourself not to be a rebel and apostate from the order of the creation, you must act like beings both above and below you. It must be the great desire of your soul that God's will may be done by you on earth as it is done in Heaven. It must be the settled purpose and intention of your heart to will nothing, design nothing, do nothing but so far as you have reason to believe that it is the will of God that you should so desire, design, and do.

'Tis as just and necessary to live in this state of heart, to think thus of God and yourself, as to think that you have any dependence upon Him. And it is as great a rebellion against God to think that your will may ever differ from His as to think that you have not received the power of willing from Him.

You are, therefore, to consider yourself as a being that has no other business in the world but to be that which God requires you to be; to have no tempers, no rules of your own, to seek no self-designs or self-ends but to fill some place and act some part in strict conformity and thankful resignation to the divine pleasure.

To think that you are your own or at your own disposal is as absurd as to think that you created and can preserve yourself. It is as plain and necessary a first principle to believe you are thus God's, that you thus belong to Him and are to act and suffer all in a thankful resignation to His pleasure as to believe that in Him you live and move and have your being.

Resignation to the divine will signifies a cheerful approbation and thankful acceptance of everything that comes from God. It is not enough patiently to submit, but we must thankfully receive and fully approve of everything that by the order of God's providence happens to us.

For there is no reason why we should be patient but what is as good and strong a reason why we should be thankful. If we were under the hands of a wise and good physician that could not mistake or do anything to us but what certainly tended to our benefit, it would not be enough to be patient and abstain from murmuring against such a physician, but it would be as great a breach of duty and gratitude to him not to be pleased and thankful for what he did as it would be to murmur at him.

Now this is our true state with relation to God; we can't be said so much as to believe in Him unless we believe Him to be of infinite wisdom. Every argument therefore for patience under His disposal of us is as strong an argument for approbation and thankfulness for everything that He does to us. And there needs no more to dispose us to this gratitude toward God than a full belief in Him, that He is this being of infinite wisdom, love, and goodness.

Do but assent to this truth in the same manner as you assent to things of which you have no doubt, and then you will cheerfully approve of everything that God has already approved for you.

For as you cannot possibly be pleased with the behavior of any person toward you but because it is for your good, is wise in itself, and the effect of His love and goodness toward you, so when you are satisfied that God does not only do that which is wise and good and kind, but that which is the effect of an infinite wisdom and love in the care of you; it will be as necessary whilst you have this faith to be thankful and pleased with everything which God chooses for you as to wish your own happiness.

Whenever, therefore, you find yourself disposed to uneasiness or murmuring at anything that is the effect of God's providence over you, you must look upon yourself as denying either the wisdom or goodness of God. For every complaint necessarily supposes this. You would never complain of your neighbor but that you suppose you can show either his unwise, unjust, or unkind behavior toward you.

Now every murmuring, impatient reflection under the providence of God is the same accusation of God. A complaint always supposes ill usage.

Hence also you may see the great necessity and piety of this thankful state of heart because the want of it implies an accusation of God's want either of wisdom or goodness in His disposal of us. It is not therefore any high degree of perfection, founded in any uncommon nicety of thinking or refined notions, but a plain principle founded in this plain belief, that God is a Being of infinite wisdom and goodness.

Now this resignation to the divine will may be considered in two respects; first, as it signifies a thankful approbation of God's general providence over the world; secondly, as it signifies a thankful acceptance of His particular providence over us.

First, every man is by the law of his creation, by the first article of his creed, obliged to consent to and acknowledge the wisdom and goodness of God in His general providence over the whole world. He is to believe that it is the effect of God's great wisdom and goodness that the world itself was formed at such a particular time and in such a manner; that the general order of nature, the whole frame of things, is contrived and formed in the best manner. He is to believe that God's providence over states and kingdoms, times and seasons, is all for the best; that the revolutions of state and changes of empire, the rise and fall of monarchies, persecutions, wars, famines, and plagues, are all permitted and conducted by God's providence to the general good of man in this state of trial.

A good man is to believe all this with the same fullness of assent as he believes that God is in every place, though he neither sees nor can comprehend the manner of His presence.

This is a noble magnificence of thought, a true religious greatness of mind, to be thus affected with God's general providence, admiring and magnifying His wisdom in all things, never murmuring at the course of the world or the state of things, but looking upon all around at Heaven and earth as a pleased spectator, and adoring that invisible hand which gives laws to all motions and overrules all events to ends suitable to the highest wisdom and goodness.

It is very common for people to allow themselves great liberty in finding fault with such things as have only God for their cause.

Everyone thinks he may justly say what a wretched, abominable climate he lives in. This man is frequently telling you what a dismal, cursed day it is and what intolerable seasons we have. Another thinks he has very little to thank God for that it is hardly worth his while to live in a world so full of changes and revolutions. But these are tempers of great impiety and show that religion has not yet its seat in the heart of those that have them.

It sounds indeed much better to murmur at the course of the world or the state of things than to murmur at providence, to complain of the seasons and weather, than to complain of God, but if these have no other cause but God and His providence it is a poor distinction to say that you are only angry at the things but not at the cause and director of them.

How sacred the whole frame of the world is, how all things are to be considered as God's and referred to Him, is fully taught by our

319

blessed Lord in the case of oaths: "But I say unto you, swear not at all; neither by heaven, for it is God's throne; nor by the earth, for it is his footstool; neither by Jerusalem, for it is the city of the great King; neither shalt thou swear by thy head, because thou canst not make one hair white or black" (Matt. 5:34, 35), that is, because the whiteness or blackness of thy hair is not thine but God's.

Here you see all things in the whole order of nature, from the highest heavens to the smallest hair, are always to be considered, not separately as they are in themselves but as in some relation to God. And if this be good reasoning, thou shalt not swear by the earth, a city, or thy hair, because these things are God's and in a certain manner belong to Him; is it not exactly the same reasoning to say, "Thou shalt not murmur at the seasons of the earth, the states of cities, and the change of times because all these things are in the hands of God, have Him for their author, are directed and governed by Him to such ends as are most suitable to His wise providence"?

If you think you can murmur at the state of things without murmuring at providence, or complain of seasons without complaining of God, hear what our blessed Lord says further upon oaths: "Whoso shall swear by the altar, sweareth by it, and by all things thereon: and whoso shall swear by the temple, sweareth by him that dwelleth therein: and he that shall swear by heaven, sweareth by the throne of God, and by him that sitteth thereon" (Matt. 23:20-22).

Now does not this scripture plainly oblige us to reason after this manner. Whoso murmurs at the course of the world murmurs at God that governs the course of the world. Whoso repines at seasons and weather and speaks impatiently of times and events repines and speaketh impatiently of God who is the sole Lord and Governor of times, seasons, and events.

As therefore, when we think of God Himself, we are to have no sentiments but of praise and thanksgiving, so when we look at those things which are under the direction of God and governed by His providence, we are to receive them with the same tempers of praise and gratitude.

And though we are not to think all things right and just and lawful which the providence of God permits, for then nothing could be unjust because nothing without His permission, yet we must adore God in the greatest public calamities, the most grievous persecutions, as things that are suffered by God, like plagues and famines, for ends suitable to His wisdom and glory in the government of the world.

There is nothing more suitable to the piety of a reasonable creature or the spirit of a Christian than thus to approve, admire, and glorify God in all the acts of His general providence, considering the whole world as His particular family, and all events as directed by His wisdom.

Everyone seems to consent to this as an undeniable truth, that all things must be as God pleases, and is not this enough to make every man pleased with them himself? And how can a man be a peevish complainer of anything that is the effect of providence but by showing that his own self-will and self-wisdom is of more weight with him than the will and wisdom of God? And what can religion be said to have done for a man whose heart is in this state?

For if he cannot thank and praise God as well in calamities and sufferings as in prosperity and happiness, he is as far from the piety of a Christian as he that only loves them that love him is from the charity of a Christian. For to thank God only for such things as you like is no more a proper act of piety than to believe only what you see is an act of faith.

Resignation and thanksgiving to God are only acts of piety when they are acts of faith, trust, and confidence in the divine goodness.

The faith of Abraham was an act of true piety because it stopped at no difficulties, was not altered or lessened by any human appearances. It first of all carried him against all show of happiness from his own kindred and country into a strange land, not knowing whither he went. It afterwards made him, against all appearances of nature, when his body was dead, when he was about a hundred years old, depend upon the promise of God, being fully persuaded that what God had promised He was able to perform. It was this same faith that against so many pleas of nature, so many appearances of reason, prevailed upon him to "Offer up Isaac . . . accounting that God was able to raise him up from the dead" (Heb. 11:17, 19).

Now this faith is the true pattern of Christian resignation to the divine pleasure; you are to thank and praise God, not only for things agreeable to you that have the appearance of happiness and comfort,

321

but when you are, like Abraham, called from all appearances of comfort to be a pilgrim in a strange land, to part with an only son, being as fully persuaded of the divine goodness in all things that happen to you as Abraham was of the divine promise when there was the least appearance of its being performed.

This is true Christian resignation to God which requires no more to the support of it than such a plain assurance of the goodness of God as Abraham had of his veracity. And if you ask yourself what greater reason Abraham had to depend upon the divine veracity than you have to depend upon the divine goodness, you will find that none can be given.

You cannot therefore look upon this as an unnecessary, high pitch of perfection, since the want of it implies the want, not of any high notions, but of a plain and ordinary faith in the most certain doctrines both of natural and revealed religion.

Thus much concerning resignation to the divine will as it signifies a thankful approbation of God's general providence. It is now to be considered as it signifies a thankful acceptance of God's particular providence over us.

Every man is to consider himself as a particular object of God's providence, under the same care and protection of God as if the world had been made for him alone. It is not by chance that any man is born at such a time, of such parents, and in such place and condition. It is as certain that every soul comes into the body at such a time and in such circumstances by the express designment[57] of God, according to some purposes of His will and for some particular ends; this is as certain as that it is by the express designment of God that some beings are angels and others are men.

It is as much by the counsel and eternal purpose of God that you should be born in your particular state and that Isaac should be the son of Abraham as that Gabriel should be an angel and Isaac a man.

The scriptures assure us that it was by divine appointment that our blessed Savior was born at Bethlehem and at such a time. Now although it was owing to the dignity of his person and the great importance of his birth that thus much of the divine counsel was declared to the world concerning the time and manner of it, yet we are as sure from the same scriptures that the time and manner of every man's coming into the world is according to some eternal purposes and direction of divine providence and in such time and place and circumstances as are directed and governed by God for particular ends of His wisdom and goodness.

This we are as certain of from plain revelation as we can be of anything. For if we are told that "not a sparrow falleth to the ground without our heavenly Father," can anything more strongly teach us that much greater beings such as human souls come not into the world without the care and direction of our heavenly Father? If it is said, "the very hairs of your head are all numbered," is it not to teach us that nothing, not the smallest things imaginable, happen to us by chance? But if the smallest things we can conceive are declared to be under the divine direction, need we or can we be more plainly taught that the greatest things of life, such as the manner of our coming into the world, our parents, the time, and other circumstances of our birth and condition, are all according to the eternal purposes, direction, and appointment of divine providence?

When the Disciples put this question to our blessed Lord concerning the blind man, saying, "Master, who did sin, this man, or his parents, that he was born blind," He that was the eternal wisdom of God made this answer, "Neither hath this man sinned, nor his parents; but that the works of God should be made manifest in him" (John 9:2, 3). Plainly declaring that the particular circumstances of every man's birth, the body that he receives and the condition and state of life into which he is born, are appointed by a secret providence which directs all things to their particular times and seasons and manner of existence, that the wisdom and works of God may be made manifest in them all.

As therefore it is thus certain that we are what we are as to birth, time, and condition of entering into the world, since all that is particular in our state is the effect of God's particular providence over us and intended for some particular ends both of his glory and our own happiness, we are by the greatest obligations of gratitude called upon to conform and resign our will to the will of God in all these respects, thankfully approving and accepting everything that is particular in our state. Praising and glorifying his name for our birth of such parents and in such circumstances of state and condition, being fully assured that it was for some reasons of infinite wisdom and goodness that we were so born into such particular states of life.

If the man above mentioned was born blind that the "works of God might be manifested in him," had he not great reason to praise God for appointing him in such a particular manner to be the instrument of His glory? And if one person is born here and another there, if one falls amongst riches and another into poverty, if one receives his flesh and blood from these parents and another from those for as particular ends as the man was born blind,[58] have not all people the greatest reason to bless God and to be thankful for their particular state and condition, because all that is particular in it is as directly intended for the glory of God and their own good as the particular blindness of that man who was so born, that "the works of God might be manifested in him"?

How noble an idea does this give us of the divine Omniscience presiding over the whole world and governing such a long chain and combination of seeming accidents and chances to the common and particular advantage of all beings? So that all persons, in such a wonderful variety of causes, accidents and events, should all fall into such particular states as were foreseen and foreordained to their best advantage, and so as to be most serviceable to the wise and glorious ends of God's government of all the world.

Had you been anything else than what you are, you had, all things considered, been less wisely provided for than you are now; you had wanted some circumstances and conditions that are best fitted to make you happy yourself and serviceable to the glory of God.

Could you see all that which God sees, all that happy chain of causes and motives which are to move and invite you to a right course of life, you would see something to make you like that state you are in as fitter for you than any other.

But as you cannot see this, so it is here that your Christian faith and trust in God is to exercise itself and render you as grateful and thankful for the happiness of your state as if you saw everything that contributes to it with your own eyes.

But now if this is the case of every man in the world, thus blessed with some particular state that is most convenient for him, how reasonable is it for every man to will that which God has already willed for him? And by a pious faith and trust in the divine goodness, thankfully adore and magnify that wise providence which he is sure has made the best choice for him of those things which he could not choose for himself.

Every uneasiness at our own state is founded upon comparing it with that of other people. Which is full as unreasonable as if a man in a dropsy should be angry at those that prescribe different things to him from those which are prescribed to people in health. For all the different states of life are like the different states of diseases; what is a remedy to one man in his state may be poison to another.

So that to murmur because you are not as some others are is as if a man in one disease should murmur that he is not treated like him that is in another. Whereas if he was to have his will, he would be killed by that which will prove the cure of another.

It is just thus in the various conditions of life; if you give yourself up to uneasiness or complain at anything in your state, you may, for ought you know, be so ungrateful to God as to murmur at that very thing which is to prove the cause of your salvation.

Had you it in your power to get that which you think it so grievous to want, it might perhaps be that very thing which of all others would most expose you to eternal damnation.

So that whether we consider the infinite goodness of God that cannot choose amiss for us, or our own great ignorance of what is most advantageous to us, there can be nothing so reasonable and pious as to have no will but that of God's, and desire nothing for ourselves in our persons, our state and condition, but that which the good providence of God appoints us.

Further, as the good providence of God thus introduces us into the world, into such states and conditions of life as are most convenient for us, so the same unerring wisdom orders all events and changes in the whole course of our lives in such a manner as to render them the fittest means to exercise and improve our virtue.

Nothing hurts us, nothing destroys us, but the ill use of that liberty with which God has entrusted us.

We are as sure that nothing happens to us by chance as that the world itself was not made by chance; we are as certain that all things happen and work together for our good as that God is goodness itself. So that a man has as much reason to will everything that happens to him because God wills it, as to think that is wisest which is directed by infinite wisdom.

This is not cheating or soothing ourselves into any false content or imaginary happiness, but is a satisfaction grounded upon as great a certainty as the being and attributes of God.

For if we are right in believing God to act over us with infinite wisdom and goodness, we cannot carry our notions of conformity and resignation to the divine will too high, nor can we ever be deceived by thinking that to be best for us which God has brought upon us.

For the providence of God is not more concerned in the government of night and day and the variety of seasons than in the common course of events that seem most to depend upon the mere wills of men. So that it is as strictly right to look upon all worldly accidents and changes, all the various turns and alterations in your own life, to be as truly the effects of divine providence as the rising and setting of the sun or the alterations of the seasons of the year. As you are, therefore, always to adore the wisdom of God in the direction of these things, so it is the same reasonable duty always to magnify God as an equal director of everything that happens to you in the course of your own life.

This holy resignation and conformity of your will to the will of God, being so much the true state of piety, I hope you will think it proper to make this hour of prayer a constant season of applying to God for so great a gift. That by thus constantly praying for it, your heart may be habitually disposed toward it and always in a state of readiness to look at everything as God's, and to consider Him in everything, that so everything that befalls you may be received in the spirit of piety and made a means of exercising some virtue.

There is nothing that so powerfully governs the heart, that so strongly excites us to wise and reasonable actions, as a true sense of God's presence. But as we cannot see or apprehend the essence of God, so nothing will so constantly keep us under a lively sense of the presence of God as this holy resignation which attributes everything to Him and receives everything as from Him.

Could we see a miracle from God, how would our thoughts be affected with a holy awe and veneration of His presence! But if we consider everything as God's doing, either by order or permission, we shall then be affected with common things, as they would be who saw a miracle.

For as there is nothing to affect you in a miracle but as it is the action of God and bespeaks His presence, so when you consider God as acting in all things and all events, then all things will become venerable to you like miracles, and fill you with the same awful sentiments of the divine presence.

Now you must not reserve the exercise of this pious temper to any particular times or occasions, or fancy how resigned you will be to God if such or such trials should happen. For this is amusing yourself with the notion or idea of resignation instead of the virtue itself.

Don't, therefore, please yourself with thinking how piously you would act and submit to God in a plague, a famine, or persecution, but be intent upon the perfection of the present day, and be assured that the best way of showing a true zeal is to make little things the occasions of great piety.

Begin, therefore, in the smallest matters and most ordinary occasions, and accustom your mind to the daily exercise of this pious temper in the lowest occurrences of life. And when a contempt, an affront, a little injury, loss, or disappointment, or the smallest events of every day continually raise your mind to God in proper acts of resignation, then you may justly hope that you shall be numbered amongst those that are resigned and thankful to God in the greatest trials and afflictions.

NOTES

57. Designment: the forming or fashioning, as with a work of art.

58. For as . . . blind: even as much as some purpose is served by the man who is born blind.

Chapter 23

Of evening prayer. Of the nature and necessity of
examination. How we are to be particular in the confession of all our sins. How we are to fill our minds
with a just horror and dread of all sin.

I am now come to six o'clock in the evening, which according
to the scripture account is called the twelfth or last hour of the day.
This is a time so proper for devotion that I suppose nothing need be
said to recommend it as a season of prayer to all people that profess
any regard to piety.

As the labor and action of every state of life is generally over at
this hour, so this is the proper time for everyone to call himself to
account and review all his behavior from the first action of the day.
The necessity of this examination is founded upon the necessity of
repentance. For if it be necessary to repent of all our sins, if the
guilt of unrepented sins still continues upon us, then it is necessary
not only that all our sins but the particular circumstances and aggravations of them be known and recollected and brought to repentance.

The scripture saith, "If we confess our sins, he is faithful and
just to forgive us our sins, and to cleanse us from all unrighteousness" (1 John 1:9). Which is as much as to say that then only our
sins are forgiven and we cleansed from the guilt and unrighteousness of them when they are thus confessed and repented of.

There seems therefore to be the greatest necessity that all our
daily actions be constantly observed and brought to account, lest by
a negligence we load ourselves with the guilt of unrepented sins.

This examination, therefore, of ourselves every evening is not
only to be considered as a commendable rule and fit for a wise man

to observe, but as something that is as necessary as a daily confession and repentance of our sins, because this daily repentance is of very little significancy[59] and loses all its chief benefit unless it be a particular confession and repentance of the sins of that day. This examination is necessary to repentance in the same manner as time is necessary. You cannot repent or express your sorrow unless you allow some time for it, nor can you repent but so far as you know what it is that you are repenting of. So that when it is said that it is necessary to examine and call your actions to account, it is only saying that it is necessary to know what, and how many things you are to repent of.

You perhaps have hitherto only used yourself to confess yourself a sinner in general and ask forgiveness in the gross, without any particular remembrance or contrition for the particular sins of that day. And by this practice you are brought to believe that the same short, general form of confession of sin in general is a sufficient repentance for every day.

Suppose another person should hold that a confession of our sins in general once at the end of every week was sufficient, and that it was as well to confess the sins of seven days all together as to have a particular repentance at the end of every day.

I know you sufficiently see the unreasonableness and impiety of this opinion and that you think it is easy enough to show the danger and folly of it.

Yet you cannot bring one argument against such an opinion but what will be as good an argument against such a daily repentance as does not call the particular sins of that day to a strict account.

For as you can bring no express text of scripture against such an opinion but must take all your arguments from the nature of repentance and the necessity of a particular repentance for particular sins, so every argument of that kind must as fully prove the necessity of being very particular in our repentance of the sins of every day. Since nothing can be justly said against leaving the sins of the whole week to be repented for in the gross but what may as justly be said against a daily repentance which considers the sins of that day only in the gross.

Would you tell such a man that a daily confession was necessary to keep up an abhorrence of sin, that the mind would grow hardened and senseless of the guilt of sin without it? And is not this as good a reason for requiring that your daily repentance be very express and particular for your daily sins? For if confession is to raise an abhorrence of sin, surely that confession which considers and lays open your particular sins, that brings them to light with all their circumstances and aggravations, that requires a particular sorrowful acknowledgment of every sin, must in a much greater degree fill the mind with an abhorrence of sin than that which only in one and the same form of words confesses you only to be a sinner in general. For as this is nothing but what the greatest Saint may justly say of himself, so the daily repeating of only such a confession has nothing in it to make you truly ashamed of your own way of life.

Again, must you not tell such a man that by leaving himself to such a weekly, general confession he would be in great danger of forgetting a great many of his sins? But is there any sense or force in this argument unless you suppose that our sins are all to be remembered and brought to a particular repentance? And is it not as necessary that our particular sins be not forgotten but particularly remembered in our daily, as in a repentance at any other time?

So that every argument for a daily confession and repentance is the same argument for the confession and repentance of the particular sins of every day.

Because daily confession has no other reason or necessity but our daily sins, and therefore is nothing of what it should be, but so far as it is a repentance and sorrowful acknowledgment of the sins of the day.

You would, I suppose, think yourself chargeable with great impiety if you was to go to bed without confessing yourself to be a sinner and asking pardon of God; you would not think it sufficient that you did so yesterday. And yet if without any regard to the present day, you only repeat the same form of words that you used yesterday, the sins of the present day may justly be looked upon to have had no repentance. For if the sins of the present day require a new confession it must be such a new confession as is proper to itself. For it is the state and condition of every day that is to determine the state and manner of your repentance in the evening; otherwise the same general form of words is rather an empty for-

mality that has the appearance of a duty than such a true performance of it as is necessary to make it truly useful to you.

Let it be supposed that on a certain day you have been guilty of
these sins, that you have told a vain lie upon yourself, ascribing
something falsely to yourself through pride, that you have been
guilty of detraction and indulged yourself in some degree of intemperance. Let it be supposed that on the next day you have lived in a
contrary manner, that you have neglected no duty of devotion and
been the rest of the day innocently employed in your proper business. Let it be supposed that on the evening of both these days you
only use the same confession in general, considering it rather as a
duty that is to be performed every night than as a repentance that is
to be suited to the particular state of the day.

Can it with any reason be said that each day has had its proper
repentance? Is it not as good sense to say there is no difference in
the guilt of these days as to say that there need be no different
repentance at the end of them? Or how can each of them have its
proper repentance but by its having a repentance as large and extensive and particular as the guilt of each day?

Again, let it be supposed that in that day, when you had been
guilty of the three notorious sins above mentioned, that in your
evening repentance you had only called one of them to mind. Is it
not plain that the other two are unrepented of and that therefore
their guilt still abides upon you? So that you are then in the state of
him who commits himself to the night without the repentance for
such a day as had betrayed him into two such great sins.

Now these are not needless particulars or such scrupulous
niceties as a man need not trouble himself about, but are such plain
truths as essentially concern the very life of piety. For if repentance
is necessary, it is full as necessary that it be rightly performed and
in due manner.

And I have entered into all these particulars only to show you
in the plainest manner that examination and a careful review of all
the actions of the day is not only to be looked upon as a good rule,
but as something as necessary as repentance itself.

If a man is to account for his expenses at night, can it be
thought a needless exactness in him to take notice of every particular expense in the day?

And if a man is to repent of his sins at night, can it be thought too great a piece of scrupulosity in him to know and call to mind what sins he is to repent of?

Further, though it should be granted that a confession in general may be a sufficient repentance for the end of such days as have only the unavoidable frailties of our nature to lament, yet even this fully proves the absolute necessity of this self-examination, for without this examination who can know that he has gone through any day in this manner?

Again, an evening repentance, which thus brings all the actions of the day to account, is not only necessary to wipe off the guilt of sin but is also the most certain way to amend and perfect our lives.

For it is only such a repentance as this that touches the heart, awakens the conscience and leaves a horror and detestation of sin upon the mind.

For instance, if it should happen that upon any particular evening all that you could charge yourself with should be this, viz., a hasty, negligent performance of your devotions or too much time spent in an impertinent conversation; if the unreasonableness of these things were fully reflected upon and acknowledged, if you was then to condemn yourself before God for them and implore His pardon and assisting grace,[60] what could be so likely a means to prevent your falling into the same faults the next day?

Or if you should fall into them again the next day, yet if they were again brought to the same examination and condemnation in the presence of God, their happening again would be such a proof to you of your own folly and weakness, would cause such a pain and remorse in your mind and fill you with such shame and confusion at yourself, as would in all probability make you exceedingly desirous of greater perfection.

Now in the case of repeated sins this would be the certain benefit that we should receive from this examination and confession, the mind would thereby be made humble, full of sorrow and deep compunction, and by degrees forced into amendment.

Whereas a formal, general confession that is only considered as an evening duty that overlooks the particular mistakes of the day and is the same whether the day be spent ill or well has little or no effect upon the mind; a man may use such a daily confession and yet go on sinning and confessing all his life without any remorse of mind or true desire of amendment.

For if your own particular sins are left out of your confession, your confessing of sin in general has no more effect upon your mind than if you had only confessed that all men in general are sinners. And there is nothing in any confession to show that it is yours but so far as it is a self-accusation, not of sin in general or such as is common to all others, but of such particular sins as are your own proper shame and reproach.

No other confession but such as thus discovers and accuses your own particular guilt can be an act of true sorrow or real concern at your own condition. And a confession that is without this sorrow and compunction of heart has nothing in it either to atone for past sins or to produce in us any true reformation and amendment of life.

To proceed: In order to make this examination still further beneficial, every man should oblige himself to a certain method in it. As every man has something particular in his nature, stronger inclinations to some vices than others, some infirmities that stick closer to him and are harder to be conquered than others, and as it is as easy for every man to know this of himself as to know whom he likes or dislikes, so it is highly necessary that these particularities of our natures and tempers should never escape a severe trial at our evening repentance: I say a severe trial because nothing but a rigorous severity against these natural tempers is sufficient to conquer them.

They are the right eyes that are not to be spared, but to be plucked out and cast from us. For as they are the infirmities of nature, so they have the strength of nature and must be treated with great opposition or they will soon be too strong for us.

He therefore who knows himself most of all subject to anger and passion must be very exact and constant in his examination of this temper every evening. He must find out every slip that he has made of that kind, whether in thought or word or action; he must shame and reproach and accuse himself before God for everything that he has said or done in obedience to his passion. He must no more allow himself to forget the examination of this temper than to forget his whole prayers.

Again, if you find that vanity is your prevailing temper that is always putting you upon the adornment of your person and catching after everything that compliments or flatters your abilities, never spare or forget this temper in your evening examination, but confess to God every vanity of thought or word or action that you have been guilty of and put yourself to all the shame and confusion for it that you can.

In this manner should all people act with regard to their chief frailty to which their nature most inclines them. And though it should not immediately do all that they would wish, yet by a constant practice it would certainly in a short time produce its desired effect.

Further, as all states and employments of life have their particular dangers and temptations and expose people more to some sins than others, so every man that wishes his own improvement should make it a necessary part of his evening examination to consider how he has avoided or fallen into such sins as are most common to his state of life.

For as our business and condition of life has great power over us, so nothing but such watchfulness as this can secure us from those temptations to which it daily exposes us.

The poor man, from his condition of life, is always in danger of repining and uneasiness, the rich man is most exposed to sensuality and indulgence, the tradesman to lying and unreasonable gains, the scholar to pride and vanity, so that in every state of life a man should always in his examination of himself have a strict eye upon those faults to which his state of life most of all exposes him.

Again, as it is reasonable to suppose that every good man has entered into, or at least proposed to himself, some method of holy living and set himself some such rules to observe as are not common to other people and only known to himself, so it should be a constant part of his night recollection to examine how, and in what degree, he has observed them and to reproach himself before God for every neglect of them.

By rules, I here mean such rules as relate to the well-ordering of our time and the business of our common life. Such rules as prescribe a certain order to all that we are to do, our business, devotion, mortifications, readings, retirements, conversation, meals, refreshments, sleep, and the like.

Now as good rules relating to all these things are certain means of great improvement and such as all serious Christians must needs propose to themselves, so they will hardly ever be observed to any purpose unless they are made the constant subject of our evening examination.

Lastly, you are not to content yourself with a hasty general review of the day but you must enter upon it with deliberation; begin with the first action of the day and proceed step by step through every particular matter that you have been concerned in and so let no time, place, or action be overlooked.

An examination thus managed will in a little time make you as different from yourself as a wise man is different from an idiot. It will give you such a newness of mind, such a spirit of wisdom and desire of perfection, as you was an entire stranger to before.

Thus much concerning the evening examination.

I proceed now to lay before you such considerations as may fill your mind with a just dread and horror of all sin, and help you to confess your own in the most passionate contrition and sorrow of heart.

Consider first how odious all sin is to God, what a mighty baseness it is and how abominable it renders sinners in the sight of God. That it is sin alone that makes the great difference betwixt an angel and the Devil, and that every sinner is, so far as he sins, a friend of the Devil's and carrying on his work against God. That sin is a greater blemish and defilement of the soul than any filth or disease is a defilement of the body. And to be content to live in sin is a much greater baseness than to desire to wallow in the mire or love any bodily impurity.

Consider how you must abhor a creature that delighted in nothing but filth and nastiness, that hated everything that was decent and clean, and let this teach you to apprehend how odious that soul that delights in nothing but the impurity of sin must appear unto God.

For all sins, whether of sensuality, pride, or falseness, or any other irregular passion, are nothing else but the filth and impure diseases of the rational soul. And all righteousness is nothing else but the purity, the decency, the beauty and perfection of that spirit which is made in the image of God.

Again, learn what horror you ought to have for the guilt of sin from the greatness of that Atonement which has been made for it.

God made the world by the breath of his mouth, by a word speaking, but the redemption of the world has been a work of longer labor.

How easily God can create beings we learn from the first chapter of Genesis, but how difficult it is for infinite mercy to forgive sins we learn from that costly Atonement, those bloody sacrifices, those pains and penances, those sicknesses and deaths which all must be undergone before the guilty sinner is fit to appear in the presence of God.

Ponder these great truths: that the Son of God was forced to become man, to be partaker of all our infirmities, to undergo a poor, painful, miserable, and contemptible life, to be persecuted, hated, and at last nailed to a cross, that by such sufferings he might render God propitious to that nature in which He suffered.

That all the bloody sacrifices and atonements of the Jewish law were to represent the necessity of this great sacrifice and the great displeasure God bore to sinners.

That the world is still under the curse of sin and certain marks of God's displeasure at it, such as famines, plagues, tempests, sickness, diseases, and death.

Consider that all the sons of Adam are to go through a painful, sickly life, denying and mortifying their natural appetites and crucifying the lusts of the flesh in order to have a share in the Atonement of our Savior's death.

That all their penances and self-denials, all their tears and repentance, are only made available by that great intercession which is still making for them at the right hand of God.

Consider these great truths, that this mysterious redemption, all these sacrifices and sufferings, both of God and man, are only to remove the guilt of sin, and then let this teach you with what tears and contrition you ought to purge yourself from it.

After this general consideration of the guilt of sin which has done so much mischief to your nature and exposed it to so great punishment and made it so odious to God that nothing less than so great an Atonement of the Son of God and so great repentance of our own can restore us to the divine favor.

Consider next your own particular share in the guilt of sin.

And if you would know with what zeal you ought to repent yourself, consider how you would exhort another sinner to repentance, and what repentance and amendment you would expect from Him whom you judged to be the greatest sinner in the world.

Now this case every man may justly reckon to be his own. And you may fairly look upon yourself to be the greatest sinner that you know in the world.

For though you may know abundance of people to be guilty of some gross sins with which you cannot charge yourself, yet you may justly condemn yourself as the greatest sinner that you know, and that for these following reasons:

First, because you know more of the folly of your own heart than you do of other people's, and can charge yourself with various sins that you only know of yourself, and cannot be sure that other sinners are guilty of them. So that as you know more of the folly, the baseness, the pride, the deceitfulness and negligence of your own heart than you do of anyone's else, so you have just reason to consider yourself as the greatest sinner that you know because you know more of the greatness of your own sins than you do of other people's.

Secondly, the greatness of our guilt arises chiefly from the greatness of God's goodness toward us, from the particular graces and blessings, the favors, the lights and instructions that we have received from Him.

Now as these graces and blessings and the multitude of God's favors toward us are the great aggravations of our sins against God, so they are only known to ourselves. And therefore every sinner knows more of the aggravations of his own guilt than he does of other people's, and consequently may justly look upon himself to be the greatest sinner that he knows.

How good God has been to other sinners, what light and instruction he has vouchsafed to them, what blessings and graces they have received from Him, how often He has touched their hearts with holy inspirations, you cannot tell. But all this you know of yourself, therefore you know greater aggravations of your own guilt and are able to charge yourself with greater ingratitude than you can charge upon other people.

And this is the reason why the greatest Saints have in all ages condemned themselves as the greatest sinners, because they knew some aggravations of their own sins which they could not know of other people's.

The right way, therefore, to fill your heart with true contrition and a deep sense of your own sins is this: You are not to consider or compare the outward form or course of your life with that of other people's and then think yourself to be less sinful than theirs.

But in order to know your own guilt you must consider your own particular circumstances, your health, your sickness, your youth or age, your particular calling, the happiness of your education, the degrees of light and instruction that you have received, the good men that you have conversed with, the admonitions that you have had, the good books that you have read, the numberless multitude of divine blessings, graces, and favors that you have received, the good motions of grace that you have resisted, the resolutions of amendment that you have often broken, and the checks of conscience that you have disregarded.

For it is from these circumstances that everyone is to state the measure and greatness of his own guilt. And as you know only these circumstances of your own sins, so you must necessarily know how to charge yourself with higher degrees of guilt than you can charge upon other people.

God Almighty knows greater sinners, it may be, than you are, because He sees and knows the circumstances of all men's sins. But your own heart, if it is faithful to you, can discover no guilt so great as your own, because it can only see in you those circumstances on which great part of the guilt of sin is founded.

You may see sins in other people that you cannot charge upon yourself, but then you know a number of circumstances of your own guilt that you cannot lay to their charge.

And perhaps that person that appears at such a distance from your virtue and so odious in your eyes would have been much better than you are had he been altogether in your circumstances and received all the same favors and graces from God that you have.

This is a very humbling reflection and very proper for those people to make who measure their virtue by comparing the outward course of their lives with that of other people's.

For look at whom you will, however different from you in his way of life, yet you can never know that he has resisted so much divine grace as you have, or that in all your circumstances he would not have been much truer to his duty than you are.

Now this is the reason why I desired you to consider how you would exhort that man to confess and bewail his sins, whom you looked upon to be one of the greatest sinners.

Because if you will deal justly you must fix the charge at home and look no further than yourself. For God has given no one any power of knowing the true greatness of any sins but his own, and therefore the greatest sinner that everyone knows is himself.

You may easily see how such a one in the outward course of his life breaks the laws of God, but then you can never say that had you been exactly in all his circumstances that you should not have broken them more than he has done.

A serious and frequent reflection upon these things will mightily tend to humble us in our own eyes, make us very apprehensive of the greatness of our own guilt and very tender in censuring and condemning other people.

For who would dare to be severe against other people when, for ought he can tell, the severity of God may be more due to him than to them? Who would exclaim against the guilt of others when he considers that he knows more of the greatness of his own guilt than he does of theirs?

How often you have resisted God's Holy Spirit, how many motives to goodness you have disregarded, how many particular blessings you have broken, how many checks and admonitions of conscience you have stifled you very well know. But how often this has been the case of other sinners, you know not. And therefore the greatest sinner that you know must be yourself.

Whenever, therefore, you are angry at sin or sinners, whenever you read or think of God's indignation and wrath at wicked men, let this teach you to be the most severe in your censure and most humble and contrite in the acknowledgment and confession of your own sins, because you know of no sinner equal to yourself.

Lastly, to conclude this chapter: Having thus examined and confessed your sins at this hour of the evening, you must afterwards look upon yourself as still obliged to betake yourself to prayer again just before you go to bed.

The subject that is most proper for your prayers at that time is death. Let your prayers therefore then be wholly upon it, reckoning up all the dangers, uncertainties, and terrors of death; let them contain everything that can affect and awaken your mind into just apprehensions of it. Let your petitions be all for right sentiments of the approach and importance of death, and beg of God that your mind may be possessed with such a sense of its nearness that you may have it always in your thoughts, do everything as in sight of it, and make every day a day for preparation for it.

Represent to your imagination that your bed is your grave, that all things are ready for your interment, that you are to have no more to do with this world and that it will be owing to God's great mercy if you ever see the light of the sun again or have another day to add to your works of piety.

And then commit yourself to sleep as into the hands of God, as one that is to have no more opportunities of doing good but is to awake amongst spirits that are separate from the body and waiting for the judgment of the last great day.

Such a solemn resignation of yourself into the hands of God every evening and parting with all the world as if you was never to see it any more, and all this in the silence and darkness of the night, is a practice that will soon have excellent effects upon your spirit.

For this time of the night is exceeding proper for such prayers and meditations, and the likeness which sleep and darkness have to death will contribute very much to make your thoughts about it the more deep and affecting. So that I hope you will not let a time so proper for such prayers be ever passed over without them.

NOTES

59. Significancy: significance, as on p. 00. Cf. Law's use of innocency (pp. 00 and 00), indifferency (p. 00), and excellency (p. 00).
60. Assisting grace: grace which assists.

Chapter 24

The conclusion. Of the excellency and greatness of a devout spirit.

I have now finished what I intended in this treatise. I have explained the nature of devotion, both as it signifies a life devoted to God and as it signifies a regular method of daily prayer. I have now only to add a word or two in recommendation of a life governed by this spirit of devotion.

For though it is as reasonable to suppose it the desire of all Christians to arrive at Christian perfection as to suppose that all sick men desire to be restored to perfect health, yet experience shows us that nothing wants more to be pressed, repeated, and forced upon our minds than the plainest rules of Christianity.

Voluntary poverty, virginity, and devout retirement have been here recommended as things not necessary yet highly beneficial to those that would make the way to perfection the most easy and certain. But Christian perfection itself is tied to no particular form of life but is to be attained, though not with the same ease, in every state of life.

This has been fully asserted in another place where it has been shown that Christian perfection "calls no one (necessarily) to a cloister, but to the full performance of those duties, which are necessary for all Christians, and common to all states of life."[61]

So that the whole of the matter is plainly this: Virginity, voluntary poverty, and such other restraints of lawful things are not necessary to Christian perfection but are much to be commended in those who choose them as helps and means of a more safe and speedy arrival at it.

It is only in this manner and in this sense that I would recommend any particularity of life, not as if perfection consisted in it, but because of its great tendency to produce and support the true spirit of Christian perfection.

But the thing which is here pressed upon all is a life of great and strict devotion which, I think, has been sufficiently shown to be equally the duty and happiness of all orders of men. Neither is there anything in any particular state of life that can be justly pleaded as a reason for any abatements of a devout spirit.

But because in this polite age of ours we have so lived away the spirit of devotion that many seem afraid even to be suspected of it, imagining great devotion to be great bigotry, that it is founded in ignorance and poorness of spirit, and that little, weak, and dejected minds are generally the greatest proficients in it.

It shall here be fully shown that great devotion is the noblest temper of the greatest and noblest souls, and that they who think it receives any advantage from ignorance and poorness of spirit are themselves not a little but entirely ignorant of the nature of devotion, the nature of God, and the nature of themselves.

People of fine parts and learning or of great knowledge in worldly matters may perhaps think it hard to have their want of devotion charged upon their ignorance. But if they will be content to be tried by reason and scripture, it may soon be made appear[62] that a want of devotion, wherever it is, either amongst the learned or unlearned, is founded in gross ignorance and the greatest blindness and insensibility that can happen to a rational creature.

And that devotion is so far from being the effect of a little and dejected mind that it must and will be always highest in the most perfect natures.

And first, who reckons it a sign of a poor, little mind for a man to be full of reverence and duty to his parents, to have the truest love and honor for his friends, or to excel in the highest instances of gratitude to his benefactor?

Are not these tempers in the highest degree in the most exalted and perfect minds?

And yet what is high devotion but the highest exercise of these tempers of duty, reverence, love, honor, and gratitude to the amiable, glorious parent, friend, and benefactor of all mankind?

Is it a true greatness of mind to reverence the authority of your parents, to fear the displeasure of your friend, to dread the reproaches of your benefactor? And must not this fear and dread and reverence be much more just and reasonable and honorable when they are in the highest degree toward God?

Now as the higher these tempers are, the more are they esteemed amongst men and are allowed to be so much the greater proofs of a true greatness of mind; so the higher and greater these same tempers are toward God, so much the more do they prove the nobility, excellence, and greatness of the mind.

So that so long as duty to parents, love to friends, and gratitude to benefactors are thought great and honorable tempers, devotion, which is nothing else but duty, love, and gratitude to God, must have the highest place amongst our highest virtues.

If a prince out of his mere goodness should send you a pardon by one of his slaves, would you think it a part of your duty to receive the slave with marks of love, esteem, and gratitude for his great kindness, in bringing you so great a gift, and at the same time think it a meanness and poorness of spirit to show love, esteem, and gratitude to the prince who of his own goodness freely sent you the pardon?

And yet this would be as reasonable as to suppose that love, esteem, honor, and gratitude are noble tempers and instances of a great soul when they are paid to our fellow creatures, but the effects of a poor, ignorant, dejected mind when they are paid to God.

Further, that part of devotion which expresses itself in sorrowful confessions and penitential tears of a broken and a contrite heart is very far from being any sign of a little and ignorant mind.

For who does not acknowledge it an instance of an ingenuous, generous, and brave mind to acknowledge a fault and ask pardon for any offence? And are not the finest and most improved minds the most remarkable for this excellent temper?

Is it not also allowed that the ingenuity and excellence of a man's spirit is much shown when his sorrow and indignation at himself rises in proportion to the folly of his crime and the goodness and greatness of the person he has offended?

Now if things are thus, then the greater any man's mind is, the more he knows of God and himself, the more will he be disposed to prostrate himself before God in all the humblest acts and expressions of repentance.

And the greater the ingenuity, the generosity, judgment, and penetration of his mind is, the more will he exercise and indulge a passionate, tender sense of God's just displeasure, and the more he knows of the greatness, the goodness, and perfection of the divine nature, the fuller of shame and confusion will he be at his own sins and ingratitude.

And on the other hand, the more dull and ignorant any soul is, the more base and ungenerous it naturally is; the more senseless it is of the goodness and purity of God, so much the more averse will it be to all acts of humble confession and repentance.

Devotion, therefore, is so far from being best suited to little ignorant minds that a true elevation of soul, a lively sense of honor, and great knowledge of God and ourselves are the greatest natural helps that our devotion hath.

And on the other hand, it shall here be made appear by variety of arguments that indevotion is founded in the most excessive ignorance.

And first, our blessed Lord and His Apostles were eminent instances of great and frequent devotion. Now if we will grant (as all Christians must grant) that their great devotion was founded in a true knowledge of the nature of devotion, the nature of God and the nature of man, then it is plain that all those that are insensible of the duty of devotion are in this excessive state of ignorance, they neither know God nor themselves, nor devotion.

For if a right knowledge in these three respects produces great devotion, as in the case of our Savior and His Apostles, then a neglect of devotion must be chargeable upon ignorance.

Again, how comes it that most people have recourse to devotion when they are in sickness, distress, or fear of death? Is it not because this state shows them more of the want of God and their own weakness than they perceive at other times? Is it not because their infirmities, their approaching end, convinces them of something which they did not half perceive before?

Now if devotion at these seasons is the effect of a better knowledge of God and ourselves, then the neglect of devotion at other times is always owing to great ignorance of God and ourselves.

Further, as indevotion is ignorance, so it is the most shameful ignorance, and such as is to be charged with the greatest folly.

This will fully appear to anyone that considers by what rules we are to judge of the excellency of any knowledge or the shamefulness of any ignorance.

Now knowledge itself would be no excellence, nor ignorance any reproach to us, but that we are rational creatures.

But if this be true, then it follows plainly that that knowledge which is most suitable to our rational nature and which most concerns us as such to know is our highest, finest knowledge; and that ignorance which relates to things that are most essential to us as rational creatures and which we are most concerned to know is of all others the most gross and shameful ignorance.

If therefore there be any things that concern us more than others, if there be any truths that are more to us than all others, he that has the fullest knowledge of these things, that sees these truths in the clearest, strongest light, has of all others as a rational creature the clearest understanding and the strongest parts.

If therefore our relation to God be our greatest relation, if our advancement in His favor be our highest advancement, he that has the highest notions of the excellence of this relation, he that most strongly perceives the highest worth and great value of holiness and virtue, that judges everything little when compared with it, proves himself to be master of the best and most excellent knowledge.

If a judge had fine skill in painting, architecture, and music but at the same time had gross and confused notions of equity and a poor, dull apprehension of the value of justice, who would scruple to reckon him a poor, ignorant judge?

If a bishop should be a man of great address and skill in the arts of preferment and understanding how to raise and enrich his family in the world, but should have no taste or sense of the maxims and principles of the Saints and fathers of the church; if he did not conceive the holy nature and great obligations of his calling and judge it better to be crucified to the world than to live idly in pomp and splendor, who would scruple to charge such a bishop with want of understanding?

If we do not judge and pronounce after this manner, our reason and judgment are but empty sounds.

But now, if a judge is to be reckoned ignorant if he does not feel and perceive the value and worth of justice, if a bishop is to be looked upon as void of understanding if he is more experienced in other things than in the exalted virtues of his apostolical calling, then all common Christians are to be looked upon as more or less knowing, accordingly as they know more or less of those great things which are the common and greatest concern of all Christians.

If a gentleman should fancy that the moon is no bigger than it appears to the eye, that it shines with its own light, that all the stars are only so many spots of light; if after reading books of astronomy he should still continue in the same opinion, most people would think he had but a poor apprehension.

But if the same person should think it better to provide for a short life here than to prepare for a glorious eternity hereafter, that it was better to be rich than to be eminent in piety, his ignorance and dullness would be too great to be compared to anything else.

There is no knowledge that deserves so much as the name of it, but that which we call judgment.

And that is the most clear and improved understanding which judges best of the value and worth of things. All the rest is but the capacity of an animal, it is but mere seeing and hearing.

And there is no excellence of any knowledge in us till we exercise our judgment and judge well of the value and worth of things.

If a man had eyes that could see beyond the stars or pierce into the heart of the earth but could not see the things that were before him or discern anything that was serviceable to him, we should reckon that he had a very bad sight.

If another had ears that received sounds from the world in the moon, but could hear nothing that was said or done upon earth, we should look upon him to be as bad as deaf.

In like manner, if a man has a memory that can retain a great many things, if he has a wit that is sharp and acute in arts and sciences but has a dull, poor apprehension of his duty and relation to God of the value of piety or the worth of moral virtue, he may very justly be reckoned to have a bad understanding. He is but like the man that can only see and hear such things as are of no benefit to him.

As certain therefore as piety, virtue, and eternal happiness are of the most concern to man, as certain as the immortality of our nature and relation to God are the most glorious circumstances of our nature, so certain is it that he who dwells most in contemplation of them, whose heart is most affected with them, who sees farthest into them, who best comprehends the value and excellency of them, who judges all worldly attainments to be mere bubbles and shadows in comparison of them, proves himself to have of all others the finest understanding and strongest judgment.

And if we don't reason after this manner or allow this method of reasoning, we have no arguments to prove that there is any such thing as a wise man or a fool.

For a man is proved to be a natural,[63] not because he wants any of his senses or is incapable of everything; but because he has no judgment and is entirely ignorant of the worth and value of things, he will perhaps choose a fine coat rather than a large estate.

And as the essence of stupidity consists in the entire want of judgment in an ignorance of the value of things, so on the other hand, the essence of wisdom and knowledge must consist in the excellency of our judgment or in the knowledge of the worth and value of things.

This therefore is an undeniable proof, that he who knows most of the value of the best things, who judges most rightly of the things which are of most concern to him, who had rather have his soul in a state of Christian perfection than the greatest share of worldly happiness, has the highest wisdom and is at the furthest distance from men that are naturals that any knowledge can place him.

On the other hand, he that can talk the learned languages and repeat a great deal of history but prefers the indulgence of his body to the purity and perfection of his soul, who is more concerned to get a name or an estate here than to live in eternal glory hereafter, is in the nearest to that natural who chooses a painted coat[64] rather than a large estate.

He is not called a natural by men but[65] he must appear to God and heavenly beings as in a more excessive state of stupidity and will sooner or later certainly appear so to himself.

But now if this be undeniably plain that we cannot prove a man to be a fool but by showing that he has no knowledge of things that are good and evil to himself, then it is undeniably plain that we cannot prove a man to be wise but by showing that he has the fullest knowledge of things that are his greatest good and his greatest evil.

If therefore God be our greatest good, if there can be no good but in His favor nor any evil but in departing from Him, then it is plain that he who judges it the best thing he can do to please God to the utmost of his power, who worships and adores Him with all his heart and soul, who had rather have a pious mind than all the dignities and honors in the world, shows himself to be in the highest state of human wisdom.

To proceed: We know how our blessed Lord acted in a human body; it was his meat and drink to do the will of His Father which is in Heaven.

And if any number of heavenly spirits were to leave their habitations in the light of God and be for a while united to human bodies, they would certainly tend toward God in all their actions and be as heavenly as they could in a state of flesh and blood.

They would certainly act in this manner because they would know that God was the only good of all spirits, and that whether they were in the body or out of the body, in Heaven or on earth, they must have every degree of their greatness and happiness from God alone.

All human spirits, therefore, the more exalted they are, the more they know their divine original; the nearer they come to heavenly spirits, by so much the more will they live to God in all their actions and make their whole life a state of devotion.

Devotion therefore is the greatest sign of a great and noble genius; it supposes a soul in its highest state of knowledge, and none but little and blinded minds that are sunk into ignorance and vanity are destitute of it.

If a human spirit should imagine some mighty prince to be greater than God, we should take it for a poor, ignorant creature; all people would acknowledge such an imagination to be the height of stupidity.

But if this same human spirit should think it better to be devoted to some mighty prince than to be devoted to God, would not this still be a greater proof of a poor, ignorant, and blinded nature?

Yet this is what all people do who think anything better, greater, or wiser than a devout life.

So that which way soever we consider this matter, it plainly appears that devotion is an instance of great judgment of an elevated nature; and the want of devotion is a certain proof of the want of understanding.

The greatest spirits of the heathen world, such as Pythagoras, Socrates, Plato, Epictetus, Marcus Antoninus, etc., owed all their greatness to the spirit of devotion.

They were full of God; their wisdom and deep contemplations tended only to deliver men from the vanity of the world, the slavery of bodily passions, that they might act as spirits that came from God and were soon to return to Him.

Again, to see the dignity and greatness of a devout spirit, we need only compare it with other tempers that are chosen in the room of it.

St. John tells us that all in the world (that is, all the tempers of a worldly life) is the lust of the flesh, the lust of the eyes, and the pride of life.

Let us therefore consider what wisdom or excellency of mind there is required to qualify a man for these delights.

Let us suppose a man given up to the pleasures of the body; surely this can be no sign of a fine mind or an excellent spirit. For if he has but the temper of an animal, he is great enough for these enjoyments.

Let us suppose him to be devoted to honors and splendors, to be fond of glitter and equipage; now if this temper required any great parts or fine understanding to make a man capable of it, it would prove the world to abound with great wits.

Let us suppose him to be in love with riches, and to be so eager in the pursuit of them as never to think he has enough; now this passion is so far from supposing any excellent sense or great understanding that blindness and folly are the best supports that it hath.

Let us lastly suppose him in another light, not singly devoted to any of these passions, but, as it mostly happens, governed by all of them in their turns; does this show a more exalted nature than to spend his days in the service of any one of them?

For to have a taste for these things and to be devoted to them is so far from arguing any tolerable parts or understanding that they are suited to the dullest, weakest minds and require only a great deal of pride and folly to be greatly admired.

But now let libertines bring any such charge as this, if they can, against devotion. They may as well endeavor to charge light with everything that belongs to darkness.

Let them but grant that there is a God and providence, and then they have granted enough to justify the wisdom and support the honor of devotion.

For if there is an infinitely wise and good Creator in whom we live, move, and have our being, whose providence governs all things in all places, surely it must be the highest act of our understanding to conceive rightly of Him; it must be the noblest instance of judgment, the most exalted temper of our nature, to worship and adore this universal providence, to conform to its laws, to study its wisdom, and to live and act everywhere as in the presence of this infinitely good and wise Creator.

Now he that lives thus, lives in the spirit of devotion.

And what can show such great parts and so fine an understanding as to live in this temper?

For if God is wisdom, surely he must be the wisest man in the world who most conforms to the wisdom of God, who best obeys His providence, who enters furthest into His designs, and does all he can that God's will may be done on earth as it is done in Heaven.

A devout man makes a true use of his reason; he sees through the vanity of the world, discovers the corruption of his nature and the blindness of his passions. He lives by a law which is not visible to vulgar eyes; he enters into the world of spirits; he compares the greatest things, sets eternity against time, and chooses rather to be forever great in the presence of God when he dies than to have the greatest share of worldly pleasures whilst he lives.

He that is devout is full of these great thoughts; he lives upon these noble reflections and conducts himself by rules and principles which can only be apprehended, admired, and loved by reason.

There is nothing therefore that shows so great a genius, nothing that so raises us above vulgar spirits, nothing that so plainly declares a heroic greatness of mind as great devotion.

When you suppose a man to be a saint or all devotion, you have raised him as much above all other conditions of life as a philosopher is above an animal.

Lastly, courage and bravery are words of a great sound and

seem to signify a heroic spirit; but yet humility, which seems to be the lowest, meanest part of devotion, is a more certain argument of a noble and courageous mind.

For humility contends with greater enemies, is more constantly engaged, more violently assaulted, bears more, suffers more, and requires greater courage to support itself than any instances of worldly bravery.

A man that dares be poor and contemptible in the eyes of the world to approve himself to God, that resists and rejects all human glory, that opposes the clamor of his passions, that meekly puts up all injuries and wrongs and dares stay for his reward till the invisible hand of God gives to everyone their proper places, endures a much greater trial and exerts a nobler fortitude than he that is bold and daring in the fire of battle.

For the boldness of a soldier, if he is a stranger to the spirit of devotion, is rather weakness than fortitude; it is at best but mad passion and heated spirits and has no more true valor in it than the fury of a tiger.

For as we cannot lift up a hand or stir a foot but by a power that is lent us from God, so bold actions that are not directed by the laws of God or so many executions of His will are no more true bravery than sedate malice is Christian patience.

Reason is our universal law that obliges us in all places and at all times; and no actions have any honor but so far as they are instances of our obedience to reason.

And it is as base and cowardly to be bold and daring against the principle of reason and justice as to be bold and daring in lying and perjury.

Would we therefore exercise a true fortitude, we must do all in the spirit of devotion, be valiant against the corruptions of the world, the lusts of the flesh, and the temptations of the Devil. For to be daring and courageous against these enemies is the noblest bravery that a human mind is capable of.

I have made this digression for the sake of those who think a great devotion to be bigotry and poorness of spirit, that by these considerations they may see how poor and mean all other tempers are if compared to it. That they may see that all worldly attainments, whether of greatness, wisdom, or bravery, are but empty sounds, and that there is nothing wise, or great, or noble in a human spirit but rightly to know and heartily worship and adore the great God that is the support and life of all spirits, whether in Heaven or on earth.

NOTES

61. See *Christian Perfection* [ed. 1726], p. 2 (Law's note, referring to his own work).
62. Appear: apparent.
63. A natural: without spiritual enlightenment or true discernment.
64. Painted coat: a highly colorful and ornamented jacket.
65. But: with the common sense, "except insofar as."

The
Spirit of Love

The Contents

THE

SPIRIT

O F

L O V E.

PART the FIRST.

In a LETTER *to a Friend.*

By *WILLIAM LAW*, A.M.

The SECOND EDITION.

L O N D O N:
Printed for J. RICHARDSON, in *Pater-noster Row.*

M DCC LIX.

The title page from the second edition of 1759.

My Dear Friend,

You had no occasion to make any apology for the manner of your letter to me, for though you very well know that I have as utter an aversion to waste my time and thoughts in matters of theological debate as in any contentions merely of a worldly nature, as knowing that the former are generally as much, if not more, hurtful to the heart of man than the latter; yet as your objections rather tend to stir up the powers of love than the wrangle of a rational debate, so I consider them only as motives and occasions of edifying both you and myself with the truth, the power and divine blessedness of the spirit of love.

You say there is nothing in all my writings that has more affected you than that spirit of love that breathes in them, and that you wish for nothing so much as to have a living sensibility of the power, life, and religion of love. But you have these two objections often rising in your mind: First, that this doctrine of pure and universal love may be too refined and imaginary, because you find that however you like it, yet you cannot attain to it, or overcome all that in your nature which is contrary to it, do what you can; and so are only able to be an admirer of that love which you cannot lay hold of. Secondly, because you find so much said in scripture of a righteousness and justice, a wrath and vengeance of God that must be atoned and satisfied, etc., that though you are in love with that description of the Deity which I have given, as a Being that is all love, yet you have some doubt whether the scripture will allow of it.

Thus stand your objections, which will fall into nothing as soon as you look at them from a right point of view, which will then be, as soon as you have found the true ground of the nature, power, and necessity of the blessed spirit of love.

Now the spirit of love has this original. God, as considered in Himself in His holy Being, before anything is brought forth by Him or out of Him, is only an eternal will to all goodness. This is the one eternal immutable God, that from eternity to

eternity changeth not, that can be neither more nor less nor anything else but an eternal will to all the goodness that is in Himself, and can come from Him. The creation of ever so many
worlds or systems of creatures adds nothing to, nor takes anything from this immutable God. He always was and always will
be the same immutable will to all goodness. So that as certainly
as He is the Creator, so certainly is He the Blesser of every
created thing, and can give nothing but blessing, goodness, and
happiness from Himself because He has in Himself nothing else
to give. It is much more possible for the sun to give forth darkness than for God to do, or be, or give forth anything but blessing and goodness. Now this is the ground and original of the
spirit of love in the creature; it is and must be a will to all goodness, and you have not the spirit of love till you have this will to
all goodness at all times and on all occasions. You may indeed do
many works of love and delight in them, especially at such times
as they are not inconvenient to you, or contradictory to your
state or temper or occurrences in life. But the spirit of love is not
in you till it is the spirit of your life, till you live freely,
willingly, and universally according to it. For every spirit acts
with freedom and universality according to what it is. It needs
no command to live its own life, or be what it is, no more than
you need bid wrath be wrathful. And therefore when love is the
spirit of your life, it will have the freedom and universality of a
spirit; it will always live and work in love, not because of this or
that, here or there, but because the spirit of love can only love,
wherever it is or goes or whatever is done to it. As the sparks
know no motion but that of flying upwards, whether it be in the
darkness of the night or in the light of the day, so the spirit of
love is always in the same course; it knows no difference of time,
place, or persons, but whether it gives or forgives, bears or forbears, it is equally doing its own delightful work, equally blessed
from itself. For the spirit of love, wherever it is, is its own blessing
and happiness because it is the truth and reality of God in
the soul, and therefore is in the same joy of life and is the same
good to itself, everywhere and on every occasion.[1]

Oh Sir! Would you know the blessing of all blessings? It is
this God of love dwelling in your soul and killing every root of

bitterness which is the pain and torment of every earthly, selfish
love. For all wants are satisfied, all disorders of nature are removed, no life is any longer a burden, every day is a day of
peace, everything you meet becomes a help to you because everything you see or do is all done in the sweet, gentle element of
love. For as love has no by-ends, wills nothing but its own increase, so everything is as oil to its flame. It must have that
which it wills and cannot be disappointed, because everything
naturally helps it to live in its own way and to bring forth its
own work. The spirit of love does not want to be rewarded,
honored, or esteemed. Its only desire is to propagate itself and
become the blessing and happiness of everything that wants it.
And therefore it meets wrath and evil and hatred and opposition
with the same one will as the light meets the darkness, only to
overcome it with all its blessings. Did you want to avoid the
wrath and ill will or to gain the favor of any persons, you might
easily miss of your ends; but if you have no will but to all goodness, everything you meet, be it what it will, must be forced to
be assistant to you. For the wrath of an enemy, the treachery of
a friend, and every other evil only helps the spirit of love to be
more triumphant, to live its own life and find all its own blessings
in a higher degree. Whether therefore you consider perfection or happiness, it is all included in the spirit of love and must
be so for this reason, because the infinitely perfect and happy
God is mere love, an unchangeable will to all goodness; and
therefore every creature must be corrupt and unhappy, so far as
it is led by any other will than the one will to all goodness. Thus
you see the ground, the nature, and perfection of the spirit of
love. Let me now in a word or two show you the necessity of it.
Now the necessity is absolute and unchangeable. No creature
can be a child of God but because the goodness of God is in it;
nor can it have any union or communion with the goodness of
the Deity till its life is a spirit of love. This is the one only band
of union betwixt God and the creature. All besides this, or that
is not this, call it by what name you will, is only so much error,
fiction, impurity, and corruption got into the creature, and must
of all necessity be entirely separated from it before it can have
that purity and holiness which alone can see God or find the di-

vine life. For as God is an immutable will to all goodness, so the divine will can unite or work with no creaturely will but that which willeth with Him only that which is good. Here the necessity is absolute; nothing will do instead of this will; all contrivances of holiness, all forms of religious piety, signify nothing without this will to all goodness. For as the will to all goodness is the whole nature of God, so it must be the whole nature of every service or religion that can be acceptable to Him. For nothing serves God or worships and adores Him but that which wills and worketh with Him. For God can delight in nothing but His own will and His own Spirit, because all goodness is included in it and can be nowhere else. And therefore everything that followeth an own will or an own spirit forsaketh the one will to all goodness, and whilst it doth so hath no capacity for the light and Spirit of God. The necessity therefore of the spirit of love is what God Himself cannot dispense with in the creature, no more than He can deny Himself or act contrary to His own holy Being. But as it was His will to all goodness that brought forth angels and the spirits of men, so He can will nothing in their existence but that they should live and work and manifest that same spirit of love and goodness which brought them into being. Everything therefore but the will and life of goodness is an apostasy in the creature and is rebellion against the whole nature of God.

There is no peace, nor ever can be for the soul of man but in the purity and perfection of its first created nature; nor can it have its purity and perfection in any other way than in and by the spirit of love. For as love is the God that created all things, so love is the purity, the perfection, and blessing of all created things; and nothing can live in God but as it lives in love. Look at every vice, pain, and disorder in human nature; it is in itself nothing else but the spirit of the creature turned from the universality of love to some self-seeking or own will in created things. So that love alone is, and only can be, the cure of every evil, and he that lives in the purity of love is risen out of the power of evil into the freedom of the one spirit of heaven. The schools[2] have given us very accurate definitions of every vice, whether it be covetousness, pride, wrath, envy, etc., and shown us how to conceive them as notionally[3] distinguished from one another. But the Christian has a much shorter way of knowing their nature and power and what they all are and do in and to himself. For call them by what names you will, or distinguish them with ever so much exactness, they are all, separately and jointly, just that same one thing, and all do that same one work as the scribes, the pharisees, hypocrites, and rabble of the Jews who crucified Christ were all but one and the same thing and all did one and the same work, however different they were in outward names. If you would therefore have a true sense of the nature and power of pride, wrath, covetousness, envy, etc., they are in their whole nature nothing else but the murderers and crucifiers of the true Christ of God; not as the High Priests did many hundred years ago, nailing His outward humanity to an outward cross, but crucifying afresh the Son of God, the holy Immanuel, who is the Christ that every man crucifies as often as he gives way to wrath, pride, envy, or covetousness, etc. For every temper or passion that is contrary to the new birth of Christ and keeps the holy Immanuel from coming to life in the soul is, in the strictest truth of the words, a murderer and killer of the Lord of life. And where pride and envy and hatred, etc., are suffered to live, there the same thing is done as when Christ was killed and Barabbas was saved alive. The Christ of God was not then first crucified when the Jews brought Him to the cross, but Adam and Eve were His first real murderers; for the death which happened to them in the day that they did eat of the earthly tree was the death of the Christ of God or the divine life in their souls. For Christ had never come into the world as a second Adam to redeem it had He not been originally the life and perfection and glory of the first Adam.[4] And He is our Atonement and reconciliation with God, because by and through Him brought to life in us, we are set again in that first state of holiness, and have Christ again in us as our first father had at his creation. For had not Christ been in our first father, as a birth of life in him, Adam had been created a mere child of wrath, in the same impurity of nature, in the same enmity with God, and in the same want of an atoning Savior as we are at this day. For God can have no delight or union with any creature but because

His well-beloved Son, the express image of His person, is found in it. This is as true of all unfallen as of all fallen creatures; the one are redeemed and the other want no redemption, only through the life of Christ dwelling in them. For as the Word, or Son of God, is the Creator of all things, and by Him everything is made that was made, so everything that is good and holy in unfallen angels is as much through His living and dwelling in them as everything that is good and holy in redeemed man is through Him. And He is just as much the preserver, the strength, and glory, and life of all the thrones and principalities of Heaven as He is the righteousness, the peace, and redemption of fallen man.[5]

This Christ of God hath many names in scripture, but they all mean only this, that He is, and alone can be, the light and life and holiness of every creature that is holy, whether in Heaven or on earth. Wherever Christ is not, there is the wrath of nature or nature left to itself and its own tormenting strength of life, to feel nothing in itself but the vain, restless contrariety of its own working properties. This is the one only origin of Hell, and every kind of curse and misery in the creature. It is nature without the Christ of God or the spirit of love ruling over it. And here you may observe that wrath has in itself the nature of Hell, and that it can have no beginning or power in any creature but so far as it has lost the Christ of God. And when Christ is everywhere, wrath and hatred will be nowhere. Whenever therefore you willingly indulge wrath or let your mind work in hatred, you not only work without Christ, but you resist Him and withstand His redeeming power over you. You do in reality what those Jews did when they said, "We will not have this man to reign over us." For Christ never was, nor can be, in any creature but purely as a spirit of love.

In all the universe of nature nothing but Heaven and heavenly creatures ever had, or could have been known, had every created will continued in that state in which it came forth out of and from God. For God can will nothing in the life of the creature but a creaturely manifestation of His own goodness, happiness and perfection. And therefore, where this is wanted, the fact is certain that the creature hath changed and lost its first state that it had from God. Everything therefore which is the vanity, the wrath, the torment and evil of man or any intelligent creature is solely the effect of his will turned from God and can come from nothing else. Misery and wickedness can have no other ground or root, for whatever wills and works with God must of all necessity partake of the happiness and perfection of God.

This therefore is a certain truth, that Hell and death, curse and misery, can never cease or be removed from the creation till the will of the creature is again as it came from God and is only a spirit of love that willeth nothing but goodness. All the whole fallen creation, stand it never so long, must groan and travail in pain; this must be its purgatory till every contrariety to the divine will is entirely taken from every creature.

Which is only saying that all the powers and properties of nature are a misery to themselves, can only work in disquiet and wrath till the birth of the Son of God brings them under the dominion and power of the spirit of love.

Thus Sir, you have seen the original, immutable ground and necessity of the spirit of love. It is no imaginary refinement or speculative curiosity, but is of the highest reality and most absolute necessity. It stands in the immutability and perfection of God, and not only every intelligent creature, be it what and where it will, but every inanimate thing must work in vanity and disquiet till it has its state in and works under the spirit of love. For as love brought forth all things, and all things were what they were and had their place and state under the working power of love, so everything that has lost its first-created state must be in restless strife and disquiet till it finds it again. There is no sort of strife, wrath, or storm in outward nature, no fermentation, vegetation, or corruption in any elementary things but what is a full proof and real effect of this truth, viz., that nature can have no rest but must be in the strife of fermentation, vegetation, and corruption, constantly doing and undoing, building and destroying, till the spirit of love has rectified all outward nature and brought it back again into that glassy sea of unity and purity in which St. John beheld the throne of God in the midst of it. For this glassy sea, which the beloved Apostle was blessed with the sight of, is the transparent, heavenly element in which all the properties and powers of nature move and work in the unity and purity of the one will of God, only known as so many endless forms of triumphing light and love. For the strife of properties, of thick against thin, hard against soft, hot against cold, etc., had no existence till angels fell, that is till they turned from God to work with nature. This is the original of all the strife, division, and materiality in the fallen world.

No fluid in this world ferments but because there is some thickness and contrariety in it which it would not have. And it ferments only for this reason, to have a unity and clearness in itself which its nature wants to have. Now when you see this in any fluid, you see the work of all fallen nature and the same that everything else is doing as well as it can in its own way; it is in a restless working and strife after a unity and purity which it can neither have nor forbear to seek. And the reason why all things are doing thus is this, because all the elements of this world, before they were brought down into their present state, had their birth and existence in the unity and purity of the heavenly glassy sea, and therefore must be always in some sort of strife and tendency after their first state, and doomed to disquiet till it is found.

This is the desire of all fallen nature in this world. It cannot be separated from it but every part must work in fermentation, vegetation, and corruption, till it is restored to its first unity and purity under the spirit of love.

Every son of fallen Adam is under this same necessity of working and striving after something that he neither is nor hath, and for the same reason, because the life of man has lost its first unity and purity and therefore must be in a working strife till all contrariety and impurity is separated from it and it finds its first state in God. All evil as well as good men, all the wisdom and folly of this life, are equally a proof of this. For the vanity of wicked men in their various ways, and the labors of good men in faith and hope, etc., proceed from the same cause, viz., from a want and desire of having and being something that they neither are nor have. The evil seek wrong and the good seek right, but they both are seekers, and for the same reason, because their present state has not that which it wants to have. And this must be the state of human life and of every creature that has fallen from its first state or has something in it that it should not have. It must do as the polluted fluid does; it must ferment and work, either right or wrong, to mend its state. The muddled wine always works right to the utmost of its power because it works according to nature, but if it had an intelligent free will it might work as vainly as man does. It might continually thicken itself, be always stirring up its own dregs, just as well as the soul of man seeks for its happiness in the lusts of the flesh, the lust of the eyes, and the pride of life. All which must of the same necessity fall away from the heart of man before it can find its happiness in God, as the dregs must separate from the wine before it can have its perfection and clearness.

Purification therefore is the one thing necessary, and nothing will do in the stead of it. But man is not purified till every earthly, wrathful, sensual, selfish, partial, self-willing temper is taken from him. He is not dying to himself till he is dying to these tempers, and he is not alive in God till he is dead to them. For he wants purification only because he has these tempers, and therefore he has not the purification which he wants till they are all separated from him. It is the purity and perfection of the divine nature that must be brought again into him, because in that purity and perfection he came forth from God and could have no less, as he was a child of God, that was to be blessed by a life in Him and from Him. For nothing impure or imperfect in its will and working can have any union with God. Nor are you to think that these words, the purity and perfection of God, are too high to be used on this occasion, for they only mean that the will of the creature, as an offspring of the divine will, must will and work with the will of God, for then it stands and lives truly and really in the purity and perfection of God, and whatever does not thus is at enmity with God and cannot have any union of life and happiness with Him and in Him.

Now nothing wills and works with God but the spirit of love, because nothing else works in God Himself. The Almighty brought forth all nature for this only end, that boundless love might have its infinity of height and depth to dwell and work in, and all the striving and working properties of nature are only to give essence and substance, life and strength, to the invisible hidden spirit of love, that it may come forth into outward activity and manifest its blessed powers, that creatures born in the strength, and out of the powers of nature, might communicate the spirit of love and goodness, give and receive mutual delight and joy to and from one another. All below this state of love is a fall from the one life of God, and the only life in which the God of love can dwell. Partiality, self, mine, thine, etc., are tempers that can only belong to creatures that have lost the power, presence, and spirit of the universal Good. They can have no place in Heaven, nor can be anywhere, but because Heaven is lost. Think not, therefore, that the spirit of pure, universal love which is the one purity and perfection of Heaven and all heavenly natures has been or can be carried too high or its absolute necessity too much asserted. For it admits of no degrees of higher or lower, and is not in being till it is absolutely pure and unmixed, no more than a line can be straight till it is absolutely free from all crookedness.

All the design of Christian redemption is to remove everything that is unheavenly, gross, dark, wrathful, and disordered from every part of this fallen world. And when you see earth and stones, storms and tempests, and every kind of evil, misery, and wickedness, you see that which Christ came into the world to remove, and not only to give a new birth to fallen man, but also to deliver all outward nature from its present vanity and evil and set it again in its first heavenly state. Now if you ask how came all things into this evil and vanity, it is because they have lost the blessed spirit of love which alone makes the happiness and perfection of every power of nature. Look at grossness, coldness, hardness, and darkness. They never could have had any existence, but because the properties of nature must appear in this manner when the light of God is no longer dwelling in them.

Nature is at first only spiritual. It has in itself nothing but the spiritual properties of the desire, which is the very being and ground of nature. But when these spiritual properties are not filled and blessed, and all held in one will by the light and love of God ruling in them, then something is found in nature which never should have been found, viz., the properties of nature in a state of visible, palpable division and contrariety to each other. And this new state of the properties of nature is the first beginning and birth and possibility of all that contrariety that is to be found betwixt hot and cold, hard and soft, thick and thin, etc., all which could have had no existence till the properties of nature lost their first unity and purity under the light and love of God, manifested and working in them. And this is the one true origin of all the materiality of this earthly system and of every struggle and contrariety that is found in material things. Had the properties of nature been kept by the creature in their first state, blessed and overcome with the light and love of heaven dwelling and working in them, no wrath or contrarity could ever have been known by any creature, and had not wrath and contrariety entered into the properties of nature, nothing thick or hard or dark, etc., could ever have been found or known in any place. Now everything that you see and know of the things of this world shows you that matter began only in and from the change of the spiritual properties of nature, and that matter is changed and altered just as the light and purity of heaven is more or less in it. How comes the flint to be in such a state of hard, dark compaction? It is because the meekness and fluidity of the light and air and water of this world have little or no existence in it. And therefore, as soon as the fire has unlocked its hard compaction and opened in it the light and air and water of this world, it becomes transparent glass and is brought so much nearer to that first glassy sea in which it once existed. For the light and air and water of this world, though all of them in a material state, yet have the most of the first heavenly nature in them, and as these are more or less in all material things, so are they nearer or farther from their first heavenly state. And as fire is the first deliverer of the flint from its hard compaction, so the last universal fire must begin the deliverance of this material system and fit everything to receive that spirit of light and love which will bring all things back again to their first glassy sea, in which the Deity dwelleth as in His throne. And thus, as the earthly fire turns flint into glass, so earth will become Heaven and the contrariety

367

of four divided elements will become one transparent brightness of glory as soon as the last fire shall have melted every grossness into its first undivided fluidity, for the light and love and majesty of God to be all in all in it. How easy and natural is it to suppose all that is earth and stones to be dissolved into water, the water to be changed into air, the air into ether, and the ether rarefied into light? Is there anything here impossible to be supposed? And how near a step is the next, to suppose all this changed or exalted into that glassy sea, which was everywhere before the angels fell? What now is become of hard, heavy, dead, divisible, corruptible matter? Is it annihilated? No; and yet nothing of it is left. All that you know of it is gone and nothing but its shadowy idea will be known in eternity. Now as this shows you how matter can lose all its material properties and go back to its first spiritual state, so it makes it very intelligible to you how the sin of angels, which was their sinful working in and with the properties of nature, could bring them out of their first spirituality into that darkness, grossness, and chaos out of which God raised this material system. See now, Sir, how unreasonably you once told me that our doctrine must suppose the eternity of matter, for throughout the whole you might easily have seen that it neither does nor can suppose it, but demonstrates the impossibility of it; shows the true origin of matter, that it is no older than sin; could have no possibility of beginning to be, but from sin, and therefore must entirely vanish when sin is entirely done away.

If matter, said you, be not made out of nothing then it must be eternal. Just as well concluded as if you had said, if snow and hail and ice are not made out of nothing, then they must be eternal. And if your senses did not force you to know how these things are created out of something and are in themselves only the properties of light and air and water, brought out of their first state into such a compaction and creation as is called snow, hail, and ice, your rational philosophy would stand to its noble conclusion, that they must be made out of nothing. Now every time you see snow or hail or ice, you see in truth and reality the creation of matter, or how this world came from some antecedent properties of nature by that same creating power or fiat of God as turns the properties of light and air and water into the different materialities of snow, hail, and ice.

The first property of nature, which is in itself a constringing,[6] attracting, compressing, and coagulating power, is that working power from whence comes all thickness, darkness, coldness, and hardness; and this is the creator of snow and hail and ice out of something that before was only the fluidity of light, air, and moisture. Now this same property of nature, directed by the will of God, was the fiat and creating power which, on the first day of this world, compacted, coagulated, or created the wrathful properties of fallen nature in the angelic kingdom into such a new state as to become earth and stones and water and a visible Heaven. And the new state of the created Heaven and earth and stones and water, etc., came forth by the fiat of God, or the working of the first property of nature, from the properties of fallen nature, just as snow and ice and hail come forth by the same fiat from the properties of light, air, and water. And the created materialities of Heaven, earth, stones, and water have no more eternity in them than there is in snow or hail or ice, but are only held for a time in their compacted or created state, by the same first astringing property[7] of nature which for a time holds snow and hail and ice in their compacted state.

Now here you see with the utmost certainty that all the matter or materiality of this world is the effect of sin and could have its beginning from nothing else. For as thickness, hardness, and darkness (which is the essence of matter) is[8] the effect of the wrathful predominant power of the first property of nature, and as no property of nature can be predominant or known as it is in itself till nature is fallen from its harmonious unity under the light and love of God dwelling in it, so you have the utmost certainty that where matter or (which is the same thing) where thickness, darkness, hardness, etc., are found, there the will of the creature has turned from God and opened a disorderly working of nature without God.

Therefore, as sure as the materiality of this world standeth in the predominant power of the first attracting, astringing property of nature, or in other words, is a thickness, darkness, hardness, etc., so sure is it that all the matter of this world has its beginning from sin and must have its end as soon as the properties of nature are again restored to their first unity and blessed harmony under the light and Spirit of God.

It is no objection to all this that Almighty God must be owned to be the true Creator of the materiality of this world. For God only brought or created it into this materiality out of the fallen sinful properties of nature, and in order to stop their sinful working and to put them into a state of recovery. He created the confused chaos of the darkened, divided, contrary properties of spiritual nature into a further, darker, harder coagulation and division, that so the fallen angels might thereby lose all power over them, and that this new materiality might become a theatre of redemption and stand its time under the dominion of the Lamb of God till all the wrath and grossness and darkness, born of the sin of angels, was fitted to return to its first heavenly purity.

And thus, though God is the Creator of the materiality of this world, yet seeing He created it out of that wrath, division, and darkness which sin had opened in nature, this truth stands firm, that sin alone is the father, first cause, and beginner of all the materiality of this world, and that when sin is removed from nature all its materiality must vanish with it. For when the properties of nature are again in the unity of the one will of light and love, then hot and cold, thick and thin, dark and hard, with every property of matter, must give up all their distinction and all the divided elements of this world lose all their materiality and division in that first heavenly spirituality of a glassy sea from whence they fell.

Now as all the whole nature of matter, its grossness, darkness, and hardness, is owing to the unequal, predominant working of the first property of nature which is an attracting, astringing, and compressing desire; so every spiritual evil, every wicked working and disorderly state of any intelligent being is all owing to the same disorderly, predominant power of the first property of nature, doing all that inwardly in the spirit of the creature, which it does in an outward grossness, darkness, and hardness. Thus, when the desire (the first property of nature) in

any intelligent creature leaves the unity and universality of the
spirit of love and contracts or shuts up itself in an own will, own
love, and self-seeking, then it does all that inwardly and
spiritually in the soul, which it does in outward grossness,
hardness, and darkness. And had not own will, own love, and
self-seeking come into the spirit of the creature, it never could
have found or felt any outward contrariety, darkness, or
hardness. For no creature can have any other outward nature but
that which is in the same state with its inward spirit, and
belongs to it as its own natural growth.

Modern metaphysics has no knowledge of the ground and
nature either of spirit or body, but supposes them not only
without any natural relation, but essentially contrary to one
another, and only held together in a forced conjunction by the
arbitrary will of God. Nay, if you was to say that God first
created a soul out of nothing, and when that is done, then takes
an understanding faculty and puts it into it, after that adds a will
and then a memory, all is independently made, as when a tailor
first makes the body of a coat and then adds sleeves or pockets to
it. Was you to say this, the schools of Descartes, Malebranche,
or Locke could have nothing to say against it.[9] And the thing is
unavoidable, for all these philosophers were so far from knowing
the ground of nature, how it is a birth from God, and all
creatures a birth from nature through the working will of God in
and by the powers of nature, as they were so far from knowing
this as to hold a creation out of nothing, so they were necessarily
excluded from every fundamental truth concerning the origin
either of body or spirit and their true relation to one another.
For a creation out of nothing leaves no room for accounting why
anything is as it is. Now every wise man is supposed to have
respect to nature in everything that he would have joined
together; he cannot suppose his work to succeed unless this be
done. But to suppose God to create man with a body and soul,
not only not naturally related but naturally impossible to be
united by any powers in either of them, is to suppose God acting
and creating man into an unnatural state, which yet he could not
do unless there was such a thing as nature antecedent to the
creation of man. And how can nature be, or have anything but

what it is and has from God? Therefore to suppose God to bring any creature into an unnatural state is to suppose Him acting contrary to Himself and to that nature which is from Him.

Yet all the metaphysics of the schools does this. It supposes God to bring a soul and a body together which have the utmost natural contrariety to each other and can only affect or act upon one another by an arbitrary will of God, willing that body and soul, held together by force, should seem to do that to one another which they have no natural or possible power to do. But the true philosophy of this matter, known only to the soul, that by a new birth from above has found its first state in and from God is this: namely, that nature is a birth or manifestation of the triune invisible Deity. And as it could only come into existence as a birth from God, so every creature or beginning thing can only come forth as a birth from and out of nature by the will of God, willing it to come forth in such a birth. And no creature can have, or be, anything but by and according to the working powers of nature; and therefore, strictly speaking, no creature can be, or be put into an unnatural state. It may indeed lose or fall from its natural perfection by the wrong use or working of its will; but then its fallen state is the natural effect of the wrong use of its will, and so it only has that which is natural to it. The truth of the matter is this: There neither is, nor can be, anything nor any effect in the whole universe of things but by the way of birth. For as the working will is the first cause or beginner of everything, so nothing can proceed further than as it is driven by the will and is a birth of it. And therefore nothing can be in anything but what is natural to its own working will and the true effect of it. Everything that is outward in any being is only a birth of its own spirit, and therefore all body, whether it be heavenly or earthly or hellish, has its whole nature and condition from its own inward spirit, and no spirit can have a body of any other properties but such as are natural to it as being its own true outward state. For body and spirit are not two separate, independent things, but are necessary to each other, and are only the inward and outward conditions of one and the same being.

Every creaturely spirit must have its own body and cannot be without it, for its body is that which makes it manifest to itself. It cannot be said to exist as a creature till in a body because it can have no sensibility of itself, nor feel nor find either that it is or what it is but in and by its own body. Its body is its first knowledge of its something and somewhere.

And now, Sir, if you ask why I have gone into this detail of the origin and nature of body and spirit when my subject was only concerning the spirit of love, it is to show you that grossness, darkness, contrariety, disquiet, and fermentation must be the state of the body and spirit till they are both made pure and luminous by the light and love of Heaven manifested in them. All darkness, grossness, and contrariety must be removed from the body before it can belong to Heaven or be united with it; but these qualities must be in the body till the soul is totally dead to self, partiality, and contrariety, and breathes only the spirit of universal love, because the state of the body has nothing of its own or from itself but is solely the outward manifestation of nothing else but that which is inwardly in the soul. Every animal of this world has nothing in its outward form or shape, every spirit, whether heavenly or hellish, has nothing in the nature and state of its body but that which is the form and growth of its own inward spirit. As no number can be anything else but that which the unities contained in it make it to be, so no body of any creature can be anything else but the coagulation or sum total of those properties of nature that are coagulated in it. And when the properties of nature are formed into the band of a creaturely union, then is its body brought forth, whether the spirit of the creature be earthly, heavenly, or hellish.

Nature, or the first properties of life, are in a state of the highest contrariety, and the highest want of something which they have not. This is their whole nature and they have nothing else in them. And this is their true ground and fitness to become a life of triumphing joy and happiness, viz., when united in the possession of that which they seek for in their contrariety. And if life, in its first root, was not this depth of strife, this strength of hunger, and sensibility of want, the fullness of heavenly joy could not be manifested in it.

You are not a stranger to the mystery of the seven properties of nature[10] which we have often spoken of; and therefore I shall shorten the matter and only say so much of them as may be of service to our present subject.

Nature, whether eternal or temporal, is that which comes not into being for its own self or to be that which it is in itself, but for the sake of something that it is not, and has not. And this is the reason why nature is only a desire; it is because it is for the sake of something else, and is also the reason why nature in itself is only a torment, because it is only a strong desire and cannot help itself to that which it wants, but is always working against itself.[11]

Now a desire that cannot be stopped nor get that which it would have has a threefold contrariety or working in it, which you may thus conceive as follows: The first and peculiar property or the one only will of the desire, as such, is to have that which it has not; and all that it can do toward having it is to act as if it were seizing it; and this is it which makes the desire to be a magic compressing, enclosing, or astringing, because that is all that it can do toward seizing of that which it would have. But the desire cannot thus magically astringe, compress, or strive to enclose without drawing and attracting: but drawing is motion, which is the highest contrariety and resistance to compressing or holding together. And thus the desire, in its magical working, sets out with two contrary properties, inseparable from one another and equal in strength; for the motion has no strength but as it is the drawing of the desire; and the desire only draws in the same degree as it wills to compress and astringe; and therefore the desire, as astringing, always begets a resistance equal to itself. Now from this great and equally strong contrariety of the two first properties of the desire magically pulling, as I may say, two contrary ways, there arises as a necessary birth from both of them a third property which is emphatically called a wheel or whirling anguish of life. For a thing that can go neither inward nor outward and yet must be and move under the equal power of both of them, must whirl or turn round; it has no possibility of doing anything else or of ceasing to do that. And that this whirling contrariety of these inseparable properties is the great anguish of life and may properly be called the hell of nature; and every lesser torment which any man finds in this mixed world has all its existence and power from the working of these three properties. For life can find no troublesome motions or sensibility of distress but so far as it comes under their power, and enters into their whirling wheel.

Now here you may observe that as this whirling anguish of life is a third state necessarily arising from the contrariety of the two first properties of the desire, so in this material system every whirling or orbicular motion of any body is solely the effect or product of the contrariety of these two first properties. For no material thing can whirl or move round till it is under the power of these two properties; that is, till it can neither go inwards nor outwards and yet is obliged to move, just as the whirling anguish of the desire then begins when it can neither go inwards nor outwards and yet must be in motion.

And this may be again another strict demonstration to you that all the matter of this world is from spiritual properties, since all its workings and effects are according to them. For if matter does nothing but according to them, it can be nothing but what it is and has from them.

Here also, that is, in these three properties of the desire, you see the ground and reason of the three great laws of matter and motion lately discovered and so much celebrated, and need no more to be told that the illustrious Sir Isaac plowed with Behmen's heifer when he brought forth the discovery of them.[12] In the mathematical system of this great philosopher these three properties, attraction, equal resistance, and the orbicular motion of the planets as the effect of them, etc., are only treated of as facts and appearances whose ground is not pretended to be known. But in our Behmen, the illuminated instrument of God, their birth and power in eternity is opened; their eternal beginning is shown, and how and why all worlds and every life of every creature, whether it be heavenly, earthly, or hellish, must be in them and from them, and can have no nature either spiritual or material, no kind of happiness or misery but according to the working power and state of these properties.

All outward nature, all inward life, is what it is and works as it works from this unceasing, powerful attraction, resistance, and whirling.

Every madness and folly of life is their immediate work and

every good spirit of wisdom and love has all its strength and activity from them. They equally support darkness and light. The one could have no powers of thickness and coldness, the other no powers of warmth, brightness, and activity but by and through these three properties acting in a different state. Not a particle of matter stirs, rises, or falls, separates from or unites with any other but under their power. Not a thought of the mind either of love or hatred, of joy or trouble, of envy or wrath, of pride and covetousness, can rise in the spirit of any creature but as these properties act and stir in it.

The next and following properties, viz., the fourth, called fire; the fifth, called the form of light and love, and the sixth, sound or understanding, only declare the gradual effects of the entrance of the Deity into the three first properties of nature, changing or bringing their strong wrathful attraction, resistance, and whirling into a life and state of triumphing joy, and fullness of satisfaction, which state of peace and joy in one another is called the seventh property, or state of nature. And this is what Behmen means by his *Ternarius Sanctus*[13] which he so often speaks of as the only place from whence he received all that he said and writ. He means by it the holy manifestation of the triune God in the seven properties of nature or Kingdom of Heaven. And from this manifestation of God in the seven properties of nature or Kingdom of Heaven, he most wonderfully opens and accounts for all that was done in the six first working days of the creation, showing how every of the six active properties had its peculiar day's work till the whole ended or rested in the sanctified, paradisiacal Sabbath of the seventh day, just as nature doth in its seventh property.

And now, Sir, you may see in the greatest clearness how everything in this world, everything in the soul and body of man, absolutely requires the one redemption of the gospel. There is but one nature in all created things, whether spiritual or material; they all stand and work upon the same ground, viz., the three first properties of nature. That only which can illuminate the soul, that alone can give brightness and purity to the body. For there is no grossness, darkness, and contrariety in the body but what strictly proceeds from the same cause that makes selfishness, wrath, envy, and torment in the soul; it is but one and the same state and working of the same three first properties of nature. All evil, whether natural or moral, whether of body or spirit, is the sole effect of the wrath and disorder of the spirits of nature working in and by themselves. And all the good, perfection, and purity of everything, whether spiritual or material, whether it be the body or spirit of man or angel, is solely from the power and presence of the supernatural Deity dwelling and working in the properties of nature. For the properties of nature are in themselves nothing else but a mere hunger, want, strife, and contrariety, till the fullness and riches of the Deity entering into them unites them all in one will and one possession of light and harmonious love, which is the one redemption of the gospel, and the one reason why nothing else but the heart or Son or light of God can purify nature and creature from all the evil they are fallen into.

For nothing can possibly deliver the soul from its selfish nature and earthly passions but that one power that can deliver matter from its present material properties and turn earth into Heaven. And that for this plain reason, because soul and body, outward nature and inward life, have but one and the same evil in them and from one and the same cause.

The Deist, therefore, who looks for life and salvation through the use of his reason, acts contrary to the whole nature of everything that he sees and knows of himself and of the nature and state of this world.[14] For from one end of it to the other, all its material state, all its gross divided elements declare that they are what they are because the light and love of Heaven is not working and manifest in them, and that nothing can take darkness, materiality, rage, storms, and tempests from them but that same heavenly light and love which was made flesh to redeem the fallen humanity first, and after that the whole material system.

Can the Deist with his reason bring the light of this world into the eyes of his body? If not, how comes it to be less absurd or more possible for reason to bring heavenly light into the soul? Can reason hinder the body from being heavy, or remove thickness and darkness from flesh and blood? Yet nothing less than such a power can possibly help the soul out of its fallen and earthly state. For the grossness of flesh and blood is the natural state of the fallen soul, and therefore nothing can purify the soul, or raise it out of its earthly, corrupt state, but that which hath all power over all that is earthy[15] and material in nature.

To pretend therefore that reason may have sufficient power to remove all hellish depravity and earthly lusts from the soul whilst it has not the least power over sweet or sour in any one particle of matter in the body is as highly absurd as if a man should pretend that he has a full power to alter the inward, invisible, vegetable life of a plant, but none at all over its outward state, colour, leaves, or fruit. The Deist therefore, and not the Christian, stands in need of continual miracles to make good his doctrine. For reason can have no pretence to amend or alter the life of the soul but so far as it can show that it has power to amend and alter the nature and state of the body.

The unbelieving Jews said of our Lord, "How can this Man forgive sins?" Christ showed them how by appealing to that power which they saw He had over the body: "Whether," says He, "is it easier to say, thy sins are forgiven thee, or to say, arise, take up thy bed, and walk?" But the delusion of the unbelieving Deist is greater than that of the Jew. For the Deist sees that his reason has no power over his body; can remove no disease, blindness, deafness, or lameness from it, and yet will pretend to have power enough from his reason to help the soul out of all its evil, not knowing that body and soul go hand in hand, and are nothing else but the inward and outward state of one and the same life, and that therefore He only, who can say to the dead body of Lazarus, "Come forth," can say to the soul, "Be thou clean." The Deist therefore, if he pleases, may style himself a natural or a moral philosopher, but with no more truth than he can call himself a healer of all the maladies of the body. And for a man to think himself a moral philosopher because he has made a choice collection of syllogisms in order to quicken and revive a divine goodness in the soul, or that no redeemer need come from Heaven because human reason when truly left to itself has great skill in chopping of logic, may justly be deemed such an ignorance of the nature of things as is seldom found in the transactions of illiterate and vulgar life. [16] But this by the by.

To return to our chief subject, the sum of all that has been said is this: All evil, be it what it will, all misery of every kind, is in its birth, working, and extent, nothing else but nature left to itself, and under the divided workings of its own hunger, wrath, and contrariety; and therefore no possibility for the natural, earthly man to escape eternal hunger, wrath, and contrariety, but solely in the way as the gospel teacheth, by denying and dying to self. On the other hand, all the goodness and perfection, all the happiness, glory, and joy that any intelligent, divine creature can be possessed of, is, and can be, from nothing else but the invisible uncreated light and Spirit of God manifesting itself in the properties of the creaturely life, filling, blessing, and uniting them all in one love and joy of life. And thus again: no possibility of man's attaining to any heavenly perfection and happiness, but only in the way of the gospel, by the union of the divine and human nature, by man's being born again from above of the word and Spirit of God. There is no possibility of any other way because there is nothing that can possibly change the first properties of life into a heavenly state but the presence and working power of the Deity united with, and working in them. And therefore the "Word was made flesh," and must of all necessity be made flesh if man is to have a heavenly nature. Now as all evil, sin, and misery have no beginning, nor power of working, but in the manifestation of nature in its divided, contrary properties, so it is certain that man has nothing to turn to, seek or aspire after but the lost spirit of love. And therefore it is, that God only can be his Redeemer, because God only is love, and love can be nowhere else but in God and where God dwelleth and worketh.

Now the difficulty which you find in attaining to this purity and universality of the spirit of love is because you seek for it, as I once told you, in the way of reasoning. You would be possessed of it only from a rational conviction of the fitness and amiableness of it. And as this clear idea does not put you immediately into the real possession of it, your reason begins to waver, and suggests to you that it may be only a fine notion that has no ground but in the power of imagination. But this, Sir, is all your own error, and as contrary to nature as if you would have your eyes do that which only your hands or feet can do for you. The spirit of love is a spirit of nature and life, and all the operations of nature and life are according to the working powers of nature, and every growth and degree of life can only arise in its own time and place from its proper cause and as the genuine effect of it. Nature and life do nothing by chance or accidentally, but everything in one uniform way. Fire, air, and light do not proceed sometimes from one thing and sometimes from another, but wherever they are, they are always born in the same manner and from the same working in the properties of nature. So in like manner, love is an immutable birth, always proceeding from the same cause, and cannot be in existence till its own true parents have brought it forth.

How unreasonable would it be to begin to doubt whether strength and health of body were real things or possible to be had because you could not by the power of your reason take possession of them? Yet this is as well as to suspect the purity and perfection of love to be only a notion, because your reason cannot bring forth its birth in your soul. For reason has no more power of altering the life and properties of the soul than of altering the life and properties of the body. That, and that only, can cast Devils and evil spirits out of the soul, that can say to the storm, "Be still," and to the leper, "Be thou clean."

The birth of love is a form or state of life, and has its fixed place in the fifth form of nature. The three first properties or forms of nature are the ground or band of life that is in itself only an extreme hunger, want, strife, and contrariety. And they are in this state, that they may become a proper fuel for the fourth form of nature, viz., the fire, to be kindled in them. You will perhaps say, "What is this fire? What is its nature? And how is it kindled? And how is it that the hunger and anguishing state of the properties are a fitness to be a fuel of this fire?" It may be answered, "This hunger and anguish of nature, in its first forms, is its fitness to be changed into a life of light, joy, and happiness: and that for this reason, because it is in this hunger and anguish only because God is not in it. For as nature comes from God, and for this only end that the Deity may manifest Heaven in it, it must stand in any hunger and anguishing state till the Deity is manifested in it. And therefore its hunger and anguish is its true fitness to be changed into a better state, and this is its fitness for the birth of the fire. For the fire means nothing and is nothing else but that which changes them into a better state. Not as if fire was a fourth, distinct thing that comes into them from without, but is only a fourth state, or condition into which the same properties are brought.

The fire then is that which changes the properties into a new and heavenly state. Therefore the fire does two things. It alters the state of nature and brings Heaven into it, and therefore it must work from a two-fold power: the Deity and nature must both be in it. It must have some strength from nature, or it could not work in nature. It must have some strength from the Deity or it could not overcome and change nature into a divine life. Now all this is only to show you that the fire can only be kindled by the entrance of the Deity, or supernatural God, into a conjunction of union with nature. And this conjunction of the Deity and nature maketh, or bringeth forth, that state or form of life which is called and truly is, fire: first, because it does that in the spiritual properties of nature which fire doth in the properties of material nature, and secondly, because it is that alone from which every fire in this world, whether in the life of animal or vegetable or inanimate matter, has its source and power and possibility of burning. The fire of this world overcomes its fuel, breaks its nature, alters its state and changes it into flame and light. But why does it do this? Whence has it this nature and power? It is because it is a true outbirth of the eternal fire which overcomes the darkness, wrath, and contrariety of nature, and changes all its properties into a life of light, joy, and glory. Not a spark of fire could be kindled in this world, nor a ray of light come from any material fire but because material nature is, in itself, nothing else but the very properties of eternal nature, standing for a time in a material state or condition; and therefore they must work in time as they do in eternity; and consequently there must be fire in this world, it must have the same birth and do the same work in its material way, which the eternal fire hath, and doth in spiritual nature.

And this is the true ground and reason why everything in this
world is delivered as far as it can be from its earthly impurity,
and brought into its highest state of existence only by fire. It is
because the eternal fire is the purifier of eternal nature and the
opener of every perfection, light, and glory in it. And if you ask
why the eternal fire is the purifier of eternal nature, the reason is
plain; it is because the eternal fire has its birth and nature and
power from the entrance of the pure, supernatural Deity into the
properties of nature, which properties must change their state
and be what they were not before, as soon as the Deity entereth
into them. Their darkness, wrath, and contrariety is driven out
of them, and they work and give forth only a life and strength of
light and joy and glory. And this two-fold operation, viz., on
one hand taking from nature its wrathful workings, and on the
other hand opening a glorious manifestation of the Deity in
them, is the whole nature and form of the fire, and is the reason
why from eternity to eternity it is and must be the purifier of
eternal nature, namely, as from eternity to eternity changing
nature into a Kingdom of Heaven. Now every fire in this world
does, and must do, the same thing in its low way to the utmost
of its power, and can do nothing else. Kindle fire where or in
what you will, it acts only as, from, and by the power of this
eternal purifying fire; and therefore it breaks and consumes the
grossness of everything, and makes all that is pure and spirituous
to come forth out of it; and therefore purification is its one only
work through all material nature, because it is a real outbirth of
that eternal fire which purifies eternal nature, and changes it into
a mere heaven of glory.

    The eternal fire is called a fourth form or state of nature
because it cannot exist but from the first three and hath its work
in the fourth place in the midst of the seven forms, changing the
three first into the three last forms of nature, that is, changing
them from their natural into a heavenly state. So that, strictly
speaking, there are but three forms of nature in answerableness
to the threefold working of the triune Deity. For the three last
are not three new or different properties but are only the three
first brought into a new state by the entrance of the triune Deity
into conjunction with them. Which entrance of the supernatural

Deity into them is the consuming of all that is bad in them and
turning all their strength into a working life of light, joy, and
heavenly glory; and therefore has the justest title to be called
fire, as having no other nature and operation in it but the known
nature of fire, and also as being that from which every fire in
this world has all its nature and power of doing as it doth.

You once, as I remember, objected to my speaking so much
in the *Appeal*,[17] etc., of the fire of life as thinking it too gross an
expression to be taken in its literal meaning when mention is
made of the eternal fire, or the fire in animal life. But, Sir, fire
has but one nature through the whole universe of things, and
material fire has not more or less of the nature of fire in it than
that which is in eternal nature because it has nothing, works
nothing but what it has, and works from thence. How easy was
it for you to have seen that the fire of the soul and the fire of the
body had but one nature? How else could they unite in their
heat? How easy also to have seen that the fire of animal life was
the same fire that burns in the kitchen? How else could the
kitchen fire be serviceable to animal life? What good could it do
you to come to a fire of wood where you wanted to have the
heat of your own life increased? In animal life the fire is kindled
and preserved in such a degree and in such circumstances as to
be life and the preservation of life, and this is its difference from
fires kindled in wood and burning it to ashes. It is the same fire,
only in a different state, that keeps up life and consumes wood,
and has no other nature in the wood than in the animal. Just as
in water that has only so much fire in it as to make it warm, and
water that is by fire made boiling hot, the same nature and
power of fire is in both but only in a different state. Now will
you say that fire is not to be literally understood when it only
makes water to be warm, because it is not red and flaming as
you see it in a burning coal? Yet this would be as well as to say
that fire is not literally to be understood in the animal life
because it is so different from that fire which you see burning in
a piece of wood. And thus, Sir, there is no foundation for any
objection to all that has been said of fire in the *Appeal*, etc. It is
one and the same great power of God in the spiritual and
material world; it is the cause of every life and the opener of

every power of nature, and its one great work through all nature and creature, animate and inanimate, is purification and exaltation; it can do nothing else and that for this plain reason, because its birth is from the entrance of the pure Deity into nature, and therefore must in its various state and degrees be only doing that which the entrance of the Deity into nature does. It must bring every natural thing into its highest state. But to go back now to the spirit of love and show you the time and place of its birth before which it can have no existence in your soul, do what you will to have it.

The fire, you see, is the first overcomer of the hungry, wrathful, self-tormenting state of the properties of nature, and it only overcomes them because it is the entrance of the pure Deity into them; and therefore that which overcomes them is the light of the Deity. And this is the true ground and reason why every right-kindled fire must give forth light and cannot do otherwise. It is because the eternal fire is only the effect or operation of the supernatural light of the Deity entering into nature; and therefore fire must give forth light because it is itself only a power of the light, and light can be nowhere in nature but as a fifth form or state of nature, brought forth by the fire. And as light thus brought forth is the first state that is lovely and delightful in nature, so the spirit of love has only its birth in the light of life, and can be nowhere else. For the properties of life have no common good, nothing to rejoice in, till the light is found, and therefore no possible beginning of the spirit of love till then.

The shock that is given to the three first properties of nature by the amazing light of the Deity breaking in upon them is the operation of the fire that consumes or takes away the wrathful strength and contrariety of the properties, and forces each of them to shrink, as it were, away from itself, and come under the power of this new-risen light. Here all strife of enmity and wrathful contrariety in the properities must cease because all† are united in the love of the light, and all equally helping one another to a higher enjoyment and delight in it. They are all one

†Here all . . . are united: the statement seems to require a verb but Law deliberately witholds "are" until the next statement, & "They are all one truine will . . ."

triune will, all doing the same thing, viz., all rejoicing in the one love of the light. And here it is, in this delightful unity of operation, that the spirit of love is born, in the fifth property or light of life, and cannot possibly rise up in any creature till the properties of its life are brought into this fifth state, thus changed and exalted into a new sensibility of life. Let me give you this similitude of the matter: Fancy to yourself a man shut up in a deep cave underground, without ever having seen a ray of the light, his body all over tortured with pain, his mind distracted with rage, himself whirling and working with the utmost fury and madness, he knows not what; and then you have an image of the first properties of life as they are in themselves before the fire had done its work in them.

Fancy this man suddenly struck, or all surrounded, with such a glare of light as in the twinkling of an eye stopped or struck dead every working of every pain and rage, both in his body and mind; and then you have an image of the operation of the fire and what it does to the first properties of nature. Now as soon as the first terror of the light has had its fiery operation, and struck nothing dead but every working sensibility of distress, fancy this man, as you now well may, in the sweetest peace of mind and bodily sensations, blessed in a new region of light, giving joy to his mind and gratification to every sense; and then the transports, the overflowings of love and delight in this new state may give you an image how the spirit of love is and must be born when fire and light have overcome and changed the state of the first properties of nature, and never till then can have any existence in any creature, nor proceed from any other cause. Thus, Sir, you may sufficiently see how vainly you attempt to possess yourself of the spirit of love by the power of your reason; and also what a vanity of all vanities there is in the religion of the Deists who will have no other perfection or divine life but what they can have from their reason, as great a contradiction to nature as if they would have no life or strength of body but that which can be had from their faculty of reasoning. For reason can no more alter or exalt any one property of life in the soul and bring it into its perfect state than it can add one cubit to the stature of the body. The perfection of every life is no way possibly to be had but as every flower comes to its perfection, viz., from its own seed and root and the various degrees of transmutation which must be gone through before the flower is found. It is strictly thus with the perfection of the soul; all its properties of life must have their true natural birth and growth from one another. The first, as its seed and root, must have their natural change into a higher state; must, like the seed of the flower, pass through death into life and be blessed with the fire and light and spirit of Heaven in their passage to it, just as the seed passes through death into life, blessed by the fire and light and air of this world till it reaches its last perfection and becomes a beautiful, sweet-smelling flower. And to think that the soul can attain its perfection any other way than by the change and exaltation of its first properties changed and exalted till it comes to have its flower is a total ignorance of the nature of things. For as whatever dies cannot have a death particular to itself but the same death in the same way and for the same reasons that any other creature, whether animal or vegetable, ever did or can die, so every life and degree of life must come into its state and condition of life in the same way and for the same reasons as life and the perfection of life comes into every other living creature, whether in Heaven or on earth. Therefore, the Deists' religion or reason, which is to raise the soul to its true perfection, is so far from being the religion of nature that it is quite unnatural and declared to be so by every working in nature. For since reason can neither give life nor death to any one thing in nature, but everything lives or dies according to the working of its own properties, everything dead and alive gives forth a demonstration that nature asks no counsel of reason, nor stays to be directed by it. Hold it therefore for a certain truth that you can have no good come into your soul but only by the one way of a birth from above, from the entrance of the Deity into the properties of your own soulish life. Nature must be set right, its properties must enter into the process of a new birth, it must work to the production of light before the spirit of love can have a birth in it. For love is delight, and delight cannot arise in any creature till its nature is in a delightful state or is possessed of that in which it must rejoice. And this is the reason why God must become man; it is because a birth of the Deity must be found in the soul, giving to nature all that it wants, or the soul can never find itself in a delightful state and only working with the spirit of love. For whilst the soul has only its natural life, it can only be in such a state as nature without God is in; viz., a mere hunger, want, contrariety, and strife, for it knows not what. Hence is all that variety of blind, restless, contrary passions which govern and torment the life of fallen man. It is because all the properties of nature must work in blindness and be doing they know not what till the light of God is found in them. Hence also it is that that which is called the wisdom, the honor, the honesty, and the religion of the natural man often does as much hurt to himself and others as his pride, ambition, self-love, envy, or revenge, and are subject to the same humor and caprice; it is because nature is no better in one motion than in another, nor can be so, till something supernatural is come into it. We often charge men, both in church and state, with changing their principles; but the charge is too hasty for no man ever did, or can change his principles but by a birth from above. The natural, called in scripture the old man, is steadily the same in heart and spirit in everything he does, whatever variety of names may be given to his actions. For self can have no motion but what is selfish, which way soever it goes, or whatever it does, either in church or state. And be assured of this, that nature in every man, whether he be learned or unlearned, is this very self and can be nothing else till a birth of the Deity is brought forth in it. There is therefore no possibility of having the spirit of love or any divine goodness from any power of nature or working of reason. It can only be had in its own time and place; and its time and place is nowhere but where nature is overcome by a birth of the life of God in the properties of the soul. And thus you see the infallible truth and absolute necessity of Christian redemption; it is the most demonstrable thing in all nature. The Deity must become man, take a birth in the fallen nature, be united to it, become the life of it or the natural man must of all necessity be forever and ever in the hell of his own hunger, anguish, contrariety, and self-torment; and all for this plain reason, because nature is and can be nothing else but this variety of self-torment, till the Deity is manifested and dwelling in it.

And now, Sir, you see also the absolute necessity of the

gospel doctrine of the cross, viz., of dying to self as the one only way to life in God. This cross, or dying to self, is the one morality that does man any good. Fancy as many rules as you will of modeling the moral behavior of man, they all do nothing because they leave nature still alive, and therefore can only help a man to a feigned, hypocritical art of concealing his own inward evil and seeming to be not under its power. And the reason why it must be so is plain; it is because nature is not possible to be reformed; it is immutable in its workings and must be always as it is and never any better or worse than its own untaught workings are. It can no more change from evil to good than darkness can work itself into light. The one work therefore of morality is the one doctrine of the cross, viz., to resist and deny nature, that a supernatural power to divine goodness may take possession of it and bring a new light into it.

In a word, there are in all the possibility of things but two states or forms of life; the one is nature and the other is God manifested in nature; and as God and nature are both within you, so you have it in your power to live and work with which you will, but are under a necessity of doing either the one or the other. There is no standing still; life goes on and is always bringing forth its realities, which way soever it goeth. You have seen that the properties of nature are, and can be, nothing else in their own life but a restless hunger, disquiet, and blind strife for they know not what, till the property of light and love has got possession of them. Now when you see this, you see the true state of every natural man, whether he be Caesar or Cato,[18] whether he gloriously murders others or only stabs himself; blind nature does all the work and must be the doer of it till the Christ of God is born in him. For the life of man can be nothing else but a hunger of covetousness, a rising up of pride, envy, and wrath, a medley of contrary passions, doing and undoing it knows not what because these workings are essential to the properties of nature; they must be always hungering and working one against another, striving to be above one another, and all this in blindness, till the light of God has helped them to one common good, in which they all willingly unite, rest, and rejoice. In a word, goodness is only a sound and virtue a mere strife of natural passions till the spirit of love is the breath of everything that lives and moves in the heart. For love is the one only blessing and goodness and God of nature; and you have no true religion, are no worshipper of the one true God but in and by that spirit of love which is God Himself living and working in you.

But here I take off my pen and shall leave the remaining part of your objection to another opportunity.

King's Cliffe, June 16, 1752.[19]   I am, etc.

NOTES

1. See *Spirit of Love*, Second Part, p. 00 (Law's note).
2. Schools: the medieval schoolmen, or scholastic philosophers, such as Saint Thomas Aquinas.
3. Notionally: speculatively, or not based on factual demonstration.
4. See *Spirit of Love*, Second Part, p. 00 (Law's note).
5. See *The Way to Divine Knowledge* [ed. 1752], p. 153 (Law's note).
6. Constringing: constricting.
7. Astringing property: possessing a constricting faculty.
8. Is: Law regards "thickness, hardness, and darkness" as a kind of trinity, or one in three, which requires a singular verb.
9. Law lumps together these rationalist thinkers, ignoring their differences; but he means to object to that theory, particularly espoused by Locke, which maintained that the human mind at birth is a blank tablet (or tabula rasa) upon which ideas and experiences are subsequently imprinted. There can thus be no sure and undeviating metaphysical position for those who lack a knowledge of the "ground of nature" (a traditional mystical term for the place in the soul that has special contact with God). Cf. Theophilus's discussion of the Ten Commandments as "an outward imitation of that which was inwardly in man" (p. 00, below), by which he implies the theory of innate ideas which Locke denied.
10. Seven properties of nature: see the Introduction, pp. 00, and Law's explanation that follows.
11. See *The Way to Divine Knowledge*, p. 00 (Law's note). Vulgar: common or ordinary.
12. On the relationship of Sir Isaac Newton (1642–1727) and William Law, and the supposed influence of Boehme on Newton, see the essay by Stephen Hobhouse in his *Selected Mystical Writings of William Law* (1(New York, 1948), Appendix Four, pp. 397-422.
13. *Ternarius Sanctus: literally, the holy ternary, or threefold life of union.*
14. *Law particularly answered the Deists in some of his earlier and polemical works. See the Introduction, pp. 00, and p. 00, below.*
15. *Earthly . . . earthy: "earthly" may be opposed to heavenly; "earthy" signifies the properties of the element* earth (cf. watery, fiery, airy).
16. See *Spirit of Love*, Second Part, p. 00 (Law's note).
17. Law is referring to his *An Appeal To all that Doubt, or Disbelieve The Truths of the Gospel, whether They be Deists, Arians, Socinians, Or Nominal Christians* (1740), and to his other works with a common theme, such as *A Demonstration of the Gross and Fundamental Errors of a late Book, called A Plain Account of the Nature and End of the Sacrament of the Lord's Supper* (1737); *The Grounds and Reasons of Christian Regeneration* (1739); and *The Spirit of Prayer* (1749), referred to below (pp. 00 and 00).
18. Caesar or Cato: the contrast between one who murders others and one who takes his own life is familiar, but Law may have had in mind Joseph Addison's sensational tragedy *Cato* (1713).
19. King Cliffe: Law writes his "Letter" as King's Cliffe, where he was living in 1752.

389

THE

SECOND PART

OF THE

SPIRIT

OF

L O V E.

IN DIALOGUES.

By *WILLIAM LAW*, A. M.

LONDON:

Printed for W. Innys and J. Richardson, in
Pater-noster-Row.

MDCCLIV.

[Price 2 s.]

The title page from the first edition of 1754.

The First Dialogue
Between
Theogenes, Eusebius, and
Theophilus

Theogenes. Dear Theophilus, this gentleman is Eusebius, a very valuable and worthy curate[20] in my neighborhood; he would not let me wait any longer for your second letter of the spirit of love, nor be content till I consented to our making you this visit. And indeed, we are both on the same errand and in equal impatience to have your full answer to that part of my objection, which you reserved for a second letter.

Theophilus. My heart embraces you both with the greatest affection, and I am much pleased at the occasion of your coming which calls me to the most delightful subject in the world, to help both you and myself to rejoice in that adorable Deity whose infinite Being is an infinity of mere love, an unbeginning, never ceasing, and forever overflowing ocean of meekness, sweetness, delight, blessing, goodness, patience, and mercy, and all this as so many blessed streams breaking out of the abyss of universal love, Father, Son, and Holy Ghost, a triune infinity of love and goodness, forever and ever giving forth nothing but the same gifts of light and love, of blessing and joy, whether before or after the fall, either of angels or men.

Look at all nature, through all its height and depth, in all its variety of working powers; it is what it is for this only end, that the hidden riches, the invisible powers, blessings, glory, and love of the unsearchable God may become visible, sensible, and manifest in it and by it.

Look at all the variety of creatures; they are what they are for this only end, that in their infinite variety, degrees, and capacities they may be as so many speaking figures, living forms of the man-

391

ifold riches and powers of nature, as so many sounds and voices, preachers, and trumpets, giving glory and praise and thanksgiving to that Deity of love which gives life to all nature and creature.

For every creature of unfallen nature, call it by what name you will, has its form, and power, and state, and place in nature for no other end but to open and enjoy, to manifest and rejoice in some share of the love and happiness and goodness of the Deity, as springing forth in the boundless height and depth of nature.

Now this is the one will and work of God in and through all nature and creature. From eternity to eternity He can will and intend nothing toward them, in them, or by them, but the communication of various degrees of His own love, goodness, and happiness to them, according to their state, and place, and capacity in nature. This is God's unchangeable disposition toward the creature; he can be nothing else but all goodness toward it because He can be nothing toward the creature but that which He is, and was, and ever shall be in Himself.

God can no more begin to have any wrath, rage, or anger in Himself after nature and creature are in a fallen state than He could have been infinite wrath and boundless rage everywhere and from all eternity. For nothing can begin to be in God, or to be in a new state in Him; everything that is in Him is essential to Him, as inseparable from Him, as unalterable in Him as the triune nature of His deity.

Theogenes. Pray, Theophilus, let me ask you, does not patience and pity and mercy begin to be in God, and only then begin, when the creature has brought itself into misery? They could have no existence in the Deity before. Why then may not a wrath and anger begin to be in God when the creature has rebelled against Him, though it neither had nor could have any existence in God before?

Theophilus. 'Tis true, Theogenes, that God can only then begin to make known His mercy and patience when the creature has lost its rectitude and happiness, yet nothing then begins to be in God or to be found in Him, but that which was always in Him in the same infinite state, viz., a will to all goodness, and which can will nothing else. And His patience and mercy which could not show forth themselves till nature and creature had brought forth misery were not new tempers or the beginning of some new disposition that was not in God before, but only new and occasional manifestations of that boundless eternal will to all goodness, which always was in God in the same height and depth. The will to all goodness, which is God Himself, began to display itself in a new way when it first gave birth to creatures. The same will to all goodness began to manifest itself in another new way when it became patience and compassion toward fallen creatures. But neither of these ways are[21] the beginning of any new tempers or qualities in God, but only new and occasional manifestations of that true eternal will to all goodness, which always was, and always will be, in the same fullness of infinity in God.

But to suppose that when the creature has abused its power, lost its happiness and plunged itself into a misery out of which it cannot deliver itself, to suppose that then there begins to be something in the holy Deity of Father, Son, and Holy Ghost that is not of the nature and essence of God and which was not there before, viz. a wrath, and fury, and vindictive vengeance, breaking out in storms of rage and resentment because the poor creature has brought misery upon itself, is an impiety and absurdity that cannot be enough abhorred. For nothing can be in God but that which He is and has from Himself, and therefore no wrath can be in the Deity itself unless God was in Himself before all nature and from all eternity an infinity of wrath.

Why are love, knowledge, wisdom, and goodness said to be infinite and eternal in God, capable of no increase or decrease, but always in the same highest state of existence? Why is His power eternal and omnipotent, His presence not here, or there, but everywhere the same? No reason can be assigned, but because nothing that is temporary, limited, or bounded can be in God. It is His nature to be that which He is, and all that He is, in an infinite, unchangeable degree, admitting neither higher, nor lower, neither here nor there, but always, and everywhere in the same unalterable state of infinity. If therefore wrath, rage, and resentment could be in the Deity itself, it must be an unbeginning, boundless, never-ceasing wrath, capable of no more, or less, no up or down, but always existing, always working, and breaking forth in the same strength, and everywhere equally burning in the height and depth of the abyssal Deity. There is no medium here; there must be either all or none, either no possibility of wrath, or no possibility of its having any bounds. And therefore, if you would not say that everything that has, or can, or ever shall proceed from God are and can be only so many effects of His eternal and omnipotent wrath, which can never cease, or be less than infinite; if you will not hold this monstrous blasphemy, you must stick close to the absolute impossibility of wrath having any existence in God. For nothing can have any existence in God, but in the way and manner as His eternity, infinity, and omnipotence have their existence in Him. Have you anything to object to this?

Theogenes. Indeed, Theophilus, both Eusebius and myself have been from the first fully satisfied with what has been said of this matter in the book of *Regeneration*, the *Appeal*, and the *Spirit of Prayer*, etc. We find it impossible to think of God as subject to wrath, or capable of being inflamed by the weakness, and folly, and irregularity of the creature. We find ourselves incapable of thinking any otherwise of God than as the one only good, or, as you express it, "an eternal immutable will to all goodness," and which can will nothing else to all eternity, but to communicate good, and blessing, and happiness, and perfection to every life, according to its capacity to receive it.

Had I a hundred lives, I could with more ease part with them all by suffering a hundred deaths than give up this lovely idea of God. Nor could I have any desire of eternity for myself if I had not hopes that, by partaking of the divine nature, I should be eternally delivered from the burden and power of my own wrath and changed into the blessed freedom of a spirit that is all love and a mere will to nothing but goodness. An eternity without this is but an eternity of trouble. For I know of no Hell either here or hereafter, but the power and working of wrath, nor any Heaven but where the God of love is all in all, and the working life of all. And therefore, that the holy Deity is all one, and blessing, and goodness, willing and working only love and goodness to everything as far as it can receive it, is a truth as deeply grounded in me as the feeling of my own existence. I ask you for no proof of this; my only difficulty is how to reconcile this idea of God to the letter of scripture. First, because the scripture speaks so much and so often of the wrath, and fury, and vindictive vengeance of God. Secondly, because the whole nature of our redemption is so plainly grounded on such a supposed degree of wrath and vengeance in God as could not be satisfied, appeased, and atoned by anything less than the death and sacrifice of the only begotten Son of God.

Theophilus. I will do more for you, Theogenes, in this matter than you seem to expect. I will not only reconcile the letter of scripture with the foregoing description of God but will show you that everything that is said of the necessity of Christ's being the only possible satisfaction and Atonement of the vindictive wrath of God is a full and absolute proof that the wrath of God spoken of never was, nor is, or possibly can be in God.

Eusebius. Oh! Theophilus, you have forced me now to speak, and I cannot contain the joy that I feel in this expectation which you have raised in me. If you can make the scriptures do all that which you have promised to Theogenes, I shall be in Paradise before I die. For to know that love alone was the beginning of nature and creature, that nothing but love encompasses the whole universe of things, that the governing hand that overrules all, the watchful eye that sees through all, is nothing but omnipotent and omniscient love using an infinity of wisdom to raise all that is fallen in nature, to save every misguided creature from the miserable works of its own hands, and make happiness and glory the perpetual inheritance of all the creation is a reflection that must be quite ravishing to every intelligent creature that is sensible of it. Thus to think of God, of providence, and eternity whilst we are in this valley and shadow of death is to have a real foretaste of the blessings of the world to come. Pray, therefore, let us hear how the letter of scripture is a proof of this God of love.

Theophilus. Before I do this, Eusebius, I think it requisite to show you in a word or two the true ground and nature of wrath in all its kinds, what it is in itself, whence it has its birth, life, and manner of existence. And then you will see with your own eyes why, and how, and where wrath or rage can, or cannot be. And until you see this fundamentally in the nature of things, you cannot be at all qualified to judge of the matter in question, but must only think and speak at random, merely as your imagination is led by the sound of words. For until we know in the nature of the thing what wrath is in itself, and why, and how it comes into existence wherever it is, we cannot say where it can enter or where it cannot. Nor can we possibly know what is meant by the satisfaction, appeasement, or atonement of wrath in any being but by knowing how, and why, and for what reason wrath can rise and work in any being; and then only can we know how any wrath, wherever raised, can be atoned or made to cease.

Now there are two things, both of them visible to your outward senses, which entirely open the true ground and nature of wrath and undeniably show what it is in itself, from whence it arises, and wherein its life, and strength, and being consists. And these two things are a tempest in the elements of this world and a raging sore in the body of man or any other animal. Now that a tempest in the elements is wrath in the elements, and a sore in the body of an animal a wrath in the state of juices of the body is a matter, I think, that needs no proof or explication. Consider, then, how or why a tempest arises in the elements, or an inflamed sore in the body, and then you have the true ground and nature of wrath. Now a tempest does not, cannot arise in the elements whilst they are in their right state, in their just mixture or union with one another. A sore does not, cannot break forth in the body whilst the body is altogether in its true state and temperature of its juices. Hence you plainly see that wrath has its whole nature and only ground of its existence in and by the disorder or bad state of the thing in which it exists and works. It can have no place of existence, no power of breaking forth, but where the thing has lost its proper perfection and is not as it ought to be. And therefore no good being that is in its proper state of goodness can, whilst it is in such a state, have any wrath or rage in it. And therefore, as a tempest of any kind in the elements is a sure proof that the elements are not in their right state, but under disorder, as a raging sore in the body is impure and corrupt and not as it should be, so in whatever mind or intelligent being wrath or rage works and breaks forth there, there is proof enough that the mind is in that same impure, corrupt, and disordered state as those elements that raise a tempest and that body which gives forth an inflamed sore. And now, Gentlemen, what think you of a supposed wrath, or rage in God; will you have such things to be in the Deity itself as cannot have place or existence even in any creature until it is become disordered and impure and has lost its proper state of goodness?

Eusebius. But pray, Theophilus, let me observe that it does not yet appear to me that there is but one wrath possible to be in nature and creature. I grant there is such a likeness in the things you have appealed to as is sufficient to justify poets, orators, or popular speakers in calling a tempest wrath, and wrath a tempest. But this will not do in our present matter; for all that you have said depends upon this, whether, in a philosophic strictness in the nature of the thing, there can only be one wrath wherever it is proceeding strictly from the same ground, and having everywhere the same nature. Now if you can prove this identity or sameness of wrath, be it where it will, either in an intelligent mind, the elements of this world, or the body of an animal, then your point is absolutely gained, and there can be no possibility for wrath to have any existence in the Deity. But as body and spirit are generally held to be quite contrary to each other in their most essential qualities, I do not know how you can sufficiently prove that they can only have one kind of wrath, or that wrath must have one and the same ground and nature, whether it be in body or spirit.

Theophilus. Wrath can have no better or other ground and nature in body than it has in spirit for this reason, because it can have no existence or manner of working in the body but what it has directly from spirit. And therefore, in every wrath that is visible in any body whatever, you have a true manifestation of the ground and nature of wrath, in whatever spirit it is. And therefore, as there is but one ground and nature of wrath in all outward things, whether they be animate or inanimate, so you have proof enough that so it is with all wrath in the spirit or mind. Because wrath in any body or outward thing is nothing else but the inward working of that spirit which manifests itself by an outward wrath in the body.

And what we call wrath in the body is truly and strictly speaking the wrath of the spirit in the body.

For you are to observe that body begins not from itself, nor is anything of itself, but is all that it is, whether pure or impure, has all that it has whether of light or darkness, and works all that it works, whether of good or evil, merely from spirit. For nothing, my friend, acts in the whole universe of things but spirit alone. And the state, condition, and degree of every spirit is only and solely opened by the state, form, condition, and qualities of the body that belongs to it. For the body can have no nature, form, condition, or quality but that which the spirit that brings it forth gives to it.

Was there no eternal, universal spirit, there could be no eternal or universal nature; that is, was not the Spirit of God everywhere, the Kingdom of Heaven, or the visible glory of God in an outward majesty of heaven, could not be everywhere. Now the Kingdom of Heaven is that to the Deity which every body is to the spirit, which liveth, worketh, and manifesteth itself in it. But the Kingdom of Heaven is not God, yet all that it is, and has, and does is only an outward manifestation of the nature, power, and working of the Spirit of God.

It is thus with every creaturely spirit and its body, which is the habitation or seat of its power; and as the spirit is in its nature, kind and degree, whether heavenly, earthly, or hellish, so is its body. Was there not creaturely spirits, there could be no creaturely bodies. And the reason why there are creaturely bodies of such various forms, shapes, and powers is because spirits come forth from God in various kinds and degrees of life, each manifesting its own nature, power, and condition by that body which proceeds from it as its own birth, or the manifestation of its own powers.

Now the spirit is not body, nor is the body spirit; they are so essentially distinct that they cannot possibly lose their difference, or be changed into one another; and yet all that is in the body is from the nature, will, and working of its spirit. There is therefore no possible room for a supposition of two kinds of wrath, or that wrath may have two natures, the one as it is in spirit, and the other as it is in body; first, because nothing can be wrathful but spirit, and secondly, because no spirit can exert or manifest wrath but in and by its body. The kindling its own body is the spirit's only wrath. And therefore, through the whole universe of things, there is and can be but one possible ground and nature of wrath, whether it be in the sore of an animal body, in a tempest of the elements, in the mind of a man, in an angel, or in Hell.

Eusebius. Enough, enough, Theophilus. You have made it sufficiently plain that wrath can be no more in God Himself than Hell can be Heaven. And therefore we ask no more of you, but only to reconcile this with the language and doctrine of the holy scriptures.

Theogenes. You are in too much haste, Eusebius; it would be better to let Theophilus proceed further in this matter. He has told us what wrath is in itself; be it where it will, I should be glad to know its one true original, or how, and where, and why it could possibly begin to be.

Theophilus. To inquire or search into the origin of wrath is the same thing as to search into the origin of evil and sin. For wrath and evil are but two words for one and the same thing. There is no evil in anything, but the working of the spirit of wrath. And when wrath is entirely suppressed, there can be no more evil, or misery, or sin in all nature and creature. This therefore is a firm truth, that nothing can be capable of wrath, or be the beginning of wrath but the creature, because nothing but the creature can be the beginner of evil and sin.

Again, the creature can have no beginning, or sensibility of wrath in itself, but by losing the living power, the living presence, and governing operation of the Spirit of God within it, or in other words, by its losing that heavenly state of existence in God and influence from Him which it had at its creation.

Now no intelligent creature, whether angel or man, can be good and happy but by partaking of, or having in itself, a two-fold life. Hence so much is said in the scripture of an inward and outward, an old and a new man. For there could be no foundation for this distinction but because every intelligent creature, created to be good and happy, must of all necessity have a two-fold life in it, or it cannot possibly be capable of goodness and happiness, nor can it possibly lose its goodness and happiness, or feel the least want of them, but by its breaking the union of this two-fold life in itself. Hence so much is said in the scripture of the quickening, raising, and reviving the inward, new man, of the new birth from above, of Christ being formed in us as the one only redemption and salvation of the soul. Hence also the fall of Adam was said to be a death, that he died the day of his sin though he lived so many hundred years after it; it was because his sin broke the union of his two-fold life and put an end to the heavenly part of it and left only one life, the life of this bestial, earthly world in him.

Now there is, in the nature of the thing, an absolute necessity of this two-fold life in every creature that is to be good and happy; and the two-fold life is this, it must have the life of nature, and the life of God in it. It cannot be a creature, and intelligent, but by having the life and properties of nature, that is, by finding itself to be a life of various sensibilities, that hath a power of understanding, willing, and desiring. This is its creaturely life, which, by the creating power of God, it hath in and from nature.

Now this is all the life that is or can be creaturely, or be a creature's natural, own life; and all this creaturely natural life, with all its various powers and sensibilities, is only a life of various appetites, hungers, and wants, and cannot possibly be anything else. God Himself cannot make a creature to be in itself, or as to its own nature, anything else but a state of emptiness, of want, of appetite, etc. He cannot make it to be good and happy, in and from its natural state: This is as impossible as for God to cease to be the one only Good. The highest life, therefore, that is natural and creaturely can go no higher than this; it can only be a bare capacity for goodness and happiness and cannot possibly be a good and happy life, but by the life of God dwelling in, and in union with it. And this is the two-fold life that of all necessity must be united in every good and perfect and happy creature.

See here the greatest of all demonstrations of the absolute necessity of the gospel redemption and salvation, and all proved from the nature of the thing. There can be no goodness and happiness for any intelligent creature, but in and by this two-fold life; and therefore the union of the divine and human life, or the Son of God incarnate in man to make man again a partaker of the divine nature, is the one only possible salvation for all the sons of fallen Adam, that is, of Adam dead to or fallen from his first union with the divine life.

Deism, therefore, or a religion of nature, pretending to make man good and happy without Christ, or the Son of God entering into union with the human nature, is the greatest of all absurdities. It is as contrary to the nature and possibilities of things as for mere emptiness to be its own fullness, mere hunger to be its own food, and mere want to be its possession of all things. For nature and creature, without the Christ of God or the divine life in union with it, is and can be nothing else but this mere emptiness, hunger, and want of all that which can alone make it good and happy. For God Himself, as I said, cannot make any creature to be good and happy by anything that is in its own created nature; and however high or noble any creature is supposed to be created, its height and nobility can consist in nothing but its higher capacity and fitness to receive a higher union with the divine life, and also a higher and more wretched misery when left to itself, as is manifest by the hellish state of the fallen angels. Their high and exalted nature was only an enlarged capacity for the divine life; and therefore, when this life was lost, their whole created nature was nothing else but the height of rage, and hellish distraction.

A plain demonstration that there can be no happiness, blessing, and goodness for any creature in Heaven or on earth but by having, as the gospel saith, Jesus Christ made unto it, wisdom, righteousness, sanctification, and peace with God.

And the reason is this; it is because goodness and happiness are absolutely inseparable from God, and can be nowhere but in God. And on the other hand, emptiness, want, insufficiency, etc., are absolutely inseparable from the creature, as such; its whole nature cannot possibly be anything else, be it what or where it will, an angel in Heaven, or a man on earth; it is and must be in its whole creaturely nature and capacity a mere hunger and emptiness, etc. And therefore all that we know of God, and all that we know of the creature, fully proves that the life of God in union with the creaturely life (which is the gospel salvation) is the one only possibility of goodness and happiness in any creature, whether in Heaven or on earth.

Hence also it is enough certain that this two-fold life must have been the original state of every intelligent creature at its first coming forth from God. It could not be brought forth by God to have only a creaturely life of nature, and be left to that; for that would be creating it under a necessity of being in misery, in want, in wrath, and all painful sensibilities. A thing more unworthy of God, and more impossible for Him to do, than to create numberless earthly animals under a necessity of being perpetually pained with hunger and thirst, without any possibility of finding anything to eat or to drink.

For no creaturely life can in itself be any higher, or better, than a state of want or a seeking for something that cannot be found in itself; and therefore, as sure as God is good, as sure as He would have intelligent beings live a life of goodness and happiness, so sure is it that such beings must of all necessity in their first existence have been blessed with a two-fold life, viz., the life of God dwelling in and united with the life of nature or created life.

Eusebius. What an important matter have you here proved in the necessity and certainty of this two-fold life in every intelligent being that is to be good and happy? For this great truth opens and asserts the certain and substantial ground of the spiritual life and shows that all salvation is and can be nothing else but the manifestation of the life of God in the soul. How clearly does this give the solid distinction between inward holiness and all outward, creaturely practices. All that God has done for man by any particular dispensations, whether by the law or the prophets, by the scriptures, or ordinances of the church, are only as helps to a holiness which they cannot give, but are only suited to the death and darkness of the earthly, creaturely life, to turn it from itself, from its own workings, and awaken in it a faith and hope, a hunger and thirst after that first union with the life of the Deity, which was lost in the fall of the first father of mankind.

How unreasonable is it to call perpetual inspiration fanaticism and enthusiasm when there cannot be the least degree of goodness or happiness in any intelligent being, but what is in its whole nature, merely and truly the breathing, the life, and the operation of God in the life of the creature? For if goodness can only be in God, if it cannot exist separate from Him, if He can only bless and sanctify not by a creaturely gift, but by Himself becoming the blessing and sanctification of the creature, then it is the highest degree of blindness to look for any goodness and happiness from anything but the immediate indwelling, union, and operation of the Deity in the life of the creature. Perpetual inspiration, therefore, is in the nature of the thing as necessary to a life of goodness, holiness, and happiness, as the perpetual respiration of the air is necessary to animal life.

For the life of the creature, whilst only creaturely and possessing nothing but itself, is Hell; that is, it is all pain and want and distress. Now nothing in the nature of the thing can make the least alteration in this creaturely life, nothing can help it to be in light and love, in peace and goodness, but the union of God with it, and the life of God working in it, because nothing but God is light, and love, and heavenly goodness. And therefore, where the life of God is not become the life and goodness of the creature, there the creature cannot have the least degree of goodness in it.

What a mistake is it, therefore, to confine inspiration to particular times and occasions, to prophets and apostles and extraordinary messengers of God, and to call it enthusiasm when the common Christian looks and trusts to be continually led and inspired by the

Spirit of God. For though all are not called to be prophets or apostles, yet all are called to be holy as He who has called them is holy, to be perfect as their heavenly Father is perfect, to be like-minded with Christ, to will only as God wills, to do all to His honor and glory, to renounce the spirit of this world, to have their conversation in heaven, to set their affections on things above, to love God with all their heart, soul, and spirit, and their neighbor as themselves.

Behold a work as great, as divine and supernatural as that of a prophet and an apostle. But to suppose that we ought and may always be in this spirit of holiness, and yet are not and ought not to be always moved and led by the breath and Spirit of God within us, is to suppose that there is a holiness and goodness which comes not from God, which is no better than supposing that there may be true prophets and apostles who have not their truth from God.

Now the holiness of the common Christian is not an occasional thing that begins and ends, or is only for such a time, or place, or action, but is the holiness of that which is always alive and stirring in us, namely, of our thoughts, wills, desires, and affections. If therefore these are always alive in us, always driving or governing our lives, if we can have no holiness or goodness but as this life of thought, will, and affection works in us, if we are all called to this inward holiness and goodness, then a perpetual, always-existing operation of the Spirit of God within us is absolutely necessary. For we cannot be inwardly led and governed by a spirit of goodness, but by being governed by the Spirit of God Himself. For the Spirit of God and the spirit of goodness are not two spirits, nor can we be said to have any more of the one than we have of the other.

Now if our thoughts, wills, and affections need only be now and then holy and good, then indeed the moving and breathing Spirit of God need only now and then govern us. But if our thoughts and affections are to be always holy and good, then the holy and good Spirit of God is to be always operating as a principle of life within us.

The scripture saith, "We are not sufficient of ourselves to think a good thought." If so, then we cannot be chargeable with not thinking and willing that which is good but upon this supposition, that there is always a supernatural power within us, ready and able to help us to the good which we cannot have from ourselves.

The difference then of a good and a bad man does not lie in this, that the one wills that which is good, and the other does not, but solely in this, that the one concurs with the living inspiring Spirit of God within him and the other resists it, and is and can be only chargeable with evil because he resists it.

Therefore whether you consider that which is good or bad in a man, they equally prove the perpetual indwelling and operation of the Spirit of God within us since we can only be bad by resisting, as we are good by yielding to the Spirit of God, both which equally suppose a perpetual operation of the Spirit of God within us.

How firmly our Established Church[22] adheres to this doctrine of the necessity of the perpetual operation of the Holy Spirit as the one only source and possibility of any degree of divine light, wisdom, virtue, and goodness in the soul of man, how earnestly she wills and requires all her members to live in the most open profession of it and in the highest conformity to it may be seen by many such prayers as these in her common, ordinary, public service.

"O God, forasmuch as without Thee, we are not able to please Thee, grant that Thy Holy Spirit may in all things direct and rule our hearts." Again, "We pray Thee, that Thy grace may always prevent and follow us, and make us continually to be given to all good works." Again, "Grant to us, Lord, we beseech Thee, the spirit to think and do always such things as be rightful, that we, who cannot do anything that is good without Thee, may by Thee be enabled to live according to Thy will." Again, "Because the frailty of man without Thee cannot but fall, keep us ever, by Thy help from all things hurtful, and lead us to all things profitable to our salvation," etc. Again, "O God, from whom all good things do come, grant to us Thy humble servants that by Thy holy inspiration we may think those things that be good, and by Thy merciful guiding may perform the same."[23] But now the true ground of all this doctrine of the necessity of the perpetual guidance and operation of the Holy Spirit lies in what has been said above of the necessity of a two-fold life in every intelligent creature, that is, to be good and happy. For if the creaturely life whilst alone or left to itself can only be want, misery, and distress, if it cannot possibly have any goodness or happiness in it till the life of God is in union with it as one life, then everything that you read in the scripture of the Spirit of God as the only principle of goodness opens itself to you as a most certain and blessed truth, about which you can have no doubt.

Theophilus. Let me only add, Eusebius, to what you have said, that from this absolute necessity of a two-fold life in every creature, that is, to be good and happy, we may in a still greater clearness see the certainty of that which we have so often spoken of at other times, namely, that the inspoken Word in Paradise, the Bruiser of the Serpent, the Seed of the Woman, the Immanuel, the Holy Jesus (for they all mean the same thing) is and was the only possible ground of salvation for fallen man. For if the two-fold life is necessary and man could not be restored to goodness and happiness but by the restored union of this two-fold life into its first state, then there was an absolute necessity in the nature of the thing that every son of Adam should have such a Seed of Heaven in the birth of his life, as could by the mediation of Christ be raised into a birth and growth of the first perfect man. This is the one original power of salvation without which no external dispensation could have done anything toward raising the fallen state of man. For nothing could be raised but what there was to be raised, nor life be given to anything but to that was capable of life. Unless, therefore, there had been a seed of life or a smothered spark of Heaven in the soul of man which wanted to come to the birth, there had been no possibility for any dispensation of God to bring forth a birth of Heaven in fallen man.

The faith of the first patriarchs could not have been in being; Moses and the prophets had come in vain had not the Christ of God lain in a state of hiddenness in every son of man. For faith, which is a will and hunger after God, could not have begun to be, or have any life in man but because there was something of the divine nature existing and hid in man. For nothing can have any longing desire but after its own likeness, nor could anything be made to desire God but that which came from Him and had the nature of Him.

The whole mediatorial office of Christ, from His birth to His sitting down in power at the right hand of God, was only for this end, to help man to a life that was fallen into death and insensibility in Him. And therefore His mediatorial power was to manifest itself by way of a new birth. In the nature of the thing nothing else was to be done, and Christ had no other way to proceed, and that for this plain reason, because life was the thing that was lost, and life wherever it is must be raised by a birth, and every birth must and can only come from its own seed.

But if Christ was to raise a new life like His own in every man, then every man must have had, originally, in the inmost spirit of his life, a Seed of Christ, or Christ as a Seed of Heaven, lying there as in a state of insensibility or death, out of which it could not arise but by the mediatorial power of Christ, who as a second Adam was to regenerate that birth of His own life, which was lost in all the natural sons of Adam the first.

But unless there was this Seed of Christ or spark of Heaven hidden in the soul, not the least beginning of man's salvation or of Christ's mediatorial office could be made. For what could begin to deny self if there was not something in man different from self? What could begin to have hope and faith and desire of a heavenly life if there was not something of Heaven hidden in his soul, and lying therein as in a state of inactivity and death till raised by the mediation of Christ into its first perfection of life, and set again in its true dominion over flesh and blood?

Eusebius. You have, Theophilus, sufficiently proved the certainty and necessity of this matter. But I should be glad if you knew how to help me to some more distinct idea and conception of it.

Theophilus. An idea is not the thing to be here sought for; it would rather hinder than help your true knowledge of it. But perhaps the following similitude may be of some use to you.

The Ten Commandments when written by God on tables of stone and given to man did not then first begin to belong to man; they had their existence in man, were born with him, they lay as a seed and power of goodness hidden in the form and make of his soul and altogether inseparable from it before they were shown to man on tables of stone. And when they were shown to man on tables of stone, they were only an outward imitation of that which was inwardly in man, though not legible because of that impurity of flesh and blood in which they were drowned and swallowed up. For the earthly nature, having overcome the divinity that was in man, it gave commandments of its own to man and required obedience to all the lusts of the flesh, the lust of the eyes, and the pride of life.

Hence it became necessary that God should give an outward knowledge of such commandments as were become inwardly unknown, unfelt, and, as it were, shut up in death in the soul.

But now, had not all that is in these commandments been really and antecedently in the soul as its own birth and nature, had they not still lain therein, and although totally suppressed yet in such a seed or remains as could be called forth into their first living state, in vain had the tables of stone been given to man; and all outward writing or teaching of the commandments had been as useless as so many instructions given to beasts or stones. If therefore you can conceive how all that is good and holy in the commandments lay hid as an unfelt, unactive power or seed of goodness till called into sensibility and stirring by laws written on tables of stone, this may help your manner of conceiving and believing how Christ as a Seed of Life or power of salvation lies in the soul as its unknown, hidden treasure till awakened and called forth into life by the mediatorial office and process of the holy Jesus.

Again, "Thou shalt love the Lord thy God with all thy heart, with all thy soul, and with all thy strength, and thy neighbor as thyself." Now these two precepts, given by the written word of God, are an absolute demonstration of the first original perfection of man and also a full and invincible proof that the same original perfection is not quite annihilated but lies in him as a hidden, suppressed seed of goodness capable of being raised up to its first perfection. For had not this divine unity, purity, and perfection of love toward God and man been man's first natural state of life, it could have nothing to do with his present state. For had any other nature, or measure, or kind of love began[24] in the first birth of his life, he could only have been called to that. For no creature has or can have a call to be above, or act above its own nature. Therefore, as sure as man is called to this unity, purity, and perfection of love, so sure is it that it was at first his natural, heavenly state, and still has its seed, or remains within him as his only power and possibility of rising up to it again. And therefore, all that man is called to, every degree of a new and perfect life, every future exaltation and glory he is to have from the mediation of Christ, is a full proof that the same perfection was originally his natural state and is still in him in such a seed or remains of existence as to admit of a perfect renewal.

And thus it is that you are to conceive of the holy Jesus, or the *Word* of God, as the hidden treasure of every human soul, born as a seed of the *Word* in the birth of the soul, immured under flesh and blood till as a daystar it arises in our hearts and changes the son of an earthly Adam into a son of God.

And was not the *Word* and *Spirit* of God in us all, antecedent to any dispensation or written word of God as a real seed of life in the birth of our own life, we could have no more fitness for the gospel redemption than the animals of this world which have nothing of Heaven in them. And to call us to love God with all our hearts, to put on Christ, to walk according to the Spirit, if these things had not their real nature and root within us, would be as vain and useless as to make rules and orders how our eyes should smell and taste, or our ears should see.

Now this mystery of an inward life hidden in man as his most precious treasure, as the ground of all that can be great or good in him and hidden only since his fall, and which only can be opened and brought forth in its first glory by Him to whom all power in Heaven and on earth is given, is a truth to which almost everything in nature bears full witness. Look where you will, nothing appears or works outwardly in any creature or in any effect of nature but what is all done from its own inward invisible spirit, not a spirit brought into it, but its own inward spirit which is an inward invisible mystery till made known or brought forth by outward appearances.

The sea neither is nor can be moved and tossed by any other wind than that which hath its birth, and life, and strength in and from the sea itself as its own wind. The sun in the firmament gives growth to everything that grows in the earth, and life to everything that lives upon it, not by giving or imparting a life from without, but only by stirring up in everything its own growth and its own life which lay as in a seed or state of death till helped to come out of it by the sun, which as an emblem of the Redeemer of the spiritual world helps every earthly thing out of its own death into its own highest state of life.

That which we call our sensations, as seeing, hearing, feeling, tasting, and smelling, are not things brought into us from without, or given unto us by any external causes, but are only so many inborn, secret states of the soul which lie in their state of hiddenness till they are occasionally awakened and brought forth into sensibility by outward occurrences. And were they not antecedently in the soul as states and forms of its own life, no outward objects could bring the soul into a sensibility of them. For nothing can have or be in any state of sensation but that which it is and hath from itself, as its own birth.

This is as certain as that a circle hath only its own roundness.

The stinking gum gives nothing to the soul, nor brings anything into sensibility but that which was before in the soul; it has only a fitness to awaken and stir up that state of the soul which lay dormant before, and which when brought into sensibility is called the sensation of bad smelling. And the odoriferous gum hath likewise but the same power, viz., a fitness to stir up that state of sensation in the soul which is called its delightful smelling. But both these sensations are only internal states of the soul which appear, or disappear, are found, or not found, just as occasions bring them into sensibility.

Again, the greatest artist in music can add no sound to his instrument, nor make it give forth any other melody but that which lieth silently hidden in it as its own inward state.

Look now at what you will, whether it be animate, or inanimate: All that it is, or has, or can be, it is and has in and from itself, as its own inward state; and all outward things can do no more to it than the hand does to the instrument, make it show forth its own inward state, either of harmony or discord.

It is strictly thus with ourselves. Not a spark of joy, of wrath, of envy, of love or grief can possibly enter into us from without, or be caused to be in us by any outward thing. This is as impossible as for the sound of metals to be put into a lump of clay. And as no metal can possibly give forth any other or higher sound than that which is enclosed within it, so we, however struck, can give forth no other or higher sound either of love, hatred, wrath, etc., than that very degree which lay before shut up within us.

The natural state of our tempers has variety of covers under which they lie concealed at times, both from ourselves and others; but when this or that accident happens to displace such or such a cover, then that which lay hid under it breaks forth. And then we vainly think that this or that outward occasion has not shown us how we are within, but has only infused or put into us a wrath, or grief, or envy which is not our natural state or of our own growth, or has all that it has from our own inward state.

But this is mere blindness and self-deceit, for it is as impossible for the mind to have any grief, or wrath, or joy, but what it has all from its own inward state, as for the instrument to give forth any other harmony or discord but that which is within and from itself.

Persons, things, and outward occurrences may strike our instrument improperly and variously, but as we are in ourselves, such is our outward sound, whatever strikes us.

If our inward state is the renewed life of Christ within us, then every thing and occasion, let it be what it will, only makes the same life to sound forth and show itself; then if one cheek is smitten, we meekly turn the other also. But if nature is alive and only under a religious cover, then every outward accident that shakes or disturbs this cover gives leave to that bad state, whether of grief, or wrath, or joy that lay hid within us to show forth itself.

But nothing at any time makes the least show or sound outwardly, but only that which lay ready within us for an outward birth, as occasion should offer.

What a miserable mistake is it therefore to place religious goodness in outward observances, in notions and opinions which good and bad men can equally receive and practice, and to treat the ready real power and operation of an inward life of God in the birth of our souls as fanaticism and enthusiasm, when not only the whole letter and spirit of scripture, but every operation in nature and creature demonstrates that the Kingdom of Heaven must be all within us, or it never can possibly belong to us. Goodness, piety, and holiness can only be ours, as thinking, willing, and desiring are ours, by being in us as a power of heaven in the birth and growth of our own life.

And now, Eusebius, how is the great controversy about religion and salvation shortened.

For since the one only work of Christ as your Redeemer is only this, to take from the earthly life of flesh and blood its usurped power and to raise the smothered spark of Heaven out of its state of death into a powerful governing life of the whole man, your one only work also under your Redeemer is fully known. And you have the utmost certainty what you are to do, where you are to seek, and in what you are to find your salvation. All that you have to do, or can do, is to oppose, resist, and, as far as you can, to renounce the evil tempers and workings of your own earthly nature. You are under the power of no other enemy, are held in no other captivity, and want no other deliverance but from the power of your own earthly self. This is the one murderer of the divine life within you. It is your own Cain that murders your own Abel. Now everything that your earthly nature does is under the influence of self-will, self-love, and self-seeking, whether it carries you to laudable or blamable practices, all is done in the nature and spirit of Cain and only helps you to such goodness as when Cain slew his brother. For every action and motion of self has the spirit of Antichrist and murders the divine life within you.

Judge not therefore of yourself by considering how many of those things you do which divines and moralists call virtue and goodness, nor how much you abstain from those things which they call sin and vice.

But daily and hourly, in every step that you take, see to the spirit that is within you whether it be Heaven or earth that guides you. And judge everything to be sin and Satan in which your earthly nature, own love, or self-seeking has any share of life in you; nor think that any goodness is brought to life in you but so far as it is an actual death to the pride, the vanity, the wrath, and selfish tempers of your fallen, earthly life.

Again, here you see where and how you are to seek your salvation, not in taking up your traveling staff, or crossing the seas to find out a new Luther or a new Calvin to clothe yourself with their opinions. No. The oracle is at home that always and only speaks the truth to you because nothing is your truth but that good and that evil which is yours within you. For salvation or damnation is no outward thing that is brought into you from without, but is only that which springs up within you as the birth and state of your own life. What you are in yourself, what is doing in yourself, is all that can be either your salvation or damnation.

For all that is our good and all that is our bad has no place nor power but within us. Again, nothing that we do is bad but for this reason, because it resists the power and working of God within us; and nothing that we do can be good but because it conforms to the Spirit of God within us. And therefore, as all that can be good and all that can be evil in us necessarily supposes a God working within us, you have the utmost certainty that God, salvation, and the Kingdom of Heaven are nowhere to be sought, or found, but within you, and that all outward religion from the fall of man to this day is not for itself, but merely for the sake of an inward and divine life which was lost when Adam died his first death in Paradise. And therefore it may well be said that circumcision is nothing, and uncircumcision is nothing, because nothing is wanted, and therefore nothing can be available but the new creature called out of its captivity under the death and darkness of flesh and blood into the light, life, and perfection of its first creation.

And thus also you have the fullest proof in what your salvation precisely consists. Not in any historic faith, or knowledge of anything absent or distant from you, not in any variety of restraints, rules, and methods of practicing virtues, not in any formality of opinion about faith and works, repentance, forgiveness of sins, or justification and sanctification, not in any truth or righteousness that you can have from yourself, from the best of men or books, but wholly and solely in the life of God, or Christ of God quickened[25] and born again in you, or in other words in the restoration and perfect union of the first two-fold life in the humanity.

Theogenes. Though all that has passed betwixt you and Eusebius concerns matters of the greatest moment, yet I must call it a digression and quite useless to me. For I have not the least doubt about any of these things you have been asserting. It is visible enough that there can be no medium in this matter; either religion must be all spiritual or all carnal, that is, we must either take up with the grossness of the Sadducees who say there is neither angel nor spirit, or with such purification as the Pharisees had from their washing of pots and vessels and tithing their mint and rue; we must, I say, either acquiesce in all this carnality, or we must profess a religion that is all spirit and life, and merely for the sake of raising up an inward spiritual life of Heaven that fell into death in our first father.

I consent also to everything that you have said of the nature and origin of wrath. That it can have no place nor possibility of beginning but solely in the creaturely nature, nor even any possibility of beginning there till the creature has died to or lost its proper state of existence in God, that is, till it has lost that life and blessing and happiness which it had in and from God at its first creation.

But I still ask, what must I do with all those scriptures which not only make God capable of being provoked to wrath and resentment, but frequently inflamed with the highest degrees of rage, fury, and vengeance that can be expressed by words?

Theophilus. I promised, you know, to remove this difficulty, and will be as good as my word. But I must first tell you that you are in much more distress about it than you need to be. For in the little book of *Regeneration*, in the *Appeal*, in the *Spirit of Prayer*, etc., which you read with such entire approbation, the whole matter is cleared up from its true ground, how wrath in the scriptures is ascribed to God and yet cannot belong to the nature of the Deity.

Thus you are told in the *Appeal*, after these two falls of two orders of creatures (that is, of angels and man), the Deity itself came to have new and strange names, new and unheard of tempers and inclinations of wrath, fury, and vengeance ascribed to it. I call them new because they began at the fall; I call them strange because they were foreign to the Deity and could not belong to God in Himself. Thus, God is said to be a consuming fire. But to whom? To the fallen angels and lost souls. But why, and how is He so to them? It is because those creatures have lost all that they had from God but the fire of their nature, and therefore God can only be found and manifested in them as a consuming fire. Now is it not justly said that God, who is nothing but infinite love, is yet in such creatures only a consuming fire? And though God be nothing but love, yet they are under the wrath and vengeance of God because they have only that fire in them which is broken off from the light and love of God and so can know or feel nothing of God but His fire of nature in them. As creatures, they can have no life but what they have in and from God; and therefore that wrathful life which they have is truly said to be a wrath or fire of God upon them. And yet it is still strictly true that there is no wrath in God Himself, that He is not changed in His temper toward the creatures, that He does not cease to be one and the same infinite fountain of goodness, infinitely flowing forth in the riches of his love upon all and every life. (Now, Sir, mind what follows as the true ground, how wrath can and cannot be ascribed to God.) God is not changed from love to wrath, but the creatures have changed their own state in nature, and so the God of nature can only be manifested in them according to their own state in nature. And, N.B., this is the true ground of rightly understanding all that is said of the wrath and vengeance of God in and upon the creatures. It is only in such a sense as the curse of God may be said to be upon them, not because anything cursed can be in or come from God, but because they have made that life which they must have in God to be a mere curse to themselves. For every creature that lives must have its life in and from God, and therefore God must be in every creature. This is as true of devils as of holy angels. But how is God in them? N.B. Why, only as He is manifested in nature. Holy angels have the triune life of God as manifested in nature, so manifested also in them, and therefore God is in them all love, goodness, majesty, and glory, and theirs is the Kingdom of Heaven.

Devils have nothing of this triune life left in them but the fire or wrath of eternal nature broken off from all light and love; and therefore the life that they can have in and from God is only and solely a life of wrath, rage, and darkness, and theirs is the Kingdom of Hell.

And because this life (though all rage and darkness) is a strength and power of life, which they must have in and from God, and which they cannot take out of His hands, therefore is their cursed, miserable, wrathful life truly and justly said to be the curse and misery, and wrath, and vengeance of God upon them, though God Himself can no more have curse, misery, wrath, and vengeance than He can have mischief, malice, or any fearful tremblings in His holy triune Deity.[26]

See now, Theogenes, what little occasion you had for your present difficulty. For here, in the above cited words, which you have been several years acquainted with, the true ground and reason is plainly shown you, how and why all the wrath, rage, and curse that is anywhere stirring in nature or breaking forth in any creature is and must be in all truth called by the scriptures the wrath, and rage, and vengeance of God, though it be the greatest of all impossibilities for rage and wrath to be in the holy Deity itself.

The scriptures therefore are literally true in all that they affirm of the wrath, etc., of God. For is it not as literally true of God that Hell and devils are His, as that Heaven and holy angels are His? Must not therefore all the wrath and rage of the one be as truly His rage and wrath and rage burning in them, as the light and joy and glory of the other is only his goodness opened and manifested in them, according to their state in nature?

Take notice of this fundamental truth.

Everything that works in nature and creature, except sin, is the working of God in nature and creature. The creature has nothing else in its power but the free use of its will; and its free will hath no other power but that of concurring with or resisting the working of God in nature. The creature with its free will can bring nothing into being, nor make any alteration in the working of nature, and so feel and find something in its state that it did not feel or find before.

Thus God, in the manifestation of Himself in and by nature, sets before every man fire and water, life and death; and man has no other power but that of entering into and uniting with either of these states, but not the least power of adding to, or taking anything from them, or of making them to be otherwise than he finds them.

For this fire and water, this life and death are nature, and have their unchangeable state in the uniform working of God in nature. And therefore, whatever is done by this fire and water, this life and death in any creature may, nay must in the strictest truth be affirmed of God as done by Him. And consequently every breathing forth of fire, or death, or rage, or curse, wherever it is, or in whatever creature, must be said, in the language of scripture, to be a provoked wrath, or fiery vengeance of God, poured forth upon the creature. And yet, everything that has been said in proof of the wrath of God shows and proves to you at the same time that it is not a wrath in the holy Deity itself.

For you see, as was said above, that God sets before man fire and water, life and death; now these things are not God, nor existent in the Deity itself; but they are that which is, and is called nature, and as they are the only things set before man, so man can go no further, reach no further, nor find, nor feel, nor be sensible of anything else but that which is to be felt or found in this nature, or fire and water, life and death which is set before him. And therefore all that man can find or feel of the wrath and vengeance of God can only be in this fire and this death, and not in the Deity itself.

Theogenes. Oh Theophilus, you have given me the utmost satisfaction on this point, and in a much better way than I imagined. I expected to have seen you glossing and criticizing away the literal expression of scriptures that affirm the wrath of God, in order to make good your point that the Deity is mere love.

But you have done the utmost justice to the letter of scripture, you have established it upon a firm and solid foundation and shown that the truth of things require it to be so, and that there can be no wrath anywhere, but what is and must be called the wrath and vengeance of God, and yet is only in nature.

What you have here said seems as if it would clear up many

passages of scripture that have raised much perplexity. Methinks I begin to see how the hardness of Pharaoh's heart, how eyes that see not and ears that hear not, may in the strictest truth be said to be of or from God, though the Deity in itself stands in the utmost contrariety to all these things, and in the utmost impossibility of willing or causing them to be.

But I must not draw you from our present matter. You have shown from the letter of scripture that nothing else is set before man but fire and water, life and death; and therefore, no possibility of wrath or love, joy or sorrow, curse or happiness to be found by man but in this state of nature set before him, or into which at his creation he is introduced as into a region of various sensibilities where all that he finds, or feels is truly God's, but not God Himself, who has His supernatural residence above and distinct from everything that is nature, fire or water, life or death.

But give me leave to mention one word of a difficulty that I yet have. You have proved that wrath, rage, vengeance, etc., can only exist or be found in nature and not in God; and yet you say that nature is nothing else but a manifestation of the hidden, invisible powers of God. But if so, must not that which is in nature be also in God? How else could nature be a manifestation of God?

Theophilus. Nature is a true manifestation of the hidden, invisible God. But you are to observe that nature, as it is in itself, in its own state, cannot have the least possible spark, or stirring of wrath, or curse, or vengeance in it, but on the contrary is from eternity to eternity a mere infinity of heavenly light, love, joy, and glory; and thus it is a true manifestation of the hidden Deity, and the greatest of proofs that the Deity itself can have no wrath in it since wrath only then begins to be in nature when nature has lost its first state.

Theogenes. This is answer enough. But now another thing starts up in my mind. For if the Deity in itself, in its supernatural state, is mere love, and only a will to all goodness, and if nature in itself is only a manifestation of this Deity of love in heavenly light and glory, if neither God nor nature have or can give forth wrath, how then can fire and water, life and death be set before man? What can they come from, or where can they exist, since God in Himself is all love; and nature, which is Kingdom of Heaven, is an infinity of joy, blessing, and happiness?

Theophilus. I will open to you all this matter to the bottom in as few words as I can.

Before God began any creation or gave birth to any creature, He was only manifested or known to Himself in His own glory and majesty; there was nothing but Himself beholding Himself in His own Kingdom of Heaven, which was, and is, and ever will be as unlimited as Himself.

Nature as well as God is and must be antecedent to all creature. For as no seeing eye could be created unless there was antecedently to it a natural visibility of things, so no creature could come into a sensibility of any natural life unless such a state of nature was antecedent to it. For no creature can begin to be in any world or state of nature, but by being created out of that world or state of nature into which it is brought to have its life. For to live in any world is the same thing as for a creature to have all that it is and has, in and from that world. And, therefore, no creature can come into any other kind of existence and life but such as can be had out of that world in which it is to live. Neither can there possibly be any other difference between created beings whether animate or inanimate but what arises from that out of which they were created. Seeing then that before the existence of the first creatures there was nothing but God and His Kingdom of Heaven, the first creatures could receive no other life but that which was in God because there was nothing living but God nor any other life but His, nor could they exist in any other place or outward state but the Kingdom of Heaven because there was none else in existence; and therefore, the first creatures must, of all necessity, be divine and heavenly, both in their inward life and outward state.

Theogenes. Here then, Theophilus, comes my question. Where is that fire and water, that life and death that is set before the creature? For as to these first creatures, nothing is set before them, nothing is within them or without them but God and the Kingdom of Heaven.

Theophilus. You should not have said there is nothing within them but God and the Kingdom of Heaven. For that which is their own creaturely nature within them is not God, nor the Kingdom of Heaven.

It has been already proved to your satisfaction that no creature can be divine, good, and happy, but by having a two-fold life united in it. And in this two-fold life of the creature is fire and water, life and death unavoidably set before it. For as its will worketh with either of these lives, so will it find either fire or water, life or death. If its will turneth from the life of God into the creaturely life, then it enters into a sensibility of that which is meant by death and fire, viz. a wrathful misery. But if the will keeps steadily given up to the Deity, then it lives in possession of that life and water which was its first and will be its everlasting heavenly joy and happiness.

But to explain this matter something deeper to you according to the mystery of all things opened by God in His chosen instrument, Jacob Behmen.

You know we have often spoken of eternal nature, that so sure as there is an eternal God, so sure is it that there is an eternal nature, as universal, as unlimited as God Himself, and everywhere working where God is and therefore everywhere equally existent, as being His Kingdom of Heaven or outward manifestation of the invisible riches, powers, and glories of the Deity.

Before or without nature, the Deity is an entire hidden, shut up, unknown, and unknowable abyss. For nature is the only ground or beginning of something; there is neither this nor that, no ground for conception, no possibility of distinction or difference; there cannot be a creature to think, nor anything to be thought upon till nature is in existence. For all the properties of sensibility and sensible life, every mode and manner of existence, all seeing, hearing, tasting, smelling, feeling, all inclinations, passions, and sensations of joy, sorrow, pain, pleasure, etc., are not in God but in nature. And therefore, God is not knowable, not a thought can begin about Him till He manifests Himself in and through and by the existence of nature, that is, till there is something that can be seen, understood, distinguished, felt, etc.

And this is eternal nature or the outbirth of the Deity, called the Kingdom of Heaven, viz., an infinity, or boundless opening of the properties, powers, wonders, and glories of the hidden Deity, and this not once done but ever doing, ever standing in the same birth, forever and ever breaking forth and springing up in new forms and openings of the abyssal Deity in the powers of nature. And out of this ocean of manifested powers of nature, the will of the Deity created hosts of heavenly beings, full of the heavenly wonders introduced into a participation of the infinity of God, to live in an eternal succession of heavenly sensations, to see and feel, to taste and find new forms of delight in an inexhaustible source of ever-changing and never-ceasing wonders of the divine glory.

Oh Theogenes! What an eternity is this, out of which and for which thy eternal soul was created? What little, crawling things are all that an earthly ambition can set before thee? Bear with patience for a while the rags of thy earthly nature, the veil and darkness of flesh and blood as the lot of thy inheritance from father Adam, but think nothing worth a thought but that which will bring thee back to thy first glory and land thee safe in the region of eternity.

But to return. Nothing is before this eternal nature but the holy, supernatural Deity; and everything that is after it is creature and has all its creaturely life and state in it and from it, either mediately or immediately.

This eternal nature hath seven chief or fountain properties that are the doers or workers of everything that is done in it and can have neither more nor less because it is a birth from or a manifestation of the Deity in nature. For the perfection of nature (as was before said of every divine and happy creature) is a union of two things, or is a two-fold state. It is nature, and it is God manifested in nature. Now God is triune and nature is triune, and hence there arises the ground of properties, three and three; and that which brings those three and three into union, or manifests the triune God in the triune nature, is another property, so that the glorious manifestation of the Deity in nature can have neither more nor less than seven chief or fountain properties from which everything that is known, found, and felt in all the universe of nature, in all the variety of creatures either in Heaven or on earth, hath its only rise, or cause, either mediately or immediately.

Theogenes. You say, Theophilus, that the triune Deity is united or manifested in triune nature, and that thence comes the glorious manifestation of God in seven heavenly properties called the Kingdom of Heaven. But how does it appear that this nature, antecedently to the entrance of the Deity into it, is triune? Or what is this triune nature before God is supposed to be in union with it?

Theophilus. It is barely a *desire*. It neither is, nor has, nor can be anything else but a desire. For desire is the only thing in which the Deity can work and manifest itself; for God can only come into that which wants and desires Him.

The Deity is an infinite plenitude, or fullness of riches and powers in and from itself; and it is only *want* and *desire* that is excluded from it and can have no existence in it. And here lies the true, immutable distinction between God and nature and shows why neither can ever be changed into the other; it is because God is a *universal all*; and nature or desire is a *universal want*, viz., to be filled with God.

Now as nature can be nothing but a desire, so nothing is in or done in any natural way but as desire does it, because desire is the all of nature. And therefore, there is no strength or substance, no power or motion, no cause or effect in nature but what is in itself a desire or the working and effect of it.

This is the true origin of attraction and all its powers in this material world. It gives essence and substance to all that is matter and the properties of matter; it holds every element in its created state, and not only earth and stones, but light and air and motion are under its dominion. From the center to the circumference of this material system, every motion, separation, union, vegetation, or corruption begins no sooner, goes on no further than as attraction works.

Take away attraction from this material system, and then it has all the annihilation it can ever possibly have.

Whence now has attraction this nature?

It is solely from hence because all nature from its eternity hath been, is, and forever can be only a *desire* and hath nothing in it but the properties of desire.

Now the essential, inseparable properties of *desire* are three and can be neither more nor less; and in this you have that tri-unity of nature which you asked after and in which the triune Deity manifesteth itself. I shall not now prove these three properties of the desire because I have done it at large and plainly enough elsewhere.[27]

But to go back now to your question where or how this fire and water, etc., can be found since God is all love and goodness and His manifestation in nature is a mere Kingdom of Heaven. They are to be found in the two-fold state of Heaven and the two-fold state of every heavenly creature.

For seeing that the perfection of nature and the perfection of the intelligent creature consists in one and the same two-fold state, you have here the plainest ground and reason why and how every good and happy and new created being must of all necessity have fire and water, life and death set before it or put into its choice.

Because it has it in its power to turn and give up its will to either of these lives, it can turn either to God or nature and therefore must have life and death, fire or water in its choice.

Now this two-fold life which makes the perfection of nature and creature is, in other words, signified by the seven heavenly properties of nature; for when God is manifested in nature, all its seven properties are in a heavenly state.

But in these seven properties, though all heavenly, lieth the ground of fire and water, etc., because a division or separation can be made in them by the will of the creature. For the three first properties are as distinct from the four following ones as God is distinct from that which wants God. And these three first properties are the essence or whole being of that desire which is and is called nature, or that which wants God.

When, therefore, the will of the creature turns from God into nature, it breaks or looses the union of the seven heavenly properties because nature, as distinct from God, has only the three first properties in it. And such a creature, having broke or lost the union of the seven properties, is fallen into the three first, which is meant by fire and death. For when the three first properties have lost God or their union with the four following ones, then they are mere nature, which in its whole being is nothing else but the strength and rage of hunger, an excess of want, of self-torment, and self-vexation. Surely now, my friend, this matter is enough explained.

Theogenes. Indeed, Theophilus, I am quite satisfied; for by this account which you have given of the ground of nature and its true and full distinction from God, you have struck a most amazing light into my mind.

For if nature is mere want and has nothing in it but a strength of want generated from the three self-tormenting properties of a desire, if God is all love, joy, and happiness, an infinite plentitude of all blessings, then the limits and bounds of good and evil, of happiness and misery are made as visibly distinct and as certainly to be known as the difference between a circle and a straight line.

To live to desire, that is, to nature, is unavoidably entering into the region of all evil and misery because nature has nothing else in it; but on the other hand, to die to desire, that is, to turn from nature to God, is to be united with the infinite source of all that is good and blessed and happy.

All that I wanted to know is now cleared up in the greatest plainness. And I have no difficulty about those passages of scripture which speak of the wrath, and fury, and vengeance of God. Wrath is His, just as all nature is His, and yet God is mere love that only rules and governs wrath as He governs the foaming waves of the sea and the madness of storms and tempests.

The following propositions are as evidently true as that two and two are four.

First, that God in His holy Deity is as absolutely free from wrath and rage and as utterly incapable of them as He is of thickness, hardness, and darkness because wrath and rage belong to nothing else, can exist in nothing else, have life in nothing else but in thickness, hardness, and darkness.

Secondly, that all wrath is disorder and can be nowhere but in nature and creature because nothing else is capable of changing from right to wrong.

Thirdly, that wrath can have no existence even in nature and creature till they have lost their first perfection which they had from God and are become that which they should not have been.

Fourthly, that all the wrath and fury and vengeance that ever did or can break forth in nature and creature is according to the strictest truth to be called and looked upon as the wrath and vengeance of God, just as the darkness as well as the light is, and is to be called His.

Oh! Theophilus, what a key have you given me to the right understanding of scripture!

For when nature and creature are known to be the only theater of evil and disorder, and the holy Deity as that governing love which wills nothing but the removal of all evil from everything as fast as infinite wisdom can find ways of doing, then whether you read of the raining of fire and brimstone or only showers of heavenly manna falling upon the earth, it is only one and the same love working in such different ways and diversity of instruments as time and place and occasion had made wise and good and beneficial.

Pharaoh with his hardened heart and St. Paul with his voice from Heaven, though so contrary to one another, were both of them the chosen vessels of the same God of love because both miraculously taken out of their own state and made to do all the good to a blind and wicked world which they were capable of doing.

And thus, Sir, are all the treasures of the wisdom and goodness of God hidden in the letter of scripture made the comfort and delight of my soul, and everything I read turns itself into a motive of loving and adoring the wonderful working of the love of God over all the various changings of nature and creature till all evil shall be extinguished and all disorder go back again to its first harmonious state of perfection.

Depart from this idea of God as an infinity of mere love, wisdom, and goodness, and then everything in the system of scripture and the system of nature only helps the reasoning mind to be miserably perplexed, as well with the mercies as with the judgments of God.

But when God is known to be omnipotent love that can do nothing but works of love, and that all nature and creature are only under the operation of love as a distempered person under the care of a kind and skillful physician who seeks nothing but the perfect recovery of his patient, then whatever is done, whether a severe caustic or a pleasant cordial is ordered, that is, whether because of its difference it may have the different name of mercy or judgment, yet all is equally well done because love is the doer of both and does both from the same principle and for the same end.

Theophilus. Oh Theogenes, now you are according to your name,[28] you are born of God. For when love is the triune God that you serve, worship, and adore, the only God in whom you desire to live and move and have your being, then of a truth God dwelleth in you, and you in God.

I shall now only add this one word more to strengthen and confirm your right understanding of all that is said of the wrath, or rage of God in the scriptures.

The Psalmist, you know, saith thus of God, "He giveth forth his ice like morsels, and who is able to abide his frosts." Now, Sir, if you know how to explain this scripture and can show how ice and frost can truly be ascribed to God as His, though absolutely impossible to have any existence in Him, then you have an easy and unerring key how the wrath and fury and vengeance that anywhere falls upon any creature is and may be truly ascribed to God as His, though fury and vengeance are as inconsistent with and as impossible to have any existence in the Deity as lumps of ice, or the hardness of intolerable frosts.

Now in this text setting forth the horror of God's ice and frost, you have the whole nature of divine wrath set before you. Search all the scriptures and you will nowhere find any wrath of God but what is bounded in nature, and is so described as to be itself a proof that it has no existence in the holy supernatural Deity.

Thus says the Psalmist again, "The earth trembled and quaked, the very foundations also of the hills shook, and were removed, because He was wroth." No wrath here but in the elements.

Again, "There went a smoke out in his presence, and a consuming fire out of his mouth, so that coals were kindled at it. The springs of water were seen and the foundations of the round world were discovered at thy chiding, O Lord, at the blasting of the breath of thy displeasure."

Now every working of the wrath of God described in scripture is strictly of a piece with this, it relates to a wrath solely confined to the powers and working properties of nature that lives and moves only in the elements of the fallen world, and no more reaches the Deity than ice or frost do.

The Apostle saith, "Avenge not yourselves, for it is written, Vengeance is mine, I will repay, saith the Lord."

This is another full proof that wrath or vengeance is not in the holy Deity itself as a quality of the divine mind; for if it was, then vengeance would belong to every child of God that was truly born of Him or he could not have the spirit of his Father, or be perfect as his Father in Heaven is perfect.

But if vengeance only belongs to God and can only be so affirmed of Him as ice and frost are His and belong to Him, if it has no other manner of working than as when it is said, "He sent out his Arrows and scattered them, He cast forth Lightnings and destroyed them," then it is certain that the divine vengeance is only in fallen nature and its disordered properties and is no more in the Deity itself than hailstones and coals of fire.

And here you have the true reason why revenge or vengeance is not allowed to man; it is because vengeance can only work in the evil or disordered properties of fallen nature. But man being himself a part of fallen nature and subject to its disordered properties is not allowed to work with them because it would be stirring up evil in himself, and that is his sin of wrath or revenge.

God therefore reserves all vengeance to Himself, not because wrathful revenge is a temper or quality that can have any place in the holy Deity but because the holy supernatural Deity, being free from all the properties of nature whence partial love and hatred spring and being in Himself nothing but an infinity of love, wisdom, and goodness, He alone knows how to overrule the disorders of nature and so to repay evil with evil that the highest good may be promoted by it.

To say therefore that vengeance is to be reserved to God is only saying in other words that all the evils in nature are to be reserved and turned over to the love of God to be healed by His goodness. And every act of what is called divine vengeance recorded in scripture may, and ought with the greatest strictness of truth, be called .n act of the divine love.

If Sodom flames and smokes with stinking brimstone, 'tis the love of God that kindled it, only to extinguish a more horrible fire. It was one and the same infinite love when it preserved Noah in the ark, when it turned Sodom into a burning lake, and overwhelmed Pharaoh in the Red Sea. And if God commanded the waters to destroy the old world, it was as high an act of the same infinite love toward that chaos as when it said to the first darkness upon the face of the deep, "Let there be Light, and there was Light."

Not a word in all scripture concerning the wrath or vengeance of God but directly teaches you these two infallible truths. First, that all the wrath spoken of worketh nowhere but in the wrathful, disordered elements and properties of fallen nature. Secondly, that all the power that God exercises over them, all that He doth at any time or on any occasion with or by them is only and solely the one work of His unchangeable love toward man.

Just as the good physician acts from only one and the same good will toward his patient when he orders bitter and sour, as when he gives the pleasant draughts.

Now suppose the good physician to have such intense love for you as to disregard your aversion toward them and to force such medicines down your throat as can alone save your life, suppose he should therefore call himself your severe physician and declare himself so rigid toward you that he would not spare you, nor suffer you go where you would to escape his bitter draughts till all means of your recovery were tried, then you would have a true and just though low representation of those bitter cups which God in His wrath forceth fallen man to drink.

Now as the bitter, sour, hot, etc., in the physician's draughts are not declarations of any the like bitterness, heat, or sourness in the spirit of the physician that uses them but are things quite distinct from the state and spirit of his mind and only manifest his care and skill in the right use of such materials toward the health of his patient, so in like manner, all the elements of fallen nature are only so many outward materials in the hands of God formed and mixed into heat and cold, into fruitful and pestilential effects, into serenity of seasons and blasting tempests, into means of health and sickness, of plenty and poverty, just as the wisdom and goodness of providence sees to be fittest to deliver man from the miserable malady of his earthly nature and help him to become heavenly minded.

If therefore it would be great folly to suppose bitterness, or heat, etc., to be in the spirit of the physician when he gives a hot or bitter medicine, much greater folly surely must it be to suppose that wrath, vengeance, or any pestilential quality is in the spirit of the holy Deity when a wrath, a vengeance, or pestilence is stirred up in the fallen elements by the providence of God as a proper remedy for the evil of this or that time or occasion.

Hear these decisive words of scripture, viz., "Whom the Lord loveth, He chasteneth." What a grossness therefore of mistake is it to conclude that wrath must be in the Deity because He chastens and threatens chastisement when you have God's own word for it that nothing but His love chasteneth. Again, thus saith the Lord, "I have smitten you with blasting and mildew. Your vineyards, and your fig trees, and your olive yards did the palmerworm devour," and then the love that did this make this complaint, "Yet ye have not returned to me." Again, "Pestilence have I sent amongst you; I have made the stink of your tents come up even into your nostrils," etc. And then the same love that did this, that made this use of the disordered elements, makes the same complaint again, "Yet have ye not returned to me" (Amos 4:9-10).

Now, Sir, how is it possible for words to give stronger proof that God is mere love, that He has no will toward fallen man but to bless Him with works of love, and this as certainly when he turns the air into a pestilence as when He makes the same air rain down manna upon the earth? Since neither the one nor the other are done but as time and place and occasion render them the fittest means to make man return and adhere to God, that is, to come out of all the evil and misery of his fallen state. What can infinite love do more, or what can it do to give greater proof that all that it does proceeds from love? And here you are to observe that this is not said from human conjecture or any imaginary idea of God, but is openly asserted, constantly affirmed and repeated in the plainest letter of scripture. But this conversation has been long enough. And I hope we shall meet again tomorrow.

The End of the First Dialogue

NOTES

20. Curate: Assisting priest.

21. Neither . . . are: thus Law, evidently influenced by "these ways."

22. Established Church: The Church of England.

23. The quotations are verbatim passages from the following collects in the Book of Common Prayer (1662), in the order Law gives: Trinity 19; Trinity 17; Trinity 9; Trinity 15; Rogation Sunday. Prevent (of Trinity 17): go before or anticipate.

24. Began: begun, a conditional use of the verb.

25. Quickened: made alive.

26. See *Appeal to all that Doubt*, etc., p. 135 (Law's note).

27. See *Way to Divine Knowledge*, p. 200 to the end; *Spirit of Love*, First Part, p. 00 to the end (Law's note).

28. According to your name: "Theogenes" is a Greek name signifying "born of God," while Theophilus means "lover of God." and Eusebius, the third participant in these holy conversations, means "one who is reverent and pious." This last figure appears also in *A Serious Call*, the name as well of the great ecclesiastical historian and scholar (c. 260–c. 340) whom Law quotes (see above, p. 00).

The Second Dialogue

Eusebius. There is no occasion to resume anything of our yesterday's discourse. The following propositions are sufficiently proved.

First, that God is an abyssal infinity of love, wisdom, and goodness, that He ever was and ever will be one and the same unchangeable will to all goodness and works of love, as incapable of any sensibility of wrath or acting under it as of falling into pain or darkness and acting under their direction.

Secondly, that all wrath, strife, discord, hatred, envy, or pride, etc., all heat and cold, all enmity in the elements, all thickness, grossness, and darkness are things that have no existence but in and from the sphere of fallen nature.

Thirdly, that all the evils of contrariety and disorder in fallen nature are only as so many materials in the hands of infinite love and wisdom, all made to work in their different ways as far as is possible to one and the same end, viz., to turn temporal evil into eternal good.

So that whether you look at light or darkness, at night or day, at fire or water, at heaven or earth, at life or death, at prosperity or adversity, at blasting winds or heavenly dews, at sickness or health, you see nothing but such a state of things in and through which the supernatural Deity wills and seeks the restoration of fallen nature and creature to their first perfection.

It now only remains that the doctrine of scripture concerning the Atonement necessary to be made by the life, sufferings, and death of Christ be explained, or in other words, the true meaning of that righteousness of justice of God that must have satisfaction done to it before man can be reconciled to God.

For this doctrine is thought by some to favor the opinion of a wrath and resentment in the Deity itself.

Theophilus. This doctrine, Eusebius, of the Atonement made by Christ, and the absolute necessity and real efficacy of it to satisfy the righteousness or justice of God, is the very ground and foundation of

Christian redemption and the life and strength of every part of it. But then, this very doctrine is so far from favoring the opinion of a wrath in the Deity itself that it is an absolute full denial of it and the strongest of demonstrations that the wrath or resentment that is to be pacified or atoned cannot possibly be in the Deity itself.

For this wrath that is to be atoned and pacified is in its whole nature nothing else but sin, or disorder in the creature. And when sin is extinguished in the creature, all the wrath that is between God and the creature is fully atoned. Search all the Bible from one end to the other, and you will find that the atonement of that which is called the divine wrath or justice and the extinguishing of sin in the creature are only different expressions for one and the same individual thing. And therefore, unless you will place sin in God, that wrath that is to be atoned or pacified cannot be placed in Him.

The whole nature of our redemption has no other end but to remove or extinguish the wrath that is between God and man. When this is removed, man is reconciled to God. Therefore, where the wrath is, or where that is which wants to be atoned, there is that which is the blamable cause of the separation between God and man; there is that which Christ came into the world to extinguish, to quench or atone. If, therefore, this wrath, which is the blamable cause of the separation between God and man, is in God Himself, if Christ died to atone or extinguish a wrath that was got into the holy Deity itself, then it must be said that Christ made an Atonement for God and not for man, that He died for the good and benefit of God and not of man, and that which is called our redemption ought rather to be called the redemption of God, as saving and delivering Him and not man from his own wrath.

This blasphemy is unavoidable if you suppose that wrath for which Christ died to be a wrath in God Himself.

Again, the very nature of Atonement absolutely shows that that which is to be atoned cannot possibly be in God nor even in any good being. For Atonement implies the alteration or removal of something that is not as it ought to be. And therefore, every creature, so long as it is good and has its proper state of goodness, neither wants nor can admit of any Atonement because it has nothing in it that wants to be altered or taken out of it. And therefore, Atonement cannot possibly have any place in God because nothing in God either wants or can receive alteration; neither can it have place in any creature but so far as it has lost or altered that which it had from God and is fallen into disorder, and then, that which brings this creature back to its first state which alters that which is wrong in it and takes its evil out of it is its true and proper Atonement.

Suppose the creature not fallen, and then there is no room nor possibility for Atonement, a plain and full proof that the work of Atonement is nothing else but the altering or quenching that which is evil in the fallen creature.

Hell, wrath, darkness, misery, and eternal death mean the same thing through all scripture, and these are the only things from which we want to be redeemed; and where there is nothing of Hell there, there is nothing of wrath, nor anything that wants or can admit of the benefits of the Atonement made by Christ.

Either, therefore, all Hell is in the essence of the holy Deity, or nothing that wants to be atoned by the merits and death of Christ can possibly be in the Deity itself.

The Apostle saith that we are by nature children of wrath, the same thing as when the Psalmist saith, "I was shapen in wickedness, and in sin hath my mother conceived me." And therefore, that wrath which wants the Atonement of the sufferings, blood, and death of Christ is no other than that sin or sinful state in which we are naturally born. But now, if this wrath could be supposed to be in the Deity itself, then it would follow that by being by nature children of wrath, we should thereby be the true children of God; we should not want any Atonement or new birth from above to make us partakers of the divine nature because that wrath that was in us would be our dwelling in God and He in us.

Again, all scripture teaches us that God wills and desires the removal or extinction of that wrath which is betwixt God and the creature, and therefore all scripture teaches that the wrath is not in God, for God cannot will the removal or alteration of anything that is in Himself; this is as impossible as for Him to will the extinction of His own omnipotence. Nor can there be anything in God contrary to, or against His own will; and yet, if God wills the extinction of a wrath that is in Himself, it must be in Him, contrary to or against His own will.

This, I presume, is enough to show you that the Atonement

made by Christ is itself the greatest of all proofs that it was not to atone or extinguish any wrath in the Deity itself, nor, indeed, any way to affect or alter any quality or temper in the divine mind, but purely and solely to overcome and remove all that death and hell, and wrath, and darkness that had opened itself in the nature, birth, and life of fallen man.

Eusebius. The truth of all this is not to be denied. And yet it is as true that all our systems of divinity give quite another account of this most important matter. The satisfaction of Christ is represented as a satisfaction made to a wrathful Deity, and the merits of the sufferings and death of Christ as that which could only avail with God to give up His own wrath and think of mercy toward man. Nay, what is still worse, if possible, the ground, and nature, and efficacy of this great transaction between God and man is often explained by debtor and creditor. Man as having contracted a debt with God that he could not pay, and God as having a right to insist upon the payment of it, and therefore only to be satisfied by receiving the death and sacrifice of Christ as a valuable consideration instead of the debt that was due to Him from man.

Theophilus. Hence you may see, Eusebius, how unreasonably complaint has been sometimes made against the *Appeal*, the *Spirit of Prayer*, etc., as introducing a philosophy into the doctrines of the gospel not enough supported by the letter of scripture, though everything there asserted has been over and over shown to be well grounded on the letter of scripture and necessarily included in the most fundamental doctrines of the gospel.

Yet they who make this complaint blindly swallow a vanity of philosophy in the most important part of gospel religion, which not only has less scripture for it than the infallibility of the Pope, but is directly contrary to the plain letter of every single text of scripture that relates to this matter, as I will now show you.

First, the Apostle saith, "God so loved the world, that He gave His only begotten Son, that all who believe in Him should not perish but have everlasting life." What becomes now of the philosophy of debtor and creditor, of a satisfaction made by Christ to a wrath in God? Is it not the grossest of all fictions and in full contrariety to the plain written word of God? "God so loved the world"; behold the degree of it. But when did He so love it? Why, before it was

432

redeemed, before He sent or gave His only Son to be the Redeemer of it. Here you see that all wrath in God antecedent to our redemption or the sacrifice of Christ for us is utterly excluded; there is no possibility for the supposition of it, it is as absolutely denied as words can do it. And therefore the infinite love, mercy, and compassion of God toward fallen man is not purchased, or procured for us by the death of Christ, but the Incarnation and sufferings of Christ come from and are given to us by the infinite antecedent love of God for us and are the gracious effects of His own love and goodness toward us.

It is needless to show you how constantly this same doctrine is asserted and repeated by all the Apostles.

Thus says St. John again, "In this was manifested the love of God toward us, because He sent his only begotten Son into the world, that we might live through Him." Again, "this is the record that God hath given unto us, eternal life; and this life is in His Son." Again, "God," saith St. Paul, "was in Christ, reconciling the world unto Himself, not imputing their trespasses to them." Which is repeated and further opened in these words, "Giving thanks unto the Father, who hath made us meet to be partakers of the inheritance of the saints in light, who hath delivered us from the power of darkness, and hath translated us into the kingdom of his dear Son" (Col. 1:12–13). And again, "Blessed be the God and Father of our Lord Jesus Christ, who hath blessed us with all spiritual blessings in heavenly places in Christ" (Eph. 1:3).

How great therefore, Eusebius, is the error, how total the disregard of scripture, and how vain the philosophy which talks of a wrath in God antecedent to our redemption, or of a debt which He could not forgive us till He had received a valuable consideration for it when all scripture from page to page tells us that all the mercy and blessing and benefits of Christ as our Savior are the free antecedent gift of God Himself to us, and bestowed upon us for no other reason, from no other motive but the infinity of His own love toward us, agreeable to what the evangelical prophet saith of God, "I am He that blotteth out transgressions for my own sake" (Isa. 43:25), that is, not for any reason or motive that can be laid before me but because I am love itself, and my own nature is my immutable reason why nothing but works of love, blessing, and goodness can come from me.

Look we now at the scripture account of the nature of the

Atonement and satisfaction of Christ, and this will further show us that it is not to atone or alter any quality or temper in the divine mind, nor for the sake of God, but purely and solely to atone, to quench, and overcome that death and wrath and hell under the power of which man was fallen.

"As in Adam all die, so in Christ shall all be made alive." This is the whole work, the whole nature, and the sole end of Christ's sacrifice of Himself; and there is not a syllable in scripture that gives you any other account of it. It all consists from the beginning to the end, in carrying on the one work of regeneration; and therefore the Apostle saith, the first Adam was made a living soul, but the last or second Adam was made a quickening spirit because sent into the world by God to quicken and revive that life from above which we lost in Adam. And He is called our Ransom, our Atonement, etc., for no other reason but because that which He did and suffered in our fallen nature was as truly an efficacious means of our being born again to a new heavenly life of Him and from Him, as that which Adam did was the true and natural cause of our being born in sin and the impurity of bestial flesh and blood.

And as Adam by what he did may be truly said to have purchased our misery and corruption, to have bought death for us, and to have sold us into a slavery under the world, the flesh, and the devil, though all that we have from him or suffer by him is only the inward working of his own nature and life within us, so according to the plain meaning of the words, Christ may be said to be our Price, our Ransom, and Atonement; though all that He does for us as buying, ransoming, and redeeming us is done wholly and solely by a birth of His own nature and spirit brought to life in us.

The Apostle saith "Christ died for our sins." Thence it is that He is the great sacrifice for sin and its true Atonement. But how and why is he so? The Apostle tells you in these words, "The sting of death is sin; but thanks be to God, who giveth us the victory through our Lord Jesus Christ"; and therefore Christ is the Atonement of our sins when by and from Him living in us we have victory over our sinful nature.

The scriptures frequently say Christ gave Himself for us. But what is the full meaning, effect, and benefit of His thus giving Himself for us? The Apostle puts this out of all doubt when he says, "Jesus Christ, who gave Himself for us, that He might redeem us from all iniquity, and purify to Himself a peculiar people . . . that He might deliver us from this present evil world . . . from the curse of the law . . . from the power of Satan . . . from the wrath to come"; or as the Apostle saith in other words, "that He might be made unto us wisdom, righteousness, and sanctification."

The whole truth therefore of the matter is plainly this. Christ given for us is neither more nor less than Christ given into us. And He is in no other sense our full, perfect, and sufficient Atonement than as His nature and spirit is born and formed in us, which so purgeth us from our sins that we are thereby in Him, and by Him dwelling in us become new creatures having our conversation in Heaven.

As Adam is truly our defilement and impurity by his birth in us, so Christ is our Atonement and purification by our being born again of Him and having thereby quickened and revived in us that first divine life which was extinguished in Adam. And therefore, as Adam purchased death for us, just so in the same manner, in the same degree, and in the same sense, Christ purchases life for us. And each of them only, and solely by their own inward life within us.

This is the one scripture account of the whole nature, the sole end, and full efficacy of all that Christ did and suffered for us. It is all comprehended in these two texts of scripture: (1) "That Christ was manifested to destroy the works of the devil; (2) That as in Adam all die, so in Christ shall all be made alive." From the beginning to the end of Christ's atoning work, no other power is ascribed to it, nothing else is intended by it as an appeaser of wrath but the destroying of all that in man which comes from the Devil, no other merits, or value, or infinite worth than that of its infinite ability and sufficiency to quicken again in all human nature that heavenly life that died in Adam.

Eusebius. Though all that is here said seems to have both the letter and spirit of scripture on its side, yet I am afraid it will be thought not enough to assert the infinite value and merits of our Savior's sufferings. For it is the common opinion of doctors that the righteousness or justice of God must have satisfaction done to it. And that nothing could avail with God as a satisfaction but the infinite worth and value of the sufferings of Christ.

Theophilus. It is true, Eusebius, that this is often, and almost always thus asserted in human writers, but it is neither the language nor the doctrine of scripture.

Not a word is there said of a righteousness or justice as an attribute in God that must be satisfied or that the sacrifice of Christ is that which satisfies the righteousness that is in God Himself.

It has been sufficiently proved to you that God wanted not to be reconciled to fallen man; that He never was anything else toward Him but love; and that His love brought forth the whole scheme of His redemption. Thence it is that the scriptures do not say that Christ came into the world to procure us the divine favor and good will for to[29] put a stop to an antecedent righteous wrath in God toward us. No, the reverse of all this is the truth, viz., that Christ and His whole mediatorial office came purely and solely from God, already so reconciled to us as to bestow an infinity of love upon us. "The God of all grace," saith the Apostle, "who hath called us to his eternal glory by Jesus Christ" (1 Pet. 5:10). Here you see Christ is not the cause or motive of God's mercy toward fallen man, but God's own love for us, His own desire of our eternal glory and happiness hath for that end given us Christ that we may be made partakers of it. The same as when it is again said, "God was in Christ reconciling the world to Himself," that is, calling and raising it out of its ungodly and miserable state.

Thus all the mystery of our redemption proclaims nothing but a God of love toward fallen man. It was the love of God that could not behold the misery of fallen man without demanding and calling for his salvation. It was love alone that wanted to have full satisfaction done to it and such a love as could not be satisfied till all that glory and happiness that was lost by the death of Adam was fully restored and regained again by the death of Christ.

Eusebius. But is there not some good sense in which righteousness or justice may be said to be satisfied by the Atonement and sacrifice of Christ?

Theophilus. Yes, most certainly there is. But then it is only that righteousness or justice that belongs to man and ought to be in him. Now righteousness, wherever it is to be, has no mercy in itself; it makes no condescensions; it is inflexibly rigid; its demands are inexorable; prayers, offerings, and entreaties have no effect upon it; it will have nothing but itself, nor will it ever cease its demands or take anything in lieu of them as a satisfaction instead of itself. Thus, "Without holiness," saith the Apostle, "no man shall see the Lord." And again, "Nothing that is defiled or impure can enter into the Kingdom of Heaven." And this is meant by righteousness being rigid and having no mercy; it cannot spare, or have pity, or hear entreaty because all its demands are righteous and good and therefore must be satisfied or fulfilled.

Now righteousness has its absolute demands upon man because man was created righteous and has lost that original righteousness which he ought to have kept in its first purity. And this is the one only righteousness or justice which Christ came into the world to satisfy, not by giving some highly valuable thing as a satisfaction to it, but by bringing back or raising up again in all human nature that holiness or righteousness which originally belonged to it. For to satisfy righteousness means neither more nor less than to fulfill it. Nor can righteousness want to have satisfaction in any being but in that being which has fallen from it, nor can it be satisfied but by restoring or fulfilling righteousness in that being which had departed from it. And therefore the Apostle saith that we are created again unto righteousness in Christ Jesus. And this is the one and only way of Christ's expiating or taking away the sins of the world, namely, by restoring to man his lost righteousness. For this end, saith the scripture, "Christ gave Himself for the church, that He might sanctify and cleanse it, that He might present it to Himself a glorious church not having spot, or wrinkle, or any such thing, but that it should be holy and without blemish" (Eph. 5:25-27).

This is the one righteousness which Christ came into the world to satisfy by fulfilling it Himself and enabling man by a new birth from Him to fulfill it. And when all unrighteousness is removed by Christ from the whole human nature, then all that righteousness is satisfied, for the doing of which Christ poured out his most precious, availing, and meritorious blood.

Eusebius. Oh Theophilus, the ground on which you stand must certainly be true. It so easily, so fully solves all difficulties and objections and enables you to give so plain and solid an account of every part of our redemption. This great point is so fully cleared up to me that I don't desire another word about it.

Theophilus. However, Eusebius, I will add a word or two more upon it that there may be no room left either for misunderstanding or denying what has been just now said of the nature of that righteousness which must have full satisfaction done to it by the atoning and redeeming work of Christ. And then you will be fully possessed of these two great truths. First, that there is no righteous wrath in the Deity itself and therefore none to be atoned there. Secondly, that though God is in Himself a mere infinity of love from whom nothing else but works of love and blessing and goodness can proceed, yet sinful men are hereby not at all delivered from that which the Apostle calls the terrors of the Lord, but that all the threatenings of woe, misery, and punishment denounced in scripture against sin and sinners both in this world and that which is to come stand all of them in their full force, and are not in the least degree weakened, or less to be dreaded because God is all love.

Everything that God hath created is right and just and good in its kind and hath its own righteousness within itself. The rectitude of its nature is its only law, and it hath no other righteousness but that of continuing in its first state. No creature is subject to any pain or punishment or guilt of sin but because it has departed from its first right state, and only does and can feel the painful loss of its own first perfection. And every intelligent creature that departs from the state of its creation is unrighteous, evil, and full of its own misery. And there is no possibility for any disordered, fallen creature to be free from its own misery and pain till it is again in its first state of perfection. This is the certain and infallible ground of the absolute necessity either of a perfect holiness in this life, or of a further purification after death before man can enter into the Kingdom of Heaven.

Now this pain and misery which is inseparable from the creature that is not in that state in which it ought to be and in which it was created is nothing else but the painful state of the creature for want of its own proper righteousness, as sickness is the painful state of the creature for want of its own proper health.

No other righteousness, no other justice, no other severe vengeance demands satisfaction or torments the sinner but that very righteousness which once was in Him, which still belongs to Him, and therefore will not suffer Him to have any rest or peace till it is again in Him as it was at the first. All, therefore, that Christ does as an Atonement for sin or as a satisfaction to righteousness is all done in and to and for man, and has no other operation but that of renewing the fallen nature of man and raising it up into its first state of original righteousness. And if this righteousness which belongs solely to man and wants no satisfaction but that of being restored and fulfilled in the human nature is sometimes called the righteousness of God, it is only so called because it is a righteousness which man had originally from God, in and by His creation; and, therefore, as it comes from God, has its whole nature and power of working as it does from God, it may very justly be called God's righteousness.

Agreeably to this way of ascribing that to God which is only in the state and condition of man, the Psalmist saith of God, "Thine arrows stick fast in me, and Thy hand presseth me sore." And yet nothing else or more is meant by it than when he saith, "My sins have taken such hold of me that I am not able to look up. . . . My wickednesses are gone over my head, and are like a sore burden too heavy for me to bear."

Now whether you call this state of man the burden of his sins and wickednesses or the arrows of the Almighty and the weight of God's hand, they mean but one and the same thing which can only be called by these different names for no other reason but this, because man's own original righteousness which he had from God makes his sinful state a pain and torment to him and lies heavy upon him in every commission of sin. And when the Psalmist again saith, "Take Thy plague away from me, I am even consumed by means of Thy heavy hand," it is only praying to be delivered from his own plague, and praying for the same thing as when he saith in other words, "Make me a clean heart, O God, and renew a right spirit within me."

Now this language of scripture which teaches us to call the pains and torments of our sins the arrows, darts, and strokes of God's hand upon us, which calls us to own the power, presence, and operation of God in all that we feel and find in our own inward state, is the language of the most exalted piety and highly suitable to that scripture which tells us that in God we live, and move, and have our being. For by teaching us to find and own the power and operation of God in everything that passes within us, it keeps us continually turned to God for all that we want and by all that we feel within ourselves, and brings us to this best of all confessions, that pain as

439

well as peace of mind is the effect and manifestation of God's infinite love and goodness toward us.

For we could not have this pain and sensibility of the burden of sin but because the love and goodness of God made us originally righteous and happy; and therefore, all the pains and torments of sin come from God's first goodness toward us and are in themselves merely and truly the arrows of His love and His blessed means of drawing us back to that first righteous state in and for which His first and never ceasing love created us.

Eusebius. The matter, therefore, plainly stands thus. There is no righteous wrath or vindictive justice in the Deity itself, which as a quality or attribute of resentment in the divine mind wants to be contented, atoned, or satisfied; but man's original righteousness which was once his peace, and happiness, and rest in God is by the fall of Adam become his tormentor, his plague that continually exercises its good vengeance upon him till it truly regains its first state in him.

Secondly, man must be under this pain, punishment, and vengeance to all eternity; there is no possibility in the nature of the thing for it to be otherwise though God be all love unless man's lost righteousness be fully again possessed by him. And, therefore, the doctrine of God's being all love, of having no wrath in Himself, has nothing in it to abate the force of those scriptures which threaten punishment to sinners, or to make them less fearful of living and dying in their sins.

Theophilus. What you say, Eusebius, is very true; but then it is but half the truth of this matter. You should have added that this doctrine is the one ground and only reason why the scriptures abound with so many declarations of woe, misery, and judgments sometimes executed and sometimes only threatened by God, and why all sinners to the end of the world must know and feel "that the wrath of God is revealed from heaven against all ungodliness and unrighteousness, and that indignation and wrath, tribulation and anguish must be upon every soul of man that doth evil" (Rom. 2:8-9).

For all these things, which the Apostle elsewhere calls the terrors of the Lord, have no ground, nothing that calls for them, nothing that vindicates the fitness and justice of them either with

440

regard to God or man but this one truth, viz., that God is in Himself a mere infinity of love from whom nothing but outflowings of love and goodness can come forth from eternity to eternity. For if God is all love, if He wills nothing toward fallen man but his full deliverance from the blind slavery and captivity of his earthly, bestial nature, then every kind of punishment, distress, and affliction that can extinguish the lusts of the flesh, the lust of the eyes, and the pride of this life may and ought to be expected from God merely because He is all love and good will toward fallen man.

To say, therefore, as some have said, if God is all love toward fallen man, how can he threaten or chastise sinners is no better than saying, if God is all goodnes in Himself and toward man, how can He do that in and to man which is for his good? As absurd as to say, if the able physician is all love, goodness, and good will toward his patients, how can he blister, purge, or scarify them, how can he order one to be trepanned and another to have a limb cut off?[30] Nay, so absurd is this reasoning that if it could be proved that God had no chastisement for sinners, the very want of this chastisement would be the greatest of all proofs that God was not all love and goodness toward man.

The meek, merciful, and compassionate Jesus who had no errand in this world but to bless and save mankind said, if thy right eye or thy right hand offend thee, pluck out the one, cut off the other, and cast them from thee. And that He said all this from mere love He adds, it is better for thee to do this than that thy whole body should be cast into Hell; therefore, if the holy Jesus had been wanting in this severity, He had been wanting in true love toward man.

And therefore, the pure, mere love of God is that alone from which sinners are justly to expect from God that no sin will pass unpunished, but that His love will visit them with every calamity and distress that can help to break and purify the bestial heart of man and awaken in him true repentance and conversion to God. It is love alone in the holy Deity that will allow no peace to the wicked, nor ever cease its judgments till every sinner is forced to confess that it is good for him that he has been in trouble, and thankfully own that not the wrath but the love of God has plucked out that right eye, cut off that right hand which he ought to have done but would not do for himself and his own salvation.

Again, this doctrine that allows of no wrath in the divine mind but places it all in the evil state of fallen nature and creature has everything in it that can prove to man the dreadful nature of sin and the absolute necessity of totally departing from it. It leaves no room for self-delusion, but puts an end to every false hope or vain seeking for relief in anything else but the total extinction of sin. And this it effectually does by showing that damnation is no foreign, separate, or imposed state that is brought in upon us or adjudged to us by the will of God, but is the inborn, natural, essential state of our own disordered nature, which is absolutely impossible in the nature of the thing to be anything else but our own hell both here and hereafter, unless all sin be separated from us and righteousness be again made our natural state by a birth of itself in us. And all this, not because God will have it so by an arbitrary act of His sovereign will, but because He cannot change His own nature or make anything to be happy and blessed, but only that which has its proper righteousness and is of one will and spirit with Himself.

If then every creature that has lost or is without the true rectitude of its nature must as such be of all necessity absolutely separated from God and necessarily under the pain and misery of a life that has lost all its own natural good, if no omnipotence or mercy or goodness of God can make it to be otherwise or give any relief to the sinner but by a total extinction of sin, by a birth of righteousness in the soul, then it fully appears that according to this doctrine, everything in God, and nature, and creature calls the sinner to an absolute renunciation of all sin as the one only possible means of salvation and leaves no room for him to deceive himself with the hopes that anything else will do instead of it. Vainly therefore is it said that if God be all love, the sinner is let loose from the dreadful apprehensions of living and dying in his sins.

On the other hand, deny this doctrine and say with the current of scholastic divines[31] that sin must be doomed to eternal pain and death unless a supposed wrath in the mind of the Deity be first atoned and satisfied, and that Christ's death was that valuable gift or offering made to God by which alone He could be moved to lay aside or extinguish His own wrath toward fallen man, say this; and then you open a wide door for licentiousness and infidelity in some and superstitious fears in others.

For if the evil, the misery, and sad effects of sin are placed in a wrath in the divine mind, what can this beget in the minds of the pious but superstitious fears about a supposed wrath in God which they can never know when it is, or is not, atoned? Every kind of superstition has its birth from this belief and cannot well be otherwise. And as to the licentious, who want to stifle all fears of gratifying all their passions, this doctrine has a natural tendency to do this for them. For if they are taught that the hurt and misery of sin is not its own natural state, not owing to its own wrath and disorder but to a wrath in the Deity, how easy is it for them to believe either that God may not be so full of wrath as is given out or that he may overcome it himself and not keep the sinner eternally in a misery that is not his own but wholly brought upon him from without by a resentment in the divine mind.

Again, this account which the schools give of the sacrifice of Christ made to atone a wrath in the Deity by the infinite value of Christ's death is that alone which helps Socinians, Deists, and infidels of all kinds to such cavils and objections to the mystery of our redemption as neither have nor can be silenced by the most able defenders of that scholastic fiction. The learning of a Grotius or Stillingfleet when defending such an account of the Atonement and satisfaction rather increases than lessens the objections to this mystery. But if you take this matter as it truly is in itself, viz., that God is in Himself all love and goodness, therefore can be nothing else but all love and goodness toward fallen man, and that fallen man is subject to no pain or misery either present or to come but what is the natural, unavoidable, essential effect of his own evil and disordered nature impossible to be altered by himself, and that the infinite, never-ceasing love of God has given Jesus Christ in all His process as the highest and only possible means that Heaven and earth can afford to save man from himself, from his own evil, misery, and death, and restore to him his original divine life. When you look at this matter in this true light, then a God all love and an Atonement for sin by Christ, not made to pacify a wrath in God but to bring forth, fulfill, and restore righteousness in the creature that had lost it, has everything in it that can make the providence of God adorable and the state of man comfortable.

Here all superstition and superstitious fears are at once totally cut off, and every work of piety is turned into a work of love. Here every false hope of every kind is taken from the licentious; they have no ground left to stand upon. Nothing to trust to as a deliverance from misery but the one total abolition of sin.

The Socinian and the infidel are here also robbed of all their philosophy against this mystery; for as it is not founded upon, does not teach an infinite resentment that could only be satisfied by an infinite Atonement as it stands not upon the ground of debtor and creditor, all their arguments which suppose it to be such are quite beside the matter and touch nothing of the truth of this blessed mystery. For it is the very reverse of all this, it declares a God that is all love and the Atonement of Christ to be nothing else in itself but the highest, most natural and efficacious means through all the possibility of things that the infinite love and wisdom of God could use to put an end to sin, and death, and Hell and restore to man his first divine state or life. I say the most natural, efficacious means through all the possibilities of nature; for there is nothing that is supernatural, however mysterious, in the whole system of our redemption; every part of it has its ground in the workings and powers of nature, and all our redemption is only nature set right, or made to be that which it ought to be.

There is nothing that is supernatural but God alone; everything besides Him is from and subject to the state of nature. It can never rise out of it, or have anything contrary to it. No creature can have either health or sickness, good or evil, or any state either from God or itself but strictly according to the capacities, powers, and workings of nature.

The mystery of our redemption, though it comes from the supernatural God, has nothing in it but what is done and to be done within the sphere and according to the powers of nature. There is nothing supernatural in it or belonging to it but that supernatural love and wisdom which brought it forth, presides over it, and will direct it till Christ as a second Adam has removed and extinguished all that evil which the first Adam brought into the human nature.

And the whole process of Jesus Christ, from His being the inspoken Word or Bruiser of the serpent given to Adam, to His birth, death, Resurrection, and Ascension into Heaven has all its ground and reason in this because nothing else in all the possibilities of nature, either in Heaven or on earth could begin, carry on, and totally effect man's deliverance from the evil of his own fallen nature.

Thus is Christ the one, full, sufficient Atonement for the sin of the whole world because He is the one only natural remedy and possible cure of all the evil that is broke[32] forth in nature, the one only natural life and resurrection of all that holiness and happiness that died in Adam. And seeing all this process of Christ is given to the world from the supernatural, antecedent, infinite love of God, therefore is it that the Apostle saith God was in Christ reconciling the world to Himself. And Christ in God is nothing else in His whole nature but that same, certain, and natural parent of a redemption to the whole human nature, as falling Adam was the certain and natural parent of a miserable life to every man that is descended from him. With this only difference, that from fallen Adam we are born in sin whether we will or no, but we cannot have that new birth which Christ has all power to bring forth in us unless the will of our heart closes with it.

But as nothing came to us from Adam but according to the powers of nature, and because He was that which He was with relation to us, so it is with Christ and our redemption by Him: All the work is grounded in and proceeds according to the powers of nature or in a way of natural efficacy or fitness to produce its effects; and everything that is found in the person, character, and condition of Christ is only there as His true and natural qualification to do all that He came to do in us and for us. That is to say, Christ was made to be that which He was; He was a seed of life in our first fallen father; He lived as a blessing of promise in the patriarchs, prophets, and Israel of God; He was born as a man of a pure virgin; He did all that He did whether as suffering, dying, conquering, rising, and ascending into Heaven only as so many things which as naturally and as truly, according to the nature of things, qualified Him to be the producer or quickener of a divine life in us, as the state and condition of Adam qualified Him to make us the slavish children of earthly, bestial flesh and blood.

This is the comfortable doctrine of our redemption: nothing in God but an infinity of love and goodness toward our fallen condition; nothing in Christ but that which had its necessity in the nature of things to make Him able to give, and us to receive, our full salvation from Him.

I will now only add that from the beginning of Deism and from the time of Socinus to this day, not a Socinian or Deist have ever seen or opposed this mystery in its true state as is undeniably plain from all their writings.

A late writer, who has as much knowledge and zeal and wit in the cause of Deism as any of his predecessors, is forced to attack our redemption by giving this false following account of it.

"That a perfectly innocent being of the highest order among intelligent natures should personate the offender and suffer in his place and stead in order to take down the wrath and resentment of the Deity against the criminal and dispose God to show mercy to Him, the Deist conceives to be both unnatural and improper and therefore not to be ascribed to God without blasphemy."

And again, "The common notion of redemption among Christians seems to represent the Deity in a disagreeable light, as implacable and revengeful," etc.[33]

What an arrow is here, I will not say, shot beside the mark but shot at nothing. Because nothing of that which he accuses is to be found in our redemption. The God of Christians is so far from being, as he says, implacable and revengeful that you have seen it proved from text to text that the whole form and manner of our redemption comes wholly from the free, antecedent, infinite love and goodness of God toward fallen man. That the innocent Christ did not suffer to quiet an angry Deity but merely as cooperating, assisting, and uniting with that love of God which desired our salvation. That He did not suffer in our place or stead but only on our account, which is a quite different matter. And to say that He suffered in our place or stead is as absurd, as contrary to scripture, as to say that He rose from the dead and ascended into Heaven in our place and stead that we might be excused from it. For His sufferings, death, Resurrection, and Ascension are all of them equally on our account, for our sake, for our good and benefit, but none of them possible to be in our stead.

And as scripture and truth affirm that He ascended into Heaven for us, though neither scripture nor truth will allow it to be in our place and stead, so for the same reasons it is strictly true that He suffered and died for us, though no more in our place or stead nor any more desirable to be so than His Ascension into Heaven for us should be in our place and stead.

I have quoted the above passage only to show you that a defender of Deism, however acute and ingenious, has not one objection to the doctrine of our redemption but what is founded on the grossest ignorance and total mistake of the whole nature of it. But when I lay this gross ignorance to the Deists' charge, I don't mean any natural dullness, want of parts, or incapacity in them to judge aright, but only that something or other, either men or books or their own way of life has hindered their seeing the true ground and real nature of Christianity as it is in itself.

Eusebius. I would fain hope, Theophilus, that from all that has been said in the *Demonstration of the Fundamental Errors of the Plain Account*, the *Appeal to all that Doubt*,[34] etc., and the rest that follow, to these dialogues in all which Christianity and Deism, with their several merits are so plainly and with so much good will and affection toward all unbelievers represented to them, all that are serious and well-minded amongst the Deists will be prevailed upon to reconsider the matter. For though some people have been hasty enough to charge those writings with fanaticism or enthusiasm as disclaiming the use of our reason in religious matters, yet this charge can be made by none but those who, having not read them, take up with hearsay censures.

For in those books, from the beginning to the end, nothing is appealed to but the natural light of the mind and the plain, known nature of things, no one is led or desired to go one step further. The use of reason is not only allowed, but asserted and proved to be of the same service to us in things of religion as in things that relate to our senses in this world (*Demonstration of Errors of the Plain Account*).

The true ground, nature, and power of faith is opened by fully proving that this saying of Christ, "According to thy Faith, so be it done unto Thee," takes in every individual of human nature; and that all men, whether Christians, Deists, idolaters, or atheists are all of them equally men of faith, all equally and absolutely governed by it and therefore must have all that they have, salvation or damnation, strictly and solely according to their faith (*Way to Divine Knowledge*).[35] All this is so evidently proved that I can't help thinking but that every considerate reader must be forced to own it.

Theogenes. All this is well said. But let us now return to the finishing of our main point which was to show that the doctrine of a

God all love does not only not destroy the necessity of Christ's death and the infinite value and merits of it but is itself the fullest proof and strongest confirmation of both.

Theophilus. How it could enter into anyone's head to charge this doctrine with destroying the necessity and merits of Christ's death is exceeding strange.

For look where you will, no other cause or reason of the death of Christ can be found but in the love of God toward fallen man. Nor could the love of God will or accept of the death of Christ but because of its absolute necessity and availing efficacy to do all that for fallen man which the love of God would have to be done for him.

God did not, could not, have or like or desire the sufferings and death of Christ for what they were in themselves or as sufferings of the highest kind. No, the higher and greater such sufferings had been, were they only considered in themselves, the less pleasing they had been to a God that wills nothing but blessing and happiness to everything capable of it.

But all that Christ was and did and suffered was infinitely prized and highly acceptable to the love of God because all that Christ was, and did, and suffered in His own person was that which gave Him full power to be a common father of life to all that died in Adam.

Had Christ wanted[36] anything that He was or did or suffered in His own person, He could not have stood in that relation to all mankind as Adam had done. Had he not been given to the first fallen man as a seed of the woman, as a light of life, enlightening every man that comes into the world, He could not have had His seed in every man as Adam had, nor been as universal a father of life as Adam was of death. Had he not in the fitness or fullness of time become a man born of a pure virgin, the first seed of life in every man must have lain only as a seed and could not have come to the fullness of the birth of a new man in Christ Jesus. For the children can have no other state of life but that which their father first had. And therefore Christ, as the father of a regenerated human race, must first stand in the fullness of that human state which was to be derived from Him into all His children.

This is the absolute necessity of Christ's being all that He was before He became man, a necessity arising from the nature of the thing. Because He could not possibly have had the relation of a father to all mankind, nor any power to be a quickener of a life of Heaven in them, but because He was both God in Himself and a Seed of God in all of them.

Now all that Christ was, and did, and suffered after He became man is from the same necessity founded in the nature of the thing. He suffered on no other account but because that which He came to do in and for the human nature was and could be nothing else in itself but a work of sufferings and death.

A crooked line cannot become straight but by having all its crookedness given up or taken from it. And there is but one way possible in nature for a crooked line to lose its crookedness.

Now the sufferings and death of Christ stand in this kind of necessity. He was made man for our salvation, that is, He took upon Him our fallen nature to bring it out of its evil crooked state and set it again in that rectitude in which it was created.

Now there was no more two ways of doing this than there are two ways of making a crooked line to become straight.

If the life of fallen nature which Christ had taken upon Him was to be overcome by Him, then every kind of suffering and dying that was a giving up or departing from the life of fallen nature was just as necessary in the nature of the thing as that the line to be made straight must give up and part with every kind and degree of its own crookedness.

And therefore the sufferings and death of Christ were, in the nature of the thing, the only possible way of His acting contrary to and overcoming all the evil that was in the fallen state of man.

The Apostle saith, "The captain of our salvation was to be made perfect through sufferings." This was the ground and reason of His sufferings. Had He been without them, He could not have been perfect in Himself as a son of man nor the restorer of perfection in all mankind. But why so? Because His perfection as a son of man, or the captain of human salvation, could only consist in His acting in and with a spirit suitable to the first created state of perfect man; that is, He must in His spirit be as much above all the good and evil of this fallen world as the first man was.

But now, He could not show that He was of this spirit, that He was under no power of fallen nature, but lived in the perfection of the first created man. He could not do this but by showing that all the good of the earthly life was renounced by Him and that all the evil which the world, the malice of men and devils could bring upon Him could not hinder His living wholly and solely to God and doing His will on earth with the same fullness as angels do it in Heaven.

But had there been any evil in all fallen nature, whether in life, death, or Hell that had not attacked Him with all its force, He could not have been said to have overcome it. And therefore so sure as Christ as the son of man was to overcome the world, death, Hell and Satan, so sure is it that all the evils which they could possibly bring upon Him were to be felt and suffered by Him as absolutely necessary in the nature of the thing, to declare His perfection and prove His superiority over them. Surely, my friend, it is now enough proved to you how a God all love toward fallen man must love, like, desire, and delight in all the sufferings of Christ which alone could enable Him as a son of man to undo and reverse all that evil which the first man had done to all his posterity.

Eusebius. Oh, Sir, in what an adorable light is this mystery now placed. And yet in no other light than that in which the plain letter of all scripture sets it. No wrath in God, no fictitious Atonement, no folly of debtor and creditor, no suffering in Christ for suffering's sake, but a Christ suffering and dying as His same victory over death and Hell as when He rose from the dead and ascended into Heaven.

Theophilus. Sure now, Eusebius, you plainly enough see wherein the infinite merits, or the availing efficacy and glorious power of the sufferings and death of Christ consist since they were that in and through which Christ Himself came out of the state of fallen nature and got power to give the same victory to all His brethren of the human race.

Wonder not therefore that the scripture so frequently ascribe all our salvation to the sufferings and death of Christ, that we are continually referred to them as the wounds and stripes by which we are healed, as the blood by which we are washed from our sins, as the price (much above gold and precious stones) by which we are bought.

Wonder not also that in the Old Testament, its service, sacrifices, and ceremonies were instituted to typify and point at the great sacrifice of Christ, and to keep up a continual hope, strong expectation, and belief of it. And that in the New Testament, the reality, the benefits, and glorious effects of Christ our Passover being actually sacrificed for us are so joyfully repeated by every Apostle.

It is because Christ, as suffering and dying, was nothing else but Christ conquering and overcoming all the false good and the hellish evil of the fallen state of man.

His Resurrection from the grave and Ascension into Heaven, though great in themselves and necessary parts of our deliverance, were yet but the consequences and genuine effects of His sufferings and death. These were in themselves the reality of His conquest; all His great work was done and effected in them and by them, and His Resurrection and Ascension was only His entering into the possession of that which His sufferings and death had gained for Him.

Wonder not then that all the true followers of Christ, the Saints of every age, have so gloried in the cross of Christ, have imputed such great things to it, have desired nothing so much as to be partakers of it, to live in constant union with it. It is because His sufferings, His death and cross were the fullness of his victory over all the works of the Devil. Not an evil in flesh and blood, not a misery of life, not a chain of death, not a power of Hell and darkness, but were all baffled, broken, and overcome by the process of a suffering and dying Christ. Well therefore may the cross of Christ be the Glory of Christians.

Eusebius. This matter is so solidly and fully cleared up that I am almost ashamed to ask you anything further about it. Yet explain a little more, if you please, how it is that the sufferings and death of Christ gave Him power to become a *common father* of life to all that died in Adam. Or how it is that we, by virtue of them, have victory over all the evil of our fallen state.

Theophilus. You are to know, Eusebius, that the Christian religion is no arbitrary system of divine worship, but is the one true, real, and only religion of nature, that is, it is wholly founded in the nature of things, has nothing in it supernatural or contrary to the powers and demands of nature, but all that it does is only in and by and according to the workings and possibilities of nature.

A religion that is not founded in nature is all fiction and falsity and as mere a nothing as an idol. For as no creature can be or have anything in it but what it is and has from the nature of things nor have anything done to it good or harm but according to the unalterable workings of nature, so no religion can be of any service but that which works with and according to the demands of nature. Nor can any fallen creature be raised out of its fallen state, even by the omnipotence of God but according to the nature of things, or the unchangeable powers of nature; for nature is the opening and manifestation of the divine omnipotence; it is God's power-world, and therefore all that God doth is and must be done in and by the powers of nature. God though omnipotent can give no existence to any creature but it must have that existence in space and time. Time cometh out of the eternity, and space cometh out of the infinity of God—God hath an omnipotent power over them, in them, and with them, to make both of them set forth and manifest the wonders of His supernatural Deity.

Yet time can only be subservient to the omnipotence of God according to the nature of time, and space can only obey His will according to the nature of space; but neither of them can by any power be made to be in a supernatural state or be anything but what they are in their own nature.

Now right and wrong, good and evil, true and false, happiness and misery, are as unchangeable in nature as time and space. And every state and quality that is creaturely, or that can belong to any creature, has its own nature as unchangeably as time and space have theirs.

Nothing, therefore, can be done to any creature supernaturally, or in a way that is without or contrary to the powers of nature; but every thing or creature that is to be helped, that is to have any good done to it, or any evil taken out of it, can only have it done so far as the powers of nature are able and rightly directed to effect it.

And this is the true ground of all divine revelation, or that help which the supernatural Deity vouchsafes to the fallen state of man. It is not to appoint an arbitrary system of religious homage to God, but solely to point out and provide for man blinded by His fallen state that one only religion that, according to the nature of things, can possibly restore to him his lost perfection. This is the truth, the goodness, and the necessity of the Christian religion; it is true and good and necessary because it is as much the one only natural and possible way of overcoming all the evil of fallen man as light is the one only natural, possible thing that can expel darkness.

And therefore it is that all the mysteries of the gospel, however high, are yet true and necessary parts of the one religion of nature because they are no higher nor otherwise than the natural state of fallen man absolutely stands in need of. His nature cannot be helped or raised out of the evils of its present state by anything less than these mysteries; and therefore, they are in the same truth and justness to be called his natural religion as that remedy which alone has full power to remove all the evil of a disease may be justly called its natural remedy.

For a religion is not to be deemed natural because it has nothing to do with revelation; but then is it the one true religion of nature when it has everything in it that our natural state stands in need of, everything that can help us out of our present evil and raise and exalt us to all the happiness which our nature is capable of having? Supposing, therefore, the Christian scheme of redemption to be all that and nothing else in itself but that which the nature of things absolutely requires it to be, it must for that very reason have its mysteries.

For the fallen, corrupt, mortal state of man absolutely requires these two things as its only salvation. First, the divine life or the life of God must be quickened again or revived in the soul of man. Secondly, there must be a resurrection of the body in a better state after death. Now nothing in the power of man or in the things of this world can effect this salvation. If, therefore, this is to be the salvation of man, then some interposition of the Deity is absolutely necessary in the nature of the thing, or man can have no religion that is sufficiently natural, that is to say, no religion that is sufficient or equal to the wants of his nature.

Now this necessary interposition of the Deity though doing nothing but in a natural way, or according to the nature of things, must be mysterious to man because it is doing something more and higher than his senses or reason ever saw done or possible to be done, either by himself or any of the powers of this world.

And this is the true ground and nature of the mysteries of Christian redemption. They are in themselves nothing else but what the nature of things requires them to be, as natural, efficacious means of our salvation, and all their power is in a natural way, or true fitness of cause for its effect, but they are mysterious to man because brought into the scheme of our redemption by the interposition of

God to work in a way and manner above and superior to all that is seen and done in the things of the world.

The mysteries, therefore, of the gospel are so far from showing the gospel not to be the one true religion of nature that they are the greatest proof of it since they are that alone which can help man to all that good which his natural state wants to have done to it.

For instance, if the salvation of man absolutely requires the revival or restoration of the divine life in the human nature, then nothing can be the one, sufficient, true religion of nature, but that which has a natural power to do this.

What a grossness of error is it, therefore, to blame that doctrine which asserts the Incarnation of the Son of God, or the necessity of the Word being made flesh, when in the nature of the thing nothing else but this very mystery can be the natural, efficacious cause of the renewal of the divine life in the human nature, or have any natural efficacy to effect our salvation?

Having now, Eusebius, established this ground, that nothing is or can be a part of true, natural religion or have any real efficacy in and from the nature of things or in the natural fitness of cause to produce its effect, you are brought into the clear view of this truth, viz., that the religion of Deism is false, and vain, and visionary, and to be rejected by every man as the mere enthusiastic, fanatic product of pure imagination, and all for this plain reason, because it quite disregards the nature of things, stands wholly upon a supernatural ground and goes as much above and as directly contrary to the powers of nature as that faith that trusts in and prays to a wooden God.

I say not this (as is too commonly done) in the spirit of accusation, or to raise an odium. No, by no means. I have the utmost aversion to such a procedure; I would no more bring a false charge against the Deist than I would bear false witness against an Apostle. And I desire to have no other temper, spirit, or behavior toward them but such as the loving God with all my heart, and loving them as I love myself requires of me. And in this spirit of love, I charge them with visionary faith and enthusiastic religion, and only so far as I have from time to time proved that they trust to be saved by that which, according to the unchangeable nature of things, can have no power of salvation in it.

For a religion not grounded in the power and nature of things is unnatural, supernatural, superrational, and is rightly called either enthusiasm, vision, fanaticism, superstition, or idolatry, just as you please. For all these are but different names for one and the same religious delusion. And every religion is this delusion but that one religion which is required by and has its efficacy in and from the unchangeable nature of things.

And thus stands the matter betwixt the Deists and myself. If I knew how to do them or the subject more justice, I would gladly do it; having no desire either for them or myself but that we may all of us be delivered from everything that separates us from God, all equal sharers of every blessing that He has for human nature, all united in that spirit of love and goodness for which he created us, and all blessed with that faith and hope to which the God of love has called us as the one, only, possible, natural, and full means of ever finding ourselves saved and redeemed from all the evils both of time and eternity.

And now, Eusebius, upon this ground, viz., (1) That there is but one true religion, and that it is the religion of nature. (2) That a religion has no pretence to be considered as the religion of nature because it rejects divine revelation and has only human reason for its guide, but wholly and solely because it has every good in it that the natural state of man wants and can receive from religion. (3) That nothing can be any religious good, or have any real efficacy as a means of salvation, but only that which has its efficacy in and from the natural power of things, or the fitness and sufficiency of cause to produce its effect. (4) That the religion of the gospel, in all its mysteries and doctrines, is wholly grounded in the natural powers of things and their fitness to produce their effects. Upon this ground, I come to answer your question, viz., how it is that the sufferings and death of Christ gave Him full power to become a common father of life to all those that died in Adam. Or how it is that we by virtue of them are delivered out of all the evils of our fallen state.

The sufferings and death of Christ have no supernatural effect, or that is above, or contrary to nature. Because the thing itself is impossible; for a thing is only therefore impossible because the nature of things will not allow of it.

The fall of all mankind in Adam is no supernatural event or

effect, but the natural and necessary consequence of our relation to him. Could Adam at his fall into this earthy[37] life have absolutely overcome every power of the world, the flesh, and the devil in the same spirit as Christ did, he had been his own redeemer, had risen out of his fall, and ascended into Paradise and been the father of a paradisiacal offspring, just as Christ when He had overcome them all rose from the dead and ascended into heaven. But Adam did not do this because it was as impossible in the nature of the thing as for a beast to raise itself into an angel. If therefore man is to come out of his fallen state, there must be something found out that, according to the nature of things, hath power to effect it. For it can no more be done supernaturally by anything else than it could by Adam.

Now the matter stood thus: The seed of all mankind was in the loins of fallen Adam. This was unalterable in the nature of the thing and therefore all mankind must come forth in his fallen state.

Neither can they ever be in any state whatever, whether earthly or heavenly, but by having an earthly man or a heavenly man for their father. For mankind as such must of all necessity be born of and have that nature which it hath from a man. And this is the true ground and absolute necessity of the one mediator, the man Christ Jesus. For seeing mankind as such must have that birth and nature which they have from man, seeing they never could have had any relation to Paradise or any possibility of partaking of it but because they had a paradisiacal man for their father, never could have had any relation to this earthly world, or any possibility of being born earthly but because they had an earthly man for their father; and seeing all this must be unalterably so forever, it plainly follows that there was an utter impossibility for the seed of Adam ever to come out of its fallen state or ever have another or better life than they had from Adam unless such a son of man could be brought into existence as had the same relation to all mankind as Adam had, was as much in them all as Adam was, and had as full power according to the nature of things to give a heavenly life to all the seed in Adam's loins as Adam had to bring them forth in earthly flesh and blood.

And now, Sir, that Christ was this very son of man, standing in the same fullness of relation to all mankind as Adam did, having his seed as really in them all as Adam had, and as truly and fully qualified according to the nature of things to be a common and universal father of life as Adam was of death to all the human race, shall in a word or two be made as plain and undeniable as that two and two are four.

The doctrine of our redemption absolutely asserts that the seed of Christ was sown into the first fallen father of mankind called the Seed of the Woman, the Bruiser of the Serpent, the ingrafted Word of life, called again in the gospel that Light which lighteth every man that cometh into the world. Therefore, Christ was in all men in that same fullness of the relation of a father to all mankind as Adam the first was. Secondly, Christ was born of Adam's flesh and blood, took the human nature upon Him and therefore stood as a human creature in the same relation to mankind as Adam did. Nothing therefore was further wanting in Christ to make Him as truly a natural father of life to all mankind as Adam was at first, but God's appointment of Him to that end.

For as Adam could not have been the natural father of mankind but because God created and appointed him for that end, so Christ could not have been the natural regenerator or redeemer of a heavenly life that was lost in all mankind but because God had appointed and brought him into the world for that end. Now that God did this, that Christ came into the world by divine appointment to be the Savior, the resurrection and life of all mankind is a truth as evident from scripture as that Adam was the first man.

And thus it appears in the utmost degree of plainness and certainty that Christ in His single person was, according to the nature of things, as fully qualified to be a common Redeemer as Adam was in his single person to be a common father of all mankind. He had his seed in all mankind as Adam had; He had the human nature as Adam had; and He had the same divine appointment as Adam had. But Christ, however qualified to be our Redeemer, could not be actually such till He had gone through and done all that by which our redemption was to be effected.

Adam, however qualified, yet could not be the father of a paradisiacal offspring till he had stood out his trial and fixed himself victorious over everything that could make trial of him. In like manner, Christ, however qualified, could not be the Redeemer of all mankind till He had also stood out His trial, had overcome all that by which Adam was overcome and had fixed Himself triumphantly in that Paradise which Adam had lost.

Now as Adam's trial was whether he would keep himself in his paradisiacal state, above and free from all that was good and evil in this earthly world, so Christ's trial was whether, as a son of man and loaded with the infirmities of fallen Adam, sacrificed to all that which the rage and malice of the world, Hell, and devils could possibly do to Him, whether He in the midst of all these evils could live and die with His spirit as contrary to them, as much above them, as unhurt by them, as Adam should have lived in Paradise.

And then it was that everything which had overcome Adam was overcome by Christ, and Christ's victory did in the nature of the thing as certainly and fully open an entrance for him and all his seed into Paradise as Adam's fall cast him and all his seed into the prison and captivity of this earthly, bestial world.

Nothing supernatural came to pass in either case but Paradise lost and Paradise regained according to the nature of things, or the real efficacy of cause to produce its effect.

Thus is your question fully answered, viz., how and why the sufferings and death of Christ enabled Him to be the author of life to all that died in Adam. Just as the fall of Adam into this world under the power of sin, death, Hell, and the Devil enabled him to be the common father of death, that is, was the natural, unavoidable cause of our being born under the same captivity, just so that life and sufferings and death of Christ which declared His breaking out from them and superiority over them must in the nature of the thing as much enable Him to be the common author of life, that is, must as certainly be the full, natural, efficacious cause of our inheriting life from Him. Because by what Christ was in Himself, by what He was in us by His whole state, character, and the divine appointment, we all had that natural union with Him and dependence upon Him as our Head in the way of redemption, as we had with Adam as our head in the way of our natural birth. So that as it must be said that because Adam fell, we must of all necessity be heirs of his fallen state, so with the same truth and from the same necessity of the thing, it must be said that because Christ our Head is risen victorious out of our fallen state we as His members and having His seed within us must be and are made heirs of all His glory. Because in all respects we are as strictly, as intimately connected with and related to Him as the one Redeemer as we are to Adam as the one father of all mankind. So that Christ by His sufferings and death become[38] in all of us our wisdom, our righteousness, our justification and redemption is the same sober and solid truth as Adam by his fall become in all of us our foolishness, our impurity, our corruption, and death.

And now, my friends, look back upon all that has been said and then tell me, is it possible more to exalt or magnify the infinite merits and availing efficacy of the sufferings and death of Christ than is done by this doctrine? Or whether everything that is said of them in scripture is not here proved from the very nature of the thing to be absolutely true? And again, whether it is not sufficiently proved to you that the sufferings and death of Christ are not only consistent with the doctrine of a God all love, but are the fullest and most absolute proof of it?

Eusebius. Indeed, Theophilus, you have so fully done for us all that we wanted to have done that we are now ready to take leave of you. As for my part, I want to return home to enjoy my Bible and delight myself with reading it in this comfortable light in which you have set the whole ground and nature of our redemption. I am now in full possession of this glorious truth that God is mere love, the most glorious truth that can possess and edify the heart of man. It drives every evil out of the soul and gives life to every spark of goodness that can possibly be kindled in it. Everything in religion is made amiable by being a service of love to the God of love.

No sacrifices, sufferings, and death have any place in religion but to satisfy and fulfill that love of God which could not be satisfied without our salvation. If the Son of God is not spared, if He is delivered up to the rage and malice of men, devils, and Hell, it is because, had we not had such a captain of our salvation made perfect through sufferings, it never could have been sung, "Oh death, where is thy sting, Oh grave, where is thy victory!" It never could have been true that "as by one man sin entered into the world, and death by sin, so by one man came the resurrection of the dead." It never could have been said "that as in Adam all die, so in Christ shall all be made alive."

Therefore, dear Theophilus, adieu. God is love, and he that hath learnt to live in the spirit of love hath learnt to live and dwell in God. Love was the beginner of all the works of God, and from eternity to eternity nothing can come from God but a variety of wonders and works of love over all nature and creature.

WILLIAM LAW

Theophilus. God prosper, Eusebius, this spark of Heaven in your soul; may it, like the seraphim's coal taken from the altar, purify your heart from all its uncleanness. But before you leave me, I beg one more conversation to be on the practical part of the spirit of love, that so doctrine and practice, hearing and doing, may go hand in hand.

The End of the Second Dialogue

NOTES

29. For to: in order to.
30. Blister . . . cut off: Law refers to various medical procedures current in his time. Blister: to raise a blister; purge: to empty the stomach, or more usually, the bowels; scarify: to make slight incisions; trepanned: to cut through the bone, especially the skull, with a trepan or surgical saw.
31. The current of scholastic divines: Law here means the Reformation theologians, primarily Luther and Calvin, who taught a penal view of the Atonement. Law later names Hugo Grotius (1583–1645), the Dutch jurist and theologian, and Bishop Edward Stillingfleet (1635–1699), for their teaching helps to promote a less harsh understanding of the Atonement and to answer the anti-Trinitarianism of Faustus Socinus (1539–1604)—the "founder" of Unitarianism—and the Deists.
32. Broke: broken.
33. See *Deism fairly stated and fully vindicated*, p. 41 (Law's note, in reference to an unsigned pamphlet published in 1746 but the work primarily of Thomas Chubb (1679–1747).
34. Eusebius refers to various works by Law. See note 17, above.
35. (*Demonstration* . . . *Way to Divine Knowledge*): Law continues (*through Eusebius*) to refer to his own books. See the reference above in n.17.
36. Wanted: stood deficient in.
37. Earthy: As above (cf. p. 00), Law uses "earthy" to express the state of being bound to, contained within, and made up by the element earth.
38. Become: may become, a conditional or subjunctive use, paralleled by the repetition later in the sentence.

The Third Dialogue

Eusebius. You have shown great good will toward us, Theophilus, in desiring another meeting before we leave you. But yet I seem to myself to have no need of that which you have proposed by this day's conversation. For this doctrine of the spirit of love cannot have more power over me or be more deeply rooted in me than it is already. It has so gained and got possession of my whole heart that everything else must be under its dominion. I can do nothing else but love; it is my whole nature, I have no taste for anything else. Can this matter be carried higher in practice?

Theophilus. No higher, Eusebius. And was this the true state of your heart, you would bid fair to leave the world as Elijah did; or like Enoch to have it said of you that you lived wholly to love, and was not. For was there nothing but this divine love alive in you, your fallen flesh and blood would be in danger of being quite burnt up by it. What you have said of yourself, you have spoken in great sincerity but in a total ignorance of yourself and the true nature of the spirit of divine love. You are as yet only charmed with the sight, or rather the sound of it; its real birth is as yet unfelt and unfound in you. Your natural complexion has a great deal of the animal meekness and softness of the lamb and the dove, your blood and spirit are of this turn; and therefore a God all love and a religion all love quite transport you; and you are so delighted with it that you fancy you have nothing in you but this God and religion of love. But, my friend, bear with me if I tell you that all this is only the good part of the spirit of this bestial world in you and may be in any unregenerate man that is of your complexion. It is so far from being a genuine fruit of divine love that if it be not well looked to, it may prove a real hindrance of it as it oftentimes does by its appearing to be that which it is not.

You have quite forgot all that was said in the letter to you on the spirit of love, that it is a birth in the soul that can only come

461

forth in its proper time and place and from its proper causes. Now nothing that is a birth can be taken in or brought into the soul by any notional conception or delightful apprehension of it. You may love it as much as you please, think it the most charming thing in the world, fancy everything but dross and dung in comparison of it, and yet have no more of its birth in you than the blind man has of that light of which he has got a most charming notion. His blindness still continues the same; he is at the same distance from the light because light can only be had by a birth of itself in seeing eyes. It is thus with the spirit of love; it is nowhere, but where it rises up as a birth.

Eusebius. But if I am got no further than this, what good have I from giving in so heartily to all that you have said of this doctrine? And to what end have you taken so much pains to assert and establish it?

Theophilus. Your error lies in this; you confound two things which are entirely distinct from each other. You make no difference betwixt the doctrine that only sets forth the nature, excellency, and necessity of the spirit of love, and the spirit of love itself, which yet are two things so different that you may be quite full of the former and at the same time quite empty of the latter. I have said everything that I could to show you the truth, excellency, and necessity of the spirit of love. It is of infinite importance to you to be well established in the belief of this doctrine. But all that I have said of it is only to induce and encourage you to buy it at its own price and to give all that for it which alone can purchase it. But if you think (as you plainly do) that you have got it because you are so highly pleased with that which you have heard of it, you only embrace the shadow instead of the substance of that which you ought to have.

Eusebius. What is the price that I must give for it?

Theophilus. You must give up all that you are, and all that you have from fallen Adam, for all that you are and have from him is that life of flesh and blood which cannot enter into the Kingdom of God.

Adam, after his fall, had nothing that was good in him, nothing that could inherit an eternal life in Heaven but the Bruiser of the Serpent or the seed of the Son of God that was inspoken into him. Everything else in him was devoted to death, that this incorruptible seed of the word might grow up into a new name in Christ Jesus.

All the doctrine of God's reprobation and election relates

wholly and solely to these two things, viz., the earthly, bestial nature from Adam, and the incorruptible Seed of the Word, or the Immanuel in every man.

Nothing is elected, is foreseen predestinated, or called according to the purpose of God, but this seed of the new man. Because the one eternal, unchangeable purpose of God toward man is only this, namely, that man should be a heavenly image or son of God; and therefore nothing can be elected or called according to the purpose of God but this seed of a heavenly birth, because nothing else is able to answer and fulfill the purpose of God; but everything else that is in man, his whole earthly, bestial nature, is from sin and is quite contrary to God's purpose in the creation of man.

On the other hand, nothing is reprobated, rejected, or cast out by God but the earthly nature which came from the fall of Adam. This is the only vessel of wrath, the son of perdition, that can have no share in the promises and blessings of God.

Here you have the whole unalterable ground of divine election and reprobation; it relates not to any particular number of people or division of mankind, but solely to the two natures that are, both of them without exception, in every individual of mankind. All that is earthly, serpentine, and devilish in every man is reprobated and doomed to destruction; and the heavenly seed of the new birth in every man is that which is chosen, ordained, and called to eternal life.

Election therefore and reprobation as respecting salvation equally relate to every man in the world because every man as such hath that in him which only is elected, and that in him which only is reprobated, namely, the earthly nature and the heavenly seed of the Word of God.

Now all this is evident from the very nature of the thing; as soon as you but suppose man at his fall to have a power of redemption or deliverance from the evil of his fallen nature engrafted into him, you then have the first unchangeable ground of election and reprobation; you are infallibly shown what it is that God elects and reprobates and the absolute impossibility of anything else being reprobated by God but that fallen, evil nature from which he is to be redeemed or of anything else being elected by God, but that seed of a new birth which is to bring forth his redemption.

Here therefore you have a full deliverance from all perplexity upon this matter and may rest yourself upon this great, comfortable, and most certain truth, that no other election or reprobation with regard to salvation ever did or can belong to any one individual son of Adam, but that very same election and reprobation which both of them happened to and took place in Adam's individual person. For all that which was in Adam, both as fallen and redeemed, must of all necessity be in every son of Adam; and no man can possibly stand in any other relation to God than Adam did, and therefore cannot have either more or less, or any other divine election and reprobation than Adam had. For from the moment of man's redemption which began at the fall when the incorruptible Seed of the Word was given into Adam, every son of Adam to the end of the world must come into it under one and the same election and reprobation with regard to God. Because the whole earthly nature from which man was to be redeemed, and the Seed of the Word by which he was to be redeemed, were both of them in every man, one as certainly as the other.

Now this being the inward, essential state of every man born into the world, having in himself all that is elected and all that is reprobated by God, hence it is that in order to publish the truth and certainty of such election and reprobation and the truth and certainty of that two-fold nature in man on which it is grounded, hence it is that the Spirit of God in holy scripture represents this matter to us by such outward figures as are yet in themselves not figurative but real proofs of it.

This is first of all done under the figures of Cain and Abel, the two first births from Adam, where the one is murdered by the other hereby demonstrating to us by this contrariety and difference of these two first births the inward real state of the father of them, namely, that the same two-fold nature was in him that discovered itself in these two first births from him.

The same thing is age after age set forth in variety of figures, more especially in Ishmael and Isaac, in Esau and Jacob. And all this, only further to confirm and establish this great truth, viz., that such strife and contrariety as appeared in the sons of the same father were not only outward representations, but full proofs of that inward strife and contrariety which not only existed in their fathers but universally in every human creature. For Cain and Abel had not come from Adam but because both their natures were antecedently in him and in the same state of opposition and contrariety to each other. And as Cain and Abel were no other than the genuine effects of the two-fold state which Adam as fallen and redeemed was then in, so every man, descended from Adam, is in himself infallibly all that which Adam was, and has as certainly his own Cain and Abel within himself as Adam had. And from the beginning to the end of the human race, all that which came to pass so remarkably in the births of Cain and Abel, Ishmael and Isaac, Esau and Jacob, all that same some way or other more or less comes to pass in every individual of mankind. In one man, his own Abel is murdered by his own Cain, and in another his own Jacob overcomes his own Esau that was born with him.

And all the good or the evil that we bring forth in our lives is from nothing else but from the strife of these two natures within us and their victory over one another. Which strife no son of Adam could ever have known anything of had not the free grace and mercy of God chosen and called all mankind to a new birth of Heaven in and out of their corrupt and fallen souls. No possible war or strife of good against evil could be in fallen man but by his having from God a seed of life in him, ordained and predestinated to overcome his earthly nature. For that which is put into him by God as the power of his redemption must be contrary to that from which he is to be redeemed.

And thus a war of good against evil set up within us by the free grace and mercy of God to us is the greatest of all demonstrations that there is but one election and but one reprobation, and that all that God rejects and reprobates is nothing else but that corrupt nature which every individual man, Abel as well as Cain, has in himself from Adam as fallen; and that all that God elects, predestinates, calls, justifies, and glorifies is nothing else but that heavenly seed which every individual man, Pharaoh as well as Moses, has in himself from Adam as redeemed.

And thus you have an unerring key to all that is said in scripture of the election falling upon Abel, Isaac, and Jacob, etc., and of the reprobation falling upon Cain, Ishmael, and Esau, not because God has respect to persons or that all men did not stand before Him in the same covenant of redemption; but the scriptures speak thus, that the true nature of God's election and reprobation may thereby be made manifest to the world.

For the earthly nature, which God only reprobates, having

broke forth in predominancy in Cain, Ishmael, and Esau, they became proper figures of that which God reprobates and were used by God as such. And the heavenly seed, which is alone elected to eternal glory, having broke forth in predominancy in Abel, Isaac, Jacob, etc., they became proper figures of that which God only elects and were used by God as such.

Nothing is here to be understood personally or according to the flesh of these persons on either side, but all that is said of them is only as they are figures of the earthly nature and heavenly seed in every man. For nothing is reprobated in Cain but that very same which is reprobated in Abel, viz. the earthly nature, nor is anything elected in Jacob but that very same which is equally elected in Esau, viz. the heavenly seed.

And now, Gentlemen, you may easily apprehend how and why a God in whose holy Deity no spark of wrath or partiality can possibly arise, but who is from eternity to eternity only flowing forth in love, goodness, and blessing to everything capable of it, could yet say of the children before they were born, or had done either good or evil, Jacob have I loved, and Esau have I hated. It is because Esau signifies the earthly, bestial nature that came from sin, and Jacob signifies the incorruptible seed of the word that is to overcome Esau and change his mortal[39] into immortality.

But now I stop, for you may perhaps think that I have here made a digression from our proposed subject.

Eusebius. A digression you may call it, if you please, Theophilus, but it is such a digression as has entirely prevented my ever having one more anxious thought about God's decrees of election and reprobation.

The matter stands now in open daylight, notwithstanding that thickness of learned darkness under which it has been hidden from the time of St. Austin to this day. And now, Sir, proceed as you please to lay open all my defects in the spirit of love; for I am earnestly desirous of being set right in so important a matter.

Theogenes. Let me first observe to Theophilus that I am afraid the matter is much worse with me than it is with you. For though this doctrine seems to have got all my heart as it is a doctrine, yet I am continually thrown out of it in practice and find myself as daily under the power of my old tempers and passions as I was before I was so full of this doctrine.

Theophilus. You are to know, my friends, that every kind of virtue and goodness may be brought into us by two different ways. They may be taught us outwardly by men, by rules and precepts, and they may be inwardly born in us, as the genuine birth of our own renewed spirit. In the former way, as we learn them only from men by rules and documents of instruction, they at best only change our outward behavior and leave our heart in its natural state and only put our passions under a forced restraint which will occasionally break forth in spite of the dead letter of precept and doctrine. Now this way of learning and attaining goodness, though thus imperfect, is yet absolutely necessary in the nature of the thing, and must first have its time, and place, and work in us; yet it is only for a time, as the law was a schoolmaster to the gospel. We must first be babes in doctrine as well as in strength before we can be men. But of all this outward instruction whether from good men or the letter of scripture, it must be said as the Apostle saith of the law, "that it maketh nothing perfect," and yet is highly necessary in order to perfection.

The true perfection and profitableness of the holy written word of God is fully set forth by St. Paul to Timothy: "From a child," saith he, "thou hast known the scriptures which are able to make thee wise unto salvation, which is by faith in Christ Jesus." Now these scriptures were the law and the prophets, for Timothy had known no other from his youth. And as they, so all other scriptures since have no other good or benefit in them but as they lead and direct us to a salvation that is not to be had in themselves but from faith in Christ Jesus. Their teaching is only to teach us where to seek and to find the fountain and source of all light and knowledge.

Of the law, saith the Apostle, "it was a schoolmaster to Christ." Of the prophets, he saith the same. "Ye have," says he, "a more sure word of prophecy, whereunto you do well, that ye take heed as unto a light that shineth in a dark place until the day dawn, and the daystar ariseth in your hearts." The same thing is to be affirmed of the letter of the New Testament; it is but our schoolmaster unto Christ, a light like that of prophecy to which we are to take great heed until Christ as the dawning of the day or the daystar ariseth in our hearts. Nor can the thing possibly be otherwise; no instruction that comes under the form of words can do more for us than sounds and words can do; they can only direct us to something that is better than themselves, that can be the true light, life, spirit, and power of holiness in us.

Eusebius. I cannot deny what you say, and yet it seems to me to derogate from[40] scripture.

Theophilus. Would you then have me to say that the written word of God is that Word of God which liveth and abideth forever; that Word, which is the wisdom and power of God; that Word, which was with God, which was God by whom all things were made; that Word of God, which was made flesh for the redemption of the world; that Word of God, of which we must be born again; that Word which lighteth every man that cometh into the world; that Word, which in Christ Jesus is become wisdom and righteousness and sanctification in us; would you have me say that all this is to be understood of the written word of God? But if this cannot possibly be, then all that I have said is granted, namely, that Jesus is alone that Word of God that can be the Light, life, and salvation of fallen man. Or how is it possible more to exalt the letter of scripture than by owning it to be a true, outward, verbal direction to the one only true Light and salvation of man?

Suppose you had been a true disciple of John the Baptist whose only office was to prepare the way to Christ, how could you have more magnified his office or declared your fidelity to him than by going from his teaching to be taught by that Christ to whom he directed you? The Baptist was indeed a burning and a shining light, and so are the holy scriptures; "but he was not that Light, but was sent to bear witness of that Light. That was the true Light, which lighteth every man that cometh into the world."

What a folly would it be to say that you had undervalued the office and character of John the Baptist because he was not allowed to be the Light itself but only a true witness of it and guide to it? Now if you can show that the written word in the Bible can have any other or higher office or power than such a ministerial one as the Baptist had, I am ready to hear you.

Eusebius. There is no possibility of doing that.

Theophilus. But if that is not possible to be done, then you are come to the full proof of this point, viz., that there are two ways of attaining knowledge, goodness, virtue, etc., the one by the ministry of outward, verbal instruction either by men or books, and the other by an inward birth of divine light, goodness, and virtue in our own renewed spirit, and that the former is only in order to the latter and of no benefit to us but as it carries us further than itself, to be united in heart and spirit with the Light and Word and Spirit of God. Just as the Baptist had been of no benefit to his disciples unless he had been their guide from himself to Christ.

But to come now closer to our subject in hand.

From this two-fold light or teaching there necessarily arises a two-fold state of virtue and goodness. For such as the teacher or teaching is, such is the state and manner of the goodness that can be had from it. Every effect must be according to the cause that produces it. If you learn virtue and goodness only from outward means, from men, or books, you may be virtuous and good according to time and place and outward forms; you may do works of humility, works of love and benevolence, use times and forms of prayer; all this virtue and goodness is suitable to this kind of teaching and may very well be had from it. But the spirit of prayer, the spirit of love, and the spirit of humility or of any other virtue are only to be attained by the operation of the Light and Spirit of God, not outwardly teaching but inwardly bringing forth a newborn spirit within us.

And now let me tell you both, that it is much to be feared that you as yet stand only under this outward teaching; your good works are only done under obedience to such rules, precepts, and doctrines as your reason assents to, but are not the fruits of a newborn spirit within you. But till you are thus renewed in the spirit of your minds, your virtues are only taught practices and grafted upon a corrupt bottom. Everything you do will be a mixture of good and bad; your humility will help you to pride, your charity to others will give nourishment to your own self-love, and as your prayers increase, so will the opinion of your own sanctity. Because till the heart is purified to the bottom and has felt the axe at the root of its evil (which cannot be done by outward instruction) everything that proceeds from it partakes of its impurity and corruption.

Now that Theogenes is only under the law or outward instruction is too plain from the complaint that he made of himself. For notwithstanding his progress in the doctrine of love, he finds all the passions of his corrupt nature still alive in him, and himself only altered in doctrine and opinion.

The same may be well suspected of you, Eusebius, who are so mistaken in the spirit of love that you fancy yourself to be wholly

469

possessed of it from no other ground but because you embrace it, as it were, with open arms, and think of nothing but living under the power of it. Whereas if the spirit of love was really born in you from its own seed, you would account for its birth and power in you in quite another manner than you have here done; you would have known the price that you had paid for it, and how many deaths you had suffered before the spirit of love came to life in you.

Eusebius. But surely, Sir, imperfect as our virtues are, we may yet, I hope, be truly said to be in a state of grace; and if so, we are under something more than mere outward instruction. Besides you very well know that it is a principle with both of us to expect all our goodness from the Spirit of God dwelling and working in us. We live in faith and hope of the divine operation; and therefore I must needs say that your censure upon us seems to be more severe than just.

Theophilus. Dear Eusebius, I censure neither of you, nor have I said one word by way of accusation. So far from it that I love and approve the state you are both in. It is good and happy for Theogenes that he feels and confesses that his natural tempers are not yet subdued by doctrine and precept. It is good and happy for you also that you are so highly delighted with the doctrine of love, for by this means each of you have your true preparation for further advancement. And though your state has this difference, yet the same error was common to both of you. You both of you thought you had as much of the spirit of love as you could, or ought to have; and therefore Theogenes wondered he had no more benefit from it, and you wondered that I should desire to lead you further into it. And therefore, to deliver you from this error, I have desired this conference upon the practical ground of the spirit of love that you may neither of you lose the benefit of that good state in which you stand.

Eusebius. Pray therefore proceed as you please. For we have nothing so much at heart as to have the truth and purity of this divine love brought forth in us. For as it is the highest perfection that I adore in God, so I can neither wish nor desire anything for myself but to be totally governed by it. I could as willingly consent to lose all my being as to find the power of love lost in my soul. Neither doctrine, nor mystery, nor precept has any delight for me but as it calls forth the birth, and growth, and exercise of that spirit which doth all that it doth toward God and man under the one law of love. Whatever therefore you can say to me, either to increase the power, manifest the defects, or remove the impediments of divine love in my soul will be heartily welcome to me.

Theophilus. I apprehend that you don't yet know what divine love is in itself, nor what is its nature and power in the soul of man. For divine love is perfect peace and joy, it is a freedom from all disquiet, it is all content and mere happiness and makes everything to rejoice in itself. Love is the Christ of God; wherever it comes, it comes as the blessing and happiness of every natural life, as the restorer of every lost perfection, a redeemer from all evil, a fulfiller of all righteousness, and a peace of God which passeth all understanding. Through all the universe of things, nothing is uneasy, unsatisfied, or restless, but because it is not governed by love, or because its nature has not reached or attained the full birth of the spirit of love. For when that is done, every hunger is satisfied, and all complaining, murmuring, accusing, resenting, revenging, and striving are as totally suppressed and overcome as the coldness, thickness, and horror of darkness are suppressed and overcome by the breaking forth of the light. If you ask why the spirit of love cannot be displeased, cannot be disappointed, cannot complain, accuse, resent, or murmur, it is because divine love desires nothing but itself; it is its own good, it has all when it has itself because nothing is good but itself and its own working; for love is God, and he that dwelleth in God, dwelleth in love; tell me now, Eusebius, are you thus blessed in the spirit of love?

Eusebius. Would you have me tell you that I am an angel? And without the infirmities of human flesh and blood?

Theophilus. No, but I would have you judge of your state of love by these angelical tempers and not by any fervor or heat that you find in yourself. For just so much and so far as you are freed from the folly of all earthly affections, from all disquiet, trouble, and complaint about this or that, just so much and so far is the spirit of love come to life in you. For divine love is a new life and new nature and introduces you into a new world; it puts an end to all your former opinions, notions, and tempers; it opens new senses in you and makes you see high to be low, and low to be high, wisdom to be foolishness, and foolishness wisdom; it makes prosperity and adversity, praise and dispraise to be equally nothing. "When I was a child," saith the Apostle, "I thought as a child, I spake as a child, but when I became a man, I put away childish things." Whilst man is under the power of nature, governed only by worldly wisdom, his life (however old he may be) is quite childish; everything about him only awakens childish thoughts and pursuits in him; all that he sees and hears, all that he desires or fears, likes or dislikes; that which he gets and that which he loses; that which he hath and that which he hath not serve only to carry him from this fiction of evil to that fiction of good, from one vanity of peace to another vanity of trouble. But when divine love is born in the soul, all childish images of good and evil are done away and all the sensibility of them is lost, as the stars lose their visibility when the sun is risen.

Theogenes. That this is the true power of the spirit of divine love, I am fully convinced from my own uneasiness at finding that my natural tempers are not overcome by it. For whence could I have this trouble but because that little dawning that I have of the spirit of love in me maketh just demands to be the one light, breath, and power of my life and to have all that is within me overcome and governed by it. And therefore I find I must either silence this small voice of new-risen love within me or have no rest from complaints and self-condemnation till my whole nature is brought into subjection to it.

Theophilus. Most rightly judged, Theogenes; and now we are fairly brought to the one great practical point on which all our proficiency in the spirit of love entirely depends. Namely, that all that we are, and all that we have from Adam as fallen, must be given up, absolutely denied and resisted, if the birth of divine love is to be brought forth in us. For all that we are by nature is in full contrariety to this divine love, nor can it be otherwise; a death to itself is its only cure, and nothing else can make it subservient to good, just as darkness cannot be altered or made better in itself or transmuted into light; it can only be subservient to the light by being lost in it and swallowed up by it.

Now this was the first state of man; all the natural properties of his creaturely life were hid in God, united in God, and glorified by the life of God manifested in them, just as the nature and qualities of darkness are lost and hid when enlightened and glorified by the light. But when man fell from, or died to the divine life, all the natural properties of his creaturely life, having lost their union in and with God, broke forth in their own natural division, contrariety, and war against one another, just as the darkness, when it has lost the light, must show forth its own coldness, horror, and other uncomfortable qualities. And as darkness, though in the utmost contrariety to light, is yet absolutely necessary to it and without which no manifestation or visibility of light could possibly be, so it is with the natural properties of the creaturely life; they are in themselves all contrariety to the divine life, and yet the divine life cannot be communicated but in them and by them.

Eusebius. I never read or heard of the darkness being necessary to light. It has been generally considered as a negative thing that was nothing in itself and only signified an absence of light; but your doctrine not only supposes darkness to be something positive that hath a strength and substantiality in itself, but also to be antecedent to the light because necessary to bring it into manifestation. I am almost afraid to hear more of this doctrine. It sounds harsh to my ears.

Theophilus. Don't be frighted, Eusebius. I will lead you into no doctrine but what is strictly conformable to the letter of scripture and the most orthodox piety. The scripture saith, "God is Light, and in Him is no darkness at all"; therefore the scripture affirmeth light to be superior, absolutely separate from, and eternally antecedent to darkness; and so do I. In this scripture you have a noble and true account of light, what it is, where it is and was, and always must be. It can never change its state or place, be altered in itself, be anywhere or in another manner than as it was and will be from and to all eternity. When God said, "Let there be Light, and there was Light," no change happened to eternal light itself, nor did any light then begin to be; but the darkness of this world then only began to receive a power or operation of the eternal light upon it, which it had not before; or eternity then began to open some resemblance of its own glory in the dark elements and shadows of time. And thus it is that I assert the priority and glory of light and put all darkness under its feet, as impossible to be anything else but its footstool.

Eusebius. I am quite delighted with this. But tell me now how it is that light can only be manifested in and by darkness.

Theophilus. The scripture saith that "God dwelleth in the Light, to which no man can approach": therefore the scripture teacheth that light in itself is and must be invisible to man, that it cannot be approached or made manifest to him but in and by something that is not light. And this is all that I said, and the very same thing that I said, when I affirmed that light cannot be manifested or have any visibility to created eyes, but in and through and by the darkness.

Light as it is in itself is only in the supernatural Deity; and that is the reason why no man or any created being can approach to it or have any sensibility of it, as it is in itself. And yet no light can come into this world but that in which God dwelt before any world was created. No light can be in time but that which was the light of eternity. If therefore the supernatural light is to manifest something of its incomprehensible glory, and make itself in some degree sensible and visible to the creature, this supernatural light must enter into nature, it must put on materiality. Now darkness is the one only materiality of light, in and through which it can become the object of creaturely eyes, and till there is darkness, there is no possible medium or power through which the supernatural light can manifest something of itself or have any of its glory visible to created eyes. And the reason why darkness can only be the materiality of light is this, it is because darkness is the one only ground of all nature and of all materiality, whether in Heaven or on earth. And therefore everything that is creaturely in nature, that has any form, figure, or substance from the highest angel in Heaven to the lowest thing upon earth, hath all that it hath of figure, form, or substantiality only and solely from darkness. Look at the glittering glory of the diamond and then you see the one medium through which the glory of the incomprehensible light can make some discovery or manifestation of itself. It matters not whether you consider Heaven or earth, eternal or temporal nature, nothing in either state can be capable of visible glory, brightness, or illumination but that which standeth in the state of the diamond and has its own thickness of darkness. And if the universe of eternal and temporal nature is everywhere light, it is because it has darkness everywhere for its dwelling place. Light, you know, is by variety of modern experiments declared to be material; the experiments are not to be disputed. And yet all these experiments are only so many proofs, not of the materiality of light, but of our doctrine, viz., that materiality is always along with visible light, and also that light can only open and display something of itself in and by darkness as its body of manifestation and visibility. But light cannot possibly be material because all materiality as such, be it what and where it will, is nothing else but so much darkness. And therefore to suppose light to be material is the same absurdity as to suppose it to be darkness; for so much materiality is so much darkness, and it is impossible to be otherwise. Again, all matter has but one nature; it admits of neither more nor less, but wherever it is, all that is material is equally there. If therefore light was material, all the materiality in the world must be light, and equally so. For no materiality could be light unless light was essential to matter as such, no more than any materiality could be extended unless extension was essential to matter as such.

Eusebius. What is it then that you understand by the materiality of light?

Theophilus. No more than I understand by the materiality of the wisdom, mercy, and goodness of God when they are made intelligible and credible to me by the materiality of paper and ink, etc. For light is as distinct from and superior to all that materiality, in and by which it gives forth some visibility of itself, as the wisdom, mercy, and goodness of God are distinct from and superior to all that written materiality, in and through which they are made in some degree intelligible and credible to human minds.

The incomprehensible Deity can make no outward revelation of His will, wisdom, and goodness but by articulate sounds, voices, or letters written on tables of stone or such like materiality. Just so the invisible, inaccessible, supernatural light can make no outward visibility of itself but through such darkness of materiality as is capable of receiving its illumination. But as the divine will, wisdom, and goodness, when making outward revelation of themselves by the materiality of things, are not therefore material, so neither is the light material when it outwardly reveals something of its invisible, incomprehensible splendor and glory by and through the materiality of darkness.

All light then that is natural and visible to the creature, whether in Heaven or on earth, is nothing else but so much darkness illuminated; and that which is called the materiality of light is only the materiality of darkness in which the light incorporateth itself.

For light can be only that same invisible, unapproachable thing which it always was in God from all eternity. And that which is called the difference of light is only the difference of that darkness through which the light gives forth different manifestations of itself. It is the same, whether it illuminates the air, water, a diamond, or any other materiality of darkness. It has no more materiality in itself when it enlightens the earth than when it enlightens the mind of an angel, when it gives color to bodies than when it gives understanding to spirits.

Sight and visibility is but one power of light, but light is all power; it is life and every joyful sensibility of life is from it. "In Him," says the Apostle, "was Light, and the Light was the life of men." Light is all things, and nothing. It is nothing because it is supernatural; it is all things because every good power and perfection of everything is from it. No joy or rejoicing in any creature, but from the power and joy of light. No meekness, benevolence, or goodness in angel, man, or any creature, but where light is the Lord of its life. Life itself begins no sooner, rises no higher, has no other glory than as the light begins it and leads it on. Sounds have no softness, flowers and gums have no sweetness, plants and fruits have no growth but as the mystery of light opens itself in them.

Whatever is delightful and ravishing, sublime and glorious in spirits, minds or bodies, either in Heaven or on earth, is from the power of the supernatural light, opening its endless wonders in them. Hell has no misery, horror, or distraction but because it has no communication with the supernatural light. And did not the supernatural light stream forth its blessings into this world through the materiality of the sun, all outward nature would be full of the horror of Hell.

And hence are all the mysteries and wonders of light in this material system so astonishingly great and unsearchable; it is because the natural light of this world is nothing else but the power and mystery of the supernatural light breaking forth and opening itself according to its omnipotence in all the various forms of elementary darkness which constitute this temporary world.

Theogenes. I could willingly hear you, Theophilus, on this subject till midnight, though it seems to lead us away from our proposed subject.

Theophilus. Not so far out of the way, Theogenes, as you may imagine; for darkness and light are the two natures that are in every man, and do all that is done in him.

The scriptures, you know, make only this division: The works of darkness are sin, and they who walk in the light are the children of God. Therefore light and darkness do everything, whether good or evil, that is done in man.

Theogenes. What is this darkness in itself, or where is it?

Theophilus. It is everywhere, where there is nature and creature. For all nature, and all that is natural in the creature, is in itself nothing else but darkness, whether it be in soul or body, in Heaven or on earth. And therefore, when the angels (though in Heaven) had lost the supernatural light, they became imprisoned in the chains of their own natural darkness. If you ask why nature must be darkness, it is because nature is not God and therefore can have no light as it is nature. For God and light are as inseparable as God and unity are inseparable. Everything, therefore, that is not God is and can be nothing else in itself but darkness, and can do nothing but in, and under, and according to the nature and powers of darkness.

Theogenes. What are the powers of darkness?

Theophilus. The powers of darkness are the workings of nature or self; for nature, darkness, and self are but three different expressions for one and the same thing.

Now every evil, wicked, wrathful, impure, unjust thought, temper, passion, or imagination that ever stirred or moved in any creature; every misery, discontent, distress, rage, horror, and torment that ever plagued the life of fallen man or angel are the very things that you are to understand by the powers or workings of darkness, nature, or self. For nothing is evil, wicked, or tormenting, but that which nature or self doth.

Theogenes. But if nature is thus the seat and source of all evil, if everything that is bad is in it and from it, how can such a nature be brought forth by a God who is all goodness?

Theophilus. Nature has all evil, and no evil in itself. Nature, as it comes forth from God, is darkness without any evil of darkness in it; for it is not darkness without or separate from light, nor could it ever have been known to have any quality of darkness in it, had it not lost that state of light in which it came forth from God only as a manifestation of the goodness, virtues, and glories of light. Again, it is nature, viz., a strife and contrariety of properties for this only end, that the supernatural good might thereby come into sensibility, be known, found, and felt, by its taking all the evil of strife and contrariety from them and becoming the union, peace, and joy of them all. Nor could the evil of strife and contrariety of will ever have had a name in all the universe of nature and creature had it all continued in that state in which it came forth from God. Lastly, it is self, viz., an own life, that so through such an own life, the universal, incomprehensible goodness, happiness, and perfections of the Deity might be possessed as properties and qualities of an own life in creaturely, finite beings.

And thus, all that is called nature, darkness, or self has not only no evil in it, but is the only true ground of all possible good.

But when the intelligent creature turns from God to self or nature, he acts unnaturally, he turns from all that which makes nature to be good, he finds nature only as it is in itself and without God. And then it is that nature or self hath all evil in it. Nothing is to be had from it or found in it but the work and working of every kind of evil, baseness, misery, and torment, and the utmost contrariety to God and all goodness. And thus also you see the plainness and certainty of our assertion that nature or self hath all evil and no evil in it.

Theogenes. I plainly enough perceive that nature or self without God manifested in it is all evil and misery. But I would, if I could, more perfectly understand the precise nature of self, or what it is that makes it to be so full of evil and misery.

Theophilus. Covetousness, envy, pride, and wrath are the four elements of self, or nature, or Hell, all of them inseparable from it. And the reason why it must be thus and cannot be otherwise is because the natural life of the creature is brought forth for the participation of some high, supernatural good in the Creator. But it could have no fitness or possible capacity to receive such good unless it was in itself both an extremity of want and an extremity of desire of some high good. When, therefore, this natural life is deprived of or fallen from God, it can be nothing else in itself but an extremity of want continually desiring, and an extremity of desire continually wanting. And hence it is that its whole life can be nothing else but a plague and torment of covetousness, envy, pride, and wrath, all which is precisely nature, self, or Hell.

Now covetousness, pride, and envy are not three different things, but only three different names for the restless workings of one and the same will or desire which, as it differently torments itself, takes different names; for nothing is in any of them but the working of a restless desire, and all this because the natural life of the creature can do nothing else but work as a desire. And therefore, when fallen from God its three first births, and which are quite inseparable from it, are covetousness, envy, and pride. It must covet because it is a desire proceeding from want; it must envy because it is a desire turned to self; it must assume and arrogate because it is a desire founded on a real want of exaltation, or a higher state.

Now wrath, which is a fourth birth from these three, can have no existence till some or all of these three are contradicted or have something done to them that is contrary to their will; and then it is that wrath is necessarily born, and not till then.

And thus you see in the highest degree of certainty what nature or self is as to its essential, constituent parts. It is the three forementioned, inseparable properties of a desire thrown into a fourth of wrath that can never cease because their will can never be gratified. For these four properties generate one another, and therefore generate their own torment. They have no outward cause, nor any inward power of altering themselves. And therefore, all self, or nature, must be in this state till some supernatural good comes into it or gets a birth in it. And therefore, every pain or disorder in the mind or body of any intelligent creature is an undeniable proof that it is in a fallen state and has lost that supernatural good for which it was created. So certain a truth is the fallen state of all mankind. And here lies the absolute, indispensable necessity of the one Christian redemption. Till fallen man is born again from above, till such a supernatural birth is brought forth in him by the eternal Word and Spirit of God, he can have no possible escape or deliverance from these four elements of self or Hell.

Whilst man, indeed, lives amongst the vanities of time, his covetousness, envy, pride, and wrath may be in a tolerable state, may help him to a mixture of peace and trouble; they may have at times their gratifications, as well as their torments. But when death has put an end to the vanity of all earthly cheats, the soul that is not born again of the supernatural Word and Spirit of God must find itself unavoidably devoured or shut up in its own, insatiable, unchangeable, self-tormenting covetousness, envy, pride, and wrath.

Oh! Theogenes, that I had power from God to take those dreadful scales from the eyes of every Deist which hinder him from seeing and feeling the infinite importance of this most certain truth!

Theogenes. God give a blessing, Theophilus, to your good prayer. And then let me tell you that you have quite satisfied my question about the nature of self. I shall never forget it, nor can I ever possibly have any doubt of the truth of it.

Theophilus. Let me however go a little deeper in the matter. All life, and all sensibility of life, is a desire; and nothing can feel or find itself to exist, but as it finds itself to have and be a desire; and therefore, all nature is a desire, and all that nature does or works is done by the working of desire. And this is the reason why all nature and the natural life of every creature is a state of want, and therefore must be a state of misery and self-torment, so long as it is mere nature or left to itself. For every desire as such is and must be made up of contrariety, as is sufficiently shown elsewhere.[41] And its essential contrariety, which it has in itself, is the one only possible sensibility of itself but because desire as such is unavoidably made up of that contrariety whence comes all feeling and felt.

Again, all natural life is nothing else but a mere desire founded in want; now want is contrary to desire, and, therefore, every natural life as such is in a state of contrariety and torment to itself. It can do nothing but work in and feel its own contrariety, and so be its own unavoidable, incessant tormentor.

Hence we may plainly see that God's bringing a sensible creature into existence is His bringing the power of desire into a creaturely state; and the power and extent of its own working desire is the bounds or limits of its own creaturely nature. And, therefore, every intelligent creature, of whatever rank in the creation, is and can be nothing else in its creaturely or natural state but a state of want; and the higher its natural state is supposed to be, the higher is its want and the greater its torment if left only in its natural state. And this is the reason of the excessive misery and depravity of the fallen angels.

Now the contrariety that is in desire and must be in it because it is a desire and the only ground of all sensibility is plainly shown you by the most undeniable appearance in outward or material nature. All that is done in outward nature is done by working of attraction. And all attraction is nothing else but an inseparable combination and incessant working of three contrary properties or laws of motion. It draws, it resists its own drawing; and from this drawing and resisting, which are necessarily equal to one another, it becomes an orbicular or whirling motion, and yet draws and resists, just as it did before.

Now this threefold contrariety in the motions or properties of attraction and by which all the elements of this material world are held and governed and made to bring forth all the wonders in all kinds of animate and inanimate things, this contrariety being the only possible ground of all material nature is a full demonstration (1) that contrariety is the one only possible ground of nature and all natural life, whether it be eternal or temporal, spiritual or material; (2) that no other contrariety is or can be in the properties or laws of attraction in this material nature but that one and the same contrariety which was from eternity in spiritual nature, is inseparable from it, and can be nowhere but in it. For time can only partake of eternity, it can have nothing in it but the working of eternity, nor be anything but what it is by the working of eternity in it. It can have nothing that is its own or peculiar to it but its transitory state, and form, and nature. It is a mere accident, has only an occasional existence; and whatever is seen or done in it is only so much of the working of eternity seen and done in it.

For attraction in the material world has not only nothing material in it but is impossible to be communicated to matter, or rather matter has no possible capacity to receive attraction. It can no more receive or obey the laws of attraction than it can make laws for angels. It is as incapable of moving or stirring itself as it is of making syllogisms. For matter is in itself only death, darkness, and inactivity and is as utterly incapable of moving itself as it is of illuminating or creating itself; nothing can be done in it and by it but that which is done by something that is not material.

Therefore, that which is called the attraction of materiality is in itself nothing else but the working of the spiritual properties of desire which has in itself those very three inseparable contrarieties which make the three contrarieties in the motions of attraction. Material nature, being an accidental, temporary, transitory outbirth from eternal nature and having no power of existing but under it and in dependence upon it, the spiritual properties of eternal nature do, as it were, materialize themselves for a time in their temporary outbirth and force matter to work as they work and to have the same contradictory motions in it which are essential to eternal nature.

And thus the three inseparable, contrary motions of matter are in the same manner and for the same reason a true ground of a material nature in time, as the three inseparable, contrary, contradictory workings of desire are a true ground of spiritual nature in eternity. And you are to observe that all that is done in matter and time is done by the same agents or spiritual properties which do all that is naturally done in eternity, in Heaven or in Hell. For nothing is the ground of happiness and glory in Heaven, nothing is the ground of misery, woe and distraction in Hell, but the working of these same contrary properties of desire which work contrariety in the attraction of matter and bring forth all the changes of life and death in this material system. They are unchangeable in their nature and are everywhere the same; they are as spiritual in Hell and on earth as they are in Heaven. Considered as in themselves, they are everywhere equally good and equally bad because they are everywhere equally the ground and only the ground for either happiness or misery. No possible happiness or sensibility of joy for any creature but where these contrary properties work, nor any possibility of misery but from them.

Now attraction, acting according to its three invariable, inseparable contrarieties of motion, stands in this material nature, exactly in the same place and for the same end and doing the same office as the three first properties of desire do in eternal or spiritual nature. For they can be or do nothing with regard to earth and time but that same which they are and do in Heaven and eternity.

In eternal nature, the three contrary properties of desire, answering exactly to the three contrary motions of material attraction, are in themselves only resistance, rage, and darkness and can be nothing else till the supernatural Deity kindles its fire of light and love in them; and then all their raging contrarieties are changed into never-ceasing sensibilities of unity, joy, and happiness.

Just so, in this material system, suppose there to be nothing in it but the contrary motions of attraction, it could be nothing else but rage against rage in the horror of darkness.

But when the same supernatural light which turns the first

fighting properties of nature into a kingdom of Heaven gives forth something of its goodness into this world through the kindled body of the sun, then all the fighting, contradictory motions of attraction serve only to bring new joys into the world and open every life and every blessing of life that can have birth in a system of transitory matter.

Theogenes. Oh Theophilus, you quite surprise me by thus showing me with so much certainty how the powers of eternity work in the things of time. Nothing is done on earth but by the unchangeable workings of the same spiritual powers which work after the same manner, both in Heaven and in Hell. I now sufficiently see how man stands in the midst of Heaven and Hell under an absolute necessity of belonging wholly to the one, or wholly to the other, as soon as this cover of materiality is taken off from him.

For matter is his only wall of partition between them, he is equally nigh to both of them; and as light and love make all the difference there is between Heaven and Hell, so nothing but a birth of light and love in the properties of his soul can possibly keep Hell out of it or bring Heaven into it.

I now also see the full truth and certainty of what you said of the nature and power of divine love, viz., "that it is perfect peace and joy, a freedom from all disquiet, making everything to rejoice in itself. That it is the Christ of God, and wherever it comes, it comes as the blessing and happiness of every natural life; as the restorer of every lost perfection; a redeemer from all evil; a fulfiller of all righteousness; and a peace of God, which passes all understanding." So that I am now a thousand times more than ever athirst after the spirit of love. I am willing to sell all and buy it; its blessing is so great and the want of it so dreadful a state that I am even afraid of lying down in my bed till every working power of my soul is given up to it, wholly possessed and governed by it.

Theophilus. You have reason for all that you say, Theogenes; for were we truly affected with things, as they are our real good or real evil, we should be much more afraid of having the serpents of covetousness, envy, pride, and wrath well nourished and kept alive within us than of being shut up in a pest house, or cast into a dungeon of venomous beasts. On the other hand, we should look upon the lofty eloquence and proud virtue of a Cicero but as the blessing of storm and tempest when compared with the heavenly tranquillity of that meek and lowly heart to which our Redeemer has called us.

I said the serpents of covetousness, envy, pride, and wrath because they are alone the real, dreadful, original serpents; and all earthly serpents are but transitory, partial, and weak outbirths of them. All evil, earthly beasts are but short-lived images or creaturely eruptions of that hellish disorder that is broke out from the fallen spiritual world; and by their manifold variety, they show us that multiplicity of evil that lies in the womb of that abyss of dark rage which (N.B.) has no maker but the three first properties of nature fallen from God and working in their darkness.

So that all evil, mischievous, ravenous, venomous beasts, though they have no life but what begins in and from this material world and totally ends at the death of their bodies, yet have they no malignity in their earthly, temporary nature but from those same wrathful properties of fallen nature which live and work in our eternal fallen souls. And therefore, though they are as different from us as time from eternity, yet wherever we see them we see so many infallible proofs of the fall of nature and the reality of Hell. For was there no Hell broke out in spiritual nature, not only no evil beast but no bestial life could ever have come into existence.

For the origin of matter and the bestial, earthly life stands thus. When the fall of angels had made their dwelling place to be a dark chaos of the first properties of nature left to themselves, the infinite wisdom and goodness of God created or compacted this spiritual chaos into a material Heaven and a material earth and commanded the light to enter into it. Hence this chaos became the ground or the materiality of a new and temporary nature in which the heavenly power of light and the properties of darkness, each of them materialized, could work together, carrying on a war of Heaven against earth so that all the evil workings of fallen spiritual nature and all the good that was to overcome it might be equally manifested both by the good and bad state of outward nature, and by that variety of good and bad living creatures that sprung up out of it. To stand in this state, viz., of a spiritual chaos changed into a materiality of light striving against darkness till the omnipotent wisdom and goodness of God, through the wonders of a first and second Adam, had made this chaotic earth to send as many angels into the highest Heaven as fell with Lucifer into the hellish chaos.

But to return. I have, I hope, sufficiently opened unto you the malignant nature of that self which dwells in and makes up the working life of every creature that has lost its right state in God, viz., that all the evil that was in the first chaos of darkness or that still is in Hell and devils, all the evil that is in material nature and material creatures whether animate or inanimate is nothing else, works in, and with nothing else but those first properties of nature which drive on the life of fallen man in covetousness, envy, pride, and wrath.

Theogenes. I could almost say that you have shown me more than enough of this monster of self, though I would not be without this knowledge of it for half the world. But now, sir, what must I do to be saved from the mouth of this lion, for he is the depth of all subtlety, the Satan that deceiveth the whole world. He can hide himself under all forms of goodness, he can watch and fast, write and instruct, pray much, and preach long, give alms to the poor, visit the sick, and yet often gets more life and strength and a more unmovable abode in these forms of virtue than he has in publicans and sinners.

Enjoin me therefore whatever you please; all rules, methods, and practices will be welcome to me if you judge them to be necessary in this matter.

Theophilus. There is no need of a number of practices or methods in this matter. For to die to self or to come from under its power is not, cannot be done by any active resistance we can make to it by the powers of nature. For nature can no more overcome or suppress itself than wrath can heal wrath. So long as nature acts, nothing but natural works are brought forth; and therefore the more labor of this kind, the more nature is fed and strengthened with its own food.

But the one true way of dying to self is most simple and plain, it wants no arts or methods, no cells, monasteries, or pilgrimages, it is equally practicable by everybody, it is always at hand, it meets you in everything, it is free from all deceit, and is never without success.

If you ask what this one, true, simple, plain, immediate and unerring way is, it is the way of patience, meekness, humility, and resignation to God. This is the truth and perfection of dying to self; it is nowhere else nor possible to be in anything else but in this state of heart.

Theogenes. The excellency and perfection of these virtues I readily acknowledge; but alas, sir, how will this prove the way of overcoming self to be so simple, plain, immediate, and unerring as you speak of? For is it not the doctrine of almost all men and all books, and confirmed by our own woeful experience, that much length of time and exercise and variety of practices and methods are necessary and scarce sufficient to the attainment of any one of these four virtues?

Theophilus. When Christ our Savior was upon earth, was there anything more simple, plain, immediate, unerring, than the way to Him? Did scribes, pharisees, publicans, and sinners want any length of time or exercise of rules and methods before they could have admission to Him, or have the benefit of faith in Him?

Theogenes. I don't understand why you put this question, nor do I see how it can possibly relate to the matter before us.

Theophilus. It not only relates to, but is the very heart and truth of the matter before us. It is not appealed to by way of illustration of our subject, but it is our subject itself, only set in a truer and stronger light. For when I refer you to patience, meekness, humility, and resignation to God as the one simple, plain, immediate, and unerring way of dying to self or being saved from it, I call it so for no other reason but because you can as easily and immediately, without art or method, by the mere turning and faith of your mind, have all the benefit of these virtues, as publicans and sinners by their turning to Christ could be helped and saved by Him.

Theogenes. But, good sir, would you have me then believe that my turning and giving up myself to these virtues is as certain and immediate a way of my being directly possessed and blessed by their good power as when sinners turned to Christ to be helped and saved by Him? Surely this is too short a way and has too much of miracle in it to be now expected.

Theophilus. I would have you strictly to believe all this in the fullest sense of the words. And also to believe that the reasons why you or anyone else are for a long time vainly endeavoring after and hardly ever attaining these first-rate virtues is because you seek them in the way they are not to be found, in a multiplicity of human rules, methods, and contrivances, and not in that simplicity of faith in which those who applied to Christ immediately obtained that which they asked of Him.

"Come unto me, all ye that labor and are heavy laden, and I will refresh you." How short and simple and certain a way to peace and comfort from the misery and burden of sin! What becomes now of your length of time and exercise, your rules and methods and roundabout ways to be delivered from self, the power of sin, and find the redeeming power and virtue of Christ? Will you say that turning to Christ in faith was once indeed the way for Jews and heathens to enter into life and be delivered from the power of their sins, but that all this happiness was at an end as soon as Pontius Pilate had nailed this good Redeemer to the cross, and so broke off all immediate union and communion between faith and Christ?

What a folly would it be to suppose that Christ, after His having finished His great work, overcome death, ascended into Heaven with all power in Heaven and on earth, was become less a Savior and gave less certain and immediate helps to those that by faith turn to Him now than when He was clothed with the infirmity of our flesh and blood upon earth? Has He less power after He has conquered than whilst He was only resisting and fighting with our enemies? Or has He less good will to assist His church, His own body, now He is in Heaven than He had to assist publicans, sinners, and heathens before He was glorified as the Redeemer of the world? And yet this must be the case if our simply turning to Him in faith and hope is not as sure a way of obtaining immediate assistance from Him now as when He was upon earth.

Theogenes. You seem, sir, to me to have stepped aside from the point in question which was not whether my turning or giving myself up to Christ in faith in Him would not do me as much good as it did to them who turned to Him when He was upon earth, but whether my turning in faith and desire to patience, meekness, humility, and resignation to God would do all that as fully for me now as faith in Christ did for those who became His disciples.

Theophilus. I have stuck closely, my friend, to the point before us. Let it be supposed that I had given you a form of prayer in these words: "O Lamb of God, that takest away the sins of the world, or O Thou bread that camest down from heaven, or Thou that art the resurrection and the life, the light and peace of all holy souls, help me to a living faith in Thee." Would you say that this was not a prayer of faith in and to Christ because it did not call Him Jesus, or the Son of God? Answer me plainly.

Theogenes. What can I answer you but that this is a most true and good prayer to Jesus, the Son of the living God? For who else but He was the Lamb of God, and the Bread that came down?

Theophilus. Well answered, my friend. When therefore I exhort you to give up yourself in faith and hope, to patience, meekness, humility, and resignation to God, what else do I do but turn you directly to so much faith and hope in the true Lamb of God? For if I ask you what the Lamb of God is and means, must you not tell me that it is and means the perfection of patience, meekness, humility, and resignation to God? Can you say it is either more or less than this? Must you not therefore say that a faith of hunger and thirst and desire of these virtues is, in spirit and truth, the one very same thing as a faith of hunger and thirst and desire of salvation through the Lamb of God? And consequently that every sincere wish and desire, every inward inclination of your heart that presses after these virtues and longs to be governed by them, is an immediate direct application to Christ, is worshipping and falling down before Him, is giving up yourself unto Him and the very perfection of faith in Him?

If you distrust my words, hear the words of Christ Himself. "Learn of me," says He, "for I am meek and lowly of heart, and ye shall find rest unto your souls." Here you have the plain truth of our two points fully asserted, first, that to be given up to, or stand in a desire of, patience, meekness, humility, and resignation to God is strictly same thing as to learn of Christ, or to have faith in Him. Secondly, that this is the one simple, short, and infallible way to overcome or be delivered from all the malignity and burden of self expressed in these words, "and ye shall find rest unto your souls."

And all this because this simple tendency or inward inclination of your heart to sink down into patience, meekness, humility, and resignation to God is truly giving up all that you are and all that you have from fallen Adam; it is perfectly leaving all that you have to follow and be with Christ, it is your highest act of faith in Him and love of Him, the most ardent and earnest declaration of your cleaving to Him with all your heart and seeking for no salvation but in Him, and from Him. And therefore all the good, and blessing, pardon, and deliverance from sin that ever happened to anyone from any kind or degree of faith and hope and application to Christ is sure to be had from this state of heart which stands continually turned to Him in a hunger and desire of being led and governed by His spirit of patience, meekness, humility, and resignation to God. Oh Theogenes, could I help you to perceive or feel what a good there is in this state of heart, you would desire it with more eagerness than the thirsty hart desireth the water brooks, you would think of nothing, desire nothing but constantly to live in it. It is a security from all evil and all delusion; no difficulty or trial either of body or mind, no temptation either within you or without you but what has its full remedy in the state of heart. You have no questions to ask of anybody, no new way that you need inquire after, no oracle that you need to consult, for whilst you shut up yourself in patience, meekness, humility, and resignation to God, you are in the very arms of Christ, your whole heart is His dwelling place and He lives and works in you as certainly as He lived in and governed that body and soul which He took from the Virgin Mary.

Learn whatever else you will from men and books, or even from Christ Himself besides or without these virtues, and you are only a poor wanderer in a barren wilderness where no water of life is to be found. For Christ is nowhere but in these virtues, and where they are there is He in His own kingdom. From morning to night, let this be the Christ that you follow, and then you will fully escape all the religious delusions that are in the world, and what is more, all the delusions of your own selfish heart.

For to seek to be saved by patience, meekness, humility of heart, and resignation to God is truly coming to God through Christ; and when these tempers live and abide in you as the spirit and aim of your life, then Christ is in you of a truth and the life that you then lead is not yours but Christ that liveth in you. For this is following Christ with all your power. You cannot possibly make more haste after Him, you have no other way of walking as He walked, no other way of being like Him, of truly believing in Him, of showing your trust in Him and dependence upon Him but by wholly giving up yourself to that which He was, viz., to patience, meekness, humility, and resignation to God.

Tell me now, have I enough proved to you the short, simple, and certain way of destroying that body of self which lives and works in the four elements of covetousness, envy, pride, and wrath?

Theogenes. Enough of all reason. But as to covetousness, I thank God I cannot charge myself with it, it has no power over me, nay I naturally abhor it. And I also now clearly see why I have been so long struggling in vain against other selfish tempers.

Theophilus. Permit me, my friend, to remove your mistake. Had covetousness no power over you, you could have no other selfish tempers to struggle against. They are all dead as soon as covetousness has done working in you. You take covetousness to relate only to the wealth of this world. But this is but one single branch of it, its nature is as large as desire, and wherever selfish desire is, there is all the evil nature of covetousness.

Now envy, pride, hatred, or wrath can have no possibility of existence in you but because there is some selfish desire alive in you that is not satisfied, not gratified, but resisted or disappointed. And therefore so long as any selfish tempers, whether of envy, uneasiness, complaint, pride, or wrath are alive in you, you have the fullest proof that all these tempers are born and bred in and from your own covetousness, that is, from that same selfish bad desire which, when it is turned to the wealth of this world, is called covetousness. For all these four elements of self or fallen nature are tied together in one inseparable band, they mutually generate and are generated from one another, they have but one common life and must all of them live, or all die together. This may show you again the absolute necessity of our one simple and certain way of dying to self and the absolute insufficiency of all human means whatever to effect it.

For consider only this, that to be angry at our own anger, to be ashamed of our own pride and strongly resolve not to be weak, is the upshot of all human endeavors, and yet all this is rather the life than the death of self. There is no help but from a total despair of all human help. When a man is brought to such an inward, full conviction as to have no more hope from all human means than he hopes to see with his hands or hear with his feet, then it is that he is truly prepared to die to self, that is, to give up all thoughts of having or doing anything that is good in any other way but that of a meek, humble, patient, total resignation of himself to God. All that we do before this conviction is in great ignorance of ourselves and full of weakness and impurity. Let our zeal be ever so wonderful, yet if it begins sooner or proceeds further, or to any other matter or in any other way than as it is led and guided by this conviction, it is full of delusion. No repentance, however long or laborious, is conversion to

God till it falls into this state. For God must do all, or all is nothing; but God cannot do all, till all is expected from Him; and all is not expected from Him till by a true and good despair of every human help, we have no hope, or trust, or longing after anything but a patient, meek, humble, total resignation to God.

And now, my dear friends, I have brought you to the very place for which I desired this day's conversation, which was to set your feet upon sure ground with regard to the spirit of love. For all that variety of matters through which we have passed has been only a variety of proofs that the spirit of divine love can have no place or possibility of birth in any fallen creature till it wills and chooses to be dead to all self in a patient, meek, humble resignation to the good power and mercy of God.

And from this state of heart also it is that the spirit of prayer is born, which is the desire of the soul turned to God. Stand, therefore, steadfastly in this will, let nothing else enter into your mind, have no other contrivance but everywhere and in everything to nourish and keep up this state of heart, and then your house is built upon a rock; you are safe from all danger; the light of Heaven and the love of God will begin their work in you, will bless and sanctify every power of your fallen soul, you will be in a readiness for every kind of virtue and good work and will know what it is to be led by the Spirit of God.

Theogenes. But, dear Theophilus, though I am so delighted with what you say that I am loath to stop you, yet permit me to mention a fear that rises up in me. Suppose I should find myself so overcome with my own darkness and selfish tempers as not to be able to sink from them into a sensibility of this meek, humble, patient, full resignation to God; what must I then do, or how shall I have the benefit of what you have taught me?

Theophilus. You are then at the very time and place of receiving the fullest benefit from it and practicing it with the greatest advantage to yourself. For though this patient, meek resignation is to be exercised with regard to all outward things and occurrences of life, yet it chiefly respects our own inward state, the troubles, perplexities, weaknesses, and disorders of our own fallen souls. And to stand turned to a patient, meek, humble resignation to God when your own impatience, wrath, pride, and irresignation attacks yourself is a higher and more beneficial performance of this duty than when you stand turned to meekness and patience when attacked by the pride or wrath or disorderly passions of other people. I say, stand turned to this patient, humble resignation, for this is your true performance of this duty at that time; and though you may have no comfortable sensibility of your performing it, yet in this state you may always have one full proof of the truth and reality of it, and that is when you seek for help no other way, nor in anything else, neither from men nor books, but wholly leave and give up yourself to be helped by the mercy of God. And thus, be your state what it will, you may always have the full benefit of this short and sure way of resigning up yourself to God. And the greater the perplexity of your distress is, the nearer you are to the greatest and best relief, provided you have but patience to expect it all from God. For nothing brings you so near to divine relief as the extremity of distress; for the goodness of God hath no other name or nature but the helper of all that wants to be helped; and nothing can possibly hinder your finding this goodness of God and every other gift and grace that you stand in need of; nothing can hinder or delay it but your turning from the only fountain of life and living water to some cracked cistern of your own making, to this or that method, opinion, division, or subdivision amongst Christians, carnally expecting some mighty things either from Samaria or Jerusalem, Paul or Apollos, which are only and solely to be had by worshipping the Father in spirit and in truth, which is then only done when your whole heart and soul and spirit trusts wholly and solely to the operation of that God within you, in whom we live, move, and have our being. And be assured of this as a most certain truth that we have neither more nor less of the divine operation within us because of this or that outward form or manner of our life but just and strictly in that degree, as our faith and hope and trust and dependence upon God is more or less in us.

What a folly then to be so often perplexed about the way to God? For nothing is the way to God, but our heart; God is nowhere else to be found, and the heart itself cannot find Him or be helped by anything else to find Him but by its own love of Him, faith in Him, dependence upon Him, resignation to Him, and expectation of all from Him.

These are short but full articles of true religion which carry salvation along with them, which make a true and full offering and oblation of our whole nature to the divine operation and also a true and full confession of the Holy Trinity in unity. For as they look wholly to the Father as blessing us with the operation of His own Word and Spirit, so they truly confess and worship the Holy Trinity of God. And as they ascribe all to, and expect all from this Deity alone, so they make the truest and best of all confessions, that there is no God but one.

Let then Arians, semi-Arians, and Socinians who puzzle their laborious brains to make paper images of a trinity for themselves have nothing from you but your pity and prayers; your foundation standeth sure whilst you look for all your salvation through the Father working life in your soul by His own Word and Spirit which dwell in Him and are one life, both in Him and you.

Theogenes. I can never enough thank you, Theophilus, for this good and comfortable answer to my scrupulous fear. It seems now as if I could always know how to find full relief in this humble, meek, patient, total resignation of myself to God. It is, as you said, a remedy that is always at hand, equally practicable at all times, and never in greater reality than when my own tempers are making war against it in my own heart.

You have quite carried your point with me; the God of patience, meekness, and love is the one God of my heart. It is now the whole bent and desire of my soul to seek for all my salvation in and through the merits and mediation of the meek, humble, patient, resigned, suffering Lamb of God who alone hath power to bring forth the blessed birth of these heavenly virtues in my soul. He is the Bread of God that came down from Heaven, of which the soul must eat, or perish and pine in everlasting hunger. He is the eternal love and meekness that left the bosom of His Father, to be Himself the Resurrection of meekness and love in all the darkened, wrathful souls of fallen men. What a comfort is it to think that this Lamb of God, Son of the Father, Light of the World, who is the Glory of Heaven and Joy of Angels is as near to us, as truly in the midst of us as He is in the midst of Heaven. And that not a thought, look, and desire of our heart that presses toward Him, longing to catch, as it were, one small spark of His heavenly nature but is in as sure a way of finding Him, touching Him, and drawing virtue from Him as the woman who was healed by longing but to touch the border of His garment.

This doctrine also makes me quite weary and ashamed of all my own natural tempers, as so many marks of the beast upon me; every whisper of my soul that stirs up impatience, uneasiness, resentment, pride, and wrath within me shall be rejected with a "get thee behind me, Satan," for it is his and has its whole nature from him. To rejoice in a resentment gratified appears now to me to be quite frightful. For what is it, in reality, but rejoicing that my own serpent of self has new life and strength given to it, and that the precious Lamb of God is denied entrance into my soul. For this is the strict truth of the matter. To give into resentment and go willingly to gratify it is calling up the courage of your own serpent and truly helping it to be more stout and valiant and successful in you; on the other hand, to give up all resentment of every kind and on every occasion, however artfully, beautifully, outwardly colored, and to sink down into the humility of meekness under all contrariety, contradiction, and injustice, always turning the other cheek to the smiter, however haughty, is the best of all prayers, the surest of all means to have nothing but Christ living and working in you as the Lamb of God that taketh away every sin that ever had power over your soul.

What a blindness was it in me to think that I had no covetousness because the love of self[42] was not felt by me! For to covet is to desire; and what can it signify whether I desire this or that? If I desire anything but that which God would have me to be and do, I stick in the mire of covetousness and must have all that evil and disquiet living and working in me, which robs misers of their peace both with God and man.

Oh sweet resignation of myself to God, happy death of every selfish desire, blessed unction of a holy life, the only driver of all evil out of my soul, be thou my guide and governor wherever I go! Nothing but thee can take me from myself, nothing but thee can lead me to God; Hell has no power where thou art; nor can Heaven hide itself from thee. Oh may I never indulge a thought, bring forth a word, or do anything for myself or others but under the influence of thy blessed inspiration.

Forgive, dear Theophilus, this transport of my soul; I could not stop it. The sight, though distant, of this heavenly Canaan, this Sabbath of the soul, freed from the miserable labor of self to rest in meekness, humility, patience, and resignation under the Spirit of God, is like the joyful voice of the Bridegroom to my soul and leaves no wish in me but to be at the marriage feast of the Lamb.

Theophilus. Thither, Theogenes, you must certainly come if you keep to the path of meekness, humility, and patience under a full resignation to God. But if you go aside from it, let the occasion seem ever so glorious, or the effects ever so wonderful to you, it is only preparing for yourself a harder death. For die you must to all and everything that you have worked or done under any other spirit but that of meekness, humility, and true resignation to God. Everything else, be it what it will, hath its rise from the fire of nature, it belongs to nothing else and must of all necessity be given up, lost, and taken from you again by fire, either here or hereafter.

For these virtues are the only wedding garment; they are the lamps and vessels well furnished with oil.

There is nothing that will do in the stead of them; they must have their own full and perfect work in you, if not before yet certainly after the death of the body, or the soul can never be delivered from its fallen wrathful state. And all this is no more than is implied in this scripture doctrine, viz., that there is no possibility of salvation but in and by a birth of the meek, humble, patient, resigned Lamb of God in our souls. And when this Lamb of God has brought forth a real birth of His own meekness, humility, and full resignation to God in our souls, then are our lamps trimmed and our virgin hearts made ready for the marriage feast.

This marriage feast signifies the entrance into the highest state of union that can be between God and the soul in this life. Or in other words, it is the birthday of the spirit of love in our souls, which whenever we attain will feast our souls with such peace and joy in God as will blot out the remembrance of everything that we called peace or joy before.

In the "Letter" on the *Spirit of Love*, you have been shown, according to the mystery of all things opened by the goodness of God in the blessed Behmen, the time and place of its birth. That it neither does nor can possibly begin any sooner than at the entrance or manifestation of the divine light in the three first wrathful, self-tormenting properties of nature, which are and must be the ground of every natural life and must be darkness, rage, and torment till the light of God, breaking in upon them, changes all their painful working into the strongest sensibilities of love, joy, and triumph in the perception and possession of a new divine life.

Now all that we have said today of the necessity of the fallen souls dying to self by meekness, patience, humility, and full resignation to God is strictly the same thing and asserted from the same ground as when it was then said that the three first properties of nature must have their wrathful activity taken from them by the light of God breaking in upon them, or manifesting itself in them. Now this was always the state of nature, it never was a state of wrath because it never was without the light of God in it. But the natural, creaturely life, having a possibility of falling and having actually fallen from God, has found and felt (what never ought to have been found and felt), viz., what nature is in itself without the manifestation of the Deity in it.

Therefore, as sure as the light of God or the entrance of the Deity into the three first properties of nature is absolutely necessary to make nature to be a heavenly kingdom of light and love, so sure and certain is it that the creaturely life that is fallen from God under the wrathful first properties of nature can have no deliverance from it, cannot have a birth of heavenly light and love by any other possible way but that of dying to self by meekness, humility, patience, and full resignation to God.

And the reason is this. It is because the will is the leader of the creaturely life, and it can have nothing but that to which its will is turned. And therefore it cannot be saved from, or raised out of the wrath of nature till its will turns from nature, and wills to be no longer driven by it. But it cannot turn from nature or show a will to come from under its power any other way than by turning and giving up itself to that meekness, humility, patience, and resignation to God, which, so far as it goes, is a leaving, rejecting, and dying to all the guidance of nature.

And thus you see that this one simple way is, according to the immutable nature of things, the one only possible and absolutely necessary way to God. It is as possible to go two contrary ways at once as to go to God any other way than this. But what is best of all, this way is absolutely infallible; nothing can defeat it. And all this infallibility is fully grounded in the two-fold character of our Savior

(1) as He is the Lamb of God, a principle and source of all meekness and humility in the soul, and (2) as He is the Light of eternity that blesses eternal nature and turns it into a Kingdom of Heaven.

For in this two-fold respect, He has a power of redeeming us, which nothing can hinder; but sooner or later, He must see all His and our enemies under His feet, and all that is fallen in Adam into death must rise and return into a unity of an eternal life in God.

For as the Lamb of God, He has all power to bring forth in us a sensibility and a weariness of our own wrathful state and a willingness to fall from it into meekness, humility, patience, and resignation to that mercy of God which alone can help us. And when we are thus weary and heavy laden and willing to get rest to our souls in meek, humble, patient resignation to God, then it is that He, as the Light of God and Heaven, joyfully breaks in upon us, turns our darkness into light, our sorrow into joy, and begins that Kingdom of God and divine love within us which will never have an end.

Need I say any more, Theogenes, to show you how to come out of the wrath of your evil earthly nature into the sweet peace and joy of the spirit of love? Neither notions, nor speculations, nor heat, nor fervor, nor rules, nor methods can bring it forth. It is the child of light and cannot possibly have any birth in you but only and solely from the light of God rising in your own soul, as it rises in heavenly beings. But the light of God cannot arise or be found in you by any art or contrivance of your own but only and solely in the way of that meekness, humility, and patience which waits, trusts, resigns to, and expects all from the inward, living, life-giving operation of the triune God within you, creating, quickening, and reviving in your fallen soul that birth and image and likeness of the Holy Trinity in which the first father of mankind was created.

Theogenes. You need say no more, Theophilus; you have not only removed that difficulty which brought us hither, but have by a variety of things fixed and confirmed us in a full belief of that great truth elsewhere asserted, namely "that there is but one salvation for all mankind, and that is the life of God in the soul. And also, that there is but one possible way for man to attain this life of God, not one for a Jew, another for a Christian, and a third for a heathen. No, God is one, human nature is one, salvation is one, and the way to it is one, and that is the desire of the soul turned to God."[43]

Therefore, dear Theophilus, adieu. If we see you no more in this life, you have sufficiently taught us how to seek and find every kind of goodness, blessing, and happiness in God alone.

The End of the Third Dialogue

NOTES

39. Change his mortal into immortality: Law alludes to 1 Cor. 15: 53, "For this corruptible must put on incorruption, and this mortal must put on immortality," that is, the flesh must be reclothed and lifted up toward God.

40. Derogate from: to lessen or impair the force of.

41. See *Way to Divine Knowledge*, p. 199, etc.; *Spirit of Love*, p. 00, etc. (Law's note).

42. Pelf: usually money, but here any kind of material possession.

43. See *Spirit of Prayer* [ed. 1752], Part I, p. 90 (Law's note).

Selected Bibliography

Bouyer, Louis. *Orthodox Spirituality and Protestant and Anglican Spirituality*. English translation of *Histoire de la Sipiritualité chrétienne*. New York, 1969.

Elton, Oliver. *A Survey of English Literature, 1730-1780*. London, 1928.

Grainger, M. *William Law and the Life of the Spirit*. London, 1948.

Hobhouse, Stephen. *Selected Mystical Writings of William Law* (1938). 2d rev. ed., New York, 1948.

————. *William Law and Eighteenth Century Quakerism*. London, 1928.

Hopkinson, Arthur W. *About William Law*. London, 1948.

Hoyles, John. *The Edges of Augustanism: The Aesthetics of Spirituality in Thomas Ken, John Byrom and William Law*. The Hague, 1972.

Hunt, Dave. *The Power of the Spirit* [an adapted version of Law's last book, *An Affectionate Address to the Clergy*]. Fort Washington, Pa., 1971.

Huxley, Aldous. *The Perennial Philosophy*. New York, 1945.

Inge, William Ralph. *Christian Mysticism*. London, 1899.

————.*Studies in the English Mystics*. London, 1905.

Law, William. *Complete Works*. London, 1762; reprinted by "G. Moreton" (G.B. Morgan), 9 vols. Brockenhurst, Hants. and Canterbury, Kent: privately printed, 1892-93.

Overton, J.H. *The Nonjurors, their Lives, Principles, and Writings*. London, 1902.

————.*William Law, Nonjuror and Mystic*. London,1881.

Palmer, W. Scott (M.E. Dowson). *Liberal and Mystical Writings of William Law* (with an introduction by William Porcher du Bose). London, 1908.

Pepler, Conrad, O.P. *The English Religious Heritage*. London, 1958.

BIBLIOGRAPHY

Spurgeon, Caroline F.E. "William Law and the Mystics," in *Cambridge History of English Literature*, ed. A.W. Ward and A.R. Waller, vol. 9 (1912), pp. 305-28.

Stephen, Leslie. *English Thought in the Eighteenth Century*. 2 vols. London, 1876.

Stoudt, John J. *Jacob Boehme: His Life and Thought*. New York, 1968.

Stranks, C.J. *Anglican Devotion*. London, 1961.

Talon, Henri, *William Law: A Study in Literary Craftsmanship*. London, 1948.

Walker, A. Keith. *William Law: His Life and Thought*. London, 1973.

Walton, Christopher. *Notes and Materials for an Adequate Biography of the Celebrated Divine and Theosopher William Law*. London: privately printed, 1854.

Whyte, Alexander. *Characters and Characters of William Law*. London, 1893.

Index to Preface, Foreword and Introduction

Index to Texts

449, 458, 488; and spirit of world, 237, 244; suffering of, 131, 241, 242, 429, 431, 432-435, 445, 446, 448-451, 455, 458, 459; tempers of, 244.

Christians, cf. Doctrine; calling of, 135, 142, 284, 286, 296; and charity, 60, 321; crucifixion of, 242; devotion of, 225, 226, 250, 300, 309; duties of, 51, 77, 240, 306; end of, 143, 287; external, 54, 55; friendship of, 301, 315; and humility, 83, 242, 250, 251; and intention, 58, 62; life of, 51, 52, 63, 76, 77, 81-83, 96, 100, 103, 113, 116, 124, 130, 136, 137, 143, 145-147, 161, 189, 192, 208, 243, 262, 284; love, 131, 296, 301, 313; and mortification, 195; perfection, 68, 142, 146, 153, 238, 282, 305, 341, 342, 347; and piety, 247; primitive, 193, 194, 225, 226, 264, 271, 310; profession of, 240; and re-birth, 236, 243; resignation of, 321-323; rules for, 341; sacrifice of, 242; self-examination of, 328-335, 339; spirit of, 55, 57, 58, 77, 78, 81, 83, 85, 121, 124, 125, 135, 142, 144, 227, 243, 246, 250, 261, 277, 278, 285, 287, 289, 321; suffering of, 242; temper of, 51, 52, 54, 77-79, 83, 86, 93, 117, 125, 147; and truth, 207; virtue of, 52, 65, 95, 126, 147, 152, 263, 268 ; and world, 78, 79, 99, 237, 240-247, 249; worthiness of, 286.

Chubb, Thomas, 460.

Church, 402; ages of, 271; attendance, 121, 139, 144, 191, 264; and Christ, 437; Established, 404, 427; fathers of, 345; glory of, 130-133; livings of, 180, 181; primitive, 193, 271; and Saints, 262; service of, 72, 141, 144, 179, 314, 404; triumphant, 311.

Cicero, 206, 483.

Classicus, 205-207.

Cladius, 283-287.

Cognatus, 179-181.

Colossians, 1:12-13, 433; 2:20, 240; 3:1, 83, 242; 3:2, 81; 3:22-23, 82.

Commandments, breaking of, 56, 65; and Christian life, 66, 124; and duty, 66; and love, 288, 296; to pray, 85; ten, 389, 406, 407.

Compassion, 117, 119, 180, 184, 274, 294, 295, 298, 315, 393, 433, 441.

Confessors, 57.

Confession, benefit of, 332; daily, 329, 330, 332; general, 329-333, 335; particular, 329, 330, 333, 335; of sin, 158, 328-339, 343, 344, 441; weekly, 329, 330.

Conscience, awakening of, 332; disregarded, 338, 339; guide, 149; lax, 245; pressing of, 65, 71, 73, 191, 228, 315; and shame, 231; strictness of 67, 69, 105, 127, 192, 278.

Consecration, of life, 96.

Contrition, 329, 335, 336, 338, 339, 343.

1 Corinthians, 6:15, 312; 6:19-20, 286; 8:9, 11-13, 277; 10:31, 77; 15:53, 498.

2 Corinthians, 1:11, 301; 5:10, 283; 5:16, 243.

Cornelius, 221, 222.

Creation, from God, 401; law of, 319, 438; from love, 357, 365,

395; of matter, 368-370; from nothing, 371; praising God, 223; purpose of, 177, 186, 187, 249, 281; and will to goodness, 360.

Creatures, as children of God, 359; Christ dwells in them, 362, 401; disorders in, 430, 431; end of, 392; exist in God, 399, 414; fallen, 363, 365, 392, 393, 431, 452, 479; first state of, 362, 363, 401, 412, 422, 429, 431, 477, 485; God in, 400; from God, 401, 414; lacking Christ, 362, 400; lose God, 412, 478, 496; lose happiness and goodness, 399, 412; nature of, 412, 417, 421, 474, 480; power of, 393, 398, 480; and redemption, 362; sanctification from, 402; state of, 400, 401, 452, 480; two-fold life of, 399-401, 404, 405, 418-421; union with God, 359, 400; variety of, 391, 398, 419; working of, 402, 414, 480, 485; and wrath, 399, 412.

Cross, bearing of, 51, 129, 184, 192, 194; of Christ, 241-243, 361, 451, 487; contemplation of, 232; doctrine of, 242, 246, 388; glory in, 451; and redemption, 336.

Daniel, 254.
David, 213, 223.
Death, and judgement, 68, 69, 71, 72; reflection on, 69-74, 340; and resurrection, 79; of self, 485, 486, 490, 491, 496; triumph over, 131; and will, 363.
Deism, 377, 378, 385, 386; 389, 400, 443, 445-447, 454, 455, 460, 480.
Deism fairly stated and fully

vindicated, 460.
Deity, cf. also Divinity, God; attributes of, 391; becomes man, 387; glory of, 418; goodness of, 359, 392, 478; hidden, 418; light of, 384, 482; is love, 357, 392, 415, 416; love of, 392, 441, 482; manifestation of, 372, 380-382, 387, 416, 419, 420, 496; power of, 377, 379, 381, 418; rejoice in, 391; and soul, 386, 387; triune, 414, 419; union with, 402; will of, 392, 418, 422, 429; working of, 394, 402, 420, 422; wrath not in, 397, 413, 415, 416, 422, 424, 425, 426, 430, 438, 440, 466.

A Demonstration of the Gross and Fundamental Errors of a late Book, 389, 447, 460.
Descartes, 371.
Desire, for God, 420, 478, 491, 494, 497; holy, 210; lack of, 62; and nature, 419, 420, 422, 478, 479, 480, 490; properties of, 374, 375, 376, 420, 481; workings of, 482.
Devil, 49, 236, 275, 309, 335, 351, 380, 414, 451, 458, 459, 485.
Devotion, cf. God; acts of, 115, 233; benefits of, 283, 304; books of, 264, 265, 269; consistency in, 78, 82, 92, 101, 121, 137, 144, 145, 146, 207, 281, 284, 287; as dedication, 47, 51, 75, 78, 83, 192, 208, 219, 341; and duty, 48, 51, 61, 100, 134, 210, 351, 342, 344; external, 48, 50, 52, 53, 57, 198, 233; failure in, 72, 87, 101, 110, 182, 191, 193, 205, 207, 226, 264, 284, 285, 286, 342, 344, 348; fervor of, 196, 199, 217, 228; forms of,

203, 212, 213, 219, 224, 227; to God, 72, 76, 78, 82, 83, 85, 122, 222, 225, 273, 341, 348; habit of, 184, 207; and happiness, 191, 280, 283, 342; and holiness, 77, 117; increase of, 204, 208, 209; lack of time for, 281; life of, 58, 75, 85, 92, 109, 113, 131, 132, 134, 139, 140, 141, 172, 179, 183, 208, 227, 229, 267, 271, 272, 277, 281, 283, 286, 342; place of, 198; practise of, 282; and prayer, 47, 49, 75, 86, 87, 112, 158, 189, 191, 192, 197, 200, 209, 214, 217, 220; preparation for, 213; private, 197, 201, 211, 219, 221, 222; and religion, 51; rules of, 88, 196, 208, 209, 226, 227, 264, 283, 284; spirit of, 86, 145, 189, 196, 203-206, 214, 223, 227, 283, 341, 342, 349, 350, 351; study of, 203, 205, 207; temper of, 213, 281; times of, 114, 140, 198, 225-228, 278, 282, 287, 328; and virtue, 218; and wisdom, 350.

Disciples, 176, 242, 244, 323.

Divinity, cf. also Deity, God; attributes of, 199; of Christ, 144; forgiveness of, 302; goodness of, 114, 135, 321, 322, 324, 344; greatness of, 344; imitation of, 117, 172; love for, 101; love of, 97, 461, 471, 472, 483; mercy of, 302; nature of, 93, 140, 148, 249, 344, 365, 379, 394; perfection of, 172, 174, 344, 365; presence, 197; promise of, 322; providence of, 323; will of, 136, 318, 322, 326, 360, 365.

Doctrine, Christian, 51, 54, 66, 79, 81, 95, 121, 124, 126, 147,

237, 249, 250, 264, 368; of common life, 51; of cross, 242, 246, 388; of election, 462; of Gospel, 65, 99, 108, 124, 142, 147, 184, 241, 311, 388, 432, 455; of Holy Spirit, 404; of humility, 251; of love, 357, 461,462,466, 469, 470, 473; of New Testament, 99, 115, 132, 237, 284; of redemption, 430, 442, 445, 447, 457, 459; and religion, 69, 87, 195, 249, 273, 323; of reprobation, 462; of Savior, 51, 56, 101; of scripture, 116, 436, 440, 495.

Duty, and charity, 102, 118, 271; and Christian life, 143, 192, 235, 306; and commandments, 66; and conscience, 67; and devotion, 48, 51, 61, 100, 134, 210, 331, 342, 344; failure in, 64, 65, 68; to God, 52, 78, 81, 90, 91, 93, 113, 125, 211, 249, 283, 343, 346; and good works, 101; and gospel, 81; and holiness, 138; and intention, 62, 64; and neighbor, 113; of ordinary life, 51, 52; and piety, 71, 110, 129, 138, 185, 247, 271; and prayer, 48, 139, 190; and public worship, 51, 53; of religion, 74, 91, 145, 172, 228; and wisdom, 89, 94, 95.

Education, Christian, 249, 250, 253, 260-279; improper, 250-252; and reason, 248; of women, 261-279.

Egyptians, 254.

Elijah, 461.

Enemies, blessing of, 51, 310; body as, 270; forgiveness of, 51, 119, 144, 157; love for, 52, 119, 295; pray for, 144, 157, 307,

311; world as 244-246; wrath of, 359.

Enoch, 461.

Envy, 250, 251, 288, 290, 292, 308, 309; and emulation, 252, 257, 260, 289.

Ephesians, 1:3, 433; 5:25-27, 437; 5:26-27, 83; 6:5, 82.

Epictetus, 249, 349.

Esau, 464-466.

Eugenius, 178.

Eusebia, 267-276.

Eusebius, 130, 131, 133.

Eve, 361.

Evil, appearance of, 59; and blessings, 119; imaginary, 150; and intention, 59; of mind, 292; nature of, 78, 361; and nature, 78, 377, 379, 388, 425, 442, 463, 477, 478; origin of, 399; overcoming, 431, 435, 449, 450, 453, 455, 458, 459, 471, 483; power of, 360, 361, 379; and spirit of love, 359; spirits, 71, 380; workings of, 478.

Faith, 402, 406, 412; acts of, 200, 321, 364; in Christ, 467, 486, 487, 488, 492; and Christianity, 249, 324; in God, 158, 218; lack of, 322; live by, 77, 132, 156, 208, 240, 447; of primitive Christians, 194; wills God, 405.

Fasting, 66, 108, 157, 190, 194, 218, 221, 222, 229, 270, 286, 305.

Father, 60, 77, 91, 100, 118, 221, 254, 281, 323, 348, 391, 393, 403, 424, 433, 492, 493.

Fear, of God, 130, 240, 255, 256, 343; as holy, 51; proper, 68, 72; and salvation, 66, 67; of world, 238-240.

Feliciana, 168-170, 172, 173.

Flatus, 164-168, 172, 173.

Flavia, 105-109, 113.

Folly, accusation of, 298; aversion to, 185; forgiveness of, 59, 69, 94; and human glory, 259; and intention, 61, 62; life of, 49, 50, 52, 57, 69-74, 98, 104, 105, 108, 113, 121, 122, 157, 166, 167, 171, 183, 207, 230, 231, 349; of mind, 261, 263, 271; and passions, 249; and repentence, 145; and world, 55, 146, 272.

Forgiveness, of brother, 101, 102, 309; cannot be given, 433; divine, 302; of enemies, 51, 119, 144, 157; of God, 59, 120, 255, 290; rule of, 101; of self, 69, 313; of sin, 101, 232, 255, 328, 329, 336, 378; temper of, 102.

Frailty, and intention, 61; of man, 55, 332; and mercy, 64, 66; of nature, 61, 62, 67, 98, 202,229,332, 334; and power, 61, 73.

Fulvius, 134, 135.

Gabriel, 322.

Galatians, 1:4, 240; 6:14, 241.

Genesis, 336; 20:7, 305.

Gentiles, 55.

Goodness, cf. Will; aspiring toward, 59, 62; consistency in, 102, 135; of Deity, 359, 392, 478; divine, 114, 135, 321, 322, 324, 387; of God, 64, 74, 119, 148, 159, 197, 200, 201, 217, 218, 256, 258, 276, 288, 293, 318, 319, 323, 325,326, 337, 350, 358, 362, 366, 389, 391-393, 401, 402, 413, 420, 423, 425, 426, 429, 433, 438, 440, 442, 443, 445, 446, 455, 466, 475, 477, 484, 492, 498; infinite, 288, 291; and intention,

59; life of, 402; of man, 231,
379; power of, 406; principle of,
404; spirit of, 360, 403; and
spirit of love, 388; and tempers,
266; ways to, 467, 468; works
of, 97, 118.
God, cf. also Deity, Divinity,
Goodness, Love, Will; adoration
of, 87, 217, 256, 320, 324, 326,
348, 350, 352, 360, 443, 470;
ascent to, 203, 226; assistance
of, 158, 228, 229, 276;
attributes of, 198, 326, 436;
becomes man, 386; belief in,
218, 318; blessings of, 72, 87,
90, 119, 120, 201, 240, 254,
255, 301-303, 306, 308, 309,
324, 337, 338, 358, 379, 389,
391, 394, 402, 433,438,, 455,
463, 466, 480, 491, 498;
blessings to, 72, 167, 172, 223,
272, 324, 427, 433; born of,
237, 240; calls of, 69, 220, 225,
272, 276, 285, 455, 465;
complaints to, 318-320, 325; as
creator, 93, 136, 150, 153, 201,
230, 254, 255, 257, 288, 293,
319, 336, 350, 358, 365, 370,
400, 401, 416, 438, 468, 478;
dedication to, 47, 51, 58, 67,
68, 75, 77, 79, 82, 83, 89, 91,
95, 96, 121, 124, 125, 130, 139,
145, 148, 158, 159, 169, 177,
186, 189, 197, 235, 240, 259,
279; devotion to, 72, 76, 78, 83,
85, 122, 130, 139, 143, 145,
159-163, 178, 184, 190, 208,
216, 222, 225, 341, 348; duties
to, 52, 59, 78, 80, 84, 91, 93,
111, 113, 125, 211, 249, 283,
343, 346; and election, 462, 463,
465; enjoyment of, 70, 83, 145,
148, 149, 169, 172, 179, 190,
193, 202, 212, 213, 216, 217,

227, 290; eternal, 186, 316;
forgiveness of, 59, 120, 255,
290, 301; as Friend, 254, 255;
gifts of, 86, 90-93, 95, 96, 98,
99, 113, 114, 125, 126, 136,
139, 140, 159, 161, 189, 196,
200, 202, 203, 210, 218, 226,
271, 287, 290, 301-303, 317,
326, 337, 338, 358, 391, 433,
492; glory of, 47, 48, 75-78,
81-83, 88, 90, 91, 94, 115, 124,
125, 127-129, 134-137, 232,
272, 276, 285, 286, 301, 321,
323, 324, 391, 392, 398, 403,
416, 419; as Good, 348, 366,
400, 401; gratitude to, 317, 320,
323-325, 343; greatness of, 199,
254, 255, 337; and happiness,
164, 168, 169, 174, 179, 257,
269, 272, 290, 296, 318, 323,
348, 358, 362, 363, 365, 392,
394, 421, 498; in Himself, 357,
392-394, 413, 417, 441, 443;
holiness of, 285, 403; honor of,
90, 134, 140, 223, 231, 232,
403; house of, 198; image of,
269, 293, 311, 312, 335, 362,
463; imitation of, 93, 97, 117,
145, 154, 258, 290; justice of,
67, 68, 159, 161, 357, 429, 430,
435, 436, 440; knowledge of,
55, 273, 343, 344, 393, 418;
Lamb of, 370, 487, 488,
493-495, 497; laws of, 94, 99,
113, 129, 136, 150, 159, 168,
297, 298, 339, 351, 407; light
of, 367, 368, 377, 387, 389,
402, 413, 469, 496, 497; majesty
of, 268, 417; manifestations of,
393, 398, 402, 414-416,
418-421, 440, 452, 465, 472,
477; mercy of, 67, 73, 74, 130,
154, 201, 246, 257, 301, 305,
336, 340, 392, 423, 433, 436,

260, 290, 300, 303, 332, 337, 465, 492; means of, 135, 138, 172, 226, 227; need for, 62, 137; and obedience, 158; pray for, 87, 91, 199, 227, 307, 308, 404; present, 62; resisted, 338; state of, 470; throne of, 190.

Grotius, Hugo, 443, 460.

The Grounds and Reasons of Christian Regeneration, 389.

Guilt, of each day, 331; greatness of, 337-339; for neglect, 285, 289, 315; removed, 332, 336; for sin, 231, 277, 313, 330-332, 335-338; for unrepented sin, 328, 331.

Gospel, commands of, 51, 65, 81, 95, 121, 245; doctrines of, 65, 99, 108, 124, 142, 147, 184, 241, 311, 388, 432, 455; history of, 237; holiness of, 95, 245; living of, 185; perfection of, 65, 67, 95, 146; piety of, 72, 207, 246; promises of, 67; and redemption, 376, 377, 400, 408; religion of, 432, 453-455, 467; and salvation, 73, 108, 400; spirit of, 170, 181, 206, 207, 244, 245, 277; study of, 206; teaching of, 379; virtues of, 144; way of, 379.

Happiness, of Christians, 147, 163; and devotion, 191, 280, 283, 342; eternal, 79, 144, 155, 162, 177, 183, 184, 187, 249, 269, 272, 301, 346; and God, 164, 168, 169, 174, 179, 257, 269, 272, 290, 296, 318, 323, 348, 358, 362, 363, 365, 392, 394, 421, 498; imaginary, 230, 326; loss of, 392, 393; man called to, 77, 281, 285; of others, 288, 290, 292, 301, 302;

and piety, 160, 167, 168, 178, 179, 181; proper, 79, 164, 177; and rational nature, 93; and religion, 154, 158, 164, 166, 167, 169, 172, 175, 186; return to, 236; and spirit of love, 358, 359; study of, 283; way to, 218, 379; and world, 163, 164, 167, 169, 172-174, 182, 183, 185, 269, 303, 309, 347.

Heaven, 70, 76, 77, 93, 95, 177, 190, 235, 307, 316, 352, 483, 494; and blessing, 395; and church, 311; desire for, 86, 115; earth to become, 367, 377; expectation of, 306; Father in, 91, 118, 348; glories of, 174, 243, 482; happiness of, 144, 158, 257; Kingdom of, 86, 154, 208, 267, 270, 300, 304, 376, 382, 398, 410, 411, 414, 416-420, 437, 438, 483; Lord of, 224; lost, 239, 366; love of, 367, 373, 377; and nature, 381, 382; perfection of, 366; and praise of God, 222-224, 232, 254; reward of, 67, 97, 132; spirit of, 360, 386; tempers of, 243; way to, 66, 77, 116, 184, 185, 189, 206, 291, 304; and will of God, 350; and Word, 362.

Heathens, 244-246, 289, 497; life of, 55, 66, 87.

Hebrews, 11:17,19, 321.

Hell, 362, 363, 394, 398, 402, 431, 441, 442, 450, 451, 458, 459, 478, 479, 482, 483, 485, 494.

High Priests, 361.

Hobhouse, Stephen, 389.

Holy Ghost, 391; temples of, 138, 193, 285, 286, 312.

Holy Spirit, 145, 196, 339, 404.

Hope, 158, 172, 194, 311, 364,

402, 406, 450, 487, 488.
Holiness, acts of, 220; aids to,
402; call to, 286, 403; and
Christ, 362; Christian, 96, 116,
137, 147, 161, 245, 286;
consistency in, 139, 144, 272;
desire for, 68, 89, 95, 266, 293;
devotion to, 77, 287; and duty,
138; and education, 250; of
God, 68; habit of, 208; and
intention, 58; lack of, 235, 437;
life of, 48, 50, 58, 59, 68, 73,
75-78, 85, 86, 89, 91, 105,
112-114, 116, 125, 127, 132,
134-136, 138-140, 142, 144,
145, 148, 213, 276, 305, 334,
402, 403, 438, 467; and love,
293, 360; principles of, 116;
progress in, 68, 95, 308; spirit
of, 77, 132, 227, 270, 285, 403;
state of, 285; striving for, 90,
286; tempers of, 74, 145-147,
202, 305; value of, 345.
Homer, 206, 304.
Horace, 206.
Humility, acts of, 202, 229, 233,
234, 273-275, 277, 469; benefits
of, 276; Christian, 83, 242, 250,
251; as Christian duty, 51, 83,
124; consistency in, 84, 101,
103, 121, 137, 144, 274, 275;
doctrine of, 253; examples of,
308; habit of, 184, 278; and
happiness, 152-154; lack of,
62-65, 84, 108, 235, 236, 266;
living in, 51, 52 68, 90, 109,
113, 125, 139, 183, 272, 286;
and man's nature, 230-232, 259;
necessity of, 278, 485-497; and
piety, 228; practise of, 235, 236,
248, 261, 275, 276, 485-497;
progress in, 235, 236, 238, 248,
262; reward of, 67, 350; rules
of, 276, 305; and sin, 231; spirit

of, 86, 91, 228, 233, 234, 236,
278, 469; temper of, 234; and
truth, 229; and virtue, 228, 229,
233, 236, 268, 275; and world,
238, 239, 246, 247.

Idleness, and church service, 72;
and intention, 61, 62; life of,
61, 62, 69, 80, 99, 105, 108,
110, 181, 191, 268, 286; and
prayer, 190-192; renouncing of,
58, 59, 158, 195, 196.
Immanuel, 361, 405, 463.
Incarnation, 433, 454.
Indulgence, life of, 189-193, 195;
renouncing of, 195, 196.
Intention, and Christians, 58, 65,
208, 238, 282; lack of, 57, 59,
62-65, 72, 73; to please God,
56-61, 67.
Isaac, 254, 321, 322, 464-466.
Isaiah, 42:25, 433.
Ishmael, 464-466.
Israel, 445.
Israelites, 254.

Jacob, 254, 464-466.
James, 5:16, 305.
Jerusalem, 320, 492.
Jews, 66, 87, 213, 225, 361, 362,
378, 497; laws of, 240, 336.
Job, 254, 305.
Job, 1:5, 307; 42:8, 305.
John, 240, 245, 293, 349, 363,
433.
John, 3:5, 81; 9:2-3, 321; 15:19,
244.
John the Baptist, 468, 469.
I John, 1:9, 328; 2:16, 245; 4:5,
240; 5:19, 240.
Joseph, 254.
Joshua, 254.
Judgement, of Christ, 283; day
of, 68, 90, 99, 100, 120 135,

514

Luther, 411, 460.
Life, cf. Christian; and chance, 59, 163, 167, 175; in Christ, 284, 410, 459; of Christ, 362; common, 47, 51-53, 61, 63, 76, 77, 83, 85-88, 93, 104, 112, 134, 139, 140-144, 147, 189, 327, 334, 341; dedication of, 47, 48, 75, 83, 89; divine, 206, 208, 473; enjoyment of, 70; eternal, 157, 168, 186, 187, 188, 193, 270, 282, 463; examination of, 66-68, 72; fullness of, 148; godly, 176; in God, 365, 439, 459; of God, 399, 402, 404, 453, 472, 497; habits of, 215; heavenly as glory, 86, 90, 91, 119, 120, 149, 150, 168, 187, 190, 269, 301, 303, 306, 346, 347, 436; inward, 375, 377, 408; natural, 471-473, 479, 480, 483, 495; of nature, 399; perfection of, 111, 280, 332, 385, 386, 394, 406; principles of, 403; properties of, 373, 379, 384, 386; purpose of, 177, 183, 281; as shadow, 79; shortness of, 272, 303; spirit of, 358; spiritual, 191, 192; states of, 96, 135, 316, 138, 139, 142, 144-146, 155,185, 186, 201, 203, 204, 208, 219, 247, 259, 272, 274, 281-283, 286, 287, 291, 302, 303, 323-325, 328, 334, 341, 342, 358, 380, 386; way to, 163; wrong way of, 48, 63, 67, 74, 77, 81,110, 113.
Light, Christ is, 476, 493, 497; and darkness, 473-476; of Deity, 384, 482; divine, 468, 495; God is, 473, 477; of God, 367, 368, 377, 387, 389, 402, 413, 469, 496, 497; and materiality, 473, 475, 476, 484; and nature, 474;

power of, 473, 476; workings of, 473.
Locke, 371, 389.
Lord, cf. Christ, Savior, Son; commands of, 65, 221; crucifixion of, 232; and devotion, 344; as fountain, 255; humility of, 253; joy of, 90, 161; love of, 287, 296; as man, 348; and prayer, 193, 199, 213, 224; precepts of, 51, 113, 147, 176, 213, 241, 244, 320, 323; presence of, 190; our representative, 242; and service, 75, 274; Spirit of, 279, 304; terrors of, 438, 440; will of, 160; work of, 172.

Malebranche, 371.
Man, cf. also Creatures, Nature, Salvation, Soul; belongs to God, 317; born of God, 424; child of God, 365, 424, 477; Christ in, 434-436, 458, 489; and common good, 288; deliverance of, 441, 444, 445, 455; and divine life, 144, 294, 410, 411, 445, 453; and divine nature, 400, 405; dwells in God, 290, 317, 365, 459, 471; end of, 249, 463; eternal, 78; exalted, 93, 290; as fallen, 67, 208, 269, 307, 362, 366, 377, 391, 405, 408, 411, 413, 425-427, 431, 433, 436, 441-443, 445, 446, 448, 450, 452, 453, 455, 456, 463, 465, 477, 479, 485; first state of, 365, 405, 407, 419, 437, 439, 444, 449, 450, 472; God in, 412; as image of God, 269, 293, 311, 312, 335, 362, 463; immortality of, 179, 186, 187, 346; as imperfect, 66, 67, 229; like God, 288; nature of, 68, 77, 78,

91, 93, 94, 98, 123, 130, 135,
142, 149, 150, 153-155, 159,
162, 175, 194, 210, 214,
229-231, 235, 237, 248, 249,
269, 281, 290, 296, 342, 344,
347, 350, 360, 379, 387, 410,
439, 445, 449, 461, 463, 464,
469, 472, 476; perfection of, 67,
68, 93, 95, 207, 248, 257, 379,
407, 450; as pilgrim, 51, 81, 83,
322; purification of, 365;
rational, 345; re-birth of, 52, 81,
145, 240, 366, 379, 388, 399,
405-407, 412, 434, 435, 437,
445, 463, 468, 469, 471, 479,
497; reconciled to God, 430;
redeemed, 138, 362, 377;
relation to God, 312, 318,
345-347, 429, 464; resists
Christ, 362; rewarded, 90; as
seeker, 364, 379; as Sons of
God, 52, 138, 283, 407; state of,
150, 159, 162, 229, 232, 249,
270, 272, 283, 296, 342, 365,
410, 439, 449, 451, 452, 453,
455, 456, 464, 466, 479;
two-fold life of, 412, 415; war
within, 270, 464, 465, 472, 493;
will of, 47, 219, 321, 324-326,
365, 404, 445.
Marcus Antoninus, 349.
Martial, 207.
Martyrs, 57, 120, 226.
Matthew, 5:22, 311; 5:28, 277;
5:34-35, 320; 18:10, 91;
18:21-22, 101; 23:20-22, 320;
25:14-30, 162; 25:21, 90; 25:30,
160.
Matilda, 263-265, 279.
Meditation, 216, 218, 232, 256,
270, 272, 281.
Meekness, of Christ, 441;
consistency in, 141; as example,
259; as habit, 101, 273, 275,

305; lack of, 63, 313; of Lord,
253, 274; necessity of, 86, 183,
217, 242; reward of, 351; of
Savior, 232, 279; way of,
485-497.
Mercy, abused, 138; of Christ,
64, 441; divine, 302; of God, 67,
73, 74, 130, 154, 201, 246, 257,
301, 305, 336, 340, 392, 423,
432, 433, 436, 442, 465, 475;
lack of, 437; promises of, 67;
and sin, 64; towards others,
119.
Metaphysics, 371, 372, 389.
Miranda, 105, 113-120, 121, 129,
131, 132.
Moderation, 112.
Moses, 212, 213, 254, 288, 405,
465.
Mundanus, 204, 205, 207.
Mortification, of body, 283; and
Christ, 131; and common life,
52, 53, 112, 132, 140, 146, 286;
of early Christians, 193-195;
earthly desires, 83, 157, 270;
habit of, 184, 208, 305; lack of,
62, 66, 108, 190, 191; and
piety, 128, 140, 192; of
passions, 145, 149, 215, 313;
and vanity, 272.
Mysticism, and quietism, 216.
Matter, creation of, 368-370;
deliverance of, 367; first state
of, 368; laws of, 375; and light,
475-476, 484; nature of, 370,
381, 475, 481, 482, 485; and
redemption, 370; workings of,
482; and world, 367, 375, 420,
481.

Nature, change in, 99, 145, 381,
382, 388, 413; of Christ, 144,
231; corrupt, 465, 469;
deliverance of, 366; and desire,

earthly, 115, 149, 153, 236,
246, 377; of envy, 252; of
holiness, 235; mortification of,
145, 149, 215; opposing of, 351,
467; and prayer, 227, 272, 309;
and reason, 350; and salvation,
67, 194; shame for, 249, 333;
and soul, 154, 158, 191-2, 202,
215; vain, 78, 82, 109, 148, 149,
174, 230, 231, 250, 263.

Passover, 451.

Paternus, 253-260.

Patience, Christian, 351; in God,
392, 393; insufficiency of, 317;
necessity of, 217, 485-497.

Paul, 68, 125, 132, 144, 193, 194,
220, 222. 240, 241, 243, 277,
283, 286, 291, 299, 300, 423,
431-437, 440, 445, 449, 467,
471, 476, 492.

Penance, 91, 117, 313, 315, 336,
343.

Penitens, 69-74.

Perfection, of Christ, 449, 450,
459; Christian, 68, 142, 146,
153, 238, 264, 282, 305, 341,
342, 347; delight in, 290; and
desire, 62, 66, 129, 131, 132,
272, 306, 335; and devotion,
280; divine, 172, 174; and faith,
322; of God, 357, 362, 363,
365, 470; of Gospel, 65, 67, 95,
146; and grace, 62; and
gratitude, 318; lack of, 65; of
life, 111, 280, 332, 385, 386,
394, 406; loss of, 248, 263, 396,
438, 452, 471, 483; and love,
294; imitation of, 90, 125; of
man, 67, 68, 93, 95, 207, 248,
257, 259, 270, 335, 379, 407,
450; and nature, 68, 168, 248,
249, 270, 360, 366, 419, 421; of
piety, 104; prayer for, 91;
progress in, 112, 129; of

religion, 153, 161; restored, **449**;
and salvation, 66; of souls, 202,
271, 347, 372, 386; state of, 68,
309, 438; striving for, 68, 90,
274, 276, 292; of virginity, 271,
272; way to, 218, 341, 379, 467,
485, 488.

Peter, 101, 118, 221, 284.

1 Peter, 1:15, 284; 2:9, 287; 2:11,
81, 83; 4:11, 287; 5:10, 436.

Pharoah, 416, 423, 425, 465.

Pharisees, 412.

Philippians, 68; 1:3-4, 300; 4:8,
95.

Piety, acts of, 216, 284, 321; and
adversity, 291; books of, 200,
206, 270, 306; calls to, 176; and
charity, 298; Christian, 278,
298; consistency in, 92, 93, 111,
122, 123, 135, 137, 139, 145,
146, 154, 186, 281, 285, 287,
315; customs, 86, 87; and
dedication, 47, 56, 57, 78, 98;
desire for, 284, 305; duty of,
71, 110, 124, 129, 138, 185,
247, 270; examples of, 262, 264,
297, 308; of gospel, 72, 207,
246; and gratitude, 318; habit
of, 146, 184; and happiness,
160, 167, 168, 178-9, 181; and
humility, 228; insufficiency of,
62, 63, 65, 69, 73, 84, 99, 109,
110, 122, 123, 138, 173, 174,
182, 212, 248, 266, 285, 289,
319, 321, 330; and intention,
58, 59; life of, 58, 72, 76, 82,
85, 86, 89, 91, 92, 105, 117,
121, 127, 129, 138, 139, 154,
161, 162, 169, 170, 172, 178,
183, 228, 235, 272, 281, 286,
331, 439; and mortification, 195;
and nature, 153; necessity of,
249; and prayer, 50, 306, 328;
progress in, 68, 104, 110, 112,

116, 235, 262, 283; and religion, 239; rules of, 77, 154; spirit of, 86, 105, 110, 287, 303, 308; value of, 346; and will of God, 325-327, 360; works of, 60, 72, 77, 161, 273, 293, 444.

Plato, 249, 349.

Plautus, 304.

Pontius Pilate, 487.

Pope, 432.

Poverty, love for, 275; of spirit, 51, 52, 108, 144, 246; voluntary, 131, 132, 341.

Power, of Christ, 405, 406, 487, 497; of Christians, 301, 306, 309; and common good, 288; of creatures, 393, 398, 480; of darkness, 477; of Deity, 418; of Devil, 236; divine, 159, 483; of evil, 360, 361, 379; of God, 77, 159, 199, 200, 220, 223, 229, 230, 231, 233, 255, 257, 276, 291, 293, 317, 348, 383, 388, 393, 400, 408, 410, 411, 416, 425, 439, 442, 448, 452, 468; of love, 290, 357, 470; of man, 162, 229, 230, 231, 232, 255, 276, 288, 291, 325, 351 388, 410, 453, 489, 491; and perfection, 62; of prayer, 226, 305; of redemption,465; of Savior, 199; of soul, 210, 214; of Spirit of love, 357, 363, 366; spiritual, 483; of tempers, 466; of willing, 317; of world, 238, 245, 246; of wrath, 394.

Prayer, cf. Devotion, God; acts of, 214, 225; at bed-time, 339, 340; benefits of, 202, 227, 302; for children, 307; commanded to, 85; and common good, 288; consistency in, 121, 141, 142, 228; daily, 196, 301, 341; and devotion, 47, 49, 75, 86, 87, 112, 158, 189, 191, 192, 200, 209, 214, 217; duty of, 48, 139, 190; in evening, 328-339; examples of, 271; external, 87, 196, 198, 209, 210, 217; and faith, 200; forms of, 75, 196, 197, 199, 200, 202, 203, 208, 209, 211, 278, 301, 469; frequency of, 227; and happiness, 191; hypocrisy in, 83-85; lack of, 66, 101, 194, 222, 226, 233; life of, 108, 114, 158, 201, 271, 281; at nine in morning, 225-279, 316; at noon, 280-315, 316; for others, 287, 292, 300-315; and passions, 227, 272; place of, 198; power of, 226, 305; preparation for, 203, 204, 222, 223; private, 47, 50, 61, 81, 115, 141, 197, 221, 310, 311; public, 47, 48, 50, 55, 61, 62, 76, 81, 141, 221; as refreshing, 196, 298; and religion, 50, 158; on rising, 189-224, 225, 226, 316; spirit of, 141, 191-193, 273, 469, 491; at three p.m., 316-327; times of, 86, 87, 92, 114, 115, 140, 184, 189, 190, 193, 95-97, 200, 201, 208, 217, 222, 225, 227, 267, 280, 283, 469; and virtue, 91, 219, 227, 228; vocal, 216; and wisdom, 48, 49.

Pride, consistency in, 84, 85, 232; effects of, 251; and fallen world, 232; guarding against, 268; habit of, 313; and humility, 84; and intention, 61; life of, 234, 235, 237, 349; of life, 77, 78, 80, 83, 85, 245, 274, 349, 406, 441; as pervasive, 235, 236; and piety, 84, 229; rejection of, 60, 140, 217, 233, 235, 274; and self-knowledge, 231, temper of,

of, 223; and hymns, 211, 223; imitation of, 108, 125, 140, 146, 184, 243, 244, 279; love of, 296; meekness of, 232, 279; merits of, 435; nature of, 199; and poverty, 275; teachings of, 51, 59, 95, 108, 143, 176, 277.

Scripture, 275; and devotion, 342; doctrine, 116, 436, 440, 495; and prayer, 200, 203, 223, 225, 227; reading of, 264, 286, 306; and religion, 193; teaching of, 59, 66, 79, 99, 108, 115, 118, 119, 124, 242, 300, 305, 320, 328, 402, 431, 467, 473; and world, 244, 246.

Selected Mystical Writings of William Law, 389.

Serena, 90.

A Serious Call, 427.

Sidon, 135.

Silas, 144, 193, 220, 222.

Sin, cf. Guilt; abolition of, 444, 488; avoided, 104, 105, 183, 334; burden of, 439, 440, 487; confession of, 158, 328-339; and conscience, 71, 245; and folly, 94, 110; and forgiveness, 101, 232, 255, 328, 329, 336, 378; of hate, 293, 312; hatred of, 294, 330, 332, 335; and human law, 137; and humility, 229; impurity of, 335; and judgement, 284; and lack of piety, 57, 110; and love, 296, 297; and man, 236; and materiality, 368, 369, 370; and mercy, 64; nature of, 231, 335, 442; origin of, 399; overcoming of, 430, 442, 450; power of, 379, 487, 494; and prayer, 226; punishment of, 440, 441; repeated, 332; repentance of, 328-339; sorrow for, 332, 333,

335; and vanity, 102.

Sloth, 68, 105, 110, 190.

Socinians, 443, 444, 446, 493.

Socinus, Faustus, 460.

Socrates, 249, 250, 349.

Sodom, 425.

Spirit, cf. World; and body, 372, 373, 397, 398; change of, 112, 243, 274; of Christ, 95, 145, 195; Christian, 55, 57, 58, 77, 78, 81, 83, 85, 121, 124, 125, 135, 142, 144, 227, 243, 246, 250; of devotion, 86, 145, 189, 196, 203-206, 214, 223, 227, 283, 341, 342, 349-351; of God, 48, 192; of gospel, 170, 181, 206, 207, 244, 245, 277; holiness of, 77, 132, 227; of humility, 86, 91, 228, 233, 234, 469; inner, 371, 372, 397, 408; perfection of, 270; of piety, 86, 105, 110, 287, 303, 308; poverty of, 51, 52, 108, 144; of prayer, 141, 191, 192, 195, 273, 469; recollection of, 198; of religion, 123, 124, 131, 185, 191, 196, 227, 228; renewed, 467, 468; of thankfulness, 218, 219; of wisdom, 308, 335, 376.

Spirit of love, blessings of, 358, 359; birth of, 470; and Christ, 362; and creation, 360; doctrine of, 357, 461, 462, 466, 469, 470, 473; and God's workings, 365, 389, 455, 491; ground of, 358, 359, 363; and happiness, 358, 359; lack of, 363, 366, 379; nature of, 357, 359; and nature, 363, 364, 380, 472, 479; necessity of, 357, 363, 462; origin of, 357, 384, 385; and passions, 388; and perfection, 359, 360, 373; power of, 357, 363, 366, 472; practice of, 470,

Thomas Aquinas, 389.
Timothy, 194, 467.
2 Timothy, 1:3, 300.
Trinity, 312, 376, 382, 391, 393, 414, 419, 493, 497.
Tyre, 135.

Vanity, assaults of, 229; and education, 263; forgiveness of, 59, 94; forsaking of, 51, 53, 57, 77, 82, 99, 122-124, 126, 127, 140, 185, 274; and intention, 61; life of, 49, 52, 53, 57, 61, 80, 104, 108, 121, 123, 160, 173, 174, 230-232, 234, 250, 263; of mind, 258, 275; and repentance, 145; and virtue, 275; and world, 55, 71, 78, 83, 98, 99, 122, 128, 146, 173, 174, 176, 237, 249, 270-272, 275, 350.
Vice, and Christians, 56, 83, 103, 105, 193; lack of, 182; and man's nature, 235, 333; and will of God, 316.
Virgin Mary, 311, 312, 489.
Virginity, 130-132, 271, 272, 276, 341.
Virtue, and charity, 273, 299, 302; Christian, 52, 65, 95, 126, 147, 152, 263, 268; desire for, 266; example of, 275, 308; glory in, 85, 258; as habit, 101; and happy death, 179; and humility, 228, 229, 233, 236, 268, 275; and intention, 63; and judgement, 284; labors of, 275; lack of, 69, 193, 228, 263, 314, 315; life of, 89, 90, 172, 183, 260, 272; and love, 292-295; love for, 67, 270; neglect of, 68, 109, 191, 286; perfection of, 218, 485; and prayer, 227, 228, 301; progress in, 64, 65, 105, 129, 227, 229, 276, 303, 308,

325, 326; rejoicing in, 292; and Saints, 249; and truth, 229; value of, 345, 346; and vice, 153; ways to, 467, 468; and will of God, 316; and world, 239, 246.

The Way to Divine Knowledge, 389, 427, 447, 460, 498.
Will, creaturely, 360, 363, 365, 369, 371, 414, 415, 418, 478, 496; divine, 136, 318, 322, 326, 360, 365; eternal, 357-359; of God, 47, 58, 75, 76, 79, 82, 90, 95, 113, 137, 140, 148, 154, 159, 160, 215, 218, 256-258, 290, 316-327, 348, 350, 351, 357, 360, 362, 364, 365, 369, 371, 392, 403, 404, 417, 427, 431, 441, 442, 448, 450, 452, 475; to goodness, 357-360, 363, 392-394, 416, 429; of Lord, 160; of man, 47, 219, 292, 321, 324-326, 365, 404, 445; resignation of, 323, 326, 327, 485-497; of soul, 372; turned from God, 418, 421, 478; turned to God, 418, 421, 422, 496.
Wisdom, and charity, 92; Christian, 74, 95, 99, 111, 124, 138; and common good, 288; consistency in, 92, 93, 121, 145, 272; divine, 159; and education, 250, 258; of God, 148; lack of, 62, 70, 239; life of, 48, 57-59, 77, 89, 91-93, 99, 104, 115, 125, 129, 140, 143-145, 169, 239, 272; of man, 231, 249, 321, 348, 468; and prayer, 48, 49; principles of, 116, 347; and religion, 166, 170, 171, 173, 174, 178, 185, 273; revealed, 240; to use of money, 114; worldly, 472.